CU00606423

AAT
INTERACTIVE TEXT

Technician Unit 17

Implementing Auditing Procedures

In this May 2000 edition

- Layout designed to be easy on the eye - and easy to use

- Icons to guide you through a 'fast track' approach if you wish

- Thorough reliable updating of material to 1 May 2000 taking into account changes to auditing standards and guidance

FOR 2000 AND 2001 DEVOLVED ASSESSMENTS

BPP Publishing
May 2000

First edition 1998
Third edition May 2000

ISBN 0 7517 6223 7 *(Previous edition 0 7517 6167 2)*

British Library Cataloguing-in-Publication Data
A catalogue record for this book
is available from the British Library

Published by

BPP Publishing Limited
Aldine House, Aldine Place
London W12 8AW

www.bpp.com

Printed in Great Britain by W M Print
Frederick Street
Walsall
West Midlands WS2 9NE

We are grateful to the Auditing Practices Board for permission to reproduce the glossary of auditing terms.

We are also grateful to the Lead Body for Accounting for permission to reproduce extracts from the Standards of Competence for Accounting, and to the AAT for permission to reproduce extracts from the mapping and Guidance Notes.

Page

HOW TO USE THIS INTERACTIVE TEXT

Aims of this Interactive Text

To provide the knowledge and practice to help you succeed in the devolved assessment for Technician Unit 17 *Implementing Auditing Procedures*.

To pass the devolved assessment you need a thorough understanding in all areas covered by the standards of competence.

To tie in with the other components of the BPP Effective Study Package to ensure you have the best possible chance of success.

Interactive Text

This covers all you need to know for the devolved assessment for Unit 17 *Implementing Auditing Procedures*. Icons clearly mark key areas of the text. Numerous activities throughout the text help you practise what you have just learnt.

Devolved Assessment Kit

When you have understood and practised the material in the Interactive Text, you will have the knowledge and experience to tackle the Devolved Assessment Kit for Unit 17 *Implementing Auditing Procedures*. This aims to get you through the devolved assessment, whether in the form of the AAT simulation or in the workplace.

Recommended approach to this Interactive Text

(a)   To achieve competence in Unit 17 (and all the other units), you need to be able to do **everything** specified by the standards. Study the Interactive Text carefully and do not skip any of it.

(b)   Learning is an **active** process. Do **all** the activities as you work through the Interactive Text so you can be sure you really understand what you have read.

(c)   After you have covered the material in the Interactive Text, work through the **Devolved Assessment Kit**.

(d)   Before you take the devolved assessment, check that you still remember the material using the following quick revision plan for each chapter.

   (i)   Read through the chapter learning objectives. Are there any gaps in your knowledge? If so, study the section again.

   (ii) Read and learn the key terms.

   (iii) Look at the devolved assessment alerts. These show the sort of things that are likely to come up.

   (iv) Read and learn the key learning points, which are a summary of the chapter.

   (v)   Do the quick quiz again. If you know what you're doing, it shouldn't take long.

   This approach is only a suggestion. Your college may well adapt it to suit your needs.

Remember this is a **practical** course.

(a)   Try to relate the material to your experience in the workplace or any other work experience you may have had.

(b)   Try to make as many links as you can to your study of the other Units at Technician level.

(c)   Keep this text, (hopefully) you will find it invaluable in your everyday work too!

TECHNICIAN QUALIFICATION STRUCTURE

The competence-based Education and Training Scheme of the Association of Accounting Technicians is based on an analysis of the work of accounting staff in a wide range of industries and types of organisation. The Standards of Competence for Accounting which students are expected to meet are based on this analysis.

The Standards identify the key purpose of the accounting occupation, which is to operate, maintain and improve systems to record, plan, monitor and report on the financial activities of an organisation, and a number of key roles of the occupation. Each key role is subdivided into units of competence, which are further divided into elements of competences. By successfully completing assessments in specified units of competence, students can gain qualifications at NVQ/SVQ levels 2, 3 and 4, which correspond to the AAT Foundation, Intermediate and Technician stages of competence respectively.

Whether you are competent in a Unit is demonstrated by means of:

- *Either* a Central Assessment (set and marked by AAT assessors)

- *Or* a Devolved Assessment (where competence is judged by an Approved Assessment Centre to whom responsibility for this is devolved)

- Or *both* Central *and* Devolved Assessment

Below we set out the overall structure of the Technician (NVQ/SVQ Level 4) stage, indicating how competence in each Unit is assessed. In the next section there is more detail about the Devolved Assessment for Unit 17.

Note that Units 8, 9 and 10 are compulsory. You can choose one out of Units 11 to 14, and then three out of Units 15 to 19.

Unit of competence	Elements of competence

| **Unit 8** Contributing to the management of costs and the enhancement of value | **8.1** Collect, analyse and disseminate information about costs |
| | **8.2** Make recommendations to reduce costs and enhance value |

Central Assessment *only*

Unit 9 Contributing to the planning and allocation of resources	**9.1** Prepare forecasts of income and expenditure
	9.2 Produce draft budget proposals
	9.3 Monitor the performance of responsiblity centres against budgets

Central Assessment *only*

Unit 10 Managing accounting systems	**10.1** Co-ordinate work activities within the accounting environment
	10.2 Identify opportunities to improve the effectiveness of an accounting system
	10.3 Prevent fraud in an accounting system

Devolved Assessment *only*

| **Unit 22** Monitor and maintain a healthy, safe and secure workplace (ASC) | **22.1** Monitor and maintain health and safety within the workplace |
| | **22.2** Monitor and maintain the security of the workplace |

Devolved Assessment *only*

| **Unit 11** Drafting financial statements (Accounting Practice, Industry and Commerce) | **11.1** Interpret financial statements |
| | **11.2** Draft limited company, sole trader and partnership year end financial statements |

Central Assessment *only*

| **Unit 12** Drafting financial statements (Central Government) | **12.1** Interpret financial statements |
| | **12.2** Draft central government financial statements |

Central Assessment *only*

| **Unit 13** Drafting financial statements (Local Government) | **13.1** Interpret financial statements |
| | **13.2** Draft local authority financial statements |

Central Assessment *only*

BPP PUBLISHING

Technician qualification structure

Unit of competence

Elements of competence

Unit 14	Drafting financial statements (National Health Service)

Central Assessment *only*

14.1	Interpret financial statements
14.2	Draft NHS accounting statements and returns

Unit 15	Operating a cash management and credit control system

Devolved Assessment *only*

15.1	Monitor and control cash receipts and payments
15.2	Manage cash balances
15.3	Grant credit
15.4	Monitor and control the collection of debts

Unit 16	Evaluating current and proposed activities

Devolved Assessment *only*

16.1	Prepare cost estimates
16.2	Recommend ways to improve cost ratios and revenue generation

Unit 17	Implementing auditing procedures

Devolved Assessment *only*

17.1	Contribute to the planning of an audit assignment
17.2	Contribute to the conduct of an audit assignment
17.3	Prepare related draft reports

Unit 18	Preparing business taxation computations

Devolved Assessment *only*

18.1	Adjust accounting profit and losses for trades and professions
18.2	Prepare capital allowances computations
18.3	Prepare Capital Gains Tax computations
18.4	Account for Income Tax payable or recoverable by a company
18.5	Prepare Corporation Tax computations and returns

Unit 19	Preparing personal taxation computations

Devolved Assessment *only*

19.1	Calculate income from employment
19.2	Prepare computations of property and investment income
19.3	Prepare Capital Gains Tax computations
19.4	Prepare personal tax returns

UNIT 17 STANDARDS OF COMPETENCE

The structure of the Standards for Unit 17

The Unit commences with a statement of the **knowledge and understanding** which underpin competence in the Unit's elements.

The Unit of Competence is then divided into **elements of competence** describing activities which the individual should be able to perform.

Each element includes:

(a) A set of **performance criteria.** This defines what constitutes competent performance.

(b) A **range statement.** This defines the situations, contexts, methods etc in which competence should be displayed.

(c) **Evidence requirements.** These state that competence must be demonstrated consistently, over an appropriate time scale with evidence of performance being provided from the appropriate sources.

(d) **Sources of evidence.** These are suggestions of ways in which you can find evidence to demonstrate that competence. These fall under the headings: 'observed performance; work produced by the candidate; authenticated testimonies from relevant witnesses; personal account of competence; other sources of evidence.' They are reproduced in full in our Devolved Assessment Kit for Unit 17.

The elements of competence for Unit 17 *Implementing Auditing Procedures* are set out below. Knowledge and understanding required for the unit as a whole are listed first, followed by the performance criteria and range statements for each element. Performance criteria are cross-referenced below to chapters in this Unit 17 *Implementing Auditing Procedures* Interactive Text.

Unit 17: Implementing Auditing Procedures

What is the unit about?

This unit relates to the **internal** and **external auditing process** and requires the candidate to be involved from planning through to the reporting stage. The candidate is responsible for the identification of control objectives and their assessment, the selection of a sample and tests, drawing appropriate conclusions from the tests and drafting the reports which give preliminary conclusions and recommendations. The unit requires the candidate to be supervised in the work.

BPP PUBLISHING

Knowledge and understanding

The business environment

- A general understanding of the legal duties of auditors: the content of reports; the definition of proper records (Elements 17.1, 17.2 & 17.3)

- A general understanding of the liability of auditors under contract and negligence including liability to third parties (Elements 17.1, 17.2 & 17.3)

- Relevant legislation, relevant auditing standards and guidelines (Elements 17.1, 17.2 & 17.3)

Accounting techniques

- Types of audit: relationship between internal and external audit (Elements 17.1, 17.2 & 17.3)

- Recording and evaluating systems: conventional symbols; flowcharts; Internal Control Questionnaires (ICQs); checklists (Elements 17.1 & 17.2)

- Verification techniques: physical examination; reperformance; third party confirmation; vouching; documentary evidence; identification of unusual items (Elements 17.1 & 17.2)

- Basic sampling techniques in auditing: confidence levels; selection techniques (random numbers, interval sampling, stratified sampling) (Elements 17.1 & 17.2)

- The use of audit files and working papers (Elements 17.1, 17.2 & 17.3)

- Auditing techniques in an IT environment (Elements 17.1 & 17.2)

- Types of tests: compliance; substantive (Elements 17.1 & 17.2)

- Management letters which include systems weaknesses, clerical/accounting mistakes, disagreement re. accounting policies or treatment (Element 17.3)

Auditing principles and theory

- Principles of control: separation of functions; need for authorisation; recording custody; vouching; verification (Elements 17.1, 17.2 & 17.3)

- Materality (Elements 17.1, 17.2 & 17.3)

- Audit isk (Elements 17.1 & 17.2)

The organisation

- Understanding that the accounting systems of an organisation are affected by its organisational structure, its administrative systems and procedures and the nature of its business transactions (Elements 17.1, 17.2 & 17.3)

- An understanding of the organisation's systems and knowledge of specific auditing procedures (Elements 17.1, 17.2 & 17.3)

Element 17.1 Contribute to the planning of an audit assignment

Performance criteria	Chapters in this Text
1 Systems under review are ascertained and clearly recorded on appropriate working papers	1-5, 7, 18
2 Control objectives are correctly identified	1-5, 7, 18
3 Risks are accurately assessed	1-5, 7, 18
4 Significant weaknesses in control are correctly recorded	1-5, 7-10, 18-19
5 Account balances to be verified and the associated risks are identified	1-5, 7, 11-16, 18
6 An appropriate sample is selected	1-5, 18
7 Appropriate tests are selected or devised in accordance with the organisation's procedures	1-5, 8-16, 18
8 Confidentiality and security procedures are followed	1-3, 5-6, 18
9 The proposed audit plan is formulated clearly in consultation with appropriate personnel and submitted for approval to the appropriate person	1-6, 18

Range statement

1   Accounting systems: purchases; sales; stock; expenses; balance sheet items; payroll

2   Types of accounting systems: manual; computerised

3   Tests: compliance; substantive

Element 17.2 Contribute to the conduct of an audit assignment

Performance criteria	Chapters in this Text
1 Tests, as specified in the audit plan, are correctly conducted, the results properly recorded and conclusions validly drawn	1-3, 5-16, 18-19
2 The existence, completeness, ownership, valuation and description of assets and liabilities is established and supported by appropriate evidence	1-3, 5-6, 8-16, 18-19
3 All matters of an unusual nature are identified and promptly referred to the audit supervisor	1-3, 5-16, 18-19
4 Material and significant errors, deficiencies or other variations from standard are identified, recorded and reported to the audit supervisor	1-3, 5-16, 18-19
5 The IT environment is examined and assessed for security	1-3, 5, 10, 18
6 Discussions with staff operating the system to be audited are conducted in a manner which promotes professional relationships between auditing and operational staff	1-3, 5-6, 18
7 Confidentiality and security procedures are followed	1-3, 5-6, 18

Range statement

1   Accounting systems: purchases; sales; stock; expenses; balance sheet items; payroll

2   Types of accounting systems: manual; computerised

3   Types of tests: compliance; substantive

BPP
PUBLISHING

Element 17.3 Prepare related draft reports

Performance criteria	Chapters in this Text
1 Clear, concise draft reports relating to the audit assignment are prepared and submitted for review and approval in accordance with organisational procedures	1-3, 5-7, 16
2 Conclusions are valid and supported by evidence	1-3, 5, 7, 16
3 Recommendations are constructive and practicable	1-3, 5, 7, 16
4 Preliminary conclusions and recommendations are discussed and agreed with the audit supervisor	1-3, 5-7, 16
5 Confidentiality and security procedures are followed	1-3, 5-6, 18

Range statement

1   Draft reports relating to: manual system; computerised system

ASSESSMENT STRATEGY

This unit is assessed by **devolved assessment**.

Devolved Assessment *(More detail can be found in the Devolved Assessment Kit)*

Devolved assessment is a means of collecting evidence of your ability to carry out practical activities and to **operate effectively in the conditions of the workplace** to the standards required. Evidence may be collected at your place of work or at an Approved Assessment Centre by means of simulations of workplace activity, or by a combination of these methods.

If the Approved Assessment Centre is a **workplace** you may be observed carrying out accounting activities as part of your normal work routine. You should collect documentary evidence of the work you have done, or contributed, in an **accounting portfolio**. Evidence collected in a portfolio can be assessed in addition to observed performance or where it is not possible to assess by observation.

Where the Approved Assessment Centre is a **college or training organisation**, devolved assessment will be by means of a combination of the following.

(a)   Documentary evidence of activities carried out at the workplace, collected by you in an **accounting portfolio**

(b)   Realistic **simulations** of workplace activities; these simulations may take the form of case studies and in-tray exercises and involve the use of primary documents and reference sources

(c)   **Projects and assignments** designed to assess the Standards of Competence

If you are unable to provide workplace evidence, you will be able to complete the assessment requirements by the alternative methods listed above.

Part A
The purpose and regulation of auditing

Chapter 1   The nature, purpose and scope of auditing

Chapter topic list

1   Introduction to this text

2   Reasons for an audit

3   Scope of an audit

4   Types of audits

5   Chronology of an audit

Learning objectives

On completion of this chapter you will be able to:

	Performance criteria	Range statement
• Explain why audits are carried out and what they involve	all	all
• List the main stages of an audit	all	all

BPP
PUBLISHING

1   INTRODUCTION TO THIS TEXT

1.1   Auditing is a fundamental business discipline. In this text we shall be studying the audit of accounts, the end product of which is a report on their truth and fairness. Since accounts are used by businesses, organisations etc to communicate how they have done, a favourable audit report sends out signals to the readers of the accounts that they can rely on the picture which the accounts give. As many of the readers will be making important decisions as a result of what they have read, the assurance given by the audit report is thus extremely important.

1.2   Thus auditing is a vital and very demanding occupation. Auditors may find themselves having to make informed judgements about a whole range of organisations and a whole range of business situations. Effective judgements can only be made if auditors understand how organisations operate and the environment in which they operate. Auditing is thus a very practical, very real-world subject.

1.3   In this chapter we start by going into detail about what the audit of accounts is designed to **achieve**, and what **assurance** it gives. We shall introduce the work of the **Auditing Practices Board**, who set the standards which auditors must follow. We shall then put audits of accounts into further context by discussing briefly what other **types** of **audit** there are. Lastly we will go into more detail about the **different stages** of an **audit** of accounts.

1.4   The rest of the text builds on the themes identified in this chapter. In Chapters 2 to 3 we shall discuss the **rules and regulations** which govern the work of auditors. In Chapters 4 to 6 we shall demonstrate how important it is for auditors to **plan** their work **thoroughly and knowledgeably,** and how auditors design their audit programme. In Chapters 7 to 10 we consider how auditors **ascertain the client's accounting system, and test the internal controls** operated by the client. In Chapters 11 to 15 we shall discuss the **detailed tests** auditors carry out to **substantiate** the figures in the accounts. Lastly, in Chapters 16 to 19 we shall consider **procedures at the end of the audit** and the contents of the all-important **audit report**.

1.5   Within the text there are a number of exercises which are designed to help you test your understanding of what you have read. You should take these seriously as illustrations of how auditing theory is applied, as it must be, in practice.

2   REASONS FOR AN AUDIT

2.1   Suppose Miles decides to set up in business writing and publishing legal textbooks. For the first couple of years all goes well. The books sell steadily and Miles derives some income from the business.

2.2   Miles however feels that he could make more income from the business if he used better equipment and if he employed other authors to write some of the textbooks. To do this however he needs more money, and he decides to obtain it by asking his rich friend Anna to invest in the business.

2.3   Anna is interested in investing but does not wish to go into partnership with Miles, as she does not wish to take an active part in the business, nor does she want to have unlimited liability (being liable to lose all her assets if necessary to settle the business's debts.) She therefore suggests to Miles that the business is incorporated as a limited company, which will mean that she only stands to lose at maximum the amount she has invested in the company should it become insolvent. Miles agrees, and the business is incorporated as a limited company with Anna owning 95% and Miles owning 5% of the shares. They both agree that Miles is to be paid a reasonable salary as managing director of the business.

2.4   At the end of the first year of trading as a limited company, Anna receives a copy of the accounts. Profits are lower than she expected, and hence the dividends she can receive are lower. Anna contacts Miles for an explanation, but is assured by him that the accounts are accurate. Anna however knows that Miles's main reward from the business is his salary, which is not dependent upon the profits. Anna feels she needs further assurance on the accounts, but she does not know a great deal about financial matters. How can she obtain the assurance she wants?

2.5   The solution is that the assurance Anna is seeking can be given by an audit of the financial statements. An auditor can provide the two things Anna requires.

- A **knowledgeable review** of the company' s business and of the accounts
- An **impartial view** since Miles' view may be partial

2.6   Hence it is important for the auditor not only to have the skills necessary to carry out a proper audit; he or she must be **independent** as well. We shall discuss the importance of auditor independence and integrity later in this text.

2.7   Other people will also read the company's accounts with interest- the company's creditors and the Inland Revenue for example. Although different readers will judge the accounts by different criteria, all readers will gain assurance from the knowledge that the accounts they have read have been subject to an audit.

Rules governing audits

2.8   The above example was that of a small company. Imagine how many people read a large company's accounts. Consider also that a number of these readers will not just be reading a single company's accounts, but will also be reading the accounts of a large number of companies, and making comparisons between them. They will want assurances when making comparisons that the reliability of the accounts does not vary from company to company. This assurance will be obtained not just from knowing each set of accounts has been audited, but knowing that each set of accounts has been audited to **common standards**.

2.9   Hence there is a need for audits to be **regulated** so that auditors follow the same standards. As we shall see in the next few chapters, auditors have to follow rules issued by a variety of bodies. Some obligations are imposed by **Parliament**; for company auditors by the Companies Act 1985. Some obligations are imposed by the professional bodies to which auditors are required to belong (such as the **AAT**).

2.10   The detailed requirements that auditors are obliged to follow are set by the **Auditing Practices Board** (APB). We shall be talking more about the Auditing Practices Board's work later, but for now we shall look at how the APB define an audit in their *Glossary of Terms*.

> **KEY TERM**
>
> An **audit** is an exercise whose objective is to enable auditors to express an opinion whether the financial statements give a true and fair view (or equivalent) of the entity's affairs at the period end and of its profit and loss (or income and expenditure) for the period then ended and have been properly prepared in accordance with the applicable reporting framework (for example relevant legislation and applicable accounting standards) or, where statutory or other specific requirements prescribe the term, whether the financial statements 'present fairly'.

2.11 This wording follows very closely that of the auditors' report on financial statements, which we will look at later. We will also look at some definitions of terms used here, in particular 'true and fair view', later on.

3 SCOPE OF AN AUDIT

3.1 In the last section we discussed the reasons for having an audit. We also mentioned the work of the Auditing Practices Board who set auditing standards which all auditors should follow.

3.2 The APB's SAS 100 *Objective and general principles governing an audit of financial statements* makes a number of important observations about the responsibilities of auditors, and the limitations of audit work.

3.3 We will discuss in detail in Chapter 2 the authority of the guidance by the Auditing Practices Board. For now you should know that SAS 100, in common with all other SASs, contains a number of Statements of Auditing Standards which auditors must follow. The first Statement of Auditing Standards in SAS 100 is as follows.

> **SAS 100.1**
>
> In undertaking an audit of financial statements auditors should:
>
> (a) carry out procedures designed to obtain sufficient appropriate audit evidence, in accordance with Auditing Standards contained in SASs, to determine with reasonable confidence whether the financial statements are free of material misstatement;
>
> (b) evaluate the overall presentation of the financial statements, in order to ascertain whether they have been prepared in accordance with relevant legislation and accounting standards; and
>
> (c) issue a report containing a clear expression of their opinion on the financial statements.

3.4 SAS 100.2 sets out the key ethical principles which govern auditors' responsibilities.

- Integrity
- Objectivity
- Independence
- Professional competence and due care
- Professional behaviour
- Confidentiality

These matters are discussed further in Chapter 2.

3.5 However auditors are not responsible for preparing the financial statements. They may assist management by providing accounting services, but ultimately the directors are responsible for the financial statements.

> 'The responsibility for the preparation and presentation of the financial statements is that of the directors of the entity. Auditors are responsible for forming and expressing an opinion on the financial statements. The audit of the financial statements does not relieve the directors of any of their responsibilities.

Limitations of audit and use of auditor judgement

3.6 SAS 100 goes on to point out that there are a number of limitations in what the auditor does. Firstly the auditor's opinion is *not* a **guarantee** of the **future viability** of the entity, or an **assurance** of **management's efficiency** and **effectiveness.** Undoubtedly the auditor pays some attention to both these matters when carrying out an audit but neither represents the main purpose of an audit.

3.7 An audit looks at what has happened **in the past,** over the period covered by the accounts, and the assets and liabilities held by the client at the end of that period. The auditors cannot guarantee what applies to the past will apply to the future.

3.8 Auditors will be primarily concerned with how the **decisions of management affect** the **financial statements.** As well as producing the audit report, auditors may recommend improved controls but they are not conducting a wide-ranging review of efficiency.

Use of auditor judgement

3.9 'Reasonable assurance' lies at the heart of what a user of financial statements can and should expect from an auditors' report. SAS 100 attempts to close the 'expectations gap' between what people think auditors do, and what auditors really do in practice. First of all, SAS 100 points out that financial statements are *not* 'absolute' or 'correct' as they represent a combination of fact and judgement.

3.10 Secondly the assurance auditors give is governed by the fact that auditors use **judgement** in deciding what audit procedures to use and what conclusions to draw, and also by the limitations of every audit.

- The fact that **auditors do not check every item** in the accounting records
- The **limitations** of **accounting** and **control systems**
- The possibility that **client staff** might **not tell the truth,** or collude in fraud
- The fact that **audit evidence indicates** what is **probable** rather than what is certain

Hence auditors can only **express an opinion**; they **cannot certify** whether **accounts are** completely **correct.**

3.11 Material misstatements may exist in financial statements and auditors will plan their work on this basis, with **professional scepticism**. SAS 100 makes it clear that, even where auditors assess the risk of litigation or adverse publicity as very low, they must still perform sufficient procedures according to auditing standards. There can never be a reason for carrying out an audit of a lower quality than that demanded by the auditing standards.

4   TYPES OF AUDITS

EXAMPLES OF STATUTORY AND NON-STATUTORY AUDITS	
Statutory audits	*Non-statutory audits*
Limited companies Building societies Trade union and employee associations Housing associations Large charities Investment businesses	Clubs Small charities Sole traders Partnerships

4.1   When carrying out **statutory** audits, auditors need to consider the **laws and regulations** that govern the audit.

4.2   Auditors may carry out **non-statutory audits** because the owners, trustees or other interested parties want them. Auditors will need to consider the internal rules or constitution of the club, society, partnership etc.

External and internal audit

4.3   We have discussed auditing in particular in the context of the APB definition quoted at the start of Section 3 of this chapter. The definition relates to the work of **external auditors**, independent persons brought in from outside an organisation to review the accounts prepared by management. **Internal auditors** perform a different role, which we will discuss briefly here, and in depth in Chapter 19.

4.4   The management of an organisation will wish to establish accounting and control systems to ensure that business activities are carried out efficiently. They will institute administrative and financial controls.

4.5   Larger organisations may appoint full-time staff whose function is to monitor and report on the running of the company's operations. **Internal audit** staff members are one type of control. Although some of the work carried out by internal auditors is similar to that performed by external auditors, there are important differences between the nature of the two functions.

DIFFERENCES BETWEEN EXTERNAL AND INTERNAL AUDITS		
	External	*Internal*
Independence	Independent of organisation	Appointed by management
Responsibilities	Fixed by statute	Decided by management
Report to	Members	Management
Scope of work	Express an opinion on truth and fairness of accounts	Consider whatever financial and operational areas management determines

5   CHRONOLOGY OF AN AUDIT

5.1   The chart on the next page outlines the main stages of an audit that are *normally* followed.

5.2   Before examining each stage in detail it is worth stating the more important duties of the auditors of a limited company. They must satisfy themselves that:

(a) **Proper accounting records** have been **kept**.

(b) The **accounts** are in **agreement** with the **accounting records**.

(c) The **accounts** have been **prepared** in accordance with the **Companies Act**, and relevant **accounting standards**.

(d) The **balance sheet** shows a **true and fair view** of the **state of the company's affairs** and the **profit and loss account** shows a **true and fair view** of the **results for the period**.

(The objects of most other audits of accounts will be broadly similar.)

5.3   Thus certain common elements form a major part of the auditors' work on any client.

(a) **Making** such **tests** and enquiries as they consider necessary to form an opinion as to the reliability of the accounting records as a basis for the preparation of accounts

(b) **Checking** the **accounts** against the underlying records

(c) **Reviewing** the **accounts** for compliance with the Companies Act and accounting standards

5.4   We will now look at the various stages identified in the diagram.

Determine audit approach

Stage 1

5.5   The first stage in any audit should be to determine its **scope** and the auditors' general approach. For statutory audits the scope is clearly laid down in the Companies Act as expanded by the Statements of Auditing Standards issued by the Auditing Practices Board. A **letter of engagement** setting out the terms of the audit will be submitted or confirmed before the start of each annual audit.

5.6   In addition to the letter of engagement auditors should prepare an **audit plan** to be placed on the audit file. The purpose of this document is to provide a record of the major areas to which the auditors attach special significance and to highlight any particular difficulties or points of concern peculiar to the audit client.

5.7   The detailed audit planning which arises from the determination of the scope of work is discussed further in Chapter 4.

Ascertain the accounting system and internal controls

Stage 2

5.8   The objective at this stage is to determine the **flow of documents** and **extent of controls** in existence. This is very much a fact-finding exercise, achieved by discussing the accounting system and document flow with all the relevant departments, including typically, sales, purchases, cash, stock and accounts personnel.

Stage 3

5.9 The objective here is to prepare a **comprehensive record** for use in evaluation of the systems. Records are in various formats.

- Charts, for example organisation charts and records of the books of account
- Narrative notes
- Internal control questionnaires (ICQs)
- Flowcharts

These documents are covered in detail in Chapter 7.

Stage 4

5.10 The auditors' objective here is to confirm that the **system recorded** is the same as that in **operation**.

5.11 After completion of the preparation (or update) of the systems records the auditors will confirm their understanding of the system by performing **walk-through tests**. These involve tracing a few transactions of each type through the system and observing the operation of controls over them. This procedure will establish whether the accounting system operates in the manner ascertained and recorded. The need for this check arises as client's staff will occasionally tell the auditors what they should be doing (the established procedures) rather than what is actually being done in practice.

5.12 Stages 2 and 3 as described above will be carried out in detail at the beginning of a new audit assignment and the results of these stages, which will be incorporated in the permanent audit file, will be reviewed and amended each year at the start of the annual audit. As part of this annual review, further walk-through tests will be carried out to confirm the system.

Assess the accounting system and internal controls

Stage 5

5.13 The purpose of **evaluating** the **systems** is to assess their reliability and formulate a basis for testing their effectiveness in practice. Following the evaluation, the auditors will be able to determine the extent of the further tests to be carried out at Stages 6 and 8 below.

Test the accounting system and internal controls

Stage 6

5.14 Given effective controls, the objective is to select and perform tests designed to establish compliance with the system, ie to **test the controls**. Auditors should consider the risk that the controls they have recorded will fail to work. They also need to check that the controls are as effective in practice as they are on paper. One of the most important points underlying modern auditing is that, if the controls are strong, the records should be reliable and consequently the amount of substantive testing (Stage 8) can be reduced.

5.15 **Tests of controls** are like walk-through checks in so far as they are concerned with the workings of the system. There are a number of differences between the two.

- Tests of controls are concerned only with those areas subject to effective control.
- Tests of controls cover a representative sample of transactions throughout the period.

A DIAGRAMMATIC REPRESENTATION OF THE SYSTEMS AUDIT

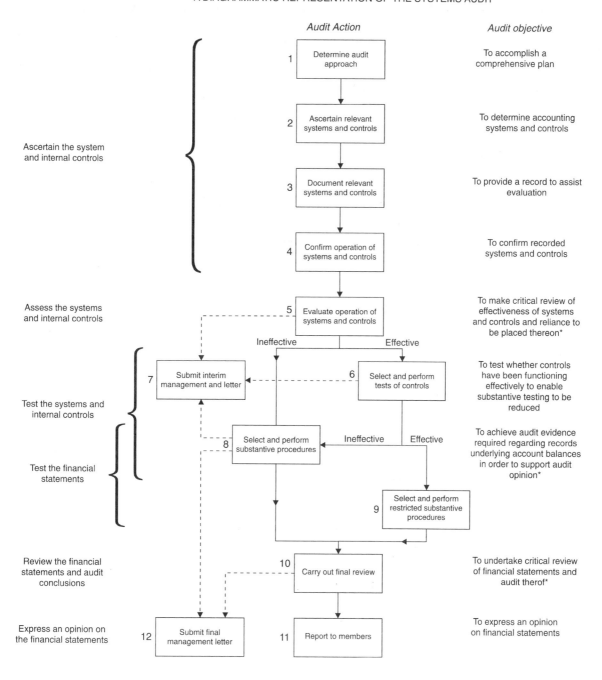

Audit Action

Audit objective

1	Determine audit approach	To accomplish a comprehensive plan
2	Ascertain relevant systems and controls	To determine accounting systems and controls
3	Document relevant systems and controls	To provide a record to assist evaluation
4	Confirm operation of systems and controls	To confirm recorded systems and controls
5	Evaluate operation of systems and controls	To make critical review of effectiveness of systems and controls and reliance to be placed thereon*

Ascertain the system and internal controls

Assess the systems and internal controls

Ineffective / Effective

7	Submit interim management and letter	
6	Select and perform tests of controls	To test whether controls have been functioning effectively to enable substantive testing to be reduced

Test the systems and internal controls

Ineffective / Effective

8	Select and perform substantive procedures	To achieve audit evidence required regarding records underlying account balances in order to support audit opinion*
9	Select and perform restricted substantive procedures	

Test the financial statements

Review the financial statements and audit conclusions

10	Carry out final review	To undertake critical review of financial statements and audit therof*

Express an opinion on the financial statements

12	Submit final management letter	
11	Report to members	To express an opinion on financial statements

———————▶ Stages in audit procedures

- - - - - - - - -▶ Contact with management

* A secondary objective of this audit action is to recommend to management improvements in systems controls and in accounting procedures and practices

BPP PUBLISHING

- Tests of control are likely to cover a larger number of items than walk-through tests.

5.16 The conclusion drawn from the results of a test of controls may be either that:

(a) The **controls** are **effective**, in which case the auditors will only need to carry out restricted substantive procedures.

(b) The **controls** are **ineffective** in practice, although they had appeared strong on paper, in which case the auditors will need to carry out more extensive substantive procedures.

5.17 Stage 6 should only be carried out if the controls are evaluated at Stage 5 as probably being effective. If the auditors know that the controls are ineffective then there is no point in carrying out tests of controls which will merely confirm what is already known. Instead the auditors should go straight on to carry out full substantive procedures (Stage 8).

Stage 7

5.18 After evaluating the systems and carrying out tests of controls, auditors normally send management a **management letter** identifying weaknesses and recommending improvements.

Test the financial statements

Stages 8 and 9

5.19 These tests are not concerned with the workings of the system, but with substantiating the figures in the **accounting records,** and eventually, in the final accounts themselves. Hence they are known as **substantive tests.**

5.20 Substantive tests also serve to assess the effect of errors, should errors exist. Before designing a substantive procedure it is essential to consider whether any errors produced could be significant. If the answer is 'NO' there is no point in performing a test.

Review the financial statements

Stage 10

5.21 The aim of the overall review is to determine the **overall reliability** of the accounts by making a critical analysis of content and presentation.

Express an opinion

5.22 There are two types of opinion given by the auditors, one statutory and one non-statutory.

Stage 11

5.23 The **report to the members** is the end product of the audit in which the auditors express their opinion of the accounts.

Stage 12

5.24 The final **letter to management** is an important non-statutory end product of the audit. Its purpose is to make further suggestions for improvements in the systems and to place on record specific points in connection with the audit and accounts.

Activity 1.1

Dan and Thomas are in partnership together. Thomas has always been responsible for the financial side of the partnership while Dan has been responsible for sales. Recently a customer has told Dan that there would be advantages for the partnership in having the accounts and accounting records audited. Dan has asked you if what the customer says is true.

Task

Explain to Dan what the advantages will be of having the partnership's accounts and records audited.

Key learning points

- An audit is essentially an **independent knowledgeable** scrutiny and review.

- In this text we shall be concentrating on **audits** of **accounts.** The aim of this type of audit is for auditors to report on whether a **true** and **fair view** is shown by the accounts.

- Auditors are regulated by statute, professional bodies and the **Auditing Practices Board** (APB).

- The APB defines the key stages of an audit as being:

  ○ Carry out procedures to obtain **sufficient appropriate audit evidence**
  ○ **Evaluate** the **presentation** of accounts
  ○ Issue a report containing a **clear expression** of **opinion.**

- The APB also points out that audits at best give **reasonable assurance** that the accounts are free from material misstatement.

- As well as audits of accounts, there are various other types of audit, statutory and non-statutory.

- **Internal auditors** are employed as part of an organisation's system of controls. Their responsibilities are determined by management and may be wide-ranging.

- The **key** stages of the audit process are:

  ○ Determine audit approach
  ○ Ascertain the accounting system and internal controls
  ○ Assess the accounting system and internal controls
  ○ Test the accounting system and internal controls
  ○ Test the financial statements (substantive testing)
  ○ Review the financial statements
  ○ Express an opinion

Quick quiz

1   Auditors normally report on whether accounts give a _____ and _____ view. Fill in the blanks.

2   What according to SAS 100 does the auditors' opinion give to financial statements?

3   What aspects of the auditors' work are particularly affected by the use of auditors' judgement?

4   What are the examples given by SAS 100 of limitations on auditing?

5   Which statute principally governs the audit of limited companies?

6   What type of tests confirm auditors' understanding of an accounting system?

13

7   What areas of a company's business would tests of control normally cover?

8   What type of test do auditors use to test the financial statements?

9   As well as reporting on the financial statements, what other type of report might auditors make at the end of the audit?

Answers to quick quiz

1   Auditors normally report on whether accounts give a **true** and **fair** view.

2   SAS 100 states that the auditors' opinion provides reasonable assurance from an independent source that the accounts present a true and fair view.

3   Auditors' judgement particularly affects the gathering of evidence and the drawing of conclusions.

4   Limitations on auditing include those resulting from:

   (a)   The impracticality of examining all items within an account balance or class of transactions
   (b)   The inherent limitations of any accounting and control system
   (c)   The possibility of collusion or misrepresentation for fraudulent purposes
   (d)   Most audit evidence being persuasive rather than conclusive

5   The Companies Act 1985 governs the audit of limited companies.

6   Walk-through tests confirm auditors' understanding of an accounting system.

7   Tests of control normally cover only those areas subject to effective internal control.

8   Substantive tests are used by auditors to test financial statements.

9   As well as issuing an audit report, auditors might also send a final letter to management.

Answers to activities

Answer 1.1

The partnership will gain the following advantages from having the books audited.

(a)   Although Dan presumably has a good idea about the partnership's sales, he may not be aware of other financial transactions of the partnership. For Dan, an audit by someone who is objective and who can understand the accounting records will give reassurance that the partnership is producing the results claimed by Thomas.

(b)   An audit may identify weaknesses in the accounting system of the business. The auditor may be able to suggest improvements which would save the partnership time and money.

(c)   Arguments between the partners will be avoided if the accounts are checked by an independent auditor. This particularly applies to partner profit shares.

(d)   The accounts will have greater credibility for other users if they are audited. For example a bank may make extra finance conditional on the partnership producing audited accounts.

Chapter 2   The auditing regulatory framework

Chapter topic list

1   Introduction

2   The structure of the UK accounting and auditing profession

3   Auditing standards

4   Professional ethics

5   Independence

Learning objectives

On completion of this chapter you will be able to:

	Performance criteria	Range statement
• Outline how the auditing profession is regulated	all	all
• Describe the purpose of Statements of Auditing Standards	all	all
• Describe the fundamental principles of ethics laid down by the AAT	all	all
• Discuss the importance of independence and confidentiality to the auditor's work	all	all

1   INTRODUCTION

1.1   This chapter summarises the roles of the various authorities that make the rules that affect auditors in this country. The Companies Act 1989 set up a system of audit regulation, administered by a number of **Recognised Supervisory Bodies.** These bodies aim to ensure that audits are conducted competently, by auditors who are '**fit and proper**'. To this end each Recognised Supervisory Body operates a **monitoring regime,** which involves periodic visits to firms by inspectors.

1.2   All auditors must follow certain standards when carrying out an audit. The body that sets those standards is the **Auditing Practices Board.** The most important guidance the Board issues is **Statements of Auditing Standards,** which contain principles and procedures that all auditors are obliged to follow.

1.3   AAT members are also subject to the AAT's **Guidelines on Professional Ethics.** These set out certain fundamental principles which all members must observe. Confidentiality is one such principle. The AAT's Guidelines try to strike a balance between stressing the importance of keeping the affairs of clients confidential, and stating that in certain instances auditors should consider (or have to) disclose client details to third parties.

1.4   Perhaps the most important guidelines are on **independence.** Auditors must not only be independent but be seen to be independent. In a number of cases it is not clear cut whether a particular situation is a threat to independence. Hence auditors must consider whether they are independent of their clients when accepting appointment as auditors, and must be alert subsequently for threats to independence.

2   THE STRUCTURE OF THE UK ACCOUNTING AND AUDITING PROFESSION

2.1   In the UK there are a large number of different accountancy, or accountancy-related, institutes and associations such as the Association of Accounting Technicians (AAT) or Chartered Institute of Management Accountants (CIMA).

2.2   All these bodies vary from each other depending on the nature of their aims and the specialisms their members wish to attain. They are all, however, characterised by various common attributes; stringent entrance requirements (examinations and practical experience), strict codes of ethics and technical updating of members. The membership of all these bodies is scattered through practice, industry, government and public bodies.

Eligibility as auditor

2.3   Membership of a Recognised Supervisory Body (discussed below) is the main criteria for eligibility as an auditor. An audit firm may be a body corporate (such as a company), a partnership, or a sole practitioner.

2.4   The Companies Act 1985 also requires an auditor to hold an 'appropriate qualification'. A person holds an 'appropriate qualification' if he or she has gained one of the following.

- Acknowledgement that he or she has met **the criteria** for appointment under CA 1985
- A **recognised qualification** obtained in the UK
- An **approved overseas qualification**

Ineligibility as auditor

2.5 Under the Companies Act 1985, a person is **ineligible** for appointment as a company auditor if he or she is any of the following.

(a) An **officer** or **employee** of the company

(b) A **partner** or **employee** of such a person

(c) A **partnership** in which such a person is a partner

(d) **Ineligible** by virtue of (a), (b) or (c) for appointment as auditor of any parent or subsidiary undertaking or a subsidiary undertaking of any parent undertaking of the company

(e) There exists between him or her or any associate (of his or hers) and the company (or company as referred to in (d) above) a **connection** of any description as may be specified in regulations laid down by Secretary of State

2.6 The legislation does *not* disqualify the following individuals from being an auditor of a limited company.

- A shareholder of the company
- A debtor or creditor of the company
- A close relative (such as a spouse or child) of an officer or employee of the company

However, the regulations of the accountancy bodies applying to their own members are stricter than statute in this respect.

2.7 Under the Companies Act 1985, a person may also be ineligible on the grounds of 'lack of independence'; the definition of lack of independence is to be determined by statutory instrument following consultation with the professional bodies.

2.8 Under s 389 CA 1985, if during his term of office a company auditor becomes ineligible for appointment to the office, he must vacate office and give notice in writing to the company.

Recognised Supervisory Bodies

2.9 The EU 8th Directive on company law requires that persons carrying out statutory audits must be approved by the authorities of EU member states. The authority to give this approval in the UK is delegated to Recognised Supervisory Bodies (RSBs). Under the new Act, an auditor must be a member of an RSB and be eligible under its own rules.

2.10 The RSBs are required to have rules to ensure that persons eligible for appointment as a company auditor are either (4(1), Sch 11, CA 1989):

- Individuals holding an appropriate qualification, or
- Firms controlled by qualified persons

2.11 The following bodies which have been designated as Recognised Supervisory Bodies include the following.

- Institute of Chartered Accountants in England and Wales (ICAEW)
- Institute of Chartered Accountants in Scotland (ICAS)
- Institute of Chartered Accountants in Ireland (ICAI)
- Association of Authorised Public Accountants (AAPA)
- Association of Chartered Certified Accountants (ACCA)

BPP PUBLISHING

2.12   Professional qualifications, which will be prerequisites for membership of an RSB, will be offered by Recognised Qualifying Bodies ('RQBs') approved by the Secretary of State.

Supervisory and monitoring roles

2.13   RSBs must also implement procedures for inspecting their registered auditors on a regular basis.

2.14   The frequency of inspection will depend on the number of partners, number of offices and number of listed company audits (these factors are also reflected in the size of annual registration fees payable). The length of the inspections depend on the size of the firm.

Activity 2.1

Who is ineligible for appointment as a company auditor?

---

3   AUDITING STANDARDS

The APB and Statements of Auditing Standards (SASs)

3.1   Auditing standards are set by the Auditing Practices Board (APB).

   (a)   The APB can issue auditing standards in its own right without having to obtain the approval of all the professional accounting bodies.

   (b)   It has strong representation from outside the accounting profession.

   (c)   It has a commitment to openness, with agenda papers being circulated to interested parties, and an annual report being published.

3.2   The APB issued a document in May 1993 entitled *The scope and authority of APB pronouncements*. The APB makes three categories of pronouncement.

   • Statements of Auditing Standards (SASs)
   • Practice Notes
   • Bulletins

3.3   The scope of **SASs** is as follows.

   'SASs contain basic principles and essential procedures ('Auditing Standards') which are indicated by bold type and with which auditors are required to comply, except where otherwise stated in the SAS concerned, in the conduct of any audit of financial statements.'

3.4   The APB also publishes SASs which apply to audits and related services other than audits of financial statements, or which apply to specific types of audits, for example audits of specialised industries.

3.5   Apart from statements in bold type, SASs also contain other material which is not prescriptive but which is designed to help auditors interpret and apply auditing standards. The APB document also states that auditing standards need not be applied to immaterial items (items which are not significant to the accounts. We shall discuss what is material and what is immaterial in later chapters.)

3.6   The authority of SASs is defined as follows.

   'Auditors who do not comply with Auditing Standards when performing company or other audits in Great Britain make themselves liable to regulatory action by the RSB with whom they are registered and which may include the withdrawal of registration and hence of eligibility to perform company audits.'

DEVOLVED ASSESSMENT ALERT

Throughout this text we emphasise the statements of basic principles and essential procedures that are contained in bold print in SASs. However, you **must** remember that these statements are designed to be practical guidance. You must therefore be able to apply the standards to practical situations; learning the standards off by heart will not be enough.

3.7 **Practice Notes** are issued 'to assist auditors in applying Auditing Standards of general application to particular circumstances and industries'.

3.8 **Bulletins** are issued 'to provide auditors with timely guidance on new or emerging issues'.

3.9 Practice Notes and Bulletins are persuasive rather than prescriptive, but they indicate good practice and have a similar status to the explanatory material in SASs. Both Practice Notes and Bulletins may be included in later SASs.

3.10 The APB standards which you should know are listed below.

Statements of Auditing Standards (SASs): APB		Issue date
Series 001/099	*Introductory matters*	
010	Scope and authority of APB pronouncements	May 93
Series 100/199	*Responsibility*	
100	Objective and general principles governing an audit of financial statements	Mar 95
110	Fraud and error	Jan 95
120	Consideration of law and regulations	Jan 95
130	The going concern basis in financial statements	Nov 94
140	Engagement letters	Mar 95
150	Subsequent events	Mar 95
160	Other information in documents containing audited financial statements	Oct 99
Series 200/299	*Planning, controlling and recording*	
200	Planning	Mar 95
210	Knowledge of the business	Mar 95
220	Materiality and the audit	Mar 95
230	Working papers	Mar 95
240	Quality control for audit work	Mar 95
Series 300/399	*Accounting systems and internal control*	
300	Accounting and internal control systems and audit risk assessments	Mar 95
Series 400/499	*Evidence*	
400	Audit evidence	Mar 95
410	Analytical procedures	Mar 95
420	Audit of accounting estimates	Mar 95
430	Audit sampling	Mar 95
440	Management representations	Mar 95
450	Opening balances and comparatives	Mar 95
460	Related parties	Nov 95
470	Overall review of financial statements	Mar 95
480	Service organisations	Jan 99

Series 500/599	*Using the work of others*	
500	Considering the work of internal audit	Mar 95
510	The relationship between principal auditors and other auditors	Mar 95
520	Using the work of an expert	Mar 95
Series 600/699	*Reporting*	
600	Auditors' report on financial statements	May 93
610	Reports to directors or management	Mar 95
-	*Glossary of terms*	Mar 95

Auditing Guidelines: APC		*Issue date*
405	Attendance at stocktaking	Oct 83
407	Auditing in a computer environment	Jun 84

3.11 Each SAS is discussed in this Study Text in the relevant chapter.

APC *The auditor's operational standard*

3.12 The matters dealt with in *The auditor's operational standard* were the cornerstones of auditing until the new auditing standards were produced. It is used as the basis for some of the old auditing guidelines which are still relevant (see above). Here is the full text.

> '*The auditor's operational standard*
>
> This Auditing Standard should be read in conjunction with the Explanatory Foreword to Auditing Standards and Guidelines. General guidance on procedures by which this auditing standard may be complied with are given in auditing guidelines:
>
> Planning, controlling and recording
> Accounting systems
> Audit evidence
> Internal controls
> Review of financial statements
>
> 1   This auditing standard applies whenever an audit is carried out.
>
> *Planning, controlling and recording*
> 2   The auditor should adequately plan, control and record his work.
>
> *Accounting systems*
> 3   The auditor should ascertain the enterprise's system of recording and processing transactions and assess its adequacy as a basis for the preparation of financial statements.
>
> *Audit evidence*
> 4   The auditor should obtain relevant and reliable audit evidence sufficient to enable him to draw reasonable conclusions therefrom.
>
> *Internal controls*
> 5   If the auditor wishes to place reliance on any internal controls, he should ascertain and evaluate those controls and perform compliance tests on their operation.
>
> *Review of financial statements*
> 6   The auditor should carry out such a review of the financial statements as is sufficient, in conjunction with the conclusions drawn from the other audit evidence obtained, to give him a reasonable basis for his opinion on the financial statements.
>
> *Effective date*
> 7   This auditing standard is effective for the audit of financial statements relating to accounting periods starting on or after 1 April 1980.'

3.13 Each of the key paragraphs 2 to 6 had an associated guideline, as indicated in the introduction to the standard. These have now been replaced by SASs.

Activity 2.2

What types of guidance do Statements of Auditing Standards (SASs) contain?

4 PROFESSIONAL ETHICS

4.1 There are a number of ethical issues which are of great importance to the client-auditor relationship. The onus is always on the auditors, not only to be ethical, but also to be *seen* to be ethical.

4.2 The AAT does not leave its members adrift with no guidance on ethical matters. Although every situation involving ethical decisions is different, basic guidelines are needed on fundamental issues. In this way, members have a measure by which to gauge their behaviour.

Guidelines on Professional Ethics

4.3 Consequently, the AAT publishes, in its annual handbook, *Guidelines on Professional Ethics*. These Guidelines state that an essential characteristic of accountants is the development of an ethical approach to the work and to clients acquired by experience and professional supervision under training and safeguarded by a strict disciplinary code.

4.4 The *Guidelines* also emphasise the public interest aspects of accountancy and the way accountants recognise and accept their responsibility to the public. Many people, not just clients, rely on the accountant's work.

Fundamental principles

4.5 The fundamental principles are very important indeed. These fundamental principles are quoted in full here as you should *learn them*.

Fundamental principles

1 **Integrity**

Members should be straightforward and honest in performing professional work.

2 **Objectivity**

Members should be fair and should not allow prejudice or bias or the influence of others to override objectivity.

3 **Professional and Technical Competence**

(a) Members should refrain from undertaking or continuing any assignments which they are not competent to carry out unless advice and assistance is obtained to ensure that the assignment is carried out satisfactorily.

(b) Members also have a continuing duty:

(i) to maintain professional knowledge and skills at a level required to ensure that a client or employer receives the advantage of competent professional service based on up-to-date developments in practice, legislation and techniques;

(ii) to maintain their technical and ethical standards in areas relevant to their work through Continuing Professional Development.

4 **Due Care**

(a) A Member, having accepted an assignment, has an obligation to carry it out with due care and reasonable despatch having regard to the nature and scope of the assignment.

> (b) Special care is required where Members undertake assignments for clients who may have little or no knowledge of accounting and taxation matters.
>
> 5 **Confidentiality**
>
> Members should respect the confidentiality of information acquired during the course of performing professional work and should not use or disclose any such information without proper and specific authority or unless there is a legal or professional right or duty to disclose.
>
> 6 **Professional behaviour**
>
> Members should act in a manner consistent with the good reputation of the profession and refrain from any conduct which might bring discredit to the profession.

4.6 The *Guidelines* then expand these fundamental principles into detailed guidance, split into two sections.

- Guidance applicable to all accounting technicians
- Guidance applicable to self-employed accounting technicians

4.7 In the case of the auditing units of competence, we need only look at **confidentiality** and **independence** (a very important auditing attribute).

Confidentiality

4.8 Confidentiality procedures are mentioned specifically in the units of competence and so it is important to look at what the AAT says on the subject.

> **Confidentiality**
>
> '1 Members have an obligation to respect the confidentiality of information about a client's or employer's affairs, or the affairs of clients or employers, acquired in the course of professional work. The duty of confidentiality continues even after the end of the relationship between the member and the employer or client.
>
> 2 Confidentiality should always be observed by members unless specific authority has been given to disclose information or there is a legal or professional duty to disclose.
>
> 3 Members have an obligation to ensure that staff under their control and persons from whom advice and assistance is obtained respect the principle of confidentiality.
>
> 4 Confidentiality concerns the matter of usage of information and not just non-disclosure or disclosure. A Member acquiring information in the course of professional work shall neither use nor appear to use that information for personal advantage or for the advantage of a third party.
>
> 5 Members have access to much confidential information about an employer's or client's affairs, or the affairs of clients of employers, not otherwise disclosed to the public. Therefore Members should be relied upon not to make unauthorised disclosure to other persons. This does not apply to disclosure of information in order to discharge their responsibilities properly according to the profession's standards.
>
> 6 The following are examples of the points which should be considered in determining the extent of which confidential information may be disclosed:
>
> (i) when disclosure is authorised. When authorisation to disclose is given by the client or the employer the interests of all the parties including those third parties whose interests might be affected should be considered;
>
> (ii) when disclosure is specifically required by law. This could lead to a Member:
>
> (a) producing documents or giving evidence in the course of legal proceedings; and
>
> (b) disclosing to the appropriate public authorities infringements of the law which might have come to light (such as money laundering);

> (iii) where there is a professional duty:
>
> (a) to comply with technical standards and ethical requirements;
>
> (b) to protect the professional interests of the Member in legal proceedings;
>
> (c) to respond to an inquiry by the AAT or by a regulatory body of an ethical, investigatory or disciplinary nature.
>
> 7 When the Member has determined that confidential information can be disclosed, the following points should be considered:
>
> (i) whether or not all the relevant facts are known and substantiated, to the extent it is practicable to do so; when the situation involves unsubstantiated fact or opinion, professional judgement should be used in determining the type of disclosure to be made if any;
>
> (ii) what type of communication is expected and to whom it will be communicated; in particular, the Member should be satisfied that the parties to whom the communication is addressed are appropriate recipients and have the authority to act on it; and
>
> (iii) whether or not the Member would incur any legal liability having made a communication and the consequences of incurring the relevant legal liability.

Security procedures

4.10 It is worth mentioning here a matter closely related to confidentiality: security. Security procedures help to maintain the confidentiality of the client. They tend to be a combination of very practical measures and detailed rules governing the technician's right to impart information about a client. A typical list of security procedures is as follows.

(a) **Do not discuss client matters** with any third party, including family and friends, even in a general way.

(b) **Do not use client information to your own gain**, nor carry on insider dealing by passing price-sensitive information to others.

(c) **Do not leave audit files unattended** at a client's premises. Lock them up at night.

(d) **Do not leave audit files** (or computer equipment) in **cars**, even in the boot, or in **unsecured private residences**.

(e) **Do not take working papers away** from the office or the client **unless strictly necessary**.

5 INDEPENDENCE

5.1 The independence of the auditor is central to his or her ability to perform an audit properly; as such it has been given a section of its own for discussion.

> **Objectivity**
>
> 1 The guidelines emphasise the need for a Member to maintain objectivity at all times. The principle of objectivity imposes the obligation on all Members to be fair minded, intellectually honest and free from conflicts of interest.
>
> 2 Members serve in many different capacities and should demonstrate their objectivity in varying circumstances.
>
> 3 Regardless of service or capacity, Members should protect the integrity of their professional services, maintain objectivity and avoid any subordination of their judgement by others.
>
> 4 Members need to bear in mind, in this context, the following factors:

(i)   whatever the nature of the professional services they provide, Members may be exposed to situations which involve the possibility of pressures and threats being exerted on them. These pressures and threats may impair their objectivity, and hence their independence;

(ii)   in dealing with independence, Members must address both:

(a)   *Independence of mind,* ie the state of mind which has regard to all considerations relevant to the task in hand but no other - independence of mind is also referred to as objectivity;

(b)   *Independence in appearance,* (or independence that can be demonstrated) ie the avoidance of situations inducing so obvious a threat to independence that an informed third party would question the Member's objectivity. Issues of independence in appearance are most likely to arise in relation to undertaking audit or other public financial reporting assignments;

(iii)   in situations which do not necessarily require independence in appearance, Members are generally able to safeguard their objectivity by analysing the threats and pressures which arise, and weighing against them the acknowledged safeguards which may be employed to negate those threats and pressures or reduce them to acceptable levels. Many safeguards arise as a result of:

(a)   a Member's normal strength of character and professionalism which enables him or her to confront the threats and pressures which may be exerted on him or her by employers or clients;

(b)   the fear of pressures of legal accountability;

(c)   the possibility of professional discipline and enforcement ;

(d)   the loss of reputation;

(iv)   Members have an obligation to ensure that personnel engaged in professional work are aware of the need to preserve their objectivity and, where appropriate, to demonstrate their independence.

Independence in reporting

5.2   The AAT states the following.

Independence in Financial Reporting and similar roles

'1   When undertaking a financial reporting assignment a self-employed Member should be independent in fact and appearance.

2   In order to safeguard their independence, Members contemplating any such assignment should consider certain matters before deciding whether to accept a new appointment, or whether to continue an existing appointment. These matters include the expectations of those directly affected by the work; the environment in which the work is to be conducted, including that within the Member's practice and the profession; the threats to objectivity which may actually arise or may appear to arise because of any expectations and the environment; and the safeguards which can be put in place to offset the risks and threats.

3   The Guidelines on Objectivity emphasise the need for the Member to maintain objectivity at all times. This is particularly so in financial reporting, and similar roles. In general, Members should be able to reach a proper and responsible decision whether or not to accept or continue an engagement based on a realistic assessment and weighing of the threats to objectivity which arise and of generally accepted safeguards which may be employed to negate those threats to objectivity or to reduce them to acceptable proportions.

4   The potential threats to objectivity and hence independence can be categorised in various ways. In essence they may arise from involvement by a Self-employed Member (or a close connection) in the client's affairs. These threats may be:

(i)   financial in nature ('self interest' threats);

(ii)   resulting from an executive, managerial, or operational involvement in the client's affairs and/or in the preparation of its accounts (a 'self-review' threat);

(iii)   arising from an emotional commitment to the client or its interest (such as to create a 'familiarity' or an 'intimidation' threat);

(iv)   or from taking a strongly proactive stance on the client's behalf (an 'advocacy' threat).'

Remember that the further guidance below applies to *all* self-employed accounting technicians, not just those acting as auditors.

Financial involvement with, or in the affairs of, clients

'Financial involvement with a client creates a self-interest threat to objectivity which is generally regarded as insurmountable. Financial involvement can arise in a number of ways, such as:

(i)   by direct or indirect financial interest;

(ii)   by loans to or from the client or any officer, director or principal shareholders of a client company. The self interest threat arising from outstanding fees is exacerbated when they become equivalent to a loan, and a Member should review the propriety of continuing to act where significant fees have been outstanding for twelve months or more. Special considerations may apply in circumstances involving Individual Voluntary Arrangements (IVAs) or other specific arrangements for payment;

(iii)   by holding a financial interest in a joint venture with a client or employee(s) of a client;

(iv)   when the receipt of fees from a client or group of connected clients represents a large proportion of the total gross fees of a Member or of the practice as a whole. The perceived threat grows with the size of the fees and is thus increased by work or services additional to the reporting assignment;

(v)   the provision of other services may also give rise to self-review, familiarity, or advocacy threats.'

5.3   The point about fees is very important. There is no hard-and-fast rule about what constitutes an unacceptable proportion of total gross fees (although the ICAEW, dealing with Registered Auditors, gives guidance of 10-15%). However, if the fees are all or a large part of fee income then the accounting technician should 'carefully consider whether independence has been impaired'.

Previous appointment in companies

AAT Guidelines

'When a Member who is self-employed is or was, within a period of two years prior to a potential assignment:

(i)   a Member of the Board, an officer or employee of a company;

(ii)   a partner of, or in the employment of, a member of the Board or an officer or employee of a company;

Then the Member would be regarded as having an insurmountable threat of a self-review nature, which would be incompatible with his or her continuing with a financial reporting assignment in relation to the company.'

BPP
PUBLISHING

Provision of other services to audit clients

> **AAT Guidelines**
>
> 'When Members provide consultancy services to clients, care should be taken when rendering advice not to report on management decisions which the Member has recommended, so as to avoid a self-review threat. The services provided by a Self-employed Member in the fields of management consultancy and taxation are advisory services which should not usurp the management functions of clients. Objectivity is not impaired by offering advisory services provided there is no involvement in, or responsibility assumed for, management decisions. Nevertheless, Members should remain aware of a possible self-review threat, and be careful not to go beyond, or appear to go beyond, the advisory function into the management sphere.'

Personal and family relationships

5.4 While not prescribing ethical requirements in detail, the *Guidelines* states the following.

> **AAT Guidelines**
>
> 'Personal and family relationships can affect objectivity. There is a particular need to ensure that an objective approach to any assignment is not endangered as a consequence of any personal or family relationship. Family relationships which will normally impose an unacceptable threat to objectivity in relation to financial reporting assignments are those in which the Member is the spouse, dependant child or relative living in a common household of the client, or vice-versa.'

Conflicts between interests of different clients

> **AAT Guidelines**
>
> 'There is, on the face of it, nothing improper in a Member or practice having two or more clients whose interests may be in conflict. In such a case however the work should be managed so as to avoid the interest of one client adversely affecting that of another. Where the acceptance or continuance of an engagement would, even with safeguards, materially prejudice the interests of any client the appointment should not be accepted or continued, or one of the appointments should be discontinued. All reasonable steps should be taken to ascertain whether any conflict of interests exists or is likely to arise, both in regard to new engagements and to any change in the circumstances of existing clients. Relationships with existing clients need to be considered before new appointments are accepted. Wherever a significant conflict between the interests of different clients or potential clients is identified, sufficient disclosure should be made to both parties so that they may make an informed decision on whether to engage or continue their relationship with the Member or practice.'

Acceptance of gifts

> **AAT Guidelines**
>
> 'Objectivity may be threatened or appear to be threatened by the acceptance by a Member, or the spouse or dependent children of a Member, of gifts, services, favours or hospitality from a client, or, in the case of an employed Member, from a work colleague or a person having or proposing to have a contractual relationship with the Member's employer.
>
> Employed Members should be aware of the difficulties which may arise from the offer or the acceptance of any gift, service, favour or hospitality which may be intended to influence the recipient or which could be interpreted by a reasonable person in full possession of the facts as likely to have that effect.'

Letters of Engagement

5.5   We will look at letters of engagement in detail in Chapter 3. In the meantime, the *Guidelines* make the following points.

> **AAT Guidelines**
>
> 'Self-employed Members should ensure that, as a matter of good practice, for each client an engagement letter is agreed. The purpose of such a letter is to provide written confirmation of the work to be undertaken and the extent of the Member's responsibilities.'

Fees and Commissions

> **AAT Guidelines**
>
> '1   Members in public practice who undertake professional services for a client assume the responsibility to perform the work with integrity and objectivity and in accordance with the appropriate technical standards. For the services rendered they are entitled to remuneration.
>
> 2   Professional fees should be a fair reflection of the value of the work performed for the client, taking into account:
>
> > (i)   the skill and knowledge required for the type of work involved;
> > (ii)   the level of training and experience of the person(s) necessarily engaged on the work;
> > (iii) the time necessarily occupied by each person engaged on the work;
> > (iv)   the degree of responsibility that the work entails.
>
> 3   Professional fees should normally be computed on the basis of agreed appropriate rates per hour or per day for the time of each person engaged on the work. These rates should be based on the fundamental premise that the organisation and conduct of the practice and the services provided to clients are well planned, controlled and managed.
>
> 4   A Member should not make a representation that specific professional services in current or future periods will be performed for either a stated fee, estimated fee or fee range if it is likely at the time of the representation that such fees will be substantially increased and the prospective client is not advised of that likelihood.
>
> 5   When undertaking work for a client it may be necessary or expedient to charge a pre-arranged fee in which event the Member should estimate a fee.
>
> 6   It is not improper for a Member to charge a client a lower fee than has previously been charged for similar services, provided the quality of the work does not suffer.
>
> 7   The following guidance relates to the charging of contingency or percentage fees:
>
> > (i)   professional services of the nature of financial reporting should not be offered or rendered to a client under an arrangement whereby no fee will be charged unless a specified finding or result is obtained or when the fee is otherwise contingent upon the findings or results of such services;
> >
> > (ii)   fees should not be regarded as being contingent if fixed by a court or other public authority;
> >
> > (iii) fees may be waived in certain circumstances, without constituting contingency fees.'

BPP
PUBLISHING

Safeguards

5.7   The ethical guidance sets out a number of safeguards which may be employed. Safeguards and procedures might include:

> **AAT Guidelines**
>
> 'Safeguards and procedures might include:
>
> (i)   educational and experience requirements for entry into the profession;
>
> (ii)   Continuing Professional Development requirements;
>
> (iii)   policies and procedures intended to promote quality control of reporting engagements;
>
> (iv)   external or internal review of a firm's quality control system;
>
> (v)   arrangements to ensure that staff are adequately aware and empowered to communicate any issue of independence and objectivity that concerns them;
>
> (vi)   where available, the involvement of an additional principal who did not take part in the conduct of the reporting assignment;
>
> (vii)   where possible, consulting a third party such as a committee of independent directors, or a professional regulatory body;
>
> (viii) where possible, arrangements to reduce the risk of conflict by compartmentalising responsibilities and knowledge in specific cases;
>
> (ix)   where possible, rotation of senior personnel;
>
> (x)   publicly visible steps, possibly including a public announcement, to explain how the risk of conflict is recognised and mitigated in a specific situation;
>
> (xi)   refusal to perform the assignment where no other appropriate course can abate the perceived problem.

Key learning points

- The Companies Act requires auditors to hold an **appropriate qualification** and to be a member of a **recognised supervisory body.**

- A person is **ineligible** to act as auditor if he is an **employee** or officer or has various other close connections with the company.

- Recognised supervisory bodies must follow a number of procedures to ensure their members are **fit** and **proper** and **competent** and that audit work is conducted **properly.**

- The Auditing Practices Board issues:
  - ° SASs
  - ° Practice Notes
  - ° Bulletins

- SASs contain **basic principles** and **procedures** with which auditors must comply as well as other material designed to help auditors.

- Rules on ethical conduct are laid down in the AAT's **Guidelines on Professional Ethics**.

- **Confidentiality** is important. Auditors can only disclose information without client permission to others in very limited circumstances.

- **Independence** is perhaps the most important characteristic of the auditor.

Quick quiz

1   What does the term appropriate qualification mean?

2   Name the three categories of pronouncement issued by the Auditing Practices Board.

3   What were the major audit areas covered by the Auditors' Operational Standard?

4   What are the basic needs that must be met if the objectives of the accountancy profession are to be fulfilled?

5   What are the fundamental principles given in *Guidelines on Professional Ethics*? (word/phrase answers will suffice)

6   Summarise the situations in which auditors can disclose confidential information.

7   Give four examples of how auditors can have a financial involvement in a client.

Answers to quick quiz

1   A person holds an appropriate qualification if he or she has gained:

    (a)   Acknowledgement that he or she has met criteria for appointment as an auditor under Companies Act 1985

    (b)   A recognised qualification obtained in the United Kingdom

    (c)   An approved overseas qualification

2   Statements of Auditing Standards
    Practice Notes
    Bulletins

3   Planning, controlling and recording
    Accounting systems
    Audit evidence
    Internal controls
    Review of financial statements

4   Credibility
    Professionalism
    Quality of service
    Confidence

5   Integrity
    Objectivity and independence
    Professional competence and due care
    Confidentiality
    Professional behaviour
    Technical standards

6   Auditors can disclose confidential information in the following circumstances.

    (a)   When disclosure is authorised

    (b)   When disclosure is specifically required by law

7   Financial involvement with clients may arise in the following ways.

    (a)   By direct or indirect financial interest

    (b)   By loans to or from the client or to or from its officers or principal shareholders

    (c)   By holding a financial interest in a joint venture with a client

    (d)   When the client's fees represent a significant proportion of the firm's income

Answers to activities

Answer 2.1

Under the Companies Act 1985, a person is *ineligible* for appointment as a company auditor if he or she is one out of:

(a)   An **officer** or **employee** of the company

(b)   A **partner** or **employee** of such a person

(c)   A **partnership** in which such a person is a partner

(d)   **Ineligible** by virtue of (a), (b) or (c) for appointment as auditor of any parent or subsidiary undertaking or a subsidiary undertaking of any parent undertaking of the company

(e)   There exists between him or her or any associate (of his or hers) and the company (or company as referred to in (d) above) a **connection** of any description as may be specified in regulations laid down by Secretary of State

Answer 2.2

SASs contain the following types of guidance.

(a)   Basic principles and essential procedures ('Auditing Standards') with which auditors must comply when carrying out an audit of financial statements

(b)   General auditing standards which apply to other types of audits and related services

(c)   Auditing Standards which apply to the audits of certain types of entity such as clients within specialist industries

(d)   Explanatory and other material designed to assist auditors in interpreting and applying Auditing Standards

Chapter 3   Appointment and removal of auditors

Chapter topic list

1   Introduction

2   Statutory requirements for appointment of auditors

3   Ethical requirements for appointment of auditors

4   Client screening

5   Engagement letters

6   Resignation and removal of auditors

7   Duties and rights of auditors

Learning objectives

On completion of this chapter you will be able to:

	Performance criteria	Range statement
• Describe the requirements relating to the appointment to, and departure from, office of auditors	all	all
• Describe the reasons for client screening procedures	all	all
• Describe the reasons for, and content of, an engagement letter	all	all
• Describe the duties and powers of auditors imposed by legislation	all	all

BPP PUBLISHING

1 INTRODUCTION

1.1 This chapter deals with how the Companies Act **affects** the rights of **auditors**. The Companies Act is extremely important since without legal backing auditors would be in a very weak position. The Companies Act provisions also protect the interests of members (to whom auditors report) if the auditors disagree with the directors or managers of the company.

1.2 We firstly consider how the **Companies Act** affects the **appointment** of auditors.

1.3 However auditors should not only consider Companies Act requirements when deciding whether to take on a new client. **Professional requirements** are important and Section 3 deals with these.

1.4 The key professional requirement is for the current and proposed auditors to **communicate** about the client's affairs. One reason for this is to preserve the integrity of the auditors' position. Thus the current and proposed auditors must ask the client for permission to discuss his affairs, but if the client refuses, the proposed auditors should decline nomination.

1.5 A second reason for the two auditors communicating is to give the proposed auditors **information** which will help them decide whether to accept nomination. Hence also there is a professional requirement for the proposed auditors to seek references about the client.

1.6 Many firms however have more stringent **screening procedures**, since auditors can suffer considerable adverse publicity (and may be sued) if they are associated with a client where things have gone wrong, for example, the client going into insolvency or a major fraud occurring). Client acceptance procedures hence aim to identify the **risks** associated with taking on the client and assess whether there are good **high level controls** such as management involvement and integrity. We discuss screening procedures in Section 4 of this chapter.

1.7 Assuming appointment is accepted, it is then necessary for the terms of the engagement to be confirmed. This is done by means of an **engagement letter**, which sets out the respective responsibilities of the auditors and directors, and details the scope of the audit. We cover engagement letters in Section 5 of this chapter.

1.8 Section 6 discusses the various ways in which auditors can **resign** or be **removed** from office. However auditors leave office, the Companies Act requires them to make a statement of whether there are any circumstances of which members and creditors ought to be aware. This is a very important duty since it allows auditors to inform members and creditors of problems they have found.

1.9 The last section of this chapter deals with other **rights and duties** of auditors, principally the right to information.

2 STATUTORY REQUIREMENTS FOR APPOINTMENT OF AUDITORS

2.1 The 1985 Act requires that the auditors should be appointed by and therefore be **answerable** to the **shareholders**.

RIGHTS OF APPOINTMENT	
Members	Appoint auditors at each **general meeting** where accounts are laid by **positive resolution** (re-appointment of existing auditor not automatic)
	Auditors hold office until conclusion of next general meeting at which accounts are laid
Directors	Can appoint auditor :
	(a) Before company's **first general meeting** at which accounts are laid; auditors hold office until conclusion of that meeting
	(b) To fill **casual vacancy**
Secretary of State	Can appoint auditors if **no auditors** are **appointed** or reappointed at general meeting at which accounts are laid

Special notice of appointment

2.2 In certain cases relating to appointment of an auditor **special notice** (28 days) is required for the appropriate resolutions at a general meeting (ss 388(3) and 391 A(1)(b) CA 1985).

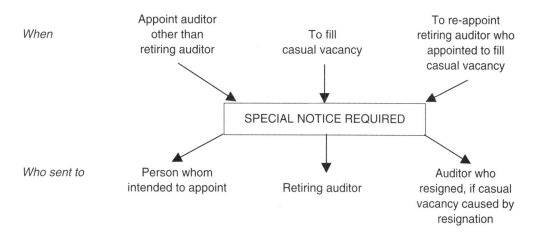

Elective regime for private companies

2.3 The Companies Act 1989 introduced a regime by which a private company may choose not to comply with some of the statutory requirements of the Companies Act. The company effects this by means of an **elective resolution**, which requires the agreement of all members entitled to vote at or attend the meeting at which the resolution is tabled.

2.4 One of the requirements a company can use an elective resolution to exempt itself from is the requirement to appoint auditors annually. If the company exempts itself from this requirement, the auditors in office will be deemed to be re-appointed annually. While the election is in force, any member may give notice in writing proposing that the auditors be removed, and the directors must convene a general meeting to decide the issue within 28 days of the notice.

2.5 A private company may also elect not to lay accounts before the members in general meeting. If the company makes such an election without making an election not to reappoint auditors annually, it must hold a general meeting annually to re-elect the auditors (s 385A CA 1985).

Remuneration

2.6   The remuneration of the auditors, which will include any sums paid by the company in respect of the auditors' expenses, will be fixed (s 390A CA 1985) either by **whoever made the appointment,** or in **such manner** as the company in **general meeting** may determine. However the auditors' remuneration is fixed, it must be disclosed in the annual accounts of the company (s 390A(3) CA 1985).

3   ETHICAL REQUIREMENTS FOR APPOINTMENT OF AUDITORS

3.1   This section covers the procedures that the auditors must undertake to ensure that their appointment is valid and that they are clear to act.

Before accepting nomination

3.2   Before a new audit client is accepted, the auditors must ensure that there are **no independence** or **other ethical problems** likely to cause conflict with the ethical code. Furthermore, new auditors should ensure that they have been appointed in a proper and legal manner.

3.3   The potential new auditors must carry out the following procedures.

ACCEPTANCE PROCEDURES	
Ensure **professionally qualified** to act	Consider whether disqualified on legal or ethical grounds
Ensure **existing resources adequate**	Consider available time, staff and technical expertise
Obtain references	Make independent enquiries if directors not personally known. (see Section 4 of this chapter)
Communicate with present auditors	Enquire whether there are reasons/circumstances behind the change which the new auditors ought to know, also courtesy
	See flowchart over page for process

Example letters

3.4   This is an example of a initial communication.

To: Retiring & Co   Certified Accountants Dear Sirs Re: New Client Co Ltd We have been asked to allow our name to go forward for nomination as auditors of the above company, and we should therefore be grateful if you would please let us know whether there are any professional reasons why we should not accept nomination....... . Acquiring & Co   Certified Accountants

3.5 The following letter would be sent if the nominee has not received a reply to the letter above within a reasonable time.

To: Retiring & Co
     Certified Accountants

Dear Sirs

                    Re: New Client Co Ltd

As we have been unable to obtain a reply to our letters of the 1 and 14 September we would inform you that, unless we hear from you by 30 September, we shall assume that there are no professional reasons preventing our acceptance of nomination as auditors of the above company and we shall allow our name to go forward. We ourselves are not aware of any reasons why we should not consent to act for this company.... .

Acquiring & Co

Certified Accountants

3.6 Having negotiated these steps the auditors will be in a position to accept the nomination, or not, as the case may be.

Procedures after accepting nomination

3.7 The following procedures should be carried out after accepting nomination.

(a) **Ensure** that the **outgoing auditors' removal** or **resignation** has been **properly conducted** in accordance with the Companies Act 1985.

The new auditors should see a valid notice of the outgoing auditors' resignation (under s 392 CA 1985), or confirm that the outgoing auditors were properly removed (under s 391 CA 1985).

(b) **Ensure** that the **new auditors' appointment is valid**. The new auditors should obtain a copy of the resolution passed at the general meeting appointing them as the company's auditors.

(c) Set up and **submit a letter of engagement** to the directors of the company (see Section 5 of this chapter).

Other matters

3.8 Where the previous auditors have **fees still owing** by the client, the new auditors need not decline appointment solely for this reason. They should decide how far they may go in helping the former auditors to obtain their fees.

3.9 Once a new appointment has taken place, the new auditors should obtain **all books and papers** which belong to the client from the old auditors. The former accountants should ensure that all such documents are transferred, *unless* they have a lien over the books because of unpaid fees. The old auditors should also pass any useful information to the new auditors if it will be of help, without charge, unless a lot of work is involved.

4 CLIENT SCREENING

4.1 As well as contacting previous auditors many firms, particularly larger firms, carry out other stringent checks on potential audit clients and their management. There are a number of reasons for these, as we will see shortly.

Appointment decision chart

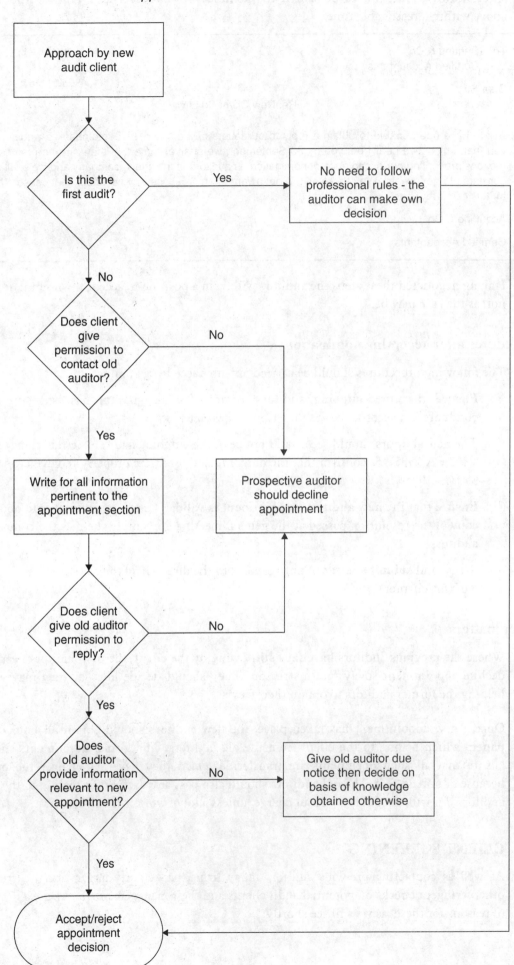

4.2   The procedures laid out here are tailored to the case of a large audit firm and a large (probably public) company audit, but the procedures may be adapted for smaller audit firms and smaller audits.

Factors for consideration

Management integrity

4.3   The integrity of those managing a company will be of great importance.

Risk

4.4   The following table contrasts low and high risk clients.

LOW RISK	HIGH RISK
Good long-term prospects	Poor recent or forecast performance
Well-financed	Likely lack of finance
Strong internal controls	Significant control weaknesses
Conservative, prudent accounting policies	Evidence of questionable integrity, doubtful accounting policies
Competent, honest management	Lack of finance director
Few unusual transactions	Significant related party or unexplained transactions

Engagement economics

4.5   Generally, the expected fees from a new client should reflect the **level of risk** expected. They should also offer the same sort of return expected of clients of this nature and reflect the overall financial strategy of the audit firm.

Relationship

4.6   The audit firm will generally want the relationship with a client to be long term. This is not only to enjoy receiving fees; it is also to allow the audit work to be enhanced by better knowledge of the client. Conflict of interest problems are significant here; the firm should establish that no existing clients will cause difficulties as competitors of the new client.

Ability to perform the work

4.7   The audit firm must have the resources to perform the work properly, as well as any relevant specialist knowledge or skills. The impact on existing engagements must be estimated, in terms of staff time and the timing of the audit.

SOURCES OF INFORMATION ABOUT NEW CLIENTS	
Enquiries of other sources	Bankers, solicitors
Review of **documents**	Most recent annual accounts, listing particulars, credit rating
Previous accountants/auditors	Previous auditors should disclose fully all relevant information
Review of **rules and standards**	Consider specific laws/standards that relate to industry

Approval

4.8 Once all the relevant procedures and information gathering has taken place, the company can be put forward for approval. The engagement partner will have completed a client acceptance form and this, along with any other relevant documentation, will be submitted to the managing partner, or whichever partner is in overall charge of accepting clients.

Activity 3.1

The directors of Compton and Edrich Limited have invited your firm to act as auditors for the year ended 31 December 19X7. They are going to ask their current auditors to resign, since they are unhappy with the service they have been given.

Tasks

(a) Describe the matters you would consider and the investigations you would carry out before accepting appointment as auditors.

(b) Describe the statutory and ethical procedures that you should follow before and after accepting appointment.

5 ENGAGEMENT LETTERS

5.1 An engagement letter sets out the terms of the audit engagement. The major purposes of an engagement letter are to:

(a) Define clearly the **extent** of the **auditors' and directors' responsibilities** and so minimise the possibility of any misunderstanding between the client and the auditors

(b) Provide **written confirmation** of the **auditors' acceptance** of the appointment, the scope of the audit, the form of their report and the scope of any non-audit services

5.2 If an engagement letter is not sent to clients, both new and existing, this will increase the risk that the directors and auditors disagree about who is responsible for what. The contents of an engagement letter should be discussed and agreed with management before it is sent.

5.3 Guidance is available in the form of the SAS 140 *Engagement letters*, which applies to audit engagements. The statements made by the standard are as follows.

SAS 140.1

The auditors and the client should agree on the terms of the engagement, which should be recorded in writing.

SAS 140.2

Auditors should agree the terms of their engagement with new clients in writing. Thereafter auditors should regularly review the terms of engagement and if appropriate agree any updating in writing.

SAS 140.3

Auditors who, before the completion of the audit, are requested to change the engagement to one which provides a different level of assurance, should consider the appropriateness of so doing. If auditors consider that it is appropriate to change the terms of engagement, they should obtain written agreement to the revised terms.

> ## SAS 140.4
>
> Auditors should ensure that the engagement letter documents and confirms their acceptance of the appointment, and includes a summary of the responsibilities of the directors and of the auditors, the scope of the engagement and the form of any reports.

Timing

5.4 The auditors should send an engagement letter to all new clients soon after their appointment as auditors and, in any event, **before** the **commencement** of the **first audit** assignment.

Content of letter

5.5 The main emphasis in the SAS is on the 'principal relevant responsibilities of the directors and the auditors and the scope of the audit'. The example in the Appendix to the SAS is reproduced below.

Form of reports

5.6 The letter should identify any reports which the auditors will submit *in addition to* the statutory audit report, such as reports to the directors/managers on material internal control weaknesses. Confidentiality aspects of such reports should be mentioned.

Other matters

5.7 The other matters which the SAS and the AAT's own guidance highlights for possible inclusion in the engagement letter are as follows.

   (a) Fees and billing arrangements

   (b) Procedures where the client has a complaint about the service

   (c) Where appropriate, arrangements concerning the involvement of other auditors and experts in some aspect of the audit and internal auditors and other staff of the entity

   (d) Arrangements, if any, to be made with the predecessor auditors, in the case of an initial audit

   (e) Any restriction of the auditors' liabilities to the client (when such possibility exists - not possible with limited companies)

   (f) Where appropriate, the country by whose laws the engagement is to be governed

   (g) A reference to any further agreements between the auditors and the client

   (h) A proposed timetable for the engagement

   (i) Ownership and lien of books and records

   (j) Action in the event of unpaid fees

   (j) The usage of work by third parties (including suitable disclaimers)

5.8 The following example of an engagement letter is for a UK limited company client. Remember that it is not necessarily comprehensive or appropriate to every audit as each client is different; it must be tailored to meet the specific requirements of the engagement.

AN EXAMPLE OF AN ENGAGEMENT LETTER

To the directors of..

The purpose of this letter is to set out the basis on which we (are to) act as auditors of the company (and its subsidiaries) and the respective areas of responsibility of the directors and of ourselves.

Responsibility of directors and auditors

1   As directors of the above company, you are responsible for ensuring that the company maintains proper accounting records and for preparing financial statements which give a true and fair view and have been prepared in accordance with the Companies Act 1985. You are also responsible for making available to us, as and when required, all the company's accounting records and all other relevant records and related information, including minutes of all management and shareholders' meetings.

2   We have a statutory responsibility to report to the members whether in our opinion the financial statements give a true and fair view of the state of the company's affairs and of the profit or loss for the year and whether they have been properly prepared in accordance with the Companies Act 1985 (or other relevant legislation). In arriving at our opinion, we are required to consider the following matters, and to report on any in respect of which we are not satisfied:

   (a)   whether proper accounting records have been kept by the company and proper returns adequate for our audit have been received from branches not visited by us;

   (b)   whether the company's balance sheet and profit and loss account are in agreement with the accounting records and returns;

   (c)   whether we have obtained all the information and explanations which we think necessary for the purposes of our audit; and

   (d)   whether the information in the directors' report is consistent with the financial statements.

   In addition, there are certain other matters which, according to the circumstances, may need to be dealt with in our report. For example, where the financial statements do not give full details of directors' remuneration or of their transactions with the company, the Companies Act requires us to disclose such matters in our report.

3   We have a professional responsibility to report if the financial statements do not comply in any material respect with applicable accounting standards, unless in our opinion the non-compliance is justified in the circumstances. In determining whether the departure is justified we consider:

   (a)   whether the departure is required in order for the financial statements to give a true and fair view; and

   (b)   whether adequate disclosure has been made concerning the departure

   Our professional responsibilities also include:

   (a)   including in our report a description of the directors' responsibilities for the financial statements where the financial statements or accompanying information do not include such a description; and

   (b)   considering whether other information in documents containing audited financial statements is consistent with those financial statements.

4   Our audit will be conducted in accordance with the Auditing Standards issued by the Auditing Practices Board, and will include such tests of transactions and of the existence, ownership and valuation of assets and liabilities as we consider necessary. We shall obtain an understanding of the accounting and internal control systems in order to assess their adequacy as a basis for the preparation of the financial statements and to establish whether proper accounting records have been maintained by the company. We shall expect to obtain such appropriate evidence as we consider sufficient to enable us to draw reasonable conclusions therefrom

5   The nature and extent of our procedures will vary according to our assessment of the company's accounting system and, where we wish to place reliance on it, the internal control system, and may cover any aspect of the business's operations. Our audit is not designed to identify all significant weaknesses in the company's systems but, if such weaknesses come to our notice during the course of our audit which we think should be brought to your attention, we shall report them to you. Any such report may not be provided to third parties without our prior written consent. Such consent will be granted only on the basis that such reports are not prepared with the interests of anyone other than the company in mind and that we accept no duty or responsibility to any other party as concerns the reports.

6   As part of our normal audit procedures, we may request you to provide written confirmation of oral representations which we have received from you during the course of the audit on matters having a material effect on the financial statements. In connection with representations and the supply of information to us generally, we draw your attention to section 389A of the Companies Act 1985 under which it is an offence for an officer of the company to mislead the auditors.

7   In order to assist us with the examination of your financial statements, we shall request sight of all documents or statements, including the chairman's statement, operating and financial review and the directors' report, which are due to be issued with the financial statements. We are also entitled to attend all general meetings of the company and to receive notice of all such meetings.

8   The responsibility for safeguarding the assets of the company and for the prevention and detection of fraud, error and non-compliance with law or regulations rests with yourselves. However, we shall endeavour to plan our audit so that we have a reasonable expectation of detecting material misstatements in the financial statements or accounting records (including those resulting from fraud, error or non-compliance with law or regulations), but our examination should not be relied upon to disclose all such material misstatements or frauds, errors or instances of non-compliance as may exist.

9   (Where appropriate). We shall not be treated as having notice, for the purposes of our audit responsibilities, of information provided to members of our firm other than those engaged on the audit (for example information provided in connection with accounting, taxation and other services).

10   Once we have issued our report we have no further direct responsibility in relation to the financial statements for that financial year. However, we expect that you will inform us of any material event occurring between the date of our report and that of the Annual General Meeting which may affect the financial statements.

Other services

11   You have requested that we provide other services in respect of ... . The terms under which we provide these other services are dealt with in a separate letter. We will also agree in a separate letter of engagement the provision of any services relating to investment business advice as defined by the Financial Services Act 1986.

Fees

12   Our fees are computed on the basis of the time spent on your affairs by the partners and our staff and on the levels of skill and responsibility involved. Unless otherwise agreed, our fees will be billed at appropriate intervals during the course of the year and will be due on presentation.

Applicable law

13   This (engagement letter) shall be governed by, and construed in accordance with, (English) law. The Courts of (England) shall have exclusive jurisdiction in relation to any claim, dispute or difference concerning the (engagement letter) and any matter arising from it. Each party irrevocably waives any right it may have to object to an action being brought in those Courts, to claim that the action has been brought in an inconvenient forum, or to claim that those Courts do not have jurisdiction.

14   Once it has been agreed, this letter will remain effective, from one audit appointment to another, until it is replaced. We shall be grateful if you could confirm in writing your agreement to these terms by signing and returning the enclosed copy of this letter, or let us know if they are not in accordance with your understanding of our terms of engagement.

Yours faithfully

Certified Accountants

Recipient of letter

5.9   The letter should be addressed to the board of directors or audit committee of the organisation to be audited. The terms of the letter should be evidenced as accepted by the organisation by the signature of an appropriate senior person.

Need for a new engagement letter

5.10   Once it has been agreed by the client, an engagement letter will, if it so provides, remain effective from one audit appointment to another until it is replaced. However, the engagement letter should be reviewed annually to ensure that it continues to reflect the client's circumstances. The SAS suggests that the following factors may make the agreement of a new letter appropriate.

- Any indication that the client **misunderstands** the objective and scope of the audit
- A **recent change of management**, board of directors or audit committee
- A **significant change in ownership**, such as a new holding company
- A **significant change** in the **nature or size** of the client's business
- Any **relevant change** in **legal** or **professional requirements**

5.11   It may be appropriate to remind the client of the original letter when the auditors decide a new engagement letter is unnecessary for any period.

Changes in the terms of an engagement

5.12   There are various reasons why there may be a change in the terms of engagement prior to completion.

(a)   A **change** in **circumstances** affecting the need for the service

(b)   A **misunderstanding** as to the nature of an audit or of the related service originally requested

(c)   A **restriction** on the **scope** of the engagement, whether imposed by management or caused by circumstances

5.13   The auditors should consider such a request for change, and the reason for it, very seriously, particularly in terms of any restriction in the scope of the engagement. Auditors may have to withdraw from the engagement.

DEVOLVED ASSESSMENT ALERT

You must be able to describe why an engagement letter is needed, and what its main contents are. Activity 3.2 tests this knowledge.

Activity 3.2

(a) Explain why it is important for auditors to send a letter of engagement to a new client prior to undertaking an audit.

(b) Describe briefly the main contents of an engagement letter.

6 RESIGNATION AND REMOVAL OF AUDITORS

Resignation

6.1 Certain provisions of the Companies Act 1985 are designed to ensure that auditors do not resign without an explanation of their action. If auditors wish to resign part-way through their term of office they must carry out the following procedures.

RESIGNATION OF AUDITORS	
1 Resignation procedures	Auditors deposit **written notice** together with **statement of circumstances** relevant to members/creditors or statement that no circumstances exist
2 Notice of resignation	Sent by **company** to Registrar of Companies within **14 days**
3 Statement of circumstances	Sent: (a) By auditors to Registrar of Companies within **28 days** (b) By company to everyone entitled to receive a copy of accounts within **14 days** (unless company applies to court because statement of circumstances defamatory)
4 Convening of general meeting	**Auditors** can **require directors** to call extraordinary general meeting to discuss circumstances of resignation Directors must send out notice for meeting within **21 days** of having received requisition by auditors Meeting must take place within **28 days** of **notice** of meeting being sent out
5 Statement prior to general meeting	**Auditors** may be required company to circulate (different) **statement of circumstances** to everyone entitled to notice of meeting
6 Other rights of auditors	Can **receive all notices** that relate to: (a) A general meeting at which their term of office would have expired (b) A general meeting where casual vacancy caused by their resignation to be filled Can **speak** at these meetings on **any matter** which **concerns them as auditors**

BPP PUBLISHING

Removal of an auditor

6.2 The detailed provisions relating to the removal of the auditors place the authority for removal of the auditors with the **members** in general meeting. The auditors *cannot* be removed by board resolution; if the directors are unhappy with the auditors, they can only try and have the auditors removed by exercising any rights they have as members.

6.3 The main object of these provisions is to **preserve the right of the members** to appoint the auditors of their choice. It also **preserves the auditors' independence** of the directors by not permitting directors, who may be in disagreement with the auditors, to dismiss them.

REMOVAL OF AUDITORS	
1 Notice of removal	**Either special notice** (28 days) with copy sent to auditor
	Or if elective resolution in place, **written resolution** to terminate auditors' appointment
	Directors must convene meeting to take place within 28 days of notice
2 Representations	**Auditors** can make **representations** on why they ought to stay in office, and may require company to state in notice representations have been made and send copy to members
3 If resolution passed	(a) Company must **notify registrar** within **14 days**
	(b) Auditors must **deposit statement of circumstances** at company's registered office **within 14 days** of ceasing to hold office
	(c) Statement must be sent to registrar within **28 days** of deposit
4 Auditor rights	Can **receive notice** of and **speak** at:
	(a) General meeting at which their term of office would have expired
	(b) General meeting where casual vacancy caused by their removal to be filled

Other types of departure from office

6.4 Auditors may be removed from office by a **resolution** at the **annual general meeting to appoint new auditors**. Special notice of 28 days is required of such a resolution, and the auditors are able, prior to the AGM, to make representations as to why they think they should stay in office.

6.5 Alternatively auditors may merely decline to offer themselves for re-election at the AGM. In these circumstances they can make representations about the resolution to appoint new auditors prior to the general meeting at which that resolution is discussed.

Statement of circumstances

6.6 Whichever way the auditors depart from office, a s 394 statement of circumstances must be deposited at the company's registered office and sent to all those entitled to receive a copy of the accounts.

6.7 The exception to this rule is that if the company or any other person feels aggrieved by the statement or any other statement made by auditors in connection with their resignation, they may apply to the court for an order that the statement need not be sent out. The application must be made within 14 days of the statement being deposited.

6.8 If the court feels that the auditors are using the statement to secure needless publicity for defamatory matters, it will direct that copies of the statement need not be sent to everyone entitled to receive a copy of the accounts. It may order the company's costs to be paid in whole or part by the auditors.

7 DUTIES AND RIGHTS OF AUDITORS

Duties

7.1 The principal statutory duties of auditors in respect of the audit of a limited company are set out in ss 235 and 237 CA 1985. Auditors are required to report on the **truth and fairness** of every balance sheet and profit and loss account laid before the company in general meeting, and also report whether these accounts have been **properly prepared in accordance with the Companies Act 1985.**

7.2 The Companies Act lists other factors which auditors must consider.

(a) **Proper accounting records** have been kept and proper returns adequate for the audit received from branches not visited.

(b) The **accounts** agree with the **accounting records** and **returns.**

(c) **All information and explanations** have been **received** as the auditors think necessary and they have had access at all times to the company's books, accounts and vouchers.

(d) **Details** of **directors' emoluments** and **other benefits** have been correctly **disclosed** in the financial statements.

(e) Particulars of **loans** and **other transactions** in favour of **directors** and others have been correctly disclosed in the financial statements.

(f) The **information** given in the **directors' report** is **consistent** with the **accounts.**

Auditors must report if any of (a) to (f) is not true.

7.3 The principal statutory rights auditors have, excepting those dealing with resignation or removal, are set out in the table below, and the following are notes on more detailed points.

s 389A(1)	*Access to records*	A right of access at all times to the books, accounts and vouchers of the company
s 389A(1)	*Information and explanations*	A right to require from the company's officers such information and explanations as they think necessary for the performance of their duties as auditors
s 390(1)(a) and (b)	*Attendance at/notices of general meetings*	A right to attend any general meetings of the company and to receive all notices of and communications relating to such meetings which any member of the company is entitled to receive
s 390(1)(c)	*Right to speak at general meetings*	A right to be heard at general meetings which they attend on any part of the business that concerns them as auditors
s 381B(2)-(4)	*Rights in relation to written resolutions*	A right to receive a copy of any written resolution proposed
s 253	*Right to require laying of accounts*	A right to give notice in writing requiring that a general meeting be held for the purpose of laying the accounts and reports before the company (if elective resolution dispensing with laying of accounts is in force)

Key learning points

- The most significant aim of the legislation relating to the **appointment** and **removal** of auditors is to ensure that auditors are ultimately answerable to the **members, not** the **directors.**

- Auditors are generally **appointed** annually at the general meeting at which accounts are laid (except when there is an elective resolution in force).

- The **present** and **proposed auditors** must **communicate** about the client.

- The proposed auditors must also ensure they are professionally qualified to act, they have sufficient resources, and they seek references.

- Most firms have **client acceptance procedures** reviewing the **management integrity** and **risk** of the prospective client, as well as the **likely profitability** of the engagement.

- An engagement letter should be sent to all new clients. The letter should **specify** the **respective responsibilities** of directors and the auditors and lay down the **scope** of the **auditors' work**.

- Auditors can leave office by one of the following means.

   ○ Resignation
   ○ Not seeking reappointment
   ○ Being removed at a general meeting before their term of office would have expired
   ○ Being removed at a general meeting at which their term of office expires

- Auditors cannot be removed by board resolution alone.

- Auditors leaving office for any reason have a duty to make a statement of **circumstances** connected with their departure.

- Auditors leaving office have other rights depending on the manner of their departure.

- Auditor **duties** include the duties to report explicitly on the **truth** and **fairness** of the accounts audited and their **compliance** with legislation.

- Auditors have a duty to **report** on other matters, such as whether proper accounting records have been kept, by **exception.**

- Auditor rights include the rights of **access** to **records** and to receive **information** and **explanations**, also rights relating to **attendance** and **speaking** at **general meetings**.

Quick quiz

1   For what period do auditors hold office?

2   (a)   When is special notice required to appoint new auditors?
     (b)   To whom must this special notice be sent?

3   Why should proposed auditors communicate with the present auditors?

4   List factors that may indicate a new client is:

     (a)   Low risk
     (b)   High risk

5   What should new auditors do once they have accepted nomination?

6   To whom should an engagement letter be addressed?

7   When should auditors issue a new engagement letter?

8   What should auditors do if they are requested to change the terms of an engagement before an audit is completed?

9   If auditors resign, what must they deposit at the company's registered office along with their statement of resignation?

10   What length of notice is required for a resolution to remove auditors before their term of office has expired?

11   What rights do auditors who are threatened with removal have?

12   Summarise the major rights concerning access to information that auditors have under the Companies Act.

Answers to quick quiz

1   Auditors are appointed at a general meeting at which accounts are laid, and hold office from the conclusion of that meeting until the conclusion of the next general meeting at which accounts are laid.

2   (a)   Special notice is required when appointing auditors:

           (i)   To appoint as auditors anyone other than the retiring auditors
           (ii)   To fill a casual vacancy in the office of auditor
           (iii)   To re-appoint as auditor a retiring auditor appointed by the directors to fill a casual vacancy

     (b)   A copy of the notice must be sent to:

           (i)   The person whom it is intended to appoint
           (ii)   The retiring auditor
           (iii)   The auditor who resigned if a casual vacancy was caused by a resignation

3   Proposed auditors should communicate with present auditors to ascertain whether there are any factors concerning the proposed change that they should consider, and also because of professional courtesy.

4   (a)   A number of factors indicate that a potential client is low risk.

           (i)   The client has a stable business.
           (ii)   The business is well-financed.
           (iii)   Internal controls are strong.
           (iv)   Accounting policies are conservative and prudent.
           (v)   Management appears honest and competent.

     (b)   A number of factors indicate that a potential client is high risk.

           (i)   Audit reports on previous accounts are qualified.
           (ii)   Internal controls are poor.
           (iii)   The client lacks a finance director or company accountant.
           (iv)   The accounting policies chosen mean that the accounts give an unduly favourable picture.
           (v)   There are significant related party transactions.

5   Once they have accepted nomination new auditors should:

     (a)   Ensure that the outgoing auditors' departure from office has been conducted in accordance with the Companies Act.

    (b)   Ensure their appointment is valid.

    (c)   Send out an appropriate letter of engagement.

6   An engagement letter should be addressed to the directors of the client.

7   Auditors should issue a new engagement letter in the following circumstances.

    (a)   The client misunderstands the objective and scope of the audit.

    (b)   There has been a significant change in management and ownership, the nature and size of the client's business, or legal and professional requirements.

8   If asked to change the terms of an engagement, auditors should consider whether the change is appropriate. If they do feel it is appropriate, they should obtain written agreement to the revised terms.

9   Along with their notice of resignation, auditors should deposit a statement *either* that there are no circumstances connected with their resignation which should be brought to members' or creditors' attention, *or* a statement of those circumstances.

10   The length of notice is 28 days.

11   Auditors have the right to make representations if they are threatened with removal. They may require the company to send these representations to members, or have them read out at the general meeting if they are not sent to members.

12   The auditors have a right of access at all times to the books, accounts and vouchers of the company, and a right to require such information and explanations as they think necessary from the company's officers.

Answers to activities

Answer 3.1

(a)   We should consider the following matters before accepting appointment as auditors.

Qualification to act
We should ensure we are qualified to act as auditors and are not disqualified on any legal or professional grounds.

Technical competence
We should consider whether the firm has the necessary expertise to carry out an effective audit, particularly if the client is in a regulated or specialised industry.

Resources
Likewise, we should consider whether we have the resources to perform the work properly, bearing in mind other staff commitments when the audit is due to take place.

Ethical matters
We should ensure no partners or staff hold shares in the potential audit client or have any other relationship which could impair independence.

We should consider whether the level of fees we are likely to obtain will compromise independence. Generally this will apply if audit fees (plus fees for other recurring work) exceed 15% of gross practice income.

We should also consider whether taking on the audit will cause conflicts of interest with other clients. In particular we should be careful if we already audit competitors of Compton and Edrich Ltd.

Risk assessment

We should consider whether the risk associated with the audit of the client will pose a significant danger to our reputation as auditors. This involves considering a number of factors.

    (i)   The viability and stability of the client's business
    (ii)   The character and involvement of management
    (iii)   The system of internal controls, particularly the client's finance and accounting function
    (iv)   The accounting policies

Replacement of previous auditors

As well as considering the above, we should also consider why the previous auditors have been replaced. The directors may be unhappy with the service provided, but we should contact the other auditors to find out if there has been any disagreement with the directors over accounting matters.

Procedures for obtaining information

When considering accepting appointment we should obtain information from the following sources.

(i)   Communication with the previous auditors
(ii)   The client's most recent annual accounts
(iii)   Other business publications of the client
(iv)   Press reports on the client's activities
(v)   Credit ratings from Dun and Bradstreet
(vi)   References from existing clients

(b)   *Before appointment*

(i)   We should request the prospective client's permission to communicate with the auditors last appointed. If such permission is refused we should decline nomination.

(ii)   On receipt of permission, we should request in writing of the auditors last appointed all information which ought to be made available to us to enable us to decide whether we are prepared to accept nomination.

(iii)   If fees are owed to the previous auditors we may still accept nomination, although we may decide that the company will be slow to pay its bills and therefore decline nomination.

After appointment

(i)   We should ensure that the outgoing auditors' removal or resignation has been properly conducted in accordance with the Companies Act 1985. We should see a valid notice of the outgoing auditors' resignation (under s 392 CA 1985), or confirm that the outgoing auditors were properly removed (under s 391 CA 1985).

(ii)   We should ensure that our appointment is valid. We should obtain a copy of the resolution passed at the meeting appointing us as the company's auditors (special notice = 28 days, ordinary resolution = simple majority > 50%).

(iii)   We should set up and submit a letter of engagement to the directors of the company.

Answer 3.2

(a)   Auditors should send out an engagement letter for the following reasons.

Defining responsibilities

An engagement letter defines the extent of auditors' and directors' responsibilities. For auditors the engagement letter states that their duties are governed by the Companies Act, not the wishes of the directors. It should also state that auditors report to the members (not the directors). For directors, the engagement letter states they are responsible for safeguarding assets, maintaining a proper system of internal control and preventing fraud. The letter should thus minimise the possibility of misunderstanding between auditors and directors.

Documenting acceptance

The engagement letter also provides confirmation in writing of the auditors' acceptance of appointment, the objective and scope of the audit and the form of the audit report.

Other matters

The letter should also lay out the basis on which fees are charged and hence minimise the possibility of arguments about fees.

The letter also sets down what the client should do if he is unhappy with the service he has been given.

(b)   The main contents and form of the engagement letter will be as follows.

(i)   It will be addressed to the directors and on the audit firm's letterhead.

(ii)   It will lay out the responsibilities of the directors of the company.

(1) Maintaining proper accounting records
(2) Ensuring the accounts show a true and fair view
(3) Accounts are prepared in accordance with CA 1985
(4) Making all records/accounts available to the auditors

(iii) It should also lay out the duties of the auditors, comprising mainly a statutory duty to report to the members their opinion on whether the accounts show a true and fair view and are prepared in accordance with CA 1985.

(iv) It should state that the audit will be conducted according to auditing standards.

(v) It should state that the accounts should normally comply with accounting standards (SSAPs and FRSs) and the auditors will report if they do not.

(vi) It should state that it is the directors' responsibility to detect fraud and error, but that audit procedures are designed so that there is a reasonable expectation of detecting material misstatements.

Other matters which might be covered include the following.

(i) Fees and billing arrangements
(ii) Procedures where the client has a complaint about the service
(iii) Arrangements to be made with the predecessor auditors, in the case of an initial audit
(iv) A reference to any further agreements between the auditors and the client
(v) A proposed timetable for the engagement
(vi) Any agreement about further services (tax, preparing accounts etc)

The letter should end by stating that it will remain effective from one audit appointment to another, until it is replaced. The directors should confirm acceptance in writing.

Part B
Planning audits

Chapter 4   Audit planning

Chapter topic list

Learning objectives

On completion of this chapter you will be able to:

	Performance criteria	Range statement
• Describe the aims of planning audits	17.1.1-17.1.9	17.1.1-17.1.3
• Describe the different types of risk and the factors that influence risk assessments	17.1.3,17.1.5, 17.1.7	17.1.1-17.1.3
• Describe the concept of materiality and what is considered when assessing the materiality level	17.1.5	17.1.1-17.1.3
• Describe how analytical procedures are used at the planning stage of the audit	17.1.5	17.1.1-17.1.3
• Draft an appropriate audit plan and programme	17.1.7,17.1.9	17.1.1-17.1.3

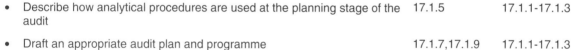

1 INTRODUCTION

1.1 This chapter covers a key stage of the audit process, audit planning. Planning above all aims to **maximise** the **effectiveness** and **efficiency** of the audit. Clearly sufficient time has to be spent on the most important areas of the accounts, those that will most influence the views of the readers. Auditors are also trying to make a profit, and hence will not wish to spend too much time on areas that are relatively unimportant.

1.2 In order to be able to plan the audit to achieve maximum efficiency and effectiveness, auditors have to have a **detailed knowledge** of the client. We discussed in Chapter 3 how auditors obtain some knowledge of the business when deciding to take on a new client. However we return to this topic in section 3 of this chapter, since the auditors will for planning purposes need a greater depth of knowledge than was obtained when accepting appointment. You should note carefully how knowledge of the business influences the rest of the planning process.

1.3 We then discuss the various tools auditors use in deciding which audit areas are the most important. A **risk-based approach** is generally used nowadays. Auditors assess three risks.

(a) The likelihood of significant errors or problems occurring (**inherent risk**)

(b) The chances that the client's controls will fail to detect errors which have occurred (**control risk**)

(c) The probability that audit procedures will not identify errors (**detection risk**)

This in turn must involve auditor judgement about the types and level of error that would be significant; hence we consider **materiality** in this chapter. A further planning procedure is **analytical review** which involves auditors considering what figures they expect to see in the accounts.

1.4 Audit planning must be properly **documented**. Auditors should prepare an **audit plan**, highlighting the most important areas of the audit and the key assumptions and judgements that have been made. Auditors should also prepare an **audit programme** at the planning stage which gives details of the audit tests to be carried out.

1.5 In the next two chapters we shall cover in more detail how the audit programme is designed, and various aspects of the conduct of the audit (who does the work and how the work is recorded and controlled).

1.6 The guidance for this Unit emphasises the importance of being able to apply planning procedures to specific practical situations.

2 AIMS OF PLANNING

2.1 An effective and efficient audit relies on proper planning procedures. The planning process is covered in general terms by SAS 200 *Planning* which states that auditors should plan the audit work so as to perform the audit in an effective manner. Other more detailed areas are covered in SAS 210 *Knowledge of the business* and the other SASs covered in this chapter.

2.2 The SAS distinguishes between the general audit strategy and the detailed audit approach.

KEY TERMS

An **audit plan** is the formulation of the general strategy for the audit, which sets the direction for the audit, describes the expected scope and conduct of the audit and provides guidance for the development of the audit programme.

An **audit programme** is a set of instructions to the audit team that sets out the audit procedures the auditors intend to adopt and may include references to other matters such as the audit objectives, timing, sample size and basis of selection for each area. It also serves as a means to control and record the proper execution of the work.

2.3 There are various objectives of planning work.

- Ensuring that **appropriate attention is devoted** to the different areas of the audit
- Ensuring that **potential problems** are **identified**
- **Facilitating review**

2.4 Good planning also helps in assigning the proper tasks to the members of the audit team.

2.5 Audit procedures should be discussed with the client's management, staff and/or audit committee in order to **co-ordinate audit work**, including that of internal audit. However, all audit procedures remain the responsibility of the external auditors.

2.6 A structured approach to planning will include a number of stages.

- **Updating knowledge of the client**
- **Preparing** the **detailed audit approach**
- Making **administrative decisions** such as staffing and budgets

These stages are considered in more detail in the next sections.

3 KNOWLEDGE OF THE BUSINESS

3.1 SAS 210 *Knowledge of the business* covers this area.

Activity 4.1

What are the major areas of business knowledge that an auditor needs when planning an audit?

SAS 210.1

Auditors should have or obtain a knowledge of the business of the entity to be audited which is sufficient to enable them to identify and understand the events, transactions and practices that may have a significant effect on the financial statements or the audit thereof.

Obtaining the knowledge

3.2 The SAS stresses that knowledge should continuously be accumulated during the audit.

BPP PUBLISHING

Sources of knowledge

3.3 The sources mentioned by the SAS are as follows.

(a) **Previous experience** of the client and its industry

(b) **Visits** to the client's premises and plant facilities

(c) **Discussion with** the client's **staff** and **directors**

(d) **Discussion with other auditors** and with legal and other advisors who have provided services to the client or within the industry

(e) **Discussion with knowledgeable people outside the client** (eg economists, industry regulators)

(f) **Publications** related to the industry (eg government statistics, surveys, texts, trade journals, reports prepared by banks and securities dealers, financial newspapers)

(g) **Legislation and regulations** that significantly affect the client

(h) **Documents produced** by the client

- Minutes of meetings
- Material sent to shareholders or filed with regulatory authorities
- Promotional literature
- Prior years' annual and financial reports
- Budgets
- Internal management reports
- Interim financial reports
- Management policy manuals
- Manuals of accounting
- Internal control systems
- Charts of accounts
- Job descriptions
- Marketing and sales plans

(i) **Professional literature** giving industry-specific guidance

Matters to consider in relation to knowledge of the business

3.4 This appendix to the SAS provides a useful list of matters to consider. We have also added a list of matters to be considered about the client's information technology systems.

KNOWLEDGE OF THE BUSINESS	
General economic factors	General level of economic activity (eg recession, growth)
	Interest rates and availability of financing
	Inflation
	Government policies
	Foreign currency rates and controls
The industry: conditions affecting the client's business	The market and competition
	Cyclical or seasonal activity
	Changes in product technology
	Business risk (eg high technology, high fashion, ease of entry for competition)
	Declining or expanding operations
	Adverse conditions (eg declining demand, excess

capacity, serious price competition)

Key ratios and operating statistics

Specific accounting practices and problems

Environmental requirements and problems

Regulatory framework

Specific or unique practices (eg relating to labour contracts, financing methods, accounting methods)

The entity: directors, management and ownership

Corporate structure: private, public, government (including any recent or planned changes)

Beneficial owners, important stakeholders and related parties (local, foreign, business reputation and experience) and any impact on the entity's transactions

The relationships between owners, directors and management

Attitudes and policies of owners

Capital structure (including any recent or planned changes)

Organisational structure

Group structure

Subsidiaries' audit arrangements

Directors' objectives, philosophy, strategic plans

Acquisitions, mergers or disposals of business activities (planned or recently executed)

Sources and methods of financing (current, historical)

Board of directors

(a) Composition

(b) Business reputation and experience of individuals

(c) Independence from and control over operating management

(d) Frequency of meetings

(e) Existence and membership of audit committee and scope of its activities

(f) Existence of policy on corporate conduct

(g) Changes in professional advisors (eg lawyers)

Operating management

(a) Experience and reputation

(b) Turnover

(c) Key financial personnel and their status in the organisation

(d) Staffing of accounting department

(e) Incentive or bonus plans as part of remuneration (eg based on profit)

(f) Use of forecasts and budgets

(g) Pressures on management (eg over-extended, dominance by one individual, support for share price, unreasonable deadlines for announcing results)

(h) Management information systems

Internal audit function (existence, quality)

Attitude to internal control environment

The entity's business: products, markets, suppliers, expenses, operations	Nature of business(es) (eg manufacturer, wholesaler, financial services, import/export)
	Location of production facilities, warehouses, offices
	Employment (eg by location, supply, wage levels, union contracts, pension commitments, government regulations)
	Products or services and markets (eg major customers and contracts, terms of payment, profit margins, market share, competitors, exports, pricing policies, reputation of products, warranties, order book, trends, marketing strategy and objectives, manufacturing processes)
	Important suppliers of goods and services (eg long-term contracts, stability of supply, terms of payment, imports, methods of delivery such as 'just in time')
	Stocks (eg locations, quantities)
	Franchises, licences, patents
	Important expense categories
	Research and development
	Foreign currency assets, liabilities and transactions by currency, hedging
	Legislation and regulations that significantly affect the entity
	Information systems: current, plans to change
	Debt structure, including covenants and restrictions
Information technology	The significance and complexity of computer processing in each significant accounting application (consider the volume of transactions, complexity of computations, electronic data interchange)
	Organisational structure of information technology activities (especially segregation of duties)
	Availability of data
Financial performance: factors concerning the entity's financial condition and profitability	Accounting policies
	Earnings and cash flow trends and forecasts
	Leasing and other financial commitments
	Availability of lines of credit
	Off balance sheet finance issues
	Foreign exchange and interest rate exposures
	Comparison with industry trends
Reporting environment: external influences which affect the directors in the preparation of the financial statements	Legislation
	Regulatory environment and requirements
	Taxation
	Accounting requirements
	Measurement and disclosure issues peculiar to the business
	Audit reporting requirements
	Users of the financial statements

Using the knowledge

3.5 Having obtained the knowledge of the entity discussed above (and below in the appendix to the SAS), the auditors must then use it to:

- **Assess risks** and identify problems
- **Plan** and **perform** the audit **effectively** and **efficiently**
- **Evaluate audit evidence**

3.6 The audit areas subject to judgement which may be affected by knowledge of the business are given by the SAS as follows.

- **Developing the overall audit plan** and the **audit programme**

- **Considering risks**

- Assessing **inherent risk** and **control risk**

- Determining a **materiality** level

- Considering the complexity of the entity's **information systems**

- Identifying areas where **special audit considerations and skills** may be necessary

- Assessing **audit evidence** to establish its appropriateness and the validity of the related financial statement assertions

- Evaluating **accounting estimates** and **representations** by the directors

- **Recognising conflicting information** (eg contradictory representations)

- **Recognising unusual circumstances** (eg undisclosed related party transactions, possible fraud or non-compliance with law or regulations)

- **Making informed enquiries** and assessing the reasonableness of answers

- **Considering the appropriateness of accounting policies** and accounts disclosures

Communication of knowledge

3.7 Knowledge of the entity can only be used effectively if it is communicated to members of the audit team. SAS 210 emphasises that audit team members must have sufficient knowledge to carry out the audit effectively.

3.8 The information will usually be provided in the planning documentation, but the partner should ensure that staff regularly share any subsequent knowledge they have gained with the rest of the team.

4   RISK IN THE AUDIT PROCESS

KEY TERMS

Audit risk is the risk that auditors may give an inappropriate opinion on the financial statements. Audit risk has three components; inherent risk, control risk and detection risk.

Inherent risk is the susceptibility of an account balance or class of transactions to material misstatement, either individually or when aggregated with misstatements in other balances or classes, irrespective of related internal controls.

Control risk is the risk that a misstatement:

(i) could occur in an account balance or class of transactions;

(ii) could be material, either individually or when aggregated with misstatements in other balances or classes; and

(iii) would not be prevented, or detected and corrected on a timely basis, by the accounting and internal control systems.

Detection risk is the risk that the auditors' substantive procedures do not detect a misstatement that exists in an account balance or class of transactions that could be material, either individually or when aggregated with misstatements in other balances or classes.

Audit risk

4.1 Audit risk is the risk that the auditors give the wrong opinion on the accounts. SAS 300 *Accounting and internal control systems and audit risk assessments* covers audit risk.

4.2 Audit risk can never be completely eliminated. The auditors are called upon to make subjective judgements in the course of forming an opinion and so fraud or error may possibly go undetected.

SAS 300.1

Auditors should:

(a) obtain an understanding of the accounting and internal control system sufficient to plan the audit and develop an effective audit approach; and

(b) use professional judgement to assess the components of audit risk and to design audit procedures to ensure it is reduced to an acceptably low level.

4.3 A **risk-centred approach** gives the auditors an overall measure of risk, and also means the extent of detailed testing required is determined by a purely risk-based perspective. A diagrammatic view of the risk-based approach is given below.

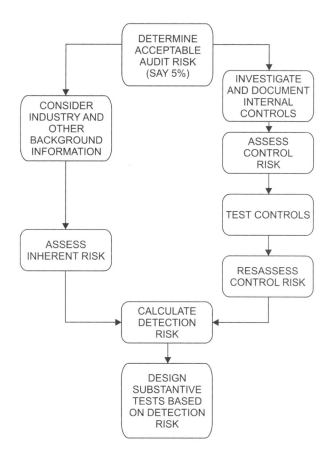

Inherent risk

4.4 Inherent risk is the risk that items will be mis-stated due to characteristics of those items, such as the fact that they are estimates or that they are important items in the accounts and hence there is a temptation to mis-state them. The auditors must use their professional judgement and all available knowledge to assess inherent risk. If no such information or knowledge is available then the inherent risk is **high**.

4.5 The results of the assessment must be properly documented and, where inherent risk is assessed as not high, then audit work may be reduced. The SAS lists the relevant factors to be considered under two headings.

SAS 300.2

... Auditors should assess inherent risk in relation to financial statement assertions ... taking account of factors relevant both to the entity as a whole and to the specific assertions.

FACTORS AFFECTING CLIENT AS A WHOLE	
Integrity and **attitude to risk** of directors and management	Domination by a single individual can cause problems
Management experience and **knowledge**	Changes in management and quality of financial management
Unusual pressures on management	Examples include tight reporting deadlines, or market or financing expectations
Nature of business	Potential problems include technological obsolescence or over-dependence on single product
Industry factors	Competitive conditions, regulatory requirements, technology developments, changes in customer demand
Information technology	Problems include lack of supporting documentation, concentration of expertise in a few people, potential for unauthorised access

FACTORS AFFECTING INDIVIDUAL ACCOUNT BALANCES OR TRANSACTIONS	
Financial statement **accounts prone to misstatement**	Accounts which require adjustment in previous period or require high degree of estimation
Complex accounts	Accounts which require expert valuations or are subjects of current professional discussion
Assets at risk of being **lost or stolen**	Cash, stock, portable fixed assets (computers)
Quality of **accounting systems**	Strength of individual departments (sales, purchases, cash etc)
Unusual transactions	Transactions for large amounts, with unusual names, not settled promptly (particularly important if they occur at period-end)
	Transactions that do not go through the system, that relate to specific clients or processed by certain individuals
Staff	Staff changes or areas of low morale

DEVOLVED ASSESSMENT ALERT

These lists are important. You should remember them when we consider substantive testing of individual audit areas in later chapters, since the factors listed affect the choice of audit tests and also the extent of testing. Audit questions often indicate problems in particular audit areas, and ask for an assessment of the risks involved.

Activity 4.2

What are likely to be the most important factors affecting the inherent risk assessment of the following clients.

(a) Queen and Sheds Ltd, a long-established family firm of brewers which leases several pubs in South-East England to tenants.

(b) Tricky Dicky Ltd, a newly-established second-hand car dealer.

(c) Prick Your Thumbs Ltd, an established manufacturer of drawing pins. The owner of all the shares of the company lives in tax exile on Jersey and takes no part in the running of the business.

(d) Blues Blues Electric Blues plc who are a fast expanding manufacturer of television and CD players currently seeking a listing on the Stock Exchange.

Control risk

4.6 Control risk is the risk that client controls fail to detect material errors.

4.7 We shall discuss and control risk in Chapter 7. For now, the most important point is that SAS 300 requires a **preliminary assessment** of **control risk** at the planning stage of the audit if the auditors intend to place some reliance on the operation of the client's control system. This assessment should be supported subsequently by tests of control.

Detection risk

4.8 Detection risk is the risk that audit procedures will fail to detect material errors.

4.9 Detection risk relates to the inability of the auditors to examine all evidence. Audit evidence is not generally 100% conclusive, and hence some detection risk will almost always be present. What auditors are seeking is to have **reasonable confidence** about the truth and fairness of the accounts.

4.10 The auditors' **inherent and control risk assessments** will influence the **nature, timing and extent of** tests on balance sheet and profit and loss account items (substantive procedures) required to reduce detection risk and thereby audit risk.

> **SAS 300.8**
>
> Regardless of the assessed levels of inherent and control risks, auditors should perform some substantive procedures for financial statement assertions of material account balances and transaction classes.

4.11 **Substantive procedures can never be abandoned entirely** because control and inherent risk can never be assessed at a low enough level. Substantive procedures may though be restricted to analytical procedures if appropriate. (Analytical procedures are discussed later in this chapter.)

4.12 Where the auditors' assessment of the components of audit risk changes during the audit, they should modify the planned substantive procedures based on the revised risk levels.

4.13 When both inherent and control risks are assessed as high, the auditors should consider whether substantive procedures can provide sufficient appropriate audit evidence to reduce detection risk, and therefore audit risk, to an acceptably low level.

4.14 When auditors determine that detection risk regarding a material financial statement assertion cannot be reduced to an acceptably low level, they should consider the implications for their audit report (discussed further in Chapter 17).

5 MATERIALITY

Audit planning

5.1 The concept of 'true and fair' is linked with the fundamental concept of materiality. The auditors' task is to decide whether accounts show a true and fair view. The auditors are not responsible for establishing whether accounts are correct in every particular for the following reasons.

(a) It can take a great deal of time and trouble to check the correctness of even a very small transaction and the resulting benefit may not justify the effort.

(b) Financial accounting inevitably involves a degree of estimation which means that financial statements can never be completely precise.

> ### KEY TERM
>
> **Materiality** is an expression of the relative significance or importance of a particular matter in the context of financial statements as a whole, or of individual financial statements.
>
> A matter is material if its omission or misstatement would reasonably influence the decisions of an addressee of the auditors' report.

5.2 Although the definition refers to the decision of the addressee of the auditors' report (ie the members of the company), their decisions may well be influenced by how the accounts are used. For example if the accounts are to be used to secure a bank loan, what is significant to the bank will influence the way members act. Hence the views of other users of the accounts must be taken into account.

5.3 Materiality is the subject of the APB's SAS 220 *Materiality and the audit*, which begins by stating the following.

> ### SAS 220.1
>
> Auditors should consider materiality and its relationship with audit risk when conducting an audit.

5.4 The SAS goes on:

> 'Auditors plan and perform the audit to be able to provide reasonable assurance that the financial statements are free of material misstatement and give a true and fair view. The assessment of what is material is a matter of professional judgement.'

5.5 Small amounts should be considered if there is a risk that they could occur more than once and together add up to an amount which is material in total. Also, qualitative aspects must be considered, for example the inaccurate and therefore misleading description of an accounting policy.

5.6 Materiality consideration will differ depending on the aspect of the financial statements being considered.

> 'Materiality is considered at both the overall financial statement level and in relation to individual account balances, classes of transactions and disclosures.'

A good example is directors' emoluments which make normal materiality considerations irrelevant, because they *must* be disclosed by the auditors if they are not disclosed correctly by the directors in the financial statements.

> ### SAS 220.2
>
> Auditors should consider materiality when determining the nature, timing and extent of audit procedures.

5.7 Materiality considerations during **audit planning** are extremely important. The assessment of materiality at this stage should be based on the most recent and reliable financial information and will help to determine an effective and efficient audit approach. Materiality assessment in conjunction with risk assessment will help the auditors to make a number of decisions.

- **What items to examine**
- Whether to use **sampling techniques**
- What **level of error** is likely to lead to a qualified audit opinion

5.8 The resulting combination of audit procedures should help to reduce detection risk to an appropriately low level.

Practical implications

5.9 Because many users of accounts are primarily interested in the **profitability** of the company, the level is often expressed as a proportion of its profits before tax.

5.10 Some argue, however, that materiality should be thought of in terms of the **size** of the business. Hence, if the company remains a fairly constant size, the materiality level should not change; similarly if the business is growing, the level of materiality will increase from year to year.

5.11 The **size** of a company can be measured in terms of turnover and total assets before deducting any liabilities (sometimes referred to in legislation as 'the balance sheet total') both of which tend not to be subject to the fluctuations which may affect profit. Note that the auditors will often calculate a range of values, such as those shown below, and then take an average or weighted average of all the figures produced as the materiality level.

Value	%
Profit before tax	5
Gross profit	½ - 1
Turnover	½ - 1
Total assets	1 - 2
Net assets	2 - 5
Profit after tax	5 - 10

5.12 The effect of planning materiality on the audit process is shown in the diagram below.

BPP PUBLISHING

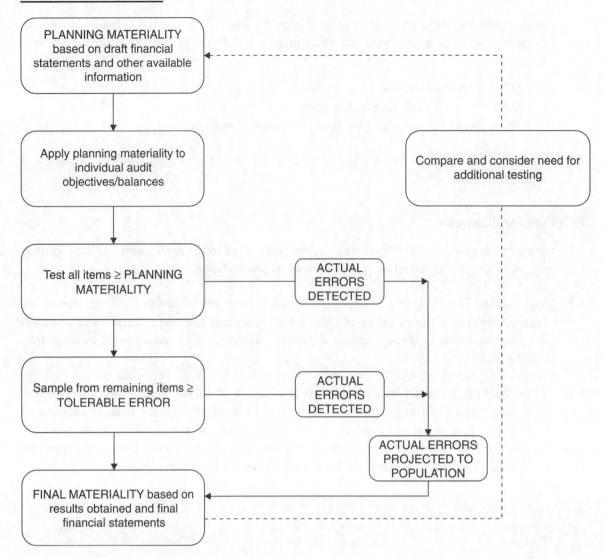

5.13 The level of materiality must be reviewed constantly as the audit progresses. Changes to audit procedures may be required for various reasons.

(a) Draft accounts are altered (due to material error and so on) and therefore overall materiality changes.

(b) External factors cause changes in the control or inherent risk estimates.

(c) Such changes as are in (b) are caused by errors found during testing.

Activity 4.3

Which measures of a client's business is an auditor likely to use when setting a level of materiality:

(a) For a client that has a stable asset base, steady turnover over the last few years, but has only made a small pre-tax profit this year owing to a large one-off expense

(b) For a client where the outside shareholders have expressed concern over declining profits over the last few years

---

6   ANALYTICAL PROCEDURES

6.1   This is our first mention of analytical procedures (or analytical review). We will cover the topic in depth in Chapter 11. For now you should understand that the purpose of analytical procedures is essentially to identify figures that are not in line with auditor expectations, and which hence require further investigation.

6.2   Analytical review can involve comparisons of current year financial information with past year information, budgets and predictions by the auditor. It can also involve comparisons between different elements of the current year financial information which are expected to have a predictable relationship with each other.

6.3   SAS 410 *Analytical procedures* deals with the subject of analytical review The SAS requires auditors to carry out analytical procedures at the planning stage of each audit, to identify areas of potential audit risk and helping in planning the nature, timing and extent of other audit procedures. We will discuss analytical review at all stages of the audit in greater detail in Chapter 11.

7   THE OVERALL AUDIT PLAN

SAS 200.2

Auditors should develop and document an overall audit plan describing the expected scope and conduct of the audit.

7.1   The SAS goes on to list matters which auditors should consider in developing the overall audit plan.

OVERALL AUDIT PLAN	
Knowledge of the entity's business	General economic factors and industry conditions
	Important characteristics of the client, (a) business, (b) principal business strategies, (c) financial performance, (d) reporting requirements, including changes since the previous audit
	The operating style and control consciousness of directors and management
	The auditors' cumulative knowledge of the accounting and control systems and any expected changes in the period
Risk and materiality	The setting of materiality for audit planning purposes
	The expected assessments of risks or error and identification of significant audit areas
	Any indication that misstatements that could have a material effect on the financial statements might arise because of fraud or for any other reason
	The identification of complex accounting areas including those involving estimates

OVERALL AUDIT PLAN

Nature, timing and extent of procedures	The relative importance and timing of tests of control and substantive procedures
	The use of information technology by the client or the auditors
	The use made of work of any internal audit function
	Procedures which need to be carried out at or before the year end
	The timing of significant phases of the preparation of the financial statements
	The audit evidence required to reduce detection risk to an acceptably low level.
Co-ordination, direction, supervision and review	The involvement of other auditors
	The involvement of experts, other third parties and internal auditors
	The number of locations
	Staffing requirements
Other matters	Any regulatory requirements arising from the decision to retain the engagement
	The possibility that the going concern basis may be inappropriate
	The terms of the engagement and any statutory responsibilities
	The nature and timing of reports or other communication with the entity that are expected under the engagement

Changes to the audit work planned

> ### SAS 200.4
>
> The audit work planned should be reviewed and, if necessary, revised during the course of the audit.

7.2 An accurate record of changes to the audit plan must be maintained in order to explain the general strategy finally adopted for the audit.

8 THE AUDIT PROGRAMME

> ### SAS 200.3
>
> Auditors should develop and document the nature, timing and extent of planned audit procedures required to implement the overall audit plan.

8.1 The audit programme may contain references to matters such as the **audit objectives, timing, sample size** and **basis of selection** for each area. The audit programme's main use is highlighted by SAS 200.

> 'It serves as a set of instructions to the audit team and as a means to control and record the proper execution of the work.'

8.2 We will discuss in the next chapter how auditors design the tests that are included in the audit programme.

DEVOLVED ASSESSMENT ALERT

You may be asked to state the matters that will be considered and the work that would be carried out in planning the audit of a client. An example is given below.

Activity 4.4

This is your first year as audit manager of Fluffy Ted Computers Ltd, a longstanding audit client of your firm.

Fluffy Ted Computers Ltd retails computer hardware buying from manufacturers and selling to the general public. The company's head office and biggest shop is in Surrey, and its warehouse is nearby. There are also a number of other shops over the South of England. The accounting records are maintained on computer at the company's head office.

When a sale is made at one of the retail outlets, the salesman orders the goods from the warehouse and they are then either delivered to the shop or directly to the customer.

In previous audits stock held at the warehouse has been less than the stock quantities shown in the accounting records. There have been problems with goods in transit. The company has also had problems identifying and valuing damaged stock and goods returned by customers.

The company allows customers to pay by instalments and there have been problems with customers failing to pay promptly in the past.

The company has opened three new retail outlets at out-of-town shopping centres. This has involved heavy capital expenditure, and has caused the company some liquidity problems. The company is currently negotiating loan finance and an increased overdraft with its bank.

Task

List and describe the matters you will consider and the work you will carry out when planning the audit.

Key learning points

- This chapter has covered some very important areas of the planning process.

- The auditors will formulate an **overall audit plan** which will be translated into a **detailed audit programme** for audit staff to follow.

- In formulating the **audit plan** the auditors will consider:

  ° Knowledge of the entity's business
  ° Risk and materiality
  ° Nature, timing and extent of procedures
  ° Co-ordination, direction, supervision and review of the audit

- Any **changes in** the audit approach during the audit should be documented very carefully.

- When a new client is acquired the auditors must obtain **knowledge of the business** from various sources.

- Important aspects of knowledge of the business are:

  ° The industry
  ° Directors, managers and ownership
  ° Products, markets, suppliers, expenses, operations
  ° Financial performance
  ° Reporting environment

- Knowledge of the business can be used to:

  ° Assess risks
  ° Develop an effective and efficient audit plan and programme
  ° Evaluate audit evidence

- **Audit risk** is the risk that the auditors may give an inappropriate opinion on the financial statements. A risk-based audit will make use of the risk model to determine the amount and extent of audit testing. Audit risk comprises **inherent, control** and **detection risk**.

- **Materiality** should be calculated at the planning stages of all audits. The calculation or estimation of materiality should be based on experience and judgement. The materiality chosen should be reviewed during the audit.

- **Analytical procedures** are very useful at the planning stage, allowing risk areas to be identified.

Quick quiz

1 Which documents set out:

    (a) The general strategy of the audit
    (b) The detailed work

2 What are the main sources of knowledge of the business mentioned by SAS 210?

3 What is audit risk?

4 What are the three components of audit risk?

5 Give examples of factors which affect the assessment of inherent risk:

    (a) For a client as a whole
    (b) For individual audit areas

6 Give examples of figures used as a basis for setting materiality.

7 What information does an audit programme usually contain?

Answers to quick quiz

1 (a) The **audit plan** sets out the general strategy of the audit.
   (b) The **audit programme** sets out the detailed work.

2   The main sources of knowledge of the business listed in SAS 210 are as follows.

   (a)   Previous experience of the client and industry
   (b)   Visits to the client
   (c)   Discussions with the client's directors and staff
   (d)   Discussions with other auditors and legal and other advisers
   (e)   Discussions with knowledgeable people outside the client
   (f)   Industry publications
   (g)   Legislation and regulations that significantly affect the client
   (h)   Documents produced by the client
   (i)   Professional literature

3   Audit risk is the risk that auditors may give an inappropriate opinion on the annual accounts.

4   The three components of audit risk are inherent, control and detection risk.

5   (a)   Factors which affect the inherent risk assessment for the client as a whole include:

      (i)   The integrity and attitude to risk of directors and management
      (ii)   Management experience and knowledge
      (iii) Unusual pressures on directors or management
      (iv)   The nature of the client's business
      (v)   Factors affecting the industry

   (b)   Factors which affect the inherent risk assessment for individual audit areas include:

      (i)   Accounts which are likely to be prone to misstatement
      (ii)   Complexity of underlying transactions
      (iii)   Degree of judgement required
      (iv)   Susceptibility of assets to loss or misappropriation
      (v)   Quality of accounting systems
      (vi)   Unusual transactions around the year-end
      (vii)   Transactions not subject to ordinary processing
      (viii) Areas where there have been significant staff changes

6   Commonly materiality is set using one or more of the following figures.

   (a)   Profit before tax
   (b)   Gross assets
   (c)   Turnover

   Less frequently the following figures are used.

   (a)   Gross profit
   (b)   Profit after tax
   (c)   Net assets

7   An audit programme usually contains:

   (a)   Audit tests
   (b)   Test objectives
   (c)   Timing of the tests
   (d)   Sample sizes
   (e)   Basis of sample detection

Answers to activities

Answer 4.1

When planning an audit auditors need to know:

(a)   How general economic factors affect the client's business
(b)   How conditions in the industry affect the client's business
(c)   The client's directors, management and ownership; their involvement, knowledge and integrity
(d)   Details of the client's business, its products, markets, supplies etc
(e)   Other factors which affect the client's financial environment
(f)   Reporting requirements which affect the accounts

(Further detail is given for these factors in Paragraph 3.4.)

BPP
PUBLISHING

Answer 4.2

Tutorial note. You may feel more confident about answering this type of question when you have completed the chapters on individual audit areas. However you should have been able to use your imagination to come up with the major points.

(a) It is likely in many aspects that the inherent risk for this client would be low. Management are likely to have sufficient expertise and knowledge, and the business may well have a good reputation.

Possible high-risk factors include the degree of competition that the pubs face. Stock valuation and valuation of properties may be complex. In addition the pubs will handle a lot of cash and thus controls will be needed against defalcations.

(b) Tricky Dicky is likely to have a high inherent risk assessment.

(i) As a new business operating in a volatile industry, the chances of business failure will be quite high.

(ii) Management may not have been able to establish sufficient internal controls or an appropriate accounting function.

(iii) Valuation of stock may be difficult.

(c) The principal factor which may indicate high inherent risk for this client would be the lack of supervision of management by the owner. Auditors would need to consider carefully how management operate and were rewarded, and any pressures on management to distort results (performance-related bonuses). Other factors indicate less of an inherent risk, the business having operated for a long time in what presumably is a fairly stable market.

(d) A number of factors indicate that the assessment of inherent risk for Blues Blues Electric Blues plc may be high.

(i) The business is seeking a Stock Exchange listing and this may put pressure on the directors to manipulate results so as to obtain a better share price.

(ii) The business will be under increased regulations once it has applied for listing.

(iii) The fact that the business is expanding quickly may indicate accounting systems and controls previously set up are no longer adequate.

(iv) Similarly the fact that the business is expanding quickly may mean it has outstripped its resources, and is having problems obtaining sufficient finance. Is this why it is seeking a listing?

Answer 4.3

(a) Because the business is stable, auditors are likely to base overall materiality on a % of turnover or gross assets, or possibly an average of both. Profit before tax is unlikely to be used overall as its fluctuation does not appear to be significant. However a different materiality level may be set when considering the one-off expense, since it may be particularly significant to readers of the accounts.

(b) Auditors are likely here to pay some attention to the level of profit when setting materiality, because the outside members regard profit as significant. However the auditors are also likely to take into account gross and net assets. Low profits will be of less significance if the business has a strong asset base, but more significance if the business is in long-term financial difficulty.

Answer 4.4

In planning the audit the following matters should be taken into consideration.

(a) We should review the previous years' audit files and note significant matters that may also affect this year's accounts.

(b) We should update our knowledge and consider whether there are significant changes that may have an impact upon this year's audit. These might include changes in:

(i) Industry and market conditions
(ii) Legislation that affect the company
(iii) Management or senior accounting staff
(iv) Products, markets or suppliers.

We would update knowledge by discussions with the client and review of industry publications and news about the industry.

(c)   We should try to obtain the management accounts and examine these to gain information about the company's trading performance. We should make comparisons between the performance of the retail outlets to see if any warrant special attention. In particular we should concentrate on the performance and viability of the three new outlets.

(d)   We should also try to obtain forecasts and budgets for the next twelve months or longer, particularly because of the company's liquidity problems. We will want to see whether cash flow is expected to improve, due perhaps to increased sales from the new outlets. We would be concerned with the assumptions on which the forecasts were based.

(e)   We should agree the timing of the audit with the company's management, in particular:

(i)   Timing of stocktake and our level of attendance
(ii)   Procedures for circularising debtors
(iii)   Timing of significant phases of the preparation of the accounts
(iv)   Extent to which analysis and summaries can be prepared by the company's employees
(v)   Relevance of any work to be carried out by the company's auditors

(f)   We should review the stock-taking procedures in detail. We should also try to obtain the results of any interim stock counts to consider whether problems still exist in the comparison between book and actual stock levels.

(g)   Having taken these factors into account, we should be able to assess risk and materiality, and decide what the general approach would be. We may be able to rely on the internal controls of the company, and hence be able to carry out control testing and reduce our substantive testing.

(h)   We will need to determine the staff to be used on the audit. The staff chosen should be suitably qualified and experienced. We will need to consider the number of staff to be used at head office and the warehouse and also how many staff will be needed at the company's stocktake.

(i)   We also need to determine which of the retail outlets will be visited. It may be the practice to visit larger outlets each year, and a selection of smaller outlets as well. This year it is likely that members of the audit team will visit the new outlets, since these are likely to be of higher risk having just opened.

(j)   Important planning decisions should be documented in the audit plan, and will also affect the audit programme, which should be drawn up at this stage.

(k)   The audit plan should also include a timetable for the principal phases of the audit, the date the audit report will be signed and an estimate of fees, costs and profits.

Chapter 5 Audit evidence and audit procedures

Chapter topic list

1   Introduction

2   Audit evidence

3   Procedures for obtaining audit evidence

4   Computer assisted audit techniques (CAATs)

5   Audit sampling

Learning objectives

On completion of this chapter you will be able to:

	Performance criteria	Range statement
• Describe the different kinds of audit evidence	all	all
• Explain the distinction between tests of control (compliance tests) and substantive tests.	17.1.7	17.1.3
• Design tests of control and substantive tests for a variety of accounting areas	17.1.7	17.1.1-17.1.3
• Describe how computer assisted audit techniques can be used in the audit	17.1.7	17.1.1-17.1.3
• Describe the factors considered when choosing a sample size and select an appropriate sample	17.1.6	17.1.1-17.1.3

BPP
PUBLISHING

1   INTRODUCTION

1.1   This chapter firstly deals with the **evidence** auditors are trying to obtain. We stressed in the last chapter that auditors aim to carry out audits effectively and efficiently; in order to do that, they must understand **how much** evidence they need to obtain, and what **quality** it needs to be. The general answer is that auditors need to obtain evidence that is **sufficient** and **appropriate**; we shall look at what these terms mean and also other general comments that can be made about audit evidence.

1.2   We saw in Chapter 1 that audit evidence is obtained by carrying out tests of control and substantive tests. We shall examine in this chapter the **evidence** auditors are attempting to obtain when carrying out these tests. We also examine the **techniques** auditors use for obtaining audit evidence, including in Section 4 computer assisted audit techniques.

1.3   We also need to discuss how auditors decide which items they will test if they adopt sampling procedures. This is not as simple as it sounds. The auditors will want to select a sample which reflects the characteristics of the population from which the sample has been selected.

1.4   The auditing standard on **audit sampling** is discussed in Section 5. Practical sampling methods range from the very simple to the very complex. The more sophisticated sampling techniques involve the use of probabilities and statistics, but we shall not be looking at these in detail.

1.5   You should particularly note how **sample sizes** are determined, methods of **sample selection** and the advantages of **statistical sampling**. You should also remember that sampling is only one type of audit test, and other tests, for example testing all high-value items, may be more appropriate in certain circumstances.

2   AUDIT EVIDENCE

> ### KEY TERM
>
> **Audit evidence** is the information auditors obtain in arriving at the conclusions on which their report is based.

2.1   In order to reach a position in which they can express a professional opinion, the auditors need to gather evidence from various sources. SAS 400 *Audit evidence* covers this area.

Sufficient appropriate audit evidence

> ### SAS 400.1
>
> Auditors should obtain sufficient appropriate audit evidence to be able to draw reasonable conclusions on which to base the audit opinion.

2.2   'Sufficiency' and 'appropriateness' are interrelated and apply to both tests of controls and substantive procedures.

- **Sufficiency** is the measure of the **quantity** of audit evidence.
- **Appropriateness** is the measure of the **quality** or **reliability** of the audit evidence.

What constitutes sufficient appropriate audit evidence for the different types of audit tests - tests of control and substantive tests - relates to what auditors are trying to assess when carrying out these tests.

Activity 5.1

Can you state which of the following tests are tests of control and which are substantive tests?

(a)   Checking that invoices have been approved by the managing director
(b)   Attending the year-end stocktake
(c)   Reviewing accounting records after the year-end for events that affect this year's accounts
(d)   Obtaining confirmation from the bank of balances held at the year-end
(e)   Checking how unauthorised personnel are prevented from entering stock-rooms
(f)   Checking if references are sought for all new major customers

---

2.3   Thus auditors are essentially looking for enough reliable audit evidence. Audit evidence usually indicates what is probable rather than what is definite (is usually persuasive rather then conclusive) so different sources are examined by the auditors. Auditors can only give reasonable assurance that the financial statements are free from misstatement, as not *all* sources of evidence will be examined.

2.4   The auditors' judgement as to what is sufficient appropriate audit evidence is influenced by various factors.

- **Assessment of risk**
- The **nature** of the **accounting and internal control systems**
- The **materiality** of the item being examined
- The **experience gained during previous audits.**
- The auditors' **knowledge of the business** and **industry**
- The **results of audit procedures**
- The **source** and **reliability of information** available

2.5   If they are unable to obtain sufficient appropriate audit evidence, the auditors may have to consider the effect on their audit report.

Tests of control

SAS 400.2

In seeking to obtain audit evidence from tests of control, auditors should consider the sufficiency and appropriateness of the audit evidence to support the assessed level of control risk.

2.6   There are two aspects of the relevant parts of the accounting and internal control systems about which auditors should seek to obtain audit evidence.

(a)   **Design**: the accounting and internal control systems are designed so as to be capable of preventing or detecting material misstatements.

(b)   **Operation**: the systems exist and have operated effectively throughout the relevant period.

Substantive procedures

> ## SAS 400.3
>
> In seeking to obtain audit evidence from substantive procedures, auditors should consider the extent to which that evidence together with any evidence from tests of controls supports the relevant financial statement assertions.

2.7 Substantive procedures are designed to obtain evidence about the financial statement assertions which are basically what the accounts say about the assets, liabilities and transactions of the client, and the events that affect the client's accounts.

FINANCIAL STATEMENT ASSERTIONS

Existence	An asset or liability exists
Rights and obligations	An asset or liability 'belongs' to the client
Occurrence	A transaction or event took place which relates to the client
Completeness	All relevant assets, liabilities, transactions and events are recorded, and there are no undisclosed items
Valuation	An asset or liability is recorded at an appropriate value
Measurement	A transaction or event is measured at a proper amount and allocated to the proper period
Presentation and disclosure	An item is disclosed, classified and described in accordance with the applicable reporting framework

An eighth assertion, **accuracy**, that all assets, liabilities, transactions and events are recorded accurately, is sometimes added.

2.8 Audit evidence is usually obtained for assets, liabilities and transactions to support each financial statement assertion and evidence from one does not compensate for failure to obtain evidence for another. However, audit tests may provide audit evidence of more than one assertion.

Reliability of evidence

2.9 The following generalisations may help in assessing the reliability of audit evidence.

(a) Audit evidence from **external sources** (eg confirmation received from a third party) is **more reliable** than that obtained from **internal sources** (the client's records).

(b) Audit evidence obtained from the **entity's records** is more reliable when the related accounting and internal **control system operates effectively**.

(c) Evidence obtained **directly by auditors** is **more reliable** than that obtained by or **from the client**.

(d) Evidence in the **form of documents and written representations** is **more reliable** than **oral representations**.

(e) **Original documents** are **more reliable** than **photocopies, telexes or faxes**.

2.10 Consistency of audit evidence from different sources will have a cumulative effect, making the evidence more persuasive.

2.11 Auditors must consider the cost-benefit relationship of obtaining evidence *but* any difficulty or expense is not in itself a valid basis for omitting a necessary procedure.

DEVOLVED ASSESSMENT ALERT

You should be able to assess how strong certain evidence is from the auditor's viewpoint, for example debtors' circularisation or third party valuation of assets. An example is given below.

Activity 5.2

Discuss the strength or weakness of the following sources of audit evidence, and the financial statement assertions to which they relate.

(a) Physical inspection of a fixed asset by an auditor

(b) Confirmation by a debtor of money owed

(c) Oral representations by management that all creditors owed money at the year-end have been included in the accounts

3 PROCEDURES FOR OBTAINING AUDIT EVIDENCE

3.1 Auditors obtain evidence by one or more of the following procedures.

PROCEDURES	
Inspection of assets	Examining or counting assets that physically exist
	Inspection confirms **existence**, gives evidence of **valuation** but does not confirm ownership
Inspection of documentation	Demonstrates that a transaction **occurs** or a balance **exists**, also that client has **rights** and **obligations** in relation to assets or liabilities
	Can also be used to **compare** documents, and hence test **consistency** of audit evidence, and to **confirm authorisation**
Observation	Involves watching a procedure being performed (eg post opening)
	Of limited use, as only confirms procedure took place when auditor watching
Inquiries	Seeking information from **client staff** or **external sources**
	Strength of evidence depends on knowledge and integrity of source of information
Confirmation	Seeking confirmation from another source of details in client's accounting records eg confirmation from bank of bank balances
Computations	Checking arithmetic of client's records eg adding up ledger account
Analytical procedures	See Chapter 11

4 COMPUTER ASSISTED AUDIT TECHNIQUES (CAATs)

4.1 Computer-based accounting systems allow auditors to use either the client's computer or another computer during their audit work. Techniques performed with computers in this way are known as Computer Assisted Audit Techniques (CAATs).

4.2 There is no mystique about using CAATs to help with auditing. You probably use common computer assisted audit techniques all the time in your daily work without realising it.

(a) Most modern accounting systems allow data to be manipulated in various ways and extracted into a **report**.

(b) Even if reporting capabilities are limited, the data can often be exported directly into a **spreadsheet** package (sometimes using simple Windows-type cut and paste facilities in very modern systems) and then analysed.

(c) Most systems have **searching** facilities that are much quicker to use than searching through print-outs by hand.

4.3 There are a variety of packages specially designed either to ease the auditing task itself, or to carry out audit interrogations of computerised data automatically. There are also a variety of ways of testing the processing that is carried out.

4.4 Auditors can use PCs such as laptops that are independent of the organisation's systems when performing CAATs.

4.5 There are various types of CAAT.

(a) **Audit interrogation software** is a computer program used for audit purposes to examine the content of the client's computer files.

(b) **Test data** is data used by the auditors for computer processing to test the operation of the client's computer programs.

(c) **Embedded audit facilities** are elements set up by the auditor which are included within the client's computer system. They allow the possibility of continuous checking.

Audit interrogation software

4.6 Interrogation software performs the sort of checks on data that auditors might otherwise have to perform by hand. Its use is particularly appropriate during substantive testing of transactions and especially balances. By using audit software, the auditors may scrutinise large volumes of data and concentrate skilled manual resources on the investigation of results, rather than on the extraction of information.

Test data

4.7 An obvious way of seeing whether a system is **processing** data in the way that it should be is to input some test data and see what happens. The expected results can be calculated in advance and then compared with the results that actually arise.

4.8 The problem with test data is that any resulting corruption of the data files has to be corrected. This is difficult with modern real-time systems, which often have built in (and highly desirable) controls to ensure that data entered *cannot* easily be removed without leaving a mark. Consequently test data is used less and less as a CAAT.

Embedded audit facilities

4.9 The results of using test data would, in any case, be completely distorted if the programs used to process it were not the ones *normally* used for processing. For example a fraudulent member of the IT department might substitute a version of the program that gave the correct results, purely for the duration of the test, and then replace it with a version that siphoned off the company's funds into his own bank account.

4.10 To allow a **continuous** review of the data recorded and the manner in which it is treated by the system, it may be possible to use CAATs referred to as 'embedded audit facilities'.

4.11 An embedded facility consists of audit modules that are incorporated into the computer element of the enterprise's accounting system.

EXAMPLES OF EMBEDDED AUDIT FACILITIES	
Integrated test facility (ITF)	Creates a **fictitious entity** within the company application, where transactions are posted to it alongside regular transactions, and actual results of fictitious entity compared with what it should have produced
Systems control and review file (SCARF)	Allows auditors to have transactions above a **certain amount** from **specific ledger account** posted to a file for later auditor review

Simulation

4.12 Simulation (or 'parallel simulation)' entails the preparation of a separate program that simulates the processing of the organisation's real system. Real data can then be passed not only through the system proper but also through the simulated program. For example the simulation program may be used to re-perform controls such as those used to identify any missing items from a sequence.

Knowledge-based systems

4.13 Decision support systems and expert systems can be used to assist with the auditors' own judgement and decisions.

Planning CAATs

4.14 In certain circumstances the auditors will need to use CAATs in order to obtain the evidence they require, whereas in other circumstances they may use CAATs to improve the efficiency or effectiveness of the audit.

4.15 In choosing the appropriate combination of CAATs and manual procedures, the auditors will need to take the following points into account.

(a) Computer programs often perform functions of which **no visible evidence** is available. In these circumstances it will frequently not be practicable for the auditors to perform tests manually.

(b) In many audit situations the auditors will have the choice of performing a test either **manually** or with the **assistance of a CAAT**. In making this choice, they will be influenced by the respective efficiency of the alternatives, which is influenced by a number of factors.

(i) The extent of tests of controls or substantive procedures achieved by both alternatives

(ii) The pattern of cost associated with the CAAT

(iii) The ability to incorporate within the use of the CAAT a number of different audit tests

BPP PUBLISHING

(c) Sometimes auditors will need to report within a comparatively **short time-scale**. In such cases it may be more efficient to use CAATs because they are quicker to apply.

(d) If using a CAAT, auditors should ensure that the **required computer facilities, computer files** and **programs are available**.

(e) The operation of some CAATs requires **frequent attendance** or access by the auditors.

Controlling CAATs

4.16 Where CAATs are used, however, particular attention should be paid to the need to **co-ordinate the work of staff** with specialist computer skills with the work of others engaged on the audit. The **technical work** should be **approved** and **reviewed** by someone with the necessary computer expertise.

Audit trails

4.17 The original purpose of an **audit trail** was to preserve details of all stages of processing on *paper*. This meant that transactions could be followed stage-by-stage through a system to ensure that they had been processed correctly.

Around the computer?

4.18 Traditionally, therefore, it was widely considered that auditors could fulfil their function without having any detailed knowledge of what was going on inside the computer.

4.19 The auditors would commonly audit **'round the computer'**, ignoring the procedures which take place within the computer programs and concentrating solely on the input and corresponding output. Audit procedures would include checking authorisation, coding and control totals of input and checking the output with source documents and clerical control totals.

Through the computer

4.20 The 'round the computer approach' is now frowned upon. Typical audit problems that arise as audit trails move further away from the hard copy trail include testing computer generated totals when no detailed analysis is available and testing the completeness of output in the absence of control totals. One of the principal problems facing the auditors is that of acquiring an understanding of the workings of electronic data processing and of the computer itself.

4.21 Auditors now customarily audit **'through the computer'**. This involves an examination of the detailed processing routines of the computer to determine whether the controls in the system are adequate to ensure complete and correct processing of all data. In these situations it will often be necessary to employ computer assisted audit techniques.

Activity 5.3

(a) What is meant by the term 'loss of audit trail' in the context of computerised accounting procedures?

(b) How can auditors gain assurance about the operation of computerised accounting procedures given the 'loss of audit trail'?

---

5   AUDIT SAMPLING

5.1   SAS 430 *Audit sampling* covers this topic in depth.

5.2   This SAS is based on the premise that auditors do not normally examine all the information available to them; it would be impractical to do so and using audit sampling will produce valid conclusions.

KEY TERMS

Audit sampling is the application of audit procedures to less than 100% of the items within an account balance or class of transactions. It enables auditors to obtain and evaluate evidence about some characteristic of the items selected in order to form a conclusion about the population sampled.

Sampling units are the individual items that make up the population.

Error is an unintentional mistake in the financial statements.

Tolerable error is the maximum error in the population that the auditors are willing to accept and still conclude that the audit objective has been achieved.

Sampling risk is the risk that the auditors' conclusion, based on a sample, may be different from the conclusion that would be reached if the entire population was subject to the same audit procedure.

Non-sampling risk is the risk that the auditors might use inappropriate procedures or might misinterpret evidence and thus fail to recognise an error.

5.3   The SAS points out that some testing procedures do *not* involve sampling.

   (a)   Testing 100% of items in a population (this should be obvious)

   (b)   Testing all items with a certain characteristic (eg over a certain value) as selection is not representative

5.4   The SAS distinguishes between **statistically based sampling**, which involves the use of techniques from which mathematically constructed conclusions about the population can be drawn, and **non-statistical or judgmental methods**, from which auditors draw a judgmental opinion about the population. However, the principles of the SAS apply to both methods.

Design of the sample

Audit objectives

5.5   Auditors must consider the **specific audit objectives** to be achieved and the audit procedures which are most likely to achieve them.

5.6   The auditors also need to consider the **nature and characteristics** of the **audit evidence** sought and **possible error conditions**. This will help them to define what constitutes an error and what population to use for sampling.

5.7   Furthermore auditors must consider the **level of error** they are prepared to accept and **how confident** they wish to be that the population does not contain an error rate greater than what is acceptable.

5.8 Thus for a test of controls auditors may wish to be 95% confident that controls have failed to work on no more than 3 occasions. For a substantive test of fixed assets, they may wish to be 90% confident that fixed assets are not mis-stated by more than £10,000.

5.9 The % confidence auditors wish to have is the '**confidence level**' and it is related to the degree of audit risk auditors are prepared to accept.

Population

5.10 The population from which the sample is drawn must be **appropriate** and **complete** for the specific audit objectives.

Sample size

> **SAS 430.3**
>
> When determining sample sizes, auditors should consider sampling risk, the amount of error that would be acceptable and the extent to which they expect to find errors.

5.11 Examples of some factors affecting sample size are given in an appendix to the SAS, reproduced here.

Table 1: Some factors influencing sample size for tests of controls	
Factor	*Impact on sample size*
Sampling risk	• The greater the reliance on the results of a test of control using audit sampling, the lower the sampling risk the auditors are willing to accept and, consequently, the larger the sample size. • The lower the assessment of control risk, the more likely the auditors are to place reliance on audit evidence from tests of control. • A high control risk assessment may result in a decision not to perform tests of control and rely entirely on substantive procedures.
Tolerable error rate	The higher the tolerable error rate the lower the sample size and vice versa.
Expected error rate	• If errors are expected, a larger sample ordinarily needs to be examined to confirm that the actual error rate is less than the tolerable error rate. • High expected error rates may result in a decision not to perform tests of control.
Number of items in population	Virtually no effect on sample size unless population is small.

Table 2: Some factors influencing sample size for substantive tests	
Factor	*Impact on sample size*
Inherent risk	• The higher the assessment of inherent risk, the more audit evidence is required to support the auditors' conclusion.
Control risk	• The higher the assessment of control risk, the greater the reliance on audit evidence obtained from substantive procedures.
Detection risk	• Sampling risk for substantive tests is one form of detection risk. The lower the sampling risk the auditors are willing to accept, the larger the sample size.
	• Other substantive procedures may provide audit evidence regarding the same financial statement assertions and reduce detection risk. This may reduce the extent of the auditors' reliance on the results of a substantive procedure using audit sampling.
	• The lower the reliance on the results of a substantive procedure using audit sampling, the higher the sampling risk the auditors are willing to accept and, consequently, the smaller the sample size.
Tolerable error rate	The higher the monetary value of the tolerable error rate the smaller the sample size and vice versa.
Expected error rate	If errors are expected, a larger sample ordinarily needs to be examined to confirm that the actual error rate is less than the tolerable error rate.
Population value	The less material the monetary value of the population to the financial statements, the smaller the sample size that may be required.
Numbers of items in population	Virtually no effect on sample size unless population is small.
Stratification	If it is appropriate to stratify the population this may lead to a smaller sample size.

Sampling risk

5.12 Sampling risk is encountered by the auditors in both tests of control and substantive procedures as follows. It is the risk of drawing a **wrong conclusion** from audit sampling. It is part of detection risk.

5.13 For tests of control, drawing a wrong conclusion means making an **incorrect assessment** (too high or too low) of **control risk.** For substantive procedures it means either stating a population is **materially mis-stated when it is not,** or stating a population is **not materially mis-stated when it is.**

5.14 The **greater** their reliance on the results of the procedure in question, the **lower** the sampling risk auditors will be willing to accept and the **larger** the sample size needs to be.

5.15 Thus if inherent risk is high, control risk is high and sampling is the only substantive procedure auditors are carrying out, then auditors are placing maximum reliance on sampling. Hence the level of sampling risk auditors will be prepared to accept will be at minimum, and sample sizes will be high.

Tolerable error

5.16   For **tests** of **control,** the tolerable error is the **maximum rate** of **deviation** from a control that auditors are willing to accept in the population and still conclude that the preliminary assessment of control risk is valid. Often this rate will be very low, since the auditor is likely to be concentrating on testing important controls.

5.17   Sometimes even a single failure of an important control will cause auditors to reject their assessment of control risk. If for example, an important control is that all major capital expenditure is approved by the board, failure to approve expenditure on one item may be an unacceptable deviation as far as the auditors are concerned.

5.18   For substantive procedures, the **tolerable error** is the **maximum monetary error** in an account balance or class of transactions, that auditors are willing to accept so that when the results of all audit procedures are considered, they are able to conclude with reasonable assurance, that the financial statements are not materially mis-stated.

5.19   Sometimes the tolerable error rate will be the materiality rate. Some accounting firms set tolerable error as being a fixed percentage of materiality, say 50% or 70% for reasons of prudence.

Expected error

5.20   Larger samples will be required when errors are expected than would be required if none were expected, in order to conclude that the *actual* error is *less* than the *tolerable* error. If the expected error rate is high then sampling may not be appropriate and auditors may have to examine 100% of a population.

Selection of the sample

SAS 430.4

Auditors should select sample items in such a way that the sample can be expected to be representative of the population in respect of the characteristics being tested.

5.21   The SAS makes a very important point.

'For a sample to be representative of the population, all items in the population are required to have an equal or known probability of being selected.'

5.22   There are a number of selection methods available, but the SAS identifies three that are commonly used.

(a)   **Random selection** ensures that all items in the population have an equal chance of selection, eg by use of random number tables.

(b)   **Systematic selection** (or interval sampling) involves selecting items using a constant interval between selections, the first interval having a random start.

Suppose the auditors decide to pick every 50th item and start at random at item number 11. They will then pick item number 61 (11 + 50), item number 111 (11 + (50 × 2)), item number 161 (11 + (50 × 3)) and so on. Auditors must when using this method, guard against the risk of errors occurring systematically in such a way as not to be detected by sampling. In our example this would be errors occurring at item number 41, 91, 141, 191 etc.

(c) **Haphazard selection** involves auditors choosing items subjectively without using formal random methods but also avoiding bias. The biggest danger of haphazard selection is that bias does in fact occur. Auditors may for example end up choosing items that are easily located, and these may not be representative. Haphazard selection is more likely to be used when auditors are using judgmental rather than statistical sampling.

5.23 In addition the auditors may also consider for certain tests:

(a) **Stratification.** This involves division of the population into a number of parts. Each sampling unit can only belong to one, specifically designed, stratum. The idea is that each stratum will contain items which have significant characteristics in common. This enables the auditors to direct audit effort towards items which, for example, contain the greatest potential monetary error.

(b) **Selection by value** is selecting the largest items within a population. This will only be appropriate if auditors believe that the size of the item is related to the risk of the item being seriously misstated.

(c) **Sequence sampling** may be used to check whether certain items have particular characteristics. For example an auditor may use a sample of 50 consecutive cheques to check whether cheques are signed by authorised signatories rather than picking 50 single cheques throughout the year. Sequence sampling may however produce samples that are not representative of the population as a whole particularly if errors occurred only during a certain part of the year.

5.24 Certain items may be tested because they are considered unusual, for example debit balances on a purchase ledger or a nil balance with a major supplier.

Statistical and judgmental sampling

5.25 As mentioned above, auditors need to decide when sampling whether to use statistical or non-statistical methods. Statistical sampling means using statistical theory to measure the impact of sampling risk and evaluate the sample results. Non-statistical sampling relies on judgement to evaluate results.

5.26 Whether statistical or non-statistical methods are used, auditors will still have to take account of risk, tolerable and expected error, and population value for substantive tests when deciding on sample sizes.

5.27 If these conditions are present, **statistical sampling** normally has the following **advantages**.

(a) At the conclusion of a test the auditors are able to state with a **definite level of confidence** that the whole population conforms to the sample result, within a stated precision limit.

(b) **Sample size** is **objectively determined**, having regard to the degree of risk the auditors are prepared to accept for each application.

(c) The process of fixing required precision and confidence levels compels the auditors to consider and **clarify their audit objectives**.

(d) The **results of tests** can be **expressed** in precise **mathematical terms**.

(e) **Bias is eliminated**.

Evaluation of sample results

> **SAS 430.5**
>
> Having carried out, on each sample item, those audit procedures which are appropriate to the particular audit objective, auditors should:
>
> (a) analyse any errors detected in the sample; and
>
> (b) draw inferences for the population as a whole.

Analysis of errors in the sample

5.28 To begin with, the auditors must consider whether the items in question are **true errors,** as they defined them before the test, eg a misposting between customer accounts will not count as an error as far as total debtors are concerned.

5.29 Assuming the problems are errors, auditors should consider the **nature and cause** of the error and any possible **effects** the error might have on other parts of the audit.

Inferences to be drawn from the population as a whole

5.30 The auditors should project the error results from the sample on to the relevant population. The projection method should be consistent with the method used to select the sampling unit. The auditors will estimate the **probable error** in the population by extrapolating the errors found in the sample. They will then estimate any **further error** that might not have been detected because of the imprecision of the sampling technique (in addition to consideration of the nature and effects of the errors).

5.31 The auditors should then compare the **projected population error** (net of adjustments made by the entity in the case of substantive procedures) to the **tolerable error,** taking account of other audit procedures relevant to the specific control or financial statement assertion.

5.32 If the projected population error *exceeds* tolerable error, then the auditors should **re-assess sampling risk.** If it is unacceptable, they should consider **extending auditing procedures** or **performing alternative procedures,** either of which may result in a proposed adjustment to the financial statements.

5.33 **Section summary**

Key stages in the sampling process are as follows.

- Determining **objectives** and **population**
- Determining **sample size**
- **Choosing method** of **sample selection**
- **Analysing** the **results** and **projecting errors**

Activity 5.4

Describe three commonly-used methods of sample selection and describe the main risks involved in using each method.

Key learning points

- The auditors must be able to evaluate all types of audit evidence in terms of its sufficiency and appropriateness.

- Evidence can be in the form of tests of controls or substantive procedures.

- Tests of control concentrate on the design and operation of controls.

- Substantive testing aims to test all the financial statement assertions.

    ° Existence
    ° Rights and obligations (ownership)
    ° Occurrence
    ° Completeness
    ° Valuation
    ° Measurement
    ° Presentation and disclosure

- The reliability of audit evidence is influenced by its source and by its nature.

- Audit evidence can be obtained by the following techniques.

    ° Inspection
    ° Observation
    ° Enquiry and confirmation
    ° Computation
    ° Analytical procedures

- Auditors may use a number of **computer assisted audit techniques** including audit interrogation software, test data and embedded audit facilities.

- The main stages of audit sampling are:

    ° Design of the sample
    ° Selection of the sample
    ° Evaluation of sample results

- **Sample sizes for tests of control** are influenced by sampling risk, tolerable error rate and expected error rate.

- **Sample sizes for substantive tests** are influenced by inherent, control and detection risk, tolerable error rate, expected error rate, population value and stratification.

- **Sample sizes** can be picked by a variety of means including random selection, systematic selection and haphazard selection.

- When **evaluating results**, auditors should:

    ° Analyse any errors considering their amount and the reasons why they have occurred
    ° Draw conclusions for the population as a whole

Quick quiz

1   What does SAS 400.1 say about the evidence that auditors should obtain?

2   When auditors are testing controls, about which two aspects are they seeking evidence?

3   List the financial statement assertions (single, two or three word descriptions will suffice).

4   What general comments can be made about audit evidence?

5   Of which type of audit procedure are the following examples?

    (a)   Physical check of fixed assets
    (b)   Watching the payment of wages
    (c)   Receiving a letter from the client's bank concerning balances held at the bank by the client
    (d)   Adding up the client's trial balance

BPP
PUBLISHING

6   What tasks are most important in controlling the use of CAATs?

7   What is the difference between auditing round the computer and auditing through the computer?

8   What is an integrated test facility (ITF)?

9   Define:

(a)   Error
(b)   Tolerable error
(c)   Sampling risk

10   Summarise the factors that affect sample sizes for substantive tests.

11   What are two stages of projection of errors onto a whole population?

Answers to quick quiz

1   SAS 400.1 states that auditors should obtain sufficient appropriate audit evidence to be able to draw reasonable conclusions on which to base their opinion.

2   When testing controls, auditors are concentrating on their design and operation.

3   The financial statement assertions are:

(a)   Existence
(b)   Rights and obligations
(c)   Occurrence
(d)   Completeness
(e)   Valuation
(f)   Measurement
(g)   Presentation and disclosure

4   General comments that can be made about audit evidence are as follows.

(a)   Audit evidence from external sources is more reliable than evidence from internal sources.

(b)   Evidence obtained form the client's records is more satisfactory if the accounting and internal control system is operating effectively.

(c)   Directly obtained audit evidence is more reliable than evidence obtained from the entity.

(d)   Written evidence is more reliable than oral evidence.

(e)   Original documents are more reliable than copies.

5   (a)   Inspection
(b)   Observation
(c)   Confirmation
(d)   Computation

6   The most important tasks in controlling the use of CAATs are:

(a)   Co-ordination of the work of specialist computer staff with the rest of the audit team
(b)   Approval and review of the work by someone with the necessary computer experience

7   Auditing 'round the computer' involves comparisons of input and output, neglecting procedures that take place within the computer.

Auditing 'through the computer' involves examination of the detailed routines that take place within the computer.

8   An integrated test facility is the creation of a fictitious entity within the framework of the regular application to which transactions are posted alongside the regular transactions.

9   (a)   An error is an unintentional mistake in the financial statements.

(b)   Tolerable error is the maximum error in the population that auditors are willing to accept and still conclude the audit objectives have been achieved.

(c)   Sampling risk is the risk that the auditors' conclusion, based on a sample, may be different from the conclusion that would be reached if the entire population was subject to the audit procedure.

10   Factors that affect the sample sizes of substantive tests are:

   (a)   Inherent risk
   (b)   Control risk
   (c)   Detection risk
   (d)   Tolerable error rate
   (e)   Expected error rate
   (f)   Population value
   (g)   Number of items (in small population)

   Stratification may also lead to smaller sample sizes.

11   The two stages of projection of an error are:

   (a)   Estimating the probable error in the population by extrapolating the errors found in the sample

   (b)   Estimating any further error that might not have been detected because of the imprecision of the sampling technique

Answers to activities

Answer 5.1

(a)   Control
(b)   Substantive
(c)   Substantive
(d)   Substantive
(e)   Control
(f)   Control

Answer 5.2

(a)   The physical inspection of an asset by auditors is inherently strong audit evidence since it is evidence obtained directly by auditors rather than from the client.

   The physical inspection of an asset gives auditors the strongest possible evidence concerning its existence.

   It also may give auditors some evidence as to valuation if for example machines appear to be obsolete or buildings appear to be derelict. More likely however auditors will require specialist assistance to value very material assets.

   Inspection also gives auditors some assurance that assets have been completely recorded. Auditors can check that all assets inspected have been recorded.

   However ownership of assets cannot be verified solely by physical inspection. Auditors will need to inspect documents of title, vehicle registration documents and so forth depending on the assets being verified.

(b)   Debtor confirmation of balances owed is inherently strong audit evidence since it is written confirmation by a third party.

   The evidence is particularly relevant to the assertions of existence (the debtor exists) and rights and obligations (the debtor owes the client money).

   Further evidence however is likely to be needed of valuation because although the debtor has acknowledged money is owed, that does not mean that the money will be paid.

(c)   Oral representations from clients about what is owed at the year-end are inherently weak evidence since they are not in writing and do not come from an independent source. Auditors should seek written confirmation of the representations, and seek confirmation from other audit evidence, for example suppliers' statements, post year-end accounting records and invoices received after the year-end.

   The representations do give some comfort on the completeness of creditors, and also the obligations of the client.

Answer 5.3

(a) Loss of audit trail means that auditors do not have full details of the accounting process that goes on within the computer, and cannot therefore check that process for accuracy. In addition auditors cannot be sure that the output of the computer is complete. Certain procedures may also take place entirely within the computer without any visible evidence.

(b) Auditors can overcome the loss of audit trail in the following ways.

   (i) Placing reliance on application and general controls. Application controls such as check digit verification or record counts can give assurance on the completeness and accuracy of processing. General controls can give assurance that the programs run have been developed properly and access to those programs is limited.

   (ii) Audit interrogation software can be used to reperform reconciliations, analyse accounts and identify items which do not fulfil criteria set down by the auditors and may therefore be subject to fraud.

   (iii) Test data can be used to see whether the system produces the results expected.

   (iv) Likewise an integrated test facility, involving the creation of a fictitious department, can be used to test the operation of processes.

   (v) The results of processing can be subject to analytical review, comparisons with previous years, budgets etc.

   (vi) Similarly the results of processing can be compared with other audit evidence, for example computer stock balances being compared with actual stock counts.

   (vii) Procedures can be reperformed manually but this is very time-consuming.

Answer 5.4

(a) **Random selection** involves using random number tables or other methods to select items. Random selection means that bias cannot affect the sample chosen; it means that all items in the population have an equal chance of being chosen.

   However, if the auditors are more concerned about some items than others, they can modify their approach, either by selecting certain items automatically because they are above a certain value, and selecting the rest of the sample by random numbers, or by stratifying the sample.

(b) **Systematic selection** involves selecting items using a constant interval between selections, the first interval having a random start.

   The main danger is that errors occur systematically in a pattern that means that none of the items in error will be selected.

(c) **Haphazard selection** involves auditors choosing items subjectively without using formal random methods but avoiding bias.

   The main danger is that bias (conscious or unconscious) does affect the auditor's judgement, and that certain items are selected because for example they are easy to obtain.

Chapter 6   Conduct of an audit

Chapter topic list

1   Introduction

2   Staffing of audits

3   Using the work of an expert and service organisations

4   Documenting the audit process

5   Quality control

Learning objectives

On completion of this chapter you will be able to:

	Performance criteria	Range statement
• Explain how audits are staffed	17.1.9	17.1.1-17.1.3
• Describe how professional relationships are promoted between audit and operational staff	17.2.6	all
• Assess whether there is a need to use the work of professional experts	17.1.7	17.1.1-17.1.3
• Explain how audit work is recorded to provide evidence of work done and how errors are recorded	17.2.1-17.2.4	17.2.1-17.2.3
• Describe the quality control procedures used on audits	17.2.1, 17.3.1, 17.3.4	17.2.1-17.2.3 17.3.1
• Employ confidentiality and security procedures	17.1.8,17.2.7, 17.3.5	all

BPP
PUBLISHING

1 INTRODUCTION

1.1 Having discussed in the last chapter how auditors decide what work they do and how much work they do, we move on to consider in this chapter who does the work, what their responsibilities are, and how audit work is recorded and controlled.

1.2 If the audit is to be carried out effectively, it is important to pick the right staff to do the work. We start this chapter by considering how audits are **staffed**, and the responsibilities of the staff who are chosen.

1.3 In addition some clients have items in their accounts which auditors do not themselves have the knowledge to assess properly; for example investment property valuation or the condition of work in progress. In these situations auditors should consider obtaining the assistance of an **expert opinion**.

1.4 We stressed in Chapter 4 the importance of recording planning properly. Similarly it is important to record the gathering of audit evidence, and hence this chapter deals with how **audit evidence is recorded** on working papers.

1.5 Lastly this chapter deals with the **control of audits**. Proper planning is of course a part of control, but auditors should be supervised throughout, and working papers reviewed. There has been increasing stress over the past few years on the procedures audit firms should implement to ensure that audit work is carried out to appropriate standards.

2 STAFFING OF AUDITS

2.1 Some audits are wholly carried out by a sole practitioner (an accountant who practices on his or her own) or a partner. More commonly however the reporting partner will take overall responsibility for the conduct of the audit and will sign the audit report. The reporting partner will however delegate aspects of the audit work such as the detailed testing to the staff of the firm.

2.2 The usual hierarchy of staff on an audit assignment is:

- Reporting partner
- Audit manager
- Supervisors/ audit seniors
- Audit assistants

2.3 When planning the audit, the partner or manager must decide **how many staff** are to be allocated to the assignment, how **experienced** (what grade) and whether any of them will require any **special knowledge, skill or experience**. The partner or manager will review the level of staffing the previous year and consider whether that level of staffing was acceptable.

Dealing with client's staff

2.4 An important skill that all staff chosen for the audit assignment should have is the ability to deal with the client staff with whom they come into contact. The *Performance Criteria* for this unit stress that discussions with staff operating the system should be conducted in a manner which **promotes professional relationships** between auditing and operational staff.

2.5 Relationships with the client will undoubtedly be enhanced if auditors aim to provide a high quality service that caters for the needs of the client.

2.6   However more specific people skills will also be needed. Negotiation skills and interviewing skills are particularly important.

2.7   Auditors should also be trying to understand what managers and staff want from the audit and how hostility to the time they have to spend dealing with auditors can be overcome. This does not mean agreeing with management and staff on every issue, but it does enable the auditors to understand why difficulties have arisen and how those difficulties can be overcome.

2.8   There are a number of signs of a poor approach to client relations.

   (a)   **Little contact** with **client managers** or **staff**

   (b)   Seeing the audit as no more than a **fault-finding exercise**, believing that managers or staff are not bothered about compliance

   (c)   **Failure to discuss findings** with client staff during the course of the audit, or failure to discuss findings at all face-to-face, but just setting them out in the audit report or management letter (a report for the client's internal use, see Chapter 7)

3   USING THE WORK OF AN EXPERT AND SERVICE ORGANISATIONS

> **KEY TERM**
>
> **An expert** is a person or firm possessing special skill, knowledge and experience in a particular field other than auditing.

3.1   Professional audit staff are highly trained and educated, but their experience and training is limited to accountancy and audit matters. In certain situations it will therefore be necessary to employ someone else with different expert knowledge.

3.2   Auditors have **sole responsibility** for their opinion, but may use the work of an expert. An expert may be engaged by a client to provide specialist advice on a particular matter which affects the financial statements, or by the auditors in order to obtain sufficient audit evidence regarding certain items in the financial statements.

Determining the need to use the work of an expert

> **SAS 520.1**
>
> When using the work performed by an expert, auditors should obtain sufficient appropriate audit evidence that such work is adequate for the purposes of an audit.

3.3   The following list of examples is given by SAS 520 of the audit evidence which might be obtained from the opinion, valuation etc of an expert.

   •   **Valuations of certain types of assets**, eg land and buildings, plant and machinery
   •   **Determination of quantities or physical condition of assets**
   •   **Determination of amounts** using specialised techniques or methods
   •   **The measurement of work completed** and **work in progress** on contracts
   •   **Legal opinions**

3.4 When considering whether to use the work of an expert, the auditors should consider various factors.

- The **importance** of the matter being considered in the context of the accounts
- The **risk of misstatement** based on the nature and complexity of the matter
- The **quantity** and **quality** of other available **relevant audit evidence**

Competence and objectivity of the expert

SAS 520.2

When planning to use the work of an expert the auditors should assess the objectivity and professional qualifications, experience and resources of the expert.

3.5 This will involve considering the expert's **professional certification,** or membership of, an appropriate professional body, and the expert's **experience and reputation** in the field in which the auditors are seeking audit evidence.

3.6 The risk that an expert's **objectivity** is **impaired** increases when the expert is **employed** by the entity or **related** in some other manner to the entity, for example having an investment in the entity.

3.7 If the auditors have **reservations** about the competence or objectivity of the expert they may need to carry out other audit procedures or obtain evidence from another expert.

3.8 The auditors should then consider the implications for their report.

The expert's scope of work

SAS 520.3

The auditors should obtain sufficient appropriate audit evidence that the expert's scope of work is adequate for the purposes of their audit.

3.9 Written instructions usually cover the expert's terms of reference and such instructions may cover such matters as follows.

- The **objectives** and **scope** of the expert's work
- A **general outline** as to the specific matters the expert's report is to cover
- The **intended use** of the expert's work
- The **extent** of the **expert's access** to appropriate records and files
- Information regarding the **assumptions and methods intended** to be used

Assessing the work of the expert

SAS 520.4

The auditors should assess the appropriateness of the expert's work as audit evidence regarding the financial statement assertions being considered.

3.10 Auditors should assess whether the substance of the expert's findings is properly reflected in the financial statements or supports the financial statement assertions. It will also require consideration of other aspects of the report.

- The **source data used**

- The **assumptions and methods used**

- **When** the expert carried out the work

- The reasons for any **changes in assumptions and methods** compared with those used in the prior period

- The **results** of the expert's work in the light of the auditors' overall knowledge of the business and the results of other audit procedures

3.11 The auditors do *not* have the expertise to judge the assumptions and methods used; these are the responsibility of the expert. However, the auditors should seek to obtain an understanding of these assumptions etc, to consider their reasonableness based on other audit evidence, knowledge of the business and so on.

3.12 Where inconsistencies arise between the expert's work and other audit evidence, then the auditors should attempt to resolve them by discussion with both the entity and the expert. Additional procedures (including use of another expert) may be necessary.

3.13 Where the audit evidence from the expert is insufficient, and there is no satisfactory alternative source of evidence, then the auditors should consider the implications for their audit report.

3.14 The SAS makes the following very important point (our italics).

> 'When the auditors are satisfied that the work of an expert provides appropriate audit evidence, *reference is not made to the work of the expert in their report.*'

Activity 6.1

The assets of Fuzzy Caterpillar Investment Ltd mostly consist of buildings in West London which are valued at open market value in the company's balance sheet. You are auditing the accounts of the company for the year ended 31 December 19X4. During the year the company re-valued its properties, using the valuations provided by Harvey Herbert, a chartered surveyor.

Tasks

(a) What work will you as auditors carry out on the valuation given by Harvey Herbert?
(b) How would your answer differ if Harvey Herbert was an employee of Fuzzy Caterpillar Ltd?

Using a service organisation

3.15 SAS 480 *Service organisations* contains a number of points relevant if the client uses a service organisation.

SAS 480.1

Auditors should identify whether a reporting entity uses service organisations and assess the effect of any such use on the procedures necessary to obtain sufficient appropriate audit evidence to determine with reasonable assurance whether the user entity's financial statements are free of material misstatement.

BPP PUBLISHING

KEY TERMS

- **Service organisation** is any entity that provides services to another.

- **User entity** is a reporting entity which uses the services of a service organisation.

- **User entity auditors** are the auditors appointed to report on the user entity's financial statements.

- **Relevant activities** are activities undertaken by a service organisation which are relevant to the audit. Relevant activities:

    (a) relate directly to the preparation of the user entity's financial statements, including the maintenance of accounting records which form the basis for those financial statements; or

    (b) relate directly to the reporting of material assets, liabilities and transactions which are required to be included or disclosed in the financial statements (excluding the charge for provision of the service concerned).

Planning

SAS 480.2

In planning the audit, user entity auditors should determine whether activities undertaken by service organisations are relevant to the audit.

3.16 SAS 480 *Service Organisations* gives a number of examples of relevant activities.

- Maintenance of the user entity's accounting records
- Other finance functions
- Custody and management of assets
- Undertaking or arranging transactions

SAS 480.3

User entity auditors should obtain and document an understanding of:

(a) the contractual terms which apply to relevant activities undertaken by service organisations; and

(b) the way that the user entity monitors the activities so as to ensure that it meets its fiduciary and other legal responsibilities.

SAS 480.4

User entity auditors should determine the effect of relevant activities on their assessment of inherent risk and the user entity's control environment.

3.17 Assessment of inherent risk may be affected by the following factors.

(a) The **nature** of the **services** provided

(b) The degree to which **authority** is **delegated** to the service organisations

(c) The **arrangements for ensuring** the **quality** of the service provided

(d) Whether the activities involve **assets** which are susceptible to **loss or misappropriation**

(e) The reputation for **integrity** of those responsible for direction and **management** of the service organisation

---

SAS 480.5

If a service organisation maintains all or part of a user entity's accounting records, user entity auditors should assess whether the arrangements affect their reporting responsibilities in relation to accounting records arising from law or regulations.

3.18 This area may cause auditors problems since it is not certain whether outsourcing the maintenance of accounting records fulfils the s 221 requirements of the Companies Act to keep proper accounting records. The terms of the outsourcing agreement and whether the user entity retains ownership of the accounting records may be relevant considerations.

Audit evidence

SAS 480.6

Based on their understanding of the aspects of the user entity's accounting system and control environment relating to relevant activities, user entity auditors should:

(a) assess whether sufficient appropriate audit evidence concerning the relevant financial statement assertions is available from records held at the user entity; and if not

(b) determine effective procedures to obtain evidence necessary for the audit either by direct access to records kept by service organisations or through information obtained from the service organisations or their auditors.

3.19 Sometimes the most efficient audit approach will be to obtain information from the user entity and confirmation from the service organisation. This approach may not always provide sufficient audit evidence, especially where the service organisation can initiate transactions or process cash receipts without user organisation approval.

3.20 In addition if the service organisation maintains accounting records for the user entity the auditors will require direct access to those records to obtain sufficient audit evidence.

3.21 There are various audit procedures that the user entity auditors might consider.

(a) **Inspecting records** or documents held by the user entity

(b) **Establishing** the **effectiveness of controls**

(c) **Obtaining representations** to confirm balances and transactions from the service organisation

(d) Performing **analytical review** procedures on the records maintained by the user entity or on the returns received from the service organisation

(e) **Inspecting records and documents** held by the service organisation

(f) **Requesting** the **service organisation auditors** or the user entity's internal audit function to perform specified procedures

(g) **Reviewing information** from the service organisation and its auditors concerning the **design and operation of its control systems**

> **SAS 480.7**
>
> When using a report issued by the service organisation auditors, the user entity's auditors should consider the scope of the work performed and assess whether the report is sufficient and appropriate for its intended use by the user auditor.

3.22   The user entity auditors should consider whether the report:

(a)   **Addresses financial statement assertions** that are relevant to the user entity auditor's examination

(b)   **Provides an adequate level of assurance** concerning relevant aspects of the **systems' design, implementation and operation** over a specified period

(c)   **Covers the period** during which the user entity auditors intend to rely on an assessment of control risk at the service organisation

Reporting

> **SAS 480.8**
>
> If user entity auditors conclude that evidence from records held by a service organisation is necessary in order to form an opinion on the user entity's financial statements and they are unable to obtain such evidence, they should
>
> (a)   include a description of the factors leading to the lack of evidence in the basis of opinion section of their report; and
>
> (b)   qualify their opinion or issue a disclaimer of opinion on the financial statements.

3.23   The SAS comments that user entity auditors are unlikely to be able to obtain sufficient appropriate evidence to express an unqualified opinion if the following three conditions exist.

(a)   The **user entity** does **not maintain adequate records** of, or **controls** over, the activities undertaken by the service organisation or cause such records to be maintained independently of the service organisation.

(b)   The **service organisation** has **not made available** a **report** from its auditors concerning the operation of aspects of its systems of controls which the user entity auditors consider sufficient for the purposes of their audit.

(c)   The **user entity auditors** are **unable** to **carry out** such **tests** as they consider appropriate at the service organisation itself, nor has it been possible for those tests to be undertaken by the service organisation's auditors.

4   DOCUMENTING THE AUDIT PROCESS

4.1   All audit work must be documented: the working papers are the tangible evidence of the work done in support of the audit opinion. SAS 230 *Working papers* covers this area.

> **KEY TERM**
>
> **Working papers** are the material the auditors prepare or obtain, and retain in connection with the performance of the audit.

Working papers may be in the form of data stored on paper, film, electronic media or other media.

Working papers support, amongst other things, the statement in the auditors' report as to the auditors' compliance or otherwise with Auditing Standards to the extent that this is important in supporting their report.

Form and content of working papers

SAS 230.2

Working papers should record the auditors' planning, the nature, timing and extent of the audit procedures performed, and the conclusions drawn from the audit evidence obtained.

SAS 230.3

Auditors should record in their working papers their reasoning on all significant matters which require the exercise of judgement, and their conclusions thereon.

4.2 Auditors cannot record everything they consider. Therefore judgement must be used as to the extent of working papers, based on:

'What would be necessary to provide an experienced auditor, with no previous connection with the audit, with an understanding of the work performed and the basis of the decisions taken.'

4.3 The form and content of working papers are affected by various matters.

(a) **Nature** of the **engagement**

(b) **Form** of the **auditors' report**

(c) **Nature** and **complexity** of the entity's **business**

(d) **Nature** and **condition** of the **entity's accounting** and **internal control systems**

(e) **Needs** in the particular circumstances for direction, supervision and review of the work of members of the audit team

(f) **Specific methodology** and technology the auditors use

4.4 The SAS warns on the use of *standardised* working papers, eg checklists, specimen letters; they:

'may improve the efficiency with which such working papers are prepared and reviewed. While they facilitate the delegation of work and provide a means to control its quality, it is never appropriate to follow mechanically a standard approach to the conduct and documentation of the audit without regard to the need to exercise professional judgement.'

4.5 While auditors utilise schedules, analyses etc prepared by the entity, they require evidence that such information is properly prepared.

Examples of working papers

4.6 These include the following.

- Information concerning the legal and organisational structure of the client
- Information concerning the client's industry, economic and legal environment
- Evidence of the planning process

- Evidence of the auditors' understanding of the accounting and internal control systems
- Evidence of inherent and control risk assessments and any revisions
- Analyses of transactions and balances
- Analyses of significant ratios and trends
- A record of the nature, timing, extent and results of auditing procedures
- Copies of communications with other auditors, experts and other third parties
- Copies of correspondence with the client.
- Reports to directors or management
- Notes of discussions with the entity's directors or management
- A summary of the significant aspects of the audit
- Copies of the approved financial statements and auditors' reports

4.7   Working papers should be **headed** as follows.

- The **name** of the **client**
- The balance sheet **date**
- The **file reference** of the working paper
- The **name** of the **person** preparing the working paper
- The **date** the working paper was **prepared**
- The **subject** of the working paper
- The **name** of the person **reviewing** the working paper
- The **date** of the **review**

4.8   Working papers should also show the following details.

- The **objective** of the work done
- The **sources of information**
- How any **sample** was **selected** and the sample size determined
- The **work done**
- A **key** to any audit ticks or symbols
- The **results obtained**
- **Analysis** of **errors** or other significant observations
- The **conclusions drawn**
- The key points highlighted including the need for further work

DEVOLVED ASSESSMENT ALERT

The lists above are critically important. In the devolved assessment itself you will be asked to prepare a number of working papers and your papers must give all the necessary detail even if the assessment does not specifically ask for it.

4.9   For recurring audits, working papers may be split between permanent and current audit files.

(a)   **Permanent audit files** are updated with new information of continuing importance such as legal documents, background information and correspondence with the client of relevance for a number of years. The file should also contain a copy of each year's final accounts.

(b)   **Current audit files** contain information relating primarily to the audit of a single period.

Confidentiality, safe custody and ownership

SAS 230.4

Auditors should adopt appropriate procedures for maintaining the confidentiality and safe custody of their working papers.

4.10 Working papers are the property of the auditors. They are not a substitute for, nor part of, the client's accounting records.

4.11 Auditors must follow ethical guidance on the confidentiality of audit working papers. They may, at their discretion, release parts of or whole working papers to the client, as long as disclosure does not undermine 'the independence or validity of the audit process'. Information should not be made available to third parties without the permission of the entity.

DEVOLVED ASSESSMENT ALERT

You should be able to discuss the uses and benefits of working papers.

Computerised working papers

4.12 **Automated** working paper packages have been developed which can make the documenting of audit work much easier. These are automatically cross referenced and balanced by the computer. Whenever an adjustment is made, the computer will automatically update all the necessary schedules.

4.13 The **advantages** of automated working papers are as follows.

(a) The **risk** of **errors** is **reduced**.

(b) The **working papers** will be **neater** and **easier to review**.

(c) The **time saved** will be **substantial** as adjustments can be made easily to all working papers, including working papers summarising the key analytical information.

(d) **Standard** forms **do not have** to be **carried** to audit locations. Forms can be designed to be called up and completed on the computer screen.

(e) **Audit working papers** can be **transmitted** for review via a modem, or fax facilities (if both the sending and receiving computers have fax boards and fax software).

Part B: Planning audits

Client: _Woodright Ltd_

Subject: _Creditors_

Year end: _31 December 1993_

Prepared by	Reviewed by
........PC...........	....
Date: _16/2/94_	Date:...............

$H^3/_1$

Work done								
	Selected a sample of trade creditors as at 31 December and reconciled the supplier's statement to the year end purchase ledger balance. Vouched any reconciling items to source documentation.							
Results								
	See $H^3/_2$							
	One credit note, relating to Woodcutter Ltd, has not been accounted for. An adjustment is required.							
	DEBIT	Trade creditors		£4,975				
	CREDIT	Purchases			£4,975	$H 1/2$		
	One other error was found, which was immaterial, and which was the fault of the supplier.							
	In view of the error found, however, we should recommend that the client management checks supplier statement reconciliations, at least on the larger accounts - management letter point							
Conclusion								
	After making the adjustment noted above, purchase ledger balances are fairly stated, as at 31 December 1993							

Activity 6.2

The auditing standard SAS 230 *Working Papers* contains the following statement on working papers.

'Auditors base their judgement as to the extent of working papers upon what would be necessary to provide an experienced auditor, with no previous connection with the audit, with an understanding of the work performed and the basis of the decisions taken.'

Task

Describe four benefits that auditors will obtain from working papers that meet the above requirement in SAS 230.

Activity 6.3

(a)   With what details should working papers of audit tests performed be headed?

(b)   What other details should working papers covering audit tests contain?

5   QUALITY CONTROL

5.1   Quality control issues come under the heading of 'planning, controlling and recording' in the Structure of Auditing Standards. They are covered by SAS 240 *Quality control for audit work*.

> **SAS 240.1**
>
> Quality control policies and procedures should be implemented both at the level of the audit firm and on individual audits.

Audit firms

> **SAS 240.2**
>
> Audit firms should establish and monitor quality control policies and procedures designed to ensure that all audits are conducted in accordance with the Auditing Standards contained in SASs and should communicate those policies and procedures to their personnel in a manner designed to provide reasonable assurance that the policies and procedures are understood and implemented.

5.2   The SAS lists the following quality control procedures which will normally be included in a firm's approach.

- **Professional requirements** (independence, objectivity, confidentiality)
- **Skills and competence**
- Consideration of whether **acceptance and retention of clients** is appropriate
- **Assignment** of work to appropriate personnel
- **Delegation,** supervision and review
- **Consultation** if problems arise
- **Monitoring** the whole range of quality control procedures

Individual audits

> **SAS 240.3**
>
> For each audit, the audit engagement partner should apply quality control procedures appropriate to the particular audit which ensure compliance with Auditing Standards.
>
> **SAS 240.4**
>
> Any work delegated to assistants should be directed, supervised and reviewed in a manner which provides reasonable assurance that such work is performed competently.

5.3 The SAS goes on to look at direction, supervision and review of assistants' work in turn.

Direction

5.4 This will involve informing assistants of:

(a) **Their responsibilities** and the objectives of the procedures they are to perform

(b) Matters such as the **nature** of the **entity's business,** and **possible accounting or auditing problems,** which may affect the procedures they are carrying out

5.5 Directions are communicated orally, both informally and at **briefing meetings** and via audit manuals, checklists and of course the **audit programme** and **overall audit plan**.

Supervision

5.6 Supervision is closely related to both direction and review and may involve elements of both. Staff with supervisory duties will perform the following functions during an audit.

(a) Monitor the progress of the audit to consider whether assistants have the **necessary skills and competence** to carry out their assigned tasks, **understand the audit directions,** and **are carrying out** the **work** in accordance with the **overall audit plan** and the **audit programme**

(b) Become informed of and **address significant accounting and auditing questions** raised during the audit

(c) **Resolve any differences of professional judgement** between personnel and consider the level of consultation that is appropriate

Review

5.7 Work performed by each assistant should be reviewed by personnel of appropriate experience to consider whether:

(a) The work has been **performed** in **accordance with the audit programme.**

(b) The work performed and the results obtained have been **adequately documented.**

(c) Any **significant matters** have been **resolved** or are reflected in audit conclusions.

(d) The **objectives** of the audit procedures have been **achieved.**

(e) The **conclusions** expressed are **consistent** with the results of the work performed and support the audit opinion.

5.8 The following should be reviewed on a timely basis.

(a) The **overall audit plan** and the **audit programme**

(b) The **assessments of inherent and control risks**

(c) The **results of control and substantive procedures** and the conclusions drawn including the results of consultations

(d) The **financial statements**, proposed audit adjustments and the proposed auditors' report

5.9 In some cases, particularly in large complex audits, personnel not involved in the audit may be asked to review some or all of the audit work, the auditors' report etc. This is sometimes called a **peer review**.

Review of audit working papers: practical points

5.10 Throughout the audit, a system of review of all working papers will be used. In the case of a large audit, the work of assistants will be reviewed by the senior/supervisor.

5.11 Each working paper should be **initialled** (or signed) and **dated** by the person who prepared it.

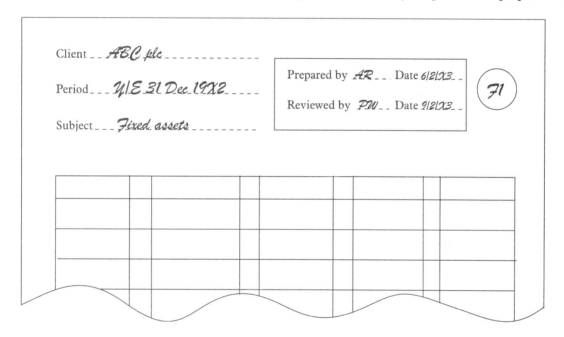

5.12 When a review takes place, the reviewer will often use a separate working paper to record queries *and* their answer.

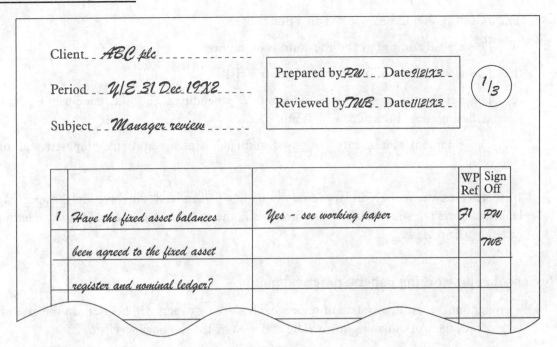

Client__ *ABC plc* _ _ _ _ _ _ _ _ _ _ _ _ _

Period __ *Y/E 31 Dec 19X2* _ _ _ _ _

Subject __ *Manager review* _ _ _ _ _ _

Prepared by *PW* _ _ Date *9/2/X3* _

Reviewed by *TWB* _ Date *1/2/X3* _

$^1/_3$

			WP Ref	Sign Off
1	*Have the fixed asset balances*	*Yes – see working paper*	*F1*	*PW*
	been agreed to the fixed asset			*TWB*
	register and nominal ledger?			

5.13 The need to sign off all working papers and queries acts as an extra check, helping to ensure that all work has been carried out and completed.

5.14 After the senior/supervisor has reviewed the work of the assistants there will usually be a **manager review**, which will cover some of the assistants' work, all of the senior/supervisor's work and an overall review of the audit work. Then there will be an **engagement partner review**, which will look at the manager's review, any controversial areas of the audit, the auditors' report etc.

Key learning points

- Audits should be carried out by staff of **appropriate skills and experience**.

- All partners and staff involved on audits have a responsibility to maintain **professional relationships** with clients.

- Auditors may only rely on other **experts** once specific procedures have been carried out.

- The **proper completion of working papers** is fundamental to the recording of audits. They should show:

  ◦ When and by whom the audit work was **performed and reviewed**
  ◦ Details of the **client**
  ◦ The **year-end**
  ◦ The **subject** of the paper

- Working papers should also show:

  ◦ The objectives of the work done
  ◦ The sources of information
  ◦ How any sample was selected and the sample size determined
  ◦ The work done
  ◦ A key to any audit ticks or symbols
  ◦ Results obtained
  ◦ Errors or other significant observations
  ◦ Conclusions drawn
  ◦ Key points highlighted

- Computerised working papers are being used more by auditors. Their main advantages are that they are **neat** and **easy to update** and the **risk of errors** is reduced.

- Major components in the quality control of individual audits are:

  ◦ Direction
  ◦ Supervision
  ◦ Review

Quick quiz

1   Can an auditor partner delegate responsibility for the audit opinion to his staff?

2   (a)   Why might auditors use the work of an expert?
     (b)   What should auditors consider when deciding whether to use the work of an expert?

3   What is the main danger of using standardised working papers?

4   What does SAS 230 say about the confidentiality of working papers?

5   What areas of quality control does SAS 240 cover?

6   What are the key tasks that should be performed when work is delegated to assistants?

Answers to quick quiz

1   No. A partner cannot delegate responsibility for the audit opinion. He can however delegate aspects of the detailed audit work.

2   (a)   Auditors might use the work of an expert to obtain sufficient audit evidence for certain items in the accounts.

     (b)   When deciding whether to use the work of an expert, auditors should consider:

            (i)   The importance of the audit area
            (ii)   The risks of misstatement
            (iii)   The quantity and quality of other audit evidence

3   The main danger of using standardised working papers is that they can mean auditors mechanically follow a standard approach to the audit without using professional judgement.

4   SAS 230 states that auditors should adopt appropriate procedures for maintaining the confidentiality and safe custody of working papers.

5   SAS 240 covers quality control procedures for audit firms and for individual auditors.

6   The key tasks that should be performed when work is delegated to assistants are as follows.

(a)   Direction. Assistants should be informed of their responsibilities and of the important factors affecting the audit.

(b)   Supervision. Assistants should be monitored to see if they are carrying out the proper work. Significant auditing and accounting issues also need to be addressed.

(c)   Review. The reviewer should check work has been performed and the audit objectives achieved. The reviewer should also ascertain whether all significant matters have been resolved, and should also see that appropriate conclusions have been drawn. The reviewer must consider whether every aspect of the audit has been appropriately documented.

Answers to activities

Answer 6.1

(a)   When assessing Harvey Herbert's work, we as auditors should consider the following.

Competence and objectivity

If Harvey Herbert is practising as a chartered surveyor he should be professionally qualified.

We should also consider what experience Harvey Herbert has of valuing similar properties within the same geographical area as the properties owned by Fuzzy Caterpillar Ltd. If he does not have experience of the type of properties owned by the company or of the areas in which they are located, then the value of his evidence is likely to be reduced.

We should also consider Harvey Herbert's reputation, and the reputation of the firm for which he works. It is likely that more reliance can be placed on a valuation from a long-established firm with a good reputation than one from a little-known small firm.

Assessing the work

We should consider the following aspects of Harvey Herbert's work.

(i)   The objectives and scope of his work. Harvey Herbert should have been aware of the purposes for which his work would be used.

(ii)   The data that Harvey Herbert used.

(iii)   The assumptions and methods employed by Harvey Herbert. In general a reasonable basis of valuation should be used. If the assumptions and methods differed significantly from those used for previous valuations of the same properties, we should satisfy ourselves that the change was for valid reasons.

(iv)   When Harvey Herbert carried out the work. If the work was carried out during the year, we should confirm that there had been no events in the months between the valuation and the year-end that would undermine the basis of the valuation.

(v)   The results of the valuation. Although we as auditors do not have the expertise to make a second valuation, we can nevertheless assess the valuation in the light of other evidence, which might include the following.

(1)   Previous valuations by Harvey Herbert can be compared against any subsequent profits or losses made on those properties, since those could indicate any tendency to over or under value the properties to a material extent.

(2)   The valuations may also be comparable with those used by other clients holding similar properties in the same locations.

We should also consider significant changes in the valuation of any of the properties since the last valuation, comparing those changes with the general behaviour of the commercial property market in the intervening period.

(b) If Harvey Herbert was employed by the company we need to consider carefully whether his lack of independence may diminish the value of his work. We may have to undertake additional audit procedures or consider obtaining a second opinion from another expert.

Answer 6.2

Four benefits that auditors will obtain from preparing working papers that meet the requirement stated in the SAS are as follows.

(a) The reporting partner needs to be satisfied that the work delegated by him has been properly performed. He can only do this by having available detailed working papers prepared by the staff who performed the work.

(b) Working papers are a record for the future of work performed and conclusions drawn, also of problems encountered. This record would be very important in the event of litigation by the client or some other party.

(c) Good working papers will aid the planning and control of future audits.

(d) The preparation of working papers encourages auditors to adopt a methodical approach, which is likely to improve the quality of their work.

Answer 6.3

(a) Working papers should be headed with:

   (i)   The name of the client
   (ii)   The balance sheet date
   (iii) The file reference of the working paper
   (iv)   The name of the person preparing the working paper
   (v)   The date the working paper was prepared
   (vi)   The subject of the working paper
   (vii) The name of the person reviewing the working paper
   (viii) The date of the review

(b) Working papers should also show:

   (i)   The objective of the work done
   (ii)   The source of information
   (iii) How any sample was selected and the sample size determined
   (iv)   The work done
   (v)   A key to any audit ticks or symbols
   (vi)   The results obtained
   (vii) Analysis of errors or other significant observations
   (viii) The conclusions drawn
   (ix)   The key points highlighted

Part C
Testing controls

Chapter 7 Internal control evaluation

Chapter topic list

1   Introduction

2   Features of accounting and control systems

3   Assessment and testing of accounting and control systems

4   Recording of accounting and control systems

5   Reporting to management

Learning objectives

On completion of this chapter you will be able to:

	Performance criteria	Range statement
• Explain what internal control means and why it is important	17.1.2	17.1.1-17.1.3
• Describe the significance of the control environment and control procedures	17.1.2	17.1.1-17.1.3
• Describe how auditors ascertain internal control systems	17.1.1	17.1.1-17.1.3
• Document systems using narrative notes, flowcharts, questionnaires and checklists	17.1.1	17.1.1-17.1.3
• Assess control risk	17.1.3, 17.1.5	17.1.1-17.1.3
• Evaluate internal control and record weaknesses	17.1.4, 17.2.1, 17.2.3, 17.2.4	17.1.1-17.1.3 17.2.1-17.2.3
• Draft reports relating to weaknesses in the accounting and control system	17.3.1-17.3.4	17.3.1

BPP PUBLISHING

1 INTRODUCTION

1.1 Having discussed in the last chapters the evidence auditors are trying to obtain when auditing accounts, we now begin to consider how auditors go about obtaining the evidence they require.

1.2 We shall first look at how auditors consider the operation of **accounting** and **internal control systems**. Auditor consideration of systems has two phases. On all audits, auditors must consider the **adequacy** of the **accounting records** and whether the accounting systems are **capable** of **producing** a **reliable set of accounts**. Auditors must also consider the context in which controls operate, the **control environment**. This involves examining the client's attitude to controls and how the business is organised, focusing particularly on the role of the directors and senior management.

1.3 The second phase of consideration is **assessment** and **testing** of the client's specific controls, the **control procedures**. This is not compulsory. Auditors will only perform detailed tests of controls if they believe that the controls are strong, and hence they will be able to place some reliance on tests of controls and reduce the amount of substantive testing they need to carry out.

1.4 We shall then go on to deal with how accounting systems and controls are **recorded**. Questionnaires are a common means of recording and assessing the strength of controls, and we shall consider Internal Control Questionnaires and Internal Control Evaluation Questionnaires.

1.5 Finally in this chapter we deal with how **control weaknesses** should be **reported** to **management** in a management letter.

1.6 We shall examine the detailed controls that businesses operate in Chapters 8 to 10. You should bear in mind the principles discussed in this chapter when considering the controls needed over specific accounting areas. You should be able to state the controls that ought to be operating, or how auditors should test the controls that are in place.

2 FEATURES OF ACCOUNTING AND CONTROL SYSTEMS

KEY TERM

An **internal control system** comprises the control environment and control procedures. It includes all the policies and procedures (internal controls) adopted by the directors and management to ensure, as far as practicable, the orderly and efficient conduct of its business, including adherence to internal policies, the safeguarding of assets, the prevention and detection of fraud and error, the accuracy and completeness of the accounting records, and the timely preparation of reliable financial information.

2.1 SAS 300 *Accounting and internal control systems and audit risk assessments* covers the whole area of controls.

Control environment

2.2 Control environment is the framework within which controls operate. The control environment is very much determined by the management of a business.

KEY TERM

Control environment is the overall attitude, awareness and actions of directors and managers regarding internal controls and their importance in the entity. The control environment encompasses the management style, and corporate culture and values shared by all employees. It provides the background against which the various other controls are operated.

2.3 The SAS adds to the definition of the control environment that a strong control environment does not, by itself, ensure the effectiveness of the overall internal control system. This is a very important point.

2.4 The following factors will be reflected in the control environment.

CONTROL ENVIRONMENT	
Philosophy and **operating style** of management	Consider attitude to controls - do management override controls? Do they neglect controls and concentrate solely on results and targets?
Organisation structure and segregation of duties	Consider delegation of authority. Segregation of duties - the principle that no single person should record and process all stages of a transaction - is vital.
Director's methods of imposing controls	Consider extent to which management supervise operations. How do they exercise control? (budgets, management accounts and internal audit)

Segregation of duties is a vital aspect of the control environment. Segregation of duties implies a number of people being involved. Hence it is more difficult for fraudulent transactions to be processed (since a number of people would have to collude in the fraud), and it is also more difficult for accidental errors to be processed (since the more people are involved, the more checking there can be).

Control procedures

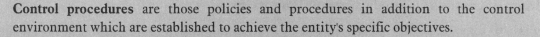

KEY TERM

Control procedures are those policies and procedures in addition to the control environment which are established to achieve the entity's specific objectives.

2.5 The definition of control procedures is extended in the SAS. Control procedures include those designed to **prevent** or to **detect** and **correct errors**. We have already discussed the importance of segregation of duties, and the SAS lists some other specific control procedures.

Approval and control of documents

2.6 Transactions should be approved by an appropriate person (eg overtime being approved by departmental managers).

Controls over computerised applications

2.7 We shall discuss these in greater detail in Chapter 10.

BPP PUBLISHING

Checking the arithmetical accuracy of records

2.8   An example of this type of control would be checking to see individual invoices have been added up correctly.

Maintaining and reviewing control accounts and trial balances

2.9   Control accounts bring together transactions in individual ledgers, trial balances bring together transactions for the organisation as a whole. Preparing these can highlight unusual transactions or accounts.

Reconciliations

2.10   Reconciliations involve comparison of a specific balance in the accounting records with what another source says that balance should be. Differences between the two figures should only be due to valid reconciling items. A good example is a bank reconciliation,

Comparing the results of cash, security and stock counts with accounting records

2.11   An example of this is a physical count of petty cash where the balance shown in the cash book should be the amount of cash in the petty cash box.

Comparing internal data with external sources of information

2.12   An example would be comparing records of goods despatched to customers with customer acknowledgement of goods that have been received.

Limiting direct physical access to assets and records

2.13   Authorised personnel alone should have access to certain assets, particularly those which are valuable or portable. An example would be ensuring the stock store is only open when the stores personnel are there, and is locked at other times.

2.14   Restricting access to records can be a particular problem in computerised systems, as we shall discuss in Chapter 10.

Internal controls and their inherent limitations

2.15   SAS 300 states that the directors of an entity will set up internal controls in the accounting system to assess the following.

(a) **Transactions** are executed in accordance with **proper authorisation**.

(b) All transactions and other events are **promptly recorded** at the **correct amount**, in the **appropriate accounts** and in the **proper accounting period**.

(c) **Access to assets** is permitted only in accordance with proper authorisation.

(d) **Recorded assets** are **compared** with the **existing assets** at reasonable intervals and appropriate action is taken with regard to any differences.

2.16   However, any internal control system can only provide the directors with **reasonable assurance** that their objectives are reached, because of **inherent limitations**. These include costs of controls not outweighing their benefits, the potential for human error, the possibility of controls being by-passed, and the fact that controls tend to be designed to cope with routine and not non-routine transactions.

2.17 These factors show why auditors cannot obtain all their evidence from tests of the systems of internal control.

Activity 7.1

What objectives should an internal control system of a company aim to fulfil?

---

3 ASSESSMENT AND TESTING OF ACCOUNTING AND CONTROL SYSTEMS

3.1 Auditors are only concerned with assessing policies and procedures which are relevant to financial statement assertions. Auditors try to:

- **Assess the adequacy** of the accounting system as a basis for preparing the accounts
- **Identify** the types of **potential misstatements** that could occur in the accounts
- **Consider factors** that affect the **risk of misstatements**
- **Design appropriate audit procedures**

Accounting system and control environment

3.2 Auditors must obtain an **understanding** of the accounting system to enable them to identify and understand:

- **Major classes of transactions** in the entity's operations
- **How such transactions** are initiated
- **Significant accounting records**, supporting documents and accounts
- The **accounting and financial reporting process**

3.3 The factors affecting the **nature, timing and extent** of the **procedures** performed in order to understand the systems include:

- **Materiality** considerations
- The **size and complexity** of the entity
- Their **assessment** of **inherent risk**
- The **complexity** of the entity's computer systems
- The **type of internal controls** involved
- The **nature of the entity's documentation** of specific internal controls

3.4 The auditors will normally update previous knowledge of the systems in the following ways.

- **Enquiries** of appropriate supervisory and other personnel
- **Inspection** of relevant documents and records produced by the systems
- **Observation** of the entity's activities and operations

3.5 Auditors must also make an assessment of whether accounting records fulfil Companies Act requirements.

Accounting records: statutory requirements

3.6 The responsibility for installing and maintaining a satisfactory accounting system rests, in the case of a company, with the directors. S 221 of the Companies Act 1985 requires that accounting records are sufficient to show and explain the company's transactions They should **disclose** with reasonable accuracy, the **financial position** of the company at any

PUBLISHING

time and enable the directors to ensure that any **balance sheet** and **profit and loss account** prepared under this Part **comply** with the requirements of the **Companies Act**.

3.7 S 221 goes on to state that the accounting records should show how **monies** have been **received** and **expended** and **record** the **assets** and **liabilities** of the company. If the company deals in goods, records should show **statements** of **stock held** at the **year end** and also **stock records** that form the basis of statements of stock held.

3.8 Directors and other company officers of a company are liable to imprisonment or a fine (or both) if found guilty of knowingly failing to comply with the above sections.

3.9 During their assessment of the systems, the auditors will obtain knowledge of the design and operation of the systems. To confirm this knowledge, '**walk-through tests**' are often performed. Walk-through tests involve tracing one or more transactions through the accounting system and observing the application of relevant aspects of the control system on these transactions.

3.10 Having assessed the accounting system and control environment, the auditors can make a **preliminary assessment** of whether the system is capable of producing reliable financial statements and of the likely mix of tests of control and substantive procedures.

Control risk

> ### SAS 300.4
>
> If auditors, … expect to be able to rely on their assessment of control risk to reduce the extent of their substantive procedures, they should make a preliminary assessment of control risk for material financial statement assertions, and should plan and perform tests of control to support that assessment.

3.11 Assessment of control risk is not necessary when the auditors decide it is likely to be **inefficient** or **impossible** to rely on any assessment to reduce their substantive testing. In such cases control risk is assumed to be **high**.

Preliminary assessment of control risk

3.12 This evaluation of the accounting and control systems' effectiveness in correcting material misstatements that will entail consideration of the **design** of the systems. Auditors should remember that some control risk will always exist as internal controls have inherent limitations (as we have seen above).

Relationship between the assessments of inherent and control risks

3.13 Where inherent risk is high, management may institute a more rigorous accounting and control systems to prevent and detect material misstatements. This interrelationship means that inherent and control risks should often be assessed in combination.

Tests of control

3.14 Tests of controls are used to confirm auditors' assessments of the **design and operation** of control systems, and to support the auditors' assessment of control risk.

KEY TERM

Tests of control are tests to obtain audit evidence about the effective operation of the accounting and internal control systems, that is, that properly designed controls identified in the preliminary assessment of control risk exist in fact and have operated effectively throughout the relevant period.

3.15 Tests of control may include the following.

(a) **Enquires** about, and observation of, internal control functions

(b) **Inspection of documents** supporting controls or events to gain audit evidence that internal controls have operated properly, for example verifying that a transaction has been authorised or a reconciliation approved

(c) **Examination** of evidence of **management views**, for example minutes of management meetings

(d) **Reperformance** of control procedures, for example reconciliation of bank accounts, to ensure they were correctly performed by the entity

(e) **Testing** of the internal controls operating on **computerised systems**

(f) **Observation of controls,** considering the manner in which the control is being operated

3.16 Auditors should consider how controls were **applied**, the **consistency** with which they were applied during the period and **by whom** they were applied.

3.17 **Changes** in the **operation** of **controls** (caused by change of staff etc) may increase control risk and tests of control may need to be modified to confirm effective operation during and after any change.

3.18 Radical changes in controls, including a periodic breakdown in controls, should be considered as **separate periods** by the auditors.

DEVOLVED ASSESSMENT ALERT

You are likely to be asked in the devolved assessment to test controls over certain aspects of the accounts. When setting out a test programme you should consider:

(a) the objectives the controls are designed to achieve. These are discussed for specific audit areas in Chapters 8 and 9. You should note now that the control considerations that are of great importance for all areas are authorisation, custody and recording.

(b) What type of test will best test the controls being operated, eg recording may be best tested by comparison of documents, custody may be best tested by observing the security arrangements over assets etc.

Interim testing

3.19 In relation to tests before the period end, the SAS states:

SAS 300.5

If intending to rely on tests of control performed in advance of the period end, auditors should obtain sufficient appropriate audit evidence as to the nature and extent of any changes in design or operation of the entity's accounting and internal control systems within the accounting period since such procedures were performed.

3.20 Further evidence must be obtained to augment the results of tests carried out at an interim audit, ie before the period end.

Final assessment of control risk

> ### SAS 300.6
>
> Having undertaken tests of control, auditors should evaluate whether the preliminary assessment of control risk is supported.

3.21 Failures of controls to operate should be investigated, but in such cases the preliminary assessment may still be supported if the failure is isolated. More frequent failures may require the level of control risk to be revised; in such cases the nature, timing and extent of the auditors' planned substantive procedures should be modified.

Communication of weaknesses

3.22 The auditors may become aware of weaknesses in the system as a result of obtaining an understanding of those systems. Such weaknesses should be reported to management according to SAS 610 *Reports to directors or management* (see Section 5).

Activity 7.2

Explain the importance of the following control procedures.

(a) Segregation of duties
(b) Bank reconciliation
(c) Comparing the results of stock counts with accounting records.

---

4 RECORDING OF ACCOUNTING AND CONTROL SYSTEMS

4.1 There are several techniques for recording accounting and internal control systems.

- Narrative notes
- Flowcharts
- Questionnaires (eg ICQ)
- Checklists

4.2 Often a combination may be used, with narrative notes and/or flowcharts recording the accounting system, and questionnaires recording controls.

4.3 Whatever method of recording the system is used, the record will usually be retained on the permanent file and updated each year.

Narrative notes

4.4 Narrative notes have the advantage of being simple to record. However they are awkward to change if written manually. Editing in future years will be easier if they are computerised. The purpose of the notes is to **describe** and **explain** the **system,** at the same time making any comments or criticisms which will help to demonstrate an intelligent understanding of the system.

4.5   For each system notes need to deal with the following questions.

- What functions are performed and by whom?
- What documents are used?
- Where do the documents originate and what is their destination?
- What sequence are retained documents filed in?
- What books are kept and where?

Narrative notes can be used to support flowcharts.

DEVOLVED ASSESSMENT ALERT

In the devolved assessment you may be required to record systems by narrative notes or update existing narrative notes.

Flowcharts

4.6   There are two methods of flowcharting in regular use.

- Document flowcharts
- Information flowcharts

Document flowcharts

4.7   Document flowcharts are more commonly used because they are relatively easy to prepare.

- *All* documents are followed through from 'cradle to grave'.
- *All* operations and controls are shown.

We shall concentrate on document flowcharts.

Information flowcharts

4.8   Information flowcharts are prepared in the reverse direction from the flow: they start with the entry in the accounting records and work back to the actual transaction. They concentrate on significant information flows and key controls and ignore any unimportant documents or copies of documents.

Design of flowcharts

4.9   Flowcharts should be kept simple, so that the overall structure or flow is clear at first sight.

(a)   There must be **conformity of symbols,** with each symbol representing one and only one thing.

(b)   The direction of the flowchart should be from **top to bottom** and from **left to right**.

(c)   There must be no **loose ends.**

(d)   The main flow should finish at the **bottom right hand corner**, not in the middle of the page.

(e)   Connecting lines should cross *only* where absolutely necessary to preserve the chart's simplicity.

Advantages and disadvantages of flowcharts

4.10 Advantages include the following.

(a) After a little experience they can be **prepared quickly**.

(b) As the information is presented in a standard form, they are fairly **easy to follow** and to review.

(c) They generally ensure that the system is **recorded in its entirety,** as all document flows have to be traced from beginning to end. Any 'loose ends' will be apparent from a quick examination.

(d) They **eliminate** the need for **extensive narrative** and can be of considerable help in highlighting the salient points of control and any weaknesses in the system.

4.11 On the other hand, flowcharts do have some disadvantages.

(a) They are **only really suitable for describing standard systems**. Procedures for dealing with unusual transactions will normally have to be recorded using narrative notes.

(b) They are useful for recording the flow of documents, but once the **records** or the assets to which they relate have **become static** they **can no longer be used for describing the controls** (for example over fixed assets).

(c) Major **amendment is difficult** without redrawing.

(d) **Time** can be **wasted** by **charting areas** that are of no **audit significance** (a criticism of *document* not information flowcharts).

4.12 Basic symbols will be used for the charting of all systems, but where the client's system involves mechanised or computerised processing, then further symbols may be required to supplement the basic ones. The basic symbols used are shown below.

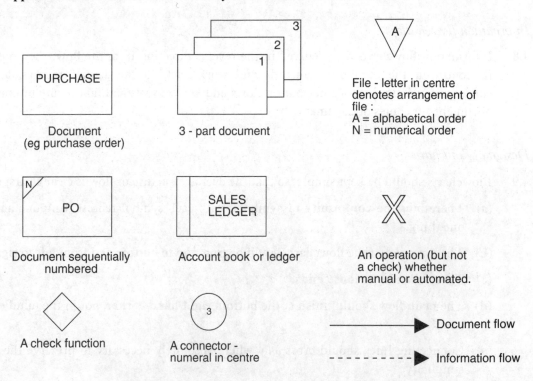

4.13 Preparation of a basic flowchart will involve the procedures laid out in the next few paragraphs.

Document flows

4.14   The symbols showing the sequence of operations taking place within the one department are joined by a vertical line as illustrated in the figure below.

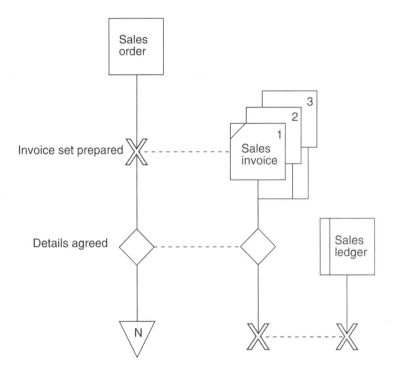

Information flows

4.15   During the course of the processing cycle it will often be found that information is transferred from one document to another. In all cases information flow is represented by a broken *horizontal* line.

Division of duties

4.16   One of the key features of any good system of internal control is that there should be a system of 'internal check'. Internal check is the requirement for a segregation of duties amongst the available staff so that one person's work is independently reviewed by another, no one person having complete responsibility for all aspects of a transaction.

4.17   This method of flowcharting shows the division of duties. This is achieved by dividing the chart into **vertical columns**. In a **smaller** enterprise there would be one column to show the duties of each **individual**, whereas in a **large** company the vertical columns would show the division of duties amongst the various **departments**.

The following figure shows, in a small company, the division of duties between Mr Major and Mr Minor.

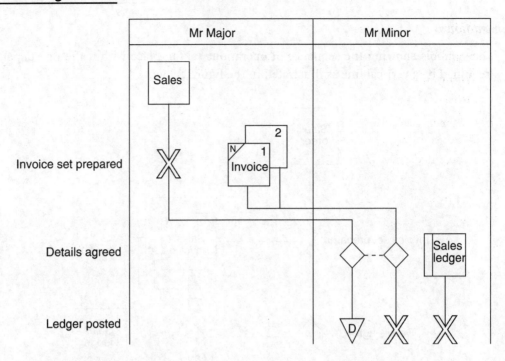

Sequence and description of operations

4.18 To facilitate ease of reference each operation shown on the chart is numbered in sequence on the chart, a separate column being used for this purpose.

4.19 Finally, the chart will be completed by the inclusion of a narrative column which will describe significant operations. Narrative should be kept to a minimum and only included where in fact it is required.

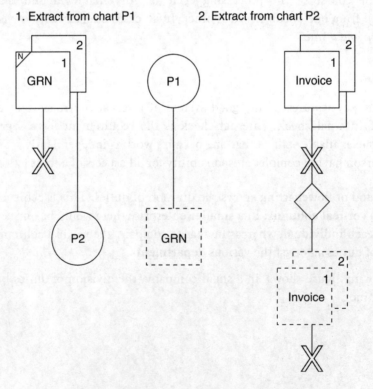

4.20 On the following pages you will find two charts which illustrate typical procedures in a company's purchasing system.

- Ordering and receiving of goods
- Approval of invoices

Questionnaires

4.21 We can look at two types of questionnaire here, each with a different purpose.

(a) **Internal Control Questionnaires (ICQs)** are used to ask whether certain controls exist.

(b) **Internal Control Evaluation Questionnaires (ICEQs)** are used to determine whether whatever controls the system contains fulfil specific objectives or can be relied on to prevent specific weaknesses.

Internal Control Questionnaires (ICQs)

4.22 The major question which internal control questionnaires are designed to answer is 'How good is the system of controls?'

4.23 Although there are many different forms of ICQ in practice, they all conform to certain basic principles.

(a) They comprise a **list of questions** designed to determine whether desirable controls are present.

(b) They are formulated so that there is one to cover each of the **major transaction cycles**.

4.24 Since it is the primary purpose of an ICQ to evaluate the system rather than describe it, one of the most effective ways of designing the questionnaire is to phrase the questions so that all the answers can be given as 'YES' or 'NO' and a 'NO' answer indicates a weakness in the system. An example would be:

Are purchase invoices checked to goods received notes before being passed for payment?	YES/NO/Comments

A 'NO' answer to that question clearly indicates a weakness in the company's payment procedures which requires further comment.

4.25 The ICQ questions below dealing with goods inward provide additional illustrations of the ICQ approach.

Goods inward

(a) Are supplies examined on arrival as to quantity and quality?

(b) Is such an examination evidenced in some way?

(c) Is the receipt of supplies recorded, perhaps by means of goods inwards notes?

(d) Are receipt records prepared by a person independent of those responsible for:

    (i)   Ordering functions
    (ii)   The processing and recording of invoices

(e) Are goods inwards records controlled to ensure that invoices are obtained for all goods received and to enable the liability for unbilled goods to be determined (by pre-numbering the records and accounting for all serial numbers)?

(f) (i)   Are goods inward records regularly reviewed for items for which no invoices have been received?

    (ii)   Are any such items investigated?

(g) Are these records reviewed by a person independent of those responsible for the receipt and control of goods?

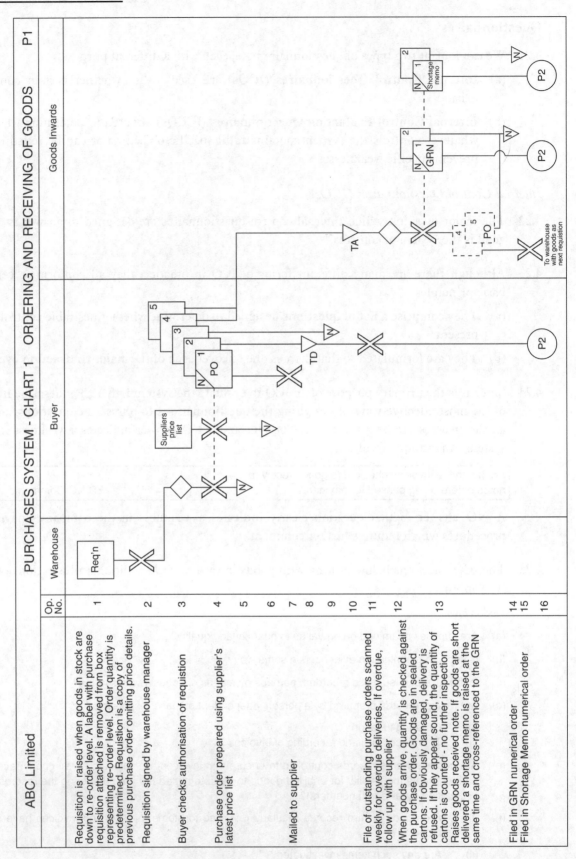

PURCHASES SYSTEM - CHART 1   ORDERING AND RECEIVING OF GOODS

Op. No.		Description
1		Requisition is raised when goods in stock are down to re-order level. A label with purchase requisition attached is removed from box representing re-order level. Order quantity is predetermined. Requisition is a copy of previous purchase order omitting price details.
2		Requisition signed by warehouse manager
3		Buyer checks authorisation of requisition
4		Purchase order prepared using supplier's latest price list
5		
6		Mailed to supplier
7		
8		
9		
10		
11		File of outstanding purchase orders scanned weekly for overdue deliveries. If overdue, follow up with supplier
12		When goods arrive, quantity is checked against the purchase order. Goods are in sealed cartons. If obviously damaged, delivery is refused. If they appear sound, the quantity of cartons is counted - no further inspection
13		Raises goods received note. If goods are short delivered a shortage memo is raised at the same time and cross-referenced to the GRN
14		Filed in GRN numerical order
15		Filed in Shortage Memo numerical order
16		

PURCHASES SYSTEM - CHART 2   APPROVAL OF INVOICES

ABC Limited

Op. No.	Description
17	Matches and checks signature on GRN, quantity and description of goods
18	
19	Invoice given sequential number and stamped with a grid for approvals
20	Invoices filed until goods arrive
21	Invoices matched with GRN and purchase order. If unmatched buyer retains until goods received. Checks quantity, price and discount terms.
22	Enters accounting code and signs approval grid. If price and quantity incorrect notes this on invoice and raises debit note (advising supplier and requesting credit). Debit notes are referenced to supplier invoice.
23	
24	
25	Check all costs and extensions on invoices over £200 and 10% of all invoices under £200
26	
27	Reviews invoices to see that package is complete and approval grid fully signed
28	

BPP PUBLISHING

4.26 Each situation must therefore be judged on its own merits and hence, although the ICQs often take the form of a standard pre-printed pack, they should be used with imagination. As using ICQs is a skilled and responsible task, the evaluation should be performed by a senior member of the audit team.

Internal Control Evaluation Questionnaires (ICEQs)

4.27 In recent years many auditing firms have developed and implemented an evaluation technique more concerned with assessing whether specific errors (or frauds) are possible rather than establishing whether certain desirable controls are present. This is achieved by reducing the control criteria for each transaction stream down to a handful of key questions (or control questions). The characteristic of these questions is that they concentrate on criteria that the controls present should fulfil.

4.28 The nature of an ICEQ can be illustrated by the following example.

Internal control evaluation questionnaire: control questions

The sales cycle

Is there reasonable assurance that:

(a) Sales are properly authorised?
(b) Sales are made to reliable payers?
(c) All goods despatched are invoiced?
(d) All invoices are properly prepared?
(e) All invoices are recorded?
(f) Invoices are properly supported?
(g) All credits to customers' accounts are valid?
(h) Cash and cheques received are properly recorded and deposited?
(i) Slow payers will be chased and that bad and doubtful debts will be provided against?
(j) All transactions are properly accounted for?
(k) Cash sales are properly dealt with?
(l) Sundry sales are controlled?
(m) At the period end the system will neither overstate nor understate debtors?

The purchases cycle

Is there reasonable assurance that:

(a) Goods or services could not be received without a liability being recorded?

(b) Receipt of goods or services is required in order to establish a liability?

(c) A liability will be recorded:

    (i)   only for authorised items; and
    (ii) at the proper amount?

(d) All payments are properly authorised?

(e) All credits due from suppliers are received?

(f) All transactions are properly accounted for?

(g) At the period end liabilities are neither overstated nor understated by the system?

(h) The balance at the bank is properly recorded at all times?

(i) Unauthorised cash payments could not be made and that the balance of petty cash is correctly stated at all times?

Wages and salaries

Is there reasonable assurance that:

(a) Employees are only paid for work done?
(b) Employees are paid the correct amount (gross and net)?
(c) The right employees actually receive the right amount?

(d)   Accounting for payroll costs and deductions is accurate?

Stock

Is there reasonable assurance that:

(a)   Stock is safeguarded from physical loss (eg fire, theft, deterioration)?
(b)   Stock records are accurate and up to date?
(c)   The recorded stock exists?
(d)   The recorded stock is owned by the company?
(e)   The cut off is reliable?
(f)   The costing system is reliable?
(g)   The stock sheets are accurately compiled?
(h)   The stock valuation is fair?

Fixed tangible assets

Is there reasonable assurance that:

(a)   Recorded assets actually exist and belong to the company?
(b)   Capital expenditure is authorised and reported?
(c)   Disposals of fixed assets are authorised and reported?
(d)   Depreciation is realistic?
(e)   Fixed assets are correctly accounted for?
(f)   Income derived from fixed assets is accounted for?

Investments

Is there reasonable assurance that:

(a)   Recorded investments belong to the company and are safeguarded from loss?

(b)   All income, rights or bonus issues are properly received and accounted for?

(c)   Investment transactions are made only in accordance with company policy and are appropriately authorised and documented?

(d)   The carrying values of investments are reasonably stated?

Management information and general controls

Is the nominal ledger satisfactorily controlled?
Are journal entries adequately controlled?
Does the organisation structure provide a clear definition of the extent and limitation of authority?
Are the systems operated by competent employees, who are adequately supported?
If there is an internal audit function, is it adequate?
Are financial planning procedures adequate?
Are periodic internal reporting procedures adequate?

4.29   Each key control question is supported by detailed control points to be considered. For example, the detailed control points to be considered in relation to key control question (b) for the expenditure cycle (Is there reasonable assurance that receipt of goods or services is required to establish a liability?) are as follows.

(1)   Is segregation of duties satisfactory?

(2)   Are controls over relevant master files satisfactory?

(3)   Is there a record that all goods received have been checked for:

    •   Weight or number?
    •   Quality and damage?

(4)   Are all goods received taken on charge in the detailed stock ledgers:

    •   By means of the goods received note?

    •   Or by means of purchase invoices?

    •   Are there, in a computerised system, sensible control totals (hash totals, money values and so on) to reconcile the stock system input with the creditors system?

(5)   Are all invoices initialled to show that:

    •   Receipt of goods has been checked against the goods received records?

131

- Receipt of services has been verified by the person using it?
- Quality of goods has been checked against the inspection?

(6) In a computerised invoice approval system are there print-outs (examined by a responsible person) of:

- Cases where order, GRN and invoice are present but they are not equal ('equal' within predetermined tolerances of minor discrepancies)?
- Cases where invoices have been input but there is no corresponding GRN?

(7) Is there adequate control over direct purchases?

(8) Are receiving documents effectively cancelled (for example cross-referenced) to prevent their supporting two invoices?

4.30 Alternatively, ICEQ questions can be phrased so that the weakness which should be prevented by a key control is highlighted, such as the following.

Question	Answer	Comments or explanation of 'yes' answer
Can goods be sent to unauthorised suppliers?		

4.31 In these cases a 'yes' answer would require an explanation, rather than a 'no' answer.

Advantages and disadvantages of ICQs and ICEQs

4.32 ICQs have various advantages.

(a) If drafted thoroughly, they can ensure **all controls** are **considered.**

(b) They are **quick** to **prepare.**

(c) They are **easy** to **use** and **control**. A manager or partner reviewing the work can easily see what has been done.

4.33 However they also have disadvantages:

(a) The client may be able to **overstate controls.**

(b) They may contain a large number of **irrelevant controls.**

(c) They can give the impression that all controls are of **equal weight**. In many systems one 'no' answer (for example lack of segregation of duties) may cancel the apparent value of a string of 'yes' answers).

(d) They may not include **unusual controls,** which are nevertheless effective in particular circumstances.

4.34 ICEQs have the following advantages:

(a) Because they are drafted in terms of **objectives** rather than specific controls, they are easier to apply to a variety of systems than **ICQs.**

(b) Answering ICEQs should enable auditors to **identify the most important controls** which they are most likely to test during control testing.

(c) ICEQs can **highlight areas of weakness** where extensive substantive testing will be required.

4.35 The principal disadvantage is that they can be **drafted vaguely,** hence **misunderstood** and important controls not identified.

5 REPORTING TO MANAGEMENT

5.1 Auditors should report any weaknesses discovered in the system of internal control to the management of the company. This report usually takes the form of a **management letter**, but other types of report are acceptable. SAS 610 *Reports to directors or management* covers this topic.

5.2 The main purposes of reports to directors or management are for auditors to communicate various points that have come to their attention during the audit.

(a) The **design** and **operation** of the **accounting and internal control systems,** including suggestions for their improvement

(b) **Other constructive advice**, for example comments on potential economies or improvements in efficiency

(c) **Other matters**, for example comments on adjusted and unadjusted errors in the financial statements or on particular accounting policies and practices

5.3 Note that such a report to management is *not* a substitute for a qualified audit report (see Chapter 17), when such a qualification is required. Inconsistencies between reports to management and the auditors' report should be avoided.

Material weaknesses in the accounting and internal control systems

> **SAS 610.2**
>
> When material weaknesses in the accounting and internal control systems are identified during the audit, auditors should report them in writing to the directors, the audit committee or an appropriate level of management on a timely basis.

5.4 A **material weakness** is one which may result in a **material misstatement** in the financial statements. If it is corrected by management, it need not be reported, but the discovery and correction should be documented.

5.5 To be effective, the report should be made **as soon as possible** after **completion** of the **audit procedures**. A written report is usual, but some matters may be raised orally with a file note to record the auditors' observation and the directors' response.

5.6 Where no report is felt to be necessary, the auditors should inform the directors that no material weaknesses have been found.

Interim letters

5.7 Where the audit work is performed on more than one visit, the auditors will normally report to management after the interim audit work has been completed as well as after the final visit.

Final letters

5.8 The final management letter can cover the following issues.

(a) **Additional matters** under the same headings as the interim letter, if sent

BPP
PUBLISHING

(b) Details of **inefficiencies** or **delays** in the agreed timetable for preparation of the accounts or of workings schedules which delayed the completion of the audit and may have resulted in increased costs

(c) Any **significant differences** between the **accounts** and any **management accounts** or budgets which not only caused audit problems but also detract from the value of management information

(d) Any results of the auditors' **analytical procedures** of which management may not be aware and may be of benefit to them

Other matters regarding reports to directors or management

5.9 If the auditors choose not to send a formal letter or report but consider it preferable to discuss any weaknesses with management, the discussion should be **minuted** or otherwise recorded in writing. Management should be provided with a copy of the note.

5.10 The auditors should explain in their report to management that it **only** includes those matters which came to their attention as a result of the audit procedures, and that it should not be regarded as a comprehensive statement of all weaknesses that exist or all improvements that might be made.

5.11 The auditors should request a **reply** to all the points raised, indicating what action management intends to take as a result of the comments made in the report.

5.12 If **previous points** have **not** been **dealt with effectively** and they are still considered significant, the auditors should enquire why action has not been taken.

5.13 The report may contain matters of varying levels of significance and thus make it difficult for senior management to identify points of significance. The auditors can deal with this by giving the report a **'tiered' structure** so that major points are dealt with by the directors or the audit committee and minor points are considered by less senior personnel.

5.14 Other points to note about the management letter are as follows.

(a) The recommendations should take the form of **suggestions** backed up by **reason and logic**.

(b) The letter should be in **formal terms** unless the client requests otherwise.

(c) **Weaknesses** that **management** are aware of but **choose not to do anything about** should be **mentioned** to protect the auditors.

(d) If management or staff have **agreed to changes**, this should be mentioned in a letter.

Third parties interested in reports to directors or management

5.15 Any report made to directors or management should be regarded as a confidential communication. The auditors should therefore not normally reveal the contents of the report to any third party without the prior written consent of the directors or management of the company.

5.16 In practice, the auditors have little control over what happens to the report once it has been despatched. Occasionally management may provide third parties with copies of the report, for example their bankers or certain regulatory authorities.

5.17 Thus care should be taken to protect the auditors' position from exposure to liability in negligence to any third parties who may seek to rely on the report. Accordingly, the auditors should state clearly in their report that it has been prepared for the private use of the client.

Specimen management letter

5.18 A specimen letter is provided below which demonstrates how the principles described in the previous paragraphs are put into practice.

DEVOLVED ASSESSMENT ALERT

You may be asked to draft paragraphs for a management letter in the devolved assessment. You should follow the format we have used.

SPECIMEN MANAGEMENT LETTER

AB & Co
Certified Accountants
29 High Street
London, N10 4KB

The Board of Directors,
Manufacturing Co Limited,
15 South Street
London, S20 1CX

1 April 198X

Members of the board,

Financial statements for the year ended 31 May 198X

In accordance with our normal practice we set out in this letter certain matters which arose as a result of our review of the accounting systems and procedures operated by your company during our recent interim audit.

We would point out that the matters dealt with in this letter came to our notice during the conduct of our normal audit procedures which are designed primarily for the purpose of expressing our opinion on the financial statements of your company. In consequence our work did not encompass a detailed review of all aspects of the system and cannot be relied on necessarily to disclose defalcations or other irregularities or to include all possible improvements in internal control.

1   *Purchases: ordering procedures*

Present system
During the course of our work we discovered that it was the practice of the stores to order certain goods from X Ltd orally without preparing either a purchase requisition or purchase order.

Implications
There is therefore the possibility of liabilities being set up for unauthorised items and at a non-competitive price.

Recommendations
We recommend that the buying department should be responsible for such orders and, if they are placed orally, an official order should be raised as confirmation.

2   *Purchase ledger reconciliation*

Present system
Although your procedures require that the purchase ledger is reconciled against the control account on the nominal ledger at the end of every month, this was not done in December or January.

Implications

The balance on the purchase ledger was short by some £2,120 of the nominal ledger control account at 31 January 198X for which no explanation could be offered. This implies a serious breakdown in the purchase invoice and/or cash payment batching and posting procedures.

Recommendations

It is important in future that this reconciliation is performed regularly by a responsible official independent of the day to day purchase ledger, cashier and nominal ledger functions.

3   *Sales ledger: credit control*

Present system

As at 28 February 198X debtors account for approximately 12 weeks' sales, although your standard credit terms are cash within 30 days of statement, equivalent to an average of about 40 days (6 weeks) of sales.

Implications

This has resulted in increased overdraft usage and difficulty in settling some key suppliers accounts on time.

Recommendations

We recommend that a more structured system of debt collection be considered using standard letters and that statements should be sent out a week earlier if possible.

4   *Preparation of payroll and maintenance of personnel records*

Present system

Under your present system, just two members of staff are entirely and equally responsible for the maintenance of personnel records and preparation of the payroll. Furthermore, the only independent check of any nature on the payroll is that the chief accountant confirms that the amount of the wages cheque presented to him for signature agrees with the total of the net wages column in the payroll. This latter check does not involve any consideration of the reasonableness of the amount of the total net wages cheque or the monies being shown as due to individual employees.

Implications

It is a serious weakness of your present system, that so much responsibility is vested in the hands of just two people. This situation is made worse by the fact that there is no clearly defined division of duties as between the two of them. In our opinion, it would be far too easy for fraud to take place in this area (eg by inserting the names of 'dummy workmen' into the personnel records and hence on to the payroll) and/or for clerical errors to go undetected.

Recommendations

(i)   Some person other than the two wages clerks be made responsible for maintaining the personnel records and for periodically (but on a surprise basis) checking them against the details on the payroll;

(ii)   The two wages clerks be allocated specific duties in relation to the preparation of the payroll, with each clerk independently reviewing the work of the other;

(iii) When the payroll is presented in support of the cheque for signature to the chief accountant, that he should be responsible for assessing the reasonableness of the overall charge for wages that week.

Our comments have been discussed with your finance director and the chief accountant and these matters will be considered by us again during future audits. We look forward to receiving your comments on the points made. Should you require any further information or explanations do not hesitate to contact us.

This letter has been produced for the sole use of your company. It must not be disclosed to a third party, or quoted or referred to, without our written consent. No responsibility is assumed by us to any other person.

We should like to take this opportunity of thanking your staff for their co-operation and assistance during the course of our audit.

Yours faithfully

ABC & Co

Activity 7.3

(a)   What are the main purposes of preparing a management letter?

(b)   What are the major advantages in each point made in the management letter being made in the format?

'Present system'
'Implication'
'Recommendations'?
Discuss what should be included under each heading.

Key learning points

- The auditors must **understand** the **accounting system** and **control environment** in order to determine the audit approach. They must also assess whether **accounting records** fulfil Companies Act requirements.

- Specific **control procedures** include the following

    ° Approval and control of documents
    ° Controls over computerised applications and the information technology environment
    ° Checking the arithmetical accuracy of the records
    ° Maintaining and reviewing control accounts and trial balances
    ° Reconciliations
    ° Comparing the results of cash, security and stock counts with accounting records
    ° Comparing internal data with external sources of information
    ° Limiting direct physical access to assets and records

- There are always inherent limitations to internal controls, including cost-benefit requirements and the possibility of controls being by-passed and over-ridden.

- Auditors should assume control risk is high, unless it is assessed, and the assessment confirmed by tests of controls.

- Tests of controls must cover the whole accounting period.

- Auditors can use a number of methods to record accounting and control systems.

    ° Narrative notes
    ° Flowcharts
    ° ICQs (which ask if various controls exist)
    ° ICEQs (which ask if controls fulfil key objectives)

- Auditors should report material control weakness to management, usually in a management letter.

Quick quiz

1   What are the main features of a business's control environment according to SAS 300?

2   What are the main limitations of a system of internal controls?

3   How do auditors confirm their understanding of accounting systems?

BPP
PUBLISHING

4   Give five examples of tests of controls by auditors.

5   What is the main disadvantage of recording systems by means of manual narrative notes?

6   In what directions should a flowchart be prepared?

7   What is the main difference between ICQs and ICEQs?

Answers to quick quiz

1   The main features of a business's control environment per SAS 300 are the overall attitude, and actions of directors and management towards internal controls. It includes the management style, and corporate culture and values of all employees

2   The main limitations of a system of internal controls are:

(a)   Costs of implementing controls may outweigh benefits.

(b)   Most internal controls are directed towards routine rather than non-routine transactions.

(c)   Mistakes may occur when controls are being operated.

(d)   Controls may be bypassed by people acting in collusion.

(e)   Controls may be over-ridden.

(f)   Changes in conditions or decreased compliance may mean control procedures become inadequate over time.

3   Auditors confirm their understanding of systems by carrying out walk-through tests.

4   Examples of control tests include:

(a)   Enquiries about and observation of internal controls
(b)   Inspection of documents
(c)   Examination of evidence of management views
(d)   Re-performance of control procedures
(e)   Testing controls on specific computerised applications or overall information technology controls

5   The main disadvantage of manual narrative notes is that they can be difficult to change.

6   Flowcharts should be prepared going from top to bottom and left to right on a page.

7   ICQs concentrate on whether specific controls exist, whereas ICEQs concentrate on whether the control system has specific strengths or can prevent specific weaknesses.

Answers to activities

Answer 7.1

It is the responsibility of directors and management to implement an appropriate system of financial and non-financial controls. Good management is itself an internal control, but other procedures must be in place as directors and senior managers cannot supervise everything, particularly in large companies. Hence overseeing an effective internal control system is how senior management discharge their responsibilities.

SAS 300 emphasises the importance of the general objective of internal controls ensuing the orderly and efficient conduct of a company's business. Clearly with the cost pressures many businesses face, they are seeking to maximise efficiency, and well-designed internal controls should be an aid, not a hindrance towards that end. Orderliness is related to efficiency, and it is also necessary so that a company fulfils its various legal obligations.

SAS 300 lists a number of further specific objectives.

Adherence to internal policies

In order for management to be able to implement their decisions, there have to be policies in place to ensure management directives are followed.

Safeguarding of assets

Safeguarding of assets is a vital objective of internal control, since directors have the responsibility of stewardship over a company's assets. Safeguarding means not only physical protection of assets but also their proper recording.

Prevention and detection of fraud and error

This objective is related to the safeguarding of assets. If the company's internal control systems cannot prevent or detect fraud or error, there would be serious legal consequences if frauds are allowed to continue, or if the company publishes inaccurate information.

Accuracy and completeness of accounting records

Directors are required by the Companies Act to maintain proper accounting records. As we have stated, this objective also relates to safeguarding of assets.

Timely preparation of financial information

Directors have a statutory responsibility to prepare accounts which show a true and fair view within time limits set by statute. Internal financial information such as management accounts and budgets also helps directors monitor what is going on, and if any areas of the business are causing concern.

Answer 7.2

(a) Segregation of duties is important because the more people that are involved in all the stages of processing a transaction, the more likely it is that fraud or error by a single person will be identified. In addition the more people that are involved, the less the changes of fraudulent collusion between them.

(b) A bank reconciliation is important because it reconciles the business's records of cash held at bank with the bank's records of cash held at bank. Written confirmation from the bank is strong evidence since it arises from an independent source and is in writing. Generally the only differences on the reconciliation should be timing differences on unpresented cheques or uncleared bankings. For large unpresented cheques and for all uncleared bankings the timing differences involved should be small.

(c) Stock is an important figure in the accounts often materially affecting both the profit and loss account and balance sheet. In addition the stock of many businesses is highly portable, and it is thus subject to a high risk of theft.

A main comparison of stock as recorded in the accounting records with actual stock held may identify differences which have to be investigated. The differences may be due to theft of stock but may also be due to failure to record stock movements properly. This may also mean that purchases or sales have been recorded incorrectly.

Answer 7.3

(a) The principal purposes of a management letter are as follows.

(i) To enable the auditors to highlight weaknesses in the accounting records, systems and controls which they have identified during the course of their audit, and which may lead to material errors

(ii) To provide management with constructive advice on various aspects of the business which the auditors may have identified during the course of the audit

(iii) To highlight matters that may have an effect on future audits

(iv) To comply with specific requirements as laid down by, for example, local authorities or housing associations

(b) In order for management letters to be effective, they must clearly describe the weaknesses, consequences and auditor suggestions. The three stage format described enables auditors to do that.

'Present system'. This section should confirm in writing auditor understanding of the system, and describe the weaknesses in precise terms.

'Implications'. Although weaknesses are stated under 'present system' their consequences may not necessarily be understood by management. A separate section on implications means that auditors can emphasise what the weaknesses mean and highlight effects on the accounts and on the safeguarding of assets.

'Recommendations'. Putting these in a separate section emphasises their importance. Clients may well view management letters negatively if recommendations are not clear. The recommendations should be practical and cost-effective and be as specific as possible, stating for instance that named members of staff should be responsible for reviews.

Chapter 8   Tests of control: income cycles

Chapter topic list

1   Introduction

2   The sales system

3   The purchases and expenses system

4   The wages system

Learning objectives

On completion of this chapter you will be able to:

	Performance criteria	Range statement
• Describe how controls are tested in the following accounting systems	17.1.4, 17.1.7,	17.1.1-17.1.3,
	17.2.1-17.2.4	17.2.1-17.2.3

- ° Sales systems
- ° Purchases systems
- ° Wages/payroll systems
- ° Expenses system

BPP
PUBLISHING

1 INTRODUCTION

1.1 In the last few chapters we have talked about controls. We have stated that on all audits auditors must ascertain the accounting system and control system. If auditors decide to rely on controls, they must test them. The next two chapters describe the controls that may operate and the tests auditors may carry out.

1.2 It is best to examine controls in terms of the various components of the accounting system. Most commonly these will be: sales, purchases, wages, expenses, cash, stock and other systems such as fixed assets and investments.

1.3 For each of the components we shall examine the controls from the client and the auditors' viewpoint. The key **objectives** that clients ought to be trying to fulfil are summarised and we shall look at **common controls** that should generally achieve those objectives (Remember however that every system is different and many of the controls listed will be more important in some systems than in others.)

1.4 As we saw in Chapter 7, auditors are concerned with the **weaknesses** that controls are aiming to prevent. For each area we shall examine the Internal Control Evaluation Questions that may be asked, and **tests of control** that auditors will often carry out to answer those questions. However the testing programme should be tailored to the controls being operated.

1.5 In this chapter we deal with sales, purchases and expenses and wages and salaries.

1.6 For **sales**, businesses want to give credit only to **customers** who will pay their debts. In addition there are various stages of the selling process- **ordering, dispatch and charging,** all of which should be **documented** and **matched** so that customers receive what they ordered and are appropriately billed. In order to keep track of who owes what and to be able to identify slow-paying customers, a **sales ledger** should be maintained.

1.7 Similarly **purchases** must be controlled. Businesses should ensure that only **properly authorised purchases** which are necessary for the business are made. Again all stages of the purchase process, ordering, receiving goods and being charged for them should be **documented** and **matched** so that the business gets what it ordered and only pays for what it ordered and received. Businesses also need to keep track of what they owe to each supplier by maintaining a **purchase ledger**. Likewise for other expenses businesses need to ensure they are authorised and recorded in the purchase ledger.

1.8 For **wages and salaries** businesses are trying to ensure that they only pay for **hours worked** and that they pay the **right staff** the **right amount**. Controls should also be in place to ensure **PAYE** and **VAT liabilities** are calculated correctly otherwise penalties may be imposed by the tax authorities.

1.9 In the devolved assessment you may need to consider the controls that should be in operation and the audit work that should be carried out. You should consider the **objectives** that the controls should be trying to achieve, and remember that audit tests should be designed to check whether the controls have fulfilled those objectives. Focusing on the objectives will help you avoid suggesting controls or audit tests which are unnecessary, whilst omitting controls or audit tests which should prevent or highlight weaknesses.

2 THE SALES SYSTEM

Aims of controls

2.1 The most important aims of the control system relating to debtors and sales are:

Ordering

- **Goods** and **services** are **only supplied** to **customers** with **good credit ratings**
- **Customers** are encouraged to **pay promptly**

Dispatch and invoicing

- All **despatches** of goods are **recorded**
- All **goods and services** sold are **correctly invoiced**
- All **invoices** raised **relate to goods and services** that have been **supplied** by the business
- **Credit notes** are only given for **valid reasons**

Recording and accounting

- All sales that have been **invoiced** are **recorded** in the general and sales ledgers
- All **credit notes** that have been **issued** are **recorded** in the general and sales ledgers
- All **entries** in the sales ledger are **made** to the **correct** sales ledger **accounts**
- **Cut-off** is applied correctly to the sales ledger
- Potentially **doubtful debts** are **identified**

Activity 8.1

What can go wrong at the following stages of the sales cycle:

(a) Ordering by customers
(b) Despatch of goods
(c) Accounting

Control considerations

2.2 The following controls relate to the **ordering** and **credit control** process; note the importance of controls over credit terms, ensuring that goods are only sent to customers who are likely to pay promptly.

- **Segregation** of duties; credit control, invoicing and stock despatch

- **Authorisation** of **credit terms** to customers

  o References/credit checks obtained
  o Authorisation by senior staff
  o Regular review

- **Authorisation** for changes in **other customer data**

  o Change of address supported by letterhead

  o Requests for deletion supported by evidence balances cleared/customer in liquidation

- **Orders** only **accepted** from **customers** who have no credit problems

- **Matching** of **customer orders** with production orders and despatch notes

- Regular **preparation** of **debtor statements**

- **Checking** of **debtors' statements**

- **Safeguarding** of **debtor statements** so that they cannot be altered before despatch

- **Review** and **follow-up** of **overdue accounts**

- **Authorisation** of **writing off** of **bad debts**

- **Dealing** with **customer queries**

2.3 The following checks relate to **despatches** and **invoice preparation**.

- **Authorisation** of **despatch of goods**
    - ○ Despatch only on sales order
    - ○ Despatch only to authorised customers
    - ○ Special authorisation of despatches of goods free of charge or on special terms

- **Examination** of **goods outwards** as to quantity, quality and condition

- **Recording** of **goods outwards**

- **Agreement** of **goods outwards records** to **customer orders, despatch notes** and **invoices**

- **Prenumbering** of despatch notes and delivery notes and regular checks on sequence

- **Condition** of **returns checked**

- Recording of goods returned on **goods returned notes**

- **Signature** of **delivery notes** by customers

- Preparation of invoices and credit notes
    - ○ **Authorisation** of **selling prices**/use of **price lists**
    - ○ **Authorisation** of **credit notes**
    - ○ **Checks on prices, quantities, extensions** and totals on invoices and credit notes
    - ○ **Custody** over blank invoices and credit notes

- Stock records updated

- Matching of sales invoices with despatch notes

2.4 The following controls relate to **accounting** and **recording**.

- **Segregation of duties:** recording sales, maintaining customer accounts and preparing statements

- **Recording** of **sales invoices** sequence and **control** over **spoilt invoices**

- **Matching** of **cash receipts** with **invoices**

- **Retention** of **customer remittance advices**

- **Separate recording** of **sales returns, price adjustments** etc

- **Cut-off procedures** to ensure goods despatched and not invoiced (or vice versa) are properly dealt with the correct period

- **Reconciliation** of **sales ledger control account**

- **Analytical review** of **sales ledger** and **profit margins**

Tests of controls

2.5 Auditors should carry out the following tests on **ordering** and **credit control** procedures.

- **Check** that **references** are being **obtained** for **all new customers**
- **Check** that all **new accounts** on the sales ledger have been **authorised** by senior staff
- **Check** that **orders** are only **accepted** from customers who are **within** their **credit terms** and **credit limits**
- **Check** that **customer orders** are being **matched** with **production orders** and **despatch notes**
- **Check** that debtor statements are **prepared** and **sent out regularly**
- **Check** that **overdue accounts** have been **followed up**
- **Check** that **all bad debts written off** have been **authorised** by management
- **Check** that **despatches** of **goods free of charge** or on **special terms** have been **authorised** by management

2.6 The following tests should be carried out over **despatches** and **invoices**.

- Verify details of **trade sales** or goods despatched notes with **sales invoices checking:**

  - **Quantities**
  - **Prices** charged with official price lists
  - **Trade discounts** have been properly dealt with
  - **Calculations** and **additions**
  - **Entries** in sales day book are correctly **analysed**
  - **VAT,** where chargeable, has been properly **dealt with**
  - **Postings** to sales ledger

- Verify details of **trade sales** with **entries in stock records.**

- Verify **non-routine** sales (scrap, fixed assets etc) with:

  - **Appropriate supporting evidence**
  - **Approval** by authorised officials
  - **Entries** in **plant register** etc

- Verify **credit notes** with:

  - **Correspondence** or other supporting evidence
  - **Approval** by authorised officials
  - **Entries** in **stock records**
  - **Entries** in **goods returned records**
  - **Calculations** and **additions**
  - **Entries** in **day book,** checking these are correctly analysed
  - **Postings** to **sales ledger**

- **Test numerical sequence** of **despatch notes** and **enquire** into **missing numbers.**

- **Test numerical sequence** of **invoices** and **credit notes, enquire** into **missing numbers** and **inspect copies** of those cancelled.

- **Test numerical sequence** of **order forms** and enquire into missing numbers.

2.7 The following tests should be carried out over **recording** and **accounting** for **sales.**

Sales day book

- **Check entries** with **invoices** and **credit notes** respectively

- **Check additions** and **cross casts**
- **Check postings** to **sales ledger control account**
- **Check postings** to **sales ledger**

Sales ledger

- **Check** entries in a **sample of accounts** to sales day book
- **Check additions** and **balances** carried down
- **Note** and **enquire** into **contra entries**
- Check that **control accounts** have been **regularly reconciled** to total of sales ledger balances
- **Scrutinise accounts** to see if credit limits have been observed

DEVOLVED ASSESSMENT ALERT

This area of control is very important.

Activity 8.2

You are the audit manager on Auckland Ltd, which manufactures computer equipment. Unfortunately the audit senior had to go off on another audit before she could draft the management letter for the final audit for the year ended 31 December 19X7. She has however left the following notes on the system.

Despatch of computer equipment

Customers have to complete a written order before any equipment is despatched. When an order is received Miss Lea in the sales section sends out a pre-numbered despatch note, which is in three parts to Miss Lang in the stock room. The goods are delivered by one of the company's delivery team who takes with him a copy of the despatch note. One copy of the despatch note is sent to Mrs Rawle in the financial accounts section and Miss Lang keeps a third copy.

If the goods are not in stock, Miss Lang sends one copy of the despatch note to the customer together with a note of when the stock is likely to arrive. She places the second copy in an awaiting goods file and destroys the third copy. When the goods arrive in stock Miss Lang notifies Miss Lea, sending her the second copy of the previous despatch note. Miss Lea places this copy in a cancelled despatches file and makes out a new despatch note, which is then processed in the usual way.

Billing

When the second copy of the despatch note of a completed order arrives in the financial accounts section, Mrs Rawle prepares a two-copy invoice. The section supervisor, Mrs McGillivray, checks the details of the invoice. One copy is sent to the customer and one copy is filed in the financial accounts section. Mrs Rawle posts the invoice details to the sales ledger. Each week the total of sales invoices for the week is posted by Miss Bamsey to the sales ledger control account.

Receipts

Customers' cheques are received in the company's post room and cheques received each day are added up. The cheques and add-list are sent to Mrs Rawle who posts the payments into the sales ledger control account. The cheques are banked by Mrs McGillivray on her way home. Miss Bamsey enters the total monies received in the cash book and sales ledger control account.

Reconciliation

Every month Miss Gallant, who is the head of the financial accounts section reconciles the sales ledger and sales ledger control account.

Tasks

Prepare a management letter highlighting weaknesses in the company's sales system and make recommendations about improvements that can remedy those weaknesses.

Activity 8.3

What tests of control can give auditors assurance that the company's system of control ensures that sales are completely recorded?

3 THE PURCHASES AND EXPENSES SYSTEM

3.1 We will follow much the same procedure for the purchases and expenses system.

Aims of controls

3.2 The most important aims of the control system relating to creditors and purchases are:

Ordering

- All **orders for,** and expenditure on, **goods and services** are properly **authorised,** and are for **goods and services** that are actually **received**

Receipt and invoicing

- All **goods** and **services received** are accurately **recorded**
- **Liabilities** are **recognised** for all **goods and services** that have been **received**
- All **credits** to which business is due are **claimed**

Recording

- All **expenditure** that is made is **recorded** correctly in the general and purchase ledger
- All **credit notes** that are received are **recorded** in the general and purchase ledger
- All **entries** in the **purchase ledger** are **made** to the **correct purchase ledger accounts**
- **Cut-off** is **applied correctly** to the purchase ledger

Activity 8.4

What can go wrong at the following stages of the purchase cycle?

(a) Ordering
(b) Receipt of goods
(c) Accounting

Control considerations

3.3 The following controls should be in place over **ordering**.

- **Central policy** for choice of suppliers

- Evidence required of **requirements** for purchase before purchase authorised (re-order quantities and re-order levels)

- **Order forms** prepared only when a purchase requisition has been received

- **Authorisation** of order forms

- **Prenumbered order forms**

- **Safeguarding** of blank order forms

- **Review** of orders not received

- **Monitoring** of **supplier terms** and taking advantage of favourable conditions (bulk order, discount)

3.4 The client should carry out the following checks on **goods received** and invoices from suppliers.

- **Examination** of goods inwards
  - Quality
  - Quantity
  - Condition

- **Recording arrival** and **acceptance** of goods (prenumbered goods received notes)

- **Comparison** of **goods received notes** with **purchase orders**

- **Referencing** of supplier invoices; numerical sequence and supplier reference

- **Checking** of **suppliers' invoices**
  - Prices, quantities, accuracy of calculation
  - Comparison with order and goods received note

3.5 The following controls should be in place over **accounting** for purchases.

- **Segregation** of **duties**: accounting and checking functions

- **Recording purchases** and **purchase returns**

- **Regular maintenance** of **purchase ledger**

- **Comparison** of **supplier statements** with **purchase ledger balances**

- **Authorisation** of **payments**
  - Authority limits
  - Confirmation that goods have been received, accord with purchase order, and are properly priced and invoiced

- **Review** of **allocation** of expenditure

- **Reconciliation** of **purchase ledger** control account to total of purchase ledger balances

- **Cut-off** accrual of unmatched goods received notes at year-end

Tests of controls

3.6 A most important test of controls is for auditors to check that all **invoices** are **supported** by authorised **purchase invoices** and **purchase orders**. The officials who approve the invoices should be operating within laid-down **authority limits.**

3.7 Auditors should carry out the following tests on **receipts of goods** and **invoices**

- Check invoices for goods, raw materials are:
  - **Supported** by **goods received notes** and **inspection notes**
  - **Entered** in **stock records**
  - **Priced correctly** by checking to **quotations, price lists** to see the price is in order
  - **Properly referenced** with a number and supplier code
  - **Correctly coded** by type of expenditure

- **Trace entry** in **record of goods returned** etc and see credit note duly received from the supplier, for invoices not passed due to defects or discrepancy

- For invoices of all types:

- ° **Check calculations** and **additions**
- ° **Check entries in purchase day book** and verify that they are correctly **analysed**
- ° **Check posting** to **purchase ledger**

- For credit notes:

  - ° **Verify** the **correctness** of credit received with correspondence
  - ° **Check entries** in **stock records**
  - ° **Check entries** in **record of returns**
  - ° **Check entries** in **purchase day book** and verify that they are correctly analysed
  - ° **Check postings** to **purchase ledger**

- Check for **returns** that **credit notes** are duly **received** from the suppliers

- Test **numerical sequence** and enquire into missing numbers of:

  - ° Purchase requisitions
  - ° Purchase orders
  - ° Goods received notes
  - ° Goods returned notes
  - ° Suppliers' invoices

- **Obtain explanations** for **items** which have been **outstanding** for a long time

  - ° Unmatched purchase requisitions
  - ° Purchase orders
  - ° Goods received notes (if invoices not received);
  - ° Unprocessed invoices

Purchase day book

3.8 The following tests should be carried out over the recording of purchases.

- Verify that invoices and credit notes recorded in the purchase day book are:

  - ° **Initialled** for prices, calculations and extensions
  - ° **Cross-referenced** to purchase orders, goods received notes etc
  - ° **Authorised** for payment

- **Check additions**

- **Check postings** to general ledger accounts and control account

- **Check postings** of entries to purchase ledger

Purchase ledger

- For a sample of accounts recorded in the purchase ledger:

  - ° **Test check entries** back into books of prime entry
  - ° **Test check additions** and **balances** forward
  - ° **Note** and **enquire** into all contra entries

- Confirm **control account balancing** has been regularly carried out during the year

- **Examine control account** for unusual entries

3.9 Once again the following question should help you to apply these 'standard' tests in a devolved assessment.

Activity 8.5

Derek Limited operates a computerised purchase system. Invoices and credit notes are posted to the purchase ledger by the purchase ledger department. The computer subsequently raises a cheque when the invoice has to be paid.

Tasks

List the controls that should be in operation:

(a) Over the addition, amendment and deletion of suppliers, ensuring that the file of suppliers' data only includes suppliers from the company's list of authorised suppliers

(b) Over purchase invoices and credit notes, to ensure only authorised purchase invoices and credit notes are posted to the purchase ledger.

Note: You may wish to read Section 2 of Chapter 10 before tackling this activity.

4 THE WAGES SYSTEM

Aims of controls

4.1 The most important aims of the control system relating to wages and salaries are:

Setting of wages and salaries

- **Employees** are **only paid** for **work** that they have **done**
- **Gross pay** has been **calculated correctly** and **authorised**

Recording of wages and salaries

- **Gross** and **net pay** and **deductions** are **accurately recorded** on the payroll
- **Wages** and **salaries paid** are **recorded correctly** in the **bank** and **cash records**

Payment of wages and salaries

- The **correct employees** are **paid**

Deductions

- Statutory and non-statutory **deductions** have been **calculated correctly** and are **authorised**
- The **correct amounts** are **paid** to the **taxation authorities**

Control considerations

4.2 While in practice separate arrangements are generally made for dealing with wages and salaries, the considerations involved are broadly similar and for convenience the two aspects are here treated together.

4.3 Responsibility for the preparation of pay sheets should be delegated to a suitable person, and adequate staff appointed to assist him. The extent to which the staff responsible for preparing wages and salaries may perform other duties should be clearly defined. In this connection full advantage should be taken where possible of the division of duties, and checks available where automatic wage-accounting systems are in use.

4.4 The following controls relate to the setting of wages and salaries.

- **Staffing** and **segregation of duties**
- **Maintenance of personnel records**

- **Authorisation**
  - ° Engagement and discharge of employees
  - ° Changes in pay rates
  - ° Overtime
  - ° Non-statutory deductions (for example pension contributions)
  - ° Advances of pay

- **Recording** of **changes** in **personnel** and **pay rates**

- **Recording** and **review** of hours worked

- **Recording** of **advances** of **pay**

- **Holiday pay** arrangements

- **Answering queries**

4.5 The following checks relate to the recording of wages and salaries.

- **Bases** for **compilation** of payroll
- **Preparation, checking** and **approval** of payroll
- Dealing with **non-routine matters**

4.6 The following controls relate to the payment of cash wages.

- **Segregation of duties**
  - ° Cash sheet preparation
  - ° Filling of pay packets
  - ° Distribution of wages

- **Custody** of cash
  - ° Encashment of cheque
  - ° Security of pay packets
  - ° Security of transit
  - ° Security of unclaimed wages

- **Verification of identity**

- **Recording** of distribution

4.7 The following controls relate to the payment of salaries.

- **Preparation** and **signing** of cheques and bank transfer lists
- **Maintenance** and **reconciliation** of wages and salaries bank account

4.8 The following controls relate to deductions from pay.

- **Maintenance** of **separate employees' records,** with which pay lists may be compared as necessary

- **Reconciliation** of **total pay** and **deductions** between one pay day and the next

- **Surprise cash counts**

- **Comparison** of actual pay totals with **budget estimates** or standard costs and the investigation of variances

- **Agreement** of **gross earnings** and **total tax deducted** with PAYE returns to the Inland Revenue

4.9 Appropriate arrangements should be made for dealing with statutory and other authorised deductions from pay, such as national insurance, PAYE, pension fund contributions, and savings held in trust. A primary consideration is the establishment of adequate controls over the **records** and **authorising** deductions.

Tests of controls

Setting of wages and salaries

4.10 Auditors should check that the **wages** and **salary summary** is approved for payment. They should confirm that procedures are operating for **authorising changes** in **rates of pay**, overtime, and holiday pay.

4.11 A particular concern will be joiners and leavers. Auditors will need to obtain evidence that staff only start being paid when they join the company, and are removed from the payroll when they leave the company. They should check that the **engagement** of **new employees** and **discharges** have been **confirmed in writing**.

4.12 Auditors will also wish to check calculations of wages and salaries. This test should be designed to check that the client is carrying out **checks** on **calculations** and also to provide substantive assurance that **wages** and **salaries** are being **calculated correctly**.

4.13 For wages, this will involve checking **calculation** of **gross pay** with:

- Authorised rates of pay

- Production records, seeing that production bonuses have been authorised and properly calculated

- Clock cards, time sheets or other evidence of hours worked. Verify that overtime has been authorised

4.14 For salaries, auditors should **verify that gross salaries and bonuses are in accordance with personnel records, letters of engagement** etc and that increases in pay have been properly authorised.

Payment of wages and salaries

4.15 If wages are paid in cash, auditors should carry out the following procedures.

- **Arrange to attend** the **pay-out** of wages to confirm that the official procedures are being followed

- **Examine receipts** given by employees; **trace unclaimed wages** to unclaimed wages book

- **Check entries** in the **unclaimed wages book** with the entries on the wages sheets

- **Check that unclaimed wages** are **banked regularly**

- **Check** that unclaimed wages books shows **reasons** why wages are unclaimed

Holiday pay

- **Verify** a sample of **payments** with the **underlying records** and **check** the **calculation** of the amounts paid

4.16 For salaries, auditors should check that comparisons are being made between payment records and they should themselves **examine paid cheques** or a **certified copy** of the **bank list** for employees paid by cheque of banks transfer.

Recording of wages and salaries

4.17 A key control auditors will be concerned with will be the reconciliation of wages and salaries.

4.18 For wages, there should have been reconciliations with:

- The **previous week's payroll**
- **Clock cards/time sheets/job cards**
- **Costing analyses, production budgets**

4.19 The total of **salaries** should be **reconciled** with the **previous week/month** or the **standard payroll.**

4.20 In addition auditors should confirm that important calculations have been checked by the clients and re-perform those calculations.

4.21 These include for wages, checking for a number of weeks:

- **Additions** of **payroll sheets**
- **Totals** of **wages sheets** selected to summary
- **Additions** and **cross-casts** of summary
- **Postings** of **summary** to **general ledger** (including control accounts)
- **Casts** of **net cash column** to cash book

4.22 For salaries, they include checking for a number of weeks/months:

- **Additions** of **payroll sheets**
- **Totals** of **salaries sheets** to **summary**
- **Additions** and **cross-casts** of **summary**
- **Postings** of **summary** to **general ledger** (including control accounts)
- **Total** of **net pay column** to cash book

Deductions

4.23 Auditors should **check** the **calculations** of **PAYE, National Insurance** and **non-statutory deductions.** For PAYE and NI they should carry out the following tests.

- **Scrutinise** the **control accounts** maintained to see **appropriate deductions** have been **made**

- **Check** to see that the **employer's contribution** for national insurance has been **correctly calculated**

- **Check** that the **payments** to the **Inland Revenue** and other bodies are **correct**

They should **check other deductions to appropriate records. For voluntary deductions, they should see** the **authority completed** by the relevant employees.

Activity 8.6

The following questions have been selected from an internal control questionnaire for wages and salaries.

Internal control questionnaire - wages and salaries

		Yes	No

1   Does an appropriate official authorise rates of pay?

2   Are written notices required for employing and terminating employment?

3   Are formal records such as time cards used for time keeping?

4   Does anyone verify rates of pay, overtime hours and computations of gross pay before the wage payments are made?

5   Does the accounting system ensure the proper recording of payroll costs in the financial records?

Tasks

(a)   Describe the internal control objective being fulfilled if the controls set out in the above questions are in effect.

(b)   Describe the audit tests which would test the effectiveness of each control and help determine any potential material error.

(c)   Identify the potential consequences for the company if the above controls were not in place.

You may answer in columnar form under the headings:

ICQ question	Internal control objective	Audit tests	Consequences

Key learning points

- The sales and purchases systems will be the most important components of most company accounting systems.

- The tests of controls of the **sales system** will be based around:

  ◦ **Selling** (authorisation)
  ◦ **Goods outwards** (custody)
  ◦ **Accounting** (recording)

- Similarly, the **purchases systems** tests will be based around:

  ◦ **Buying** (authorisation)
  ◦ **Goods inwards** (custody)
  ◦ **Accounting** (recording)

- Important **tests of control** by auditors include:

  ◦ Checking documentation for correct details, calculations and authorisation
  ◦ Comparing documents
  ◦ Checking completeness of documentation sequences

- Note that all weaknesses discovered in these tests will be included in a **report to management**.

- Obviously, most manufacturing companies will have a large payroll. **Wages and salaries** are usually dealt with in very different ways, but they are often grouped together for audit testing purposes.

- Key controls over **wages** cover:

  ◦ Documentation and authorisation of staff changes
  ◦ Calculation of wages and salaries
  ◦ Payment of wages and salaries
  ◦ Authorisation of deductions

Quick quiz

1 What are the key elements in authorisation of credit terms to customers?

2 What should auditors check when reviewing sales invoices?

3 How can a company ensure that quantities of goods ordered do not exceed those that are required?

4 What are the important checks that should be made on invoices received from suppliers?

5 What tests should auditors carry out on credit notes received?

6 What are the most important authorisation controls over amounts to be paid to employees?

7 How should auditors confirm that wages have been paid at the correct rate to individual employees?

Answers to quick quiz

1 References and credit checks should be obtained before customers are given credit. Credit limits should be authorised by senior staff and should be regularly reviewed.

2 When checking sales invoices, auditors should check:

   (a) Quantities
   (b) Prices charged with price lists
   (c) Correct calculation of discounts
   (d) Calculations and additions
   (e) Invoices have been correctly entered and analysed in the sales day book
   (f) VAT has been properly dealt with
   (g) Invoices have been posted to the sales ledger

3 A company can ensure goods ordered do not exceed requirements by setting re-order quantities and re-order limits.

4   Invoices from suppliers should be checked for correctness of prices and quantities and accuracy of calculation. They should be compared with purchase orders and goods received notes.

5   Auditors should:

(a)   Verify the correctness of credit notes with previous correspondence.

(b)   Confirm by reviewing stock records and records of returns that goods have been returned.

(c)   Check credit notes have been correctly accounted for by checking entries in the purchase day book and purchase ledger.

6   The most important authorisation controls over wages and salaries are controls over:

(a)   Engagement and discharge of employees
(b)   Changes in pay rates
(c)   Overtime
(d)   Non-statutory deductions
(e)   Advances of pay

7   Auditors should confirm that wages have been paid at the correct rate by checking calculation of gross pay to:

(a)   Authorised rates of pay
(b)   Production records
(c)   Clock cards, time sheets or other evidence of hours worked

Answers to activities

Answer 8.1

(a)   Orders may never be recorded.
      The goods may never be sent.
      Goods may be sold to a customer who is unable to pay.

(b)   Goods may never be despatched.
      Damaged or incorrect goods may be despatched.
      The customer may never receive the goods.

(c)   Goods may never be invoiced.
      Invoicing errors may occur.
      Accounts may remain overdue.
      Accounts may not be correctly updated.

Answer 8.2

XYZ & Co
Chartered Accountants
10 Kinson Street
Northbourne
NN10 1MM
25 February 19X8

Board of Directors
Auckland Ltd
11 Moordown Road
Winton
NN11 1 WW

Dear Sirs

Points arising from the audit for the year ended 31 December 19X7

In accordance with our normal practice, we set out in this letter certain matters which arose as a result of our review of the accounting system and procedures operated by your company during our recent audit visit.

We would point out that the matters dealt with in this letter came to our notice during the conduct of our normal audit procedures which are designed primarily for the purpose of expressing our opinion of the financial statements of your company. In consequence, our work cannot be relied on necessarily to disclose defalcations or other irregularities or to be regarded as a comprehensive statement of all weaknesses that exist or of all improvements that might be made.

This report has been prepared for the sole use of your company. Its contents should not be disclosed to a third party without our written consent. No responsibility is assumed by us to any other person.

Sales, debtors and cash collection system

Sales and despatch

(a)   Present system

There is no check when orders are received as to whether:

(i)   They are from an established credit customer, or

(ii)   The customer is within their credit limit.

Implication

Goods can be supplied to a bad credit risk.

Recommendations

(i)   Credit ratings/references should be obtained for all customers and a credit limit set.

(ii)   Miss Lea should ensure individual orders do not place customers above their credit limit and evidence the order as such.

(b)   Present system

No evidence is obtained from customers that they have accepted delivery of their goods.

Implication

Bad debts may occur if customers claim that they have not received goods.

Recommendation

Customers should sign a copy of the despatch note which should then be returned to Auckland Ltd as proof of delivery.

Invoicing

Present system

Sequentially pre-numbered invoices are not used and there is no checking between orders, despatch notes and invoices.

Implications

(i)   Customer goodwill may be lost as it is not possible to check that all orders have been fulfilled correctly.

(ii)   Sales and debtors may be understated because there is no guarantee that invoices are eventually raised in respect of goods despatched.

Recommendations

(i)   Sequentially pre-numbered invoices should be used. Despatch notes should be matched and filed with order forms. A sequence check should be periodically performed to chase up unfulfilled orders.

(ii)   Invoices should be matched and filed with order forms and despatch notes in sequence order. A periodic sequence check would reveal uninvoiced sales.

(iii)   A sequence check on sales invoice posting should also be carried out monthly.

Cash receipts

Present system

Mrs Rawle is responsible for recording of both invoices and cheques received in the sales ledger.

Implication

It is possible for Mrs Rawle to suppress the recording of sales invoices and then misappropriate the cheques on receipt from customers without any need for collusion with another member of staff.

Recommendation

There must be segregation of duties between recording of invoices and recording payments received. The cheques received should be sent directly to Mrs McGillivray alongside a copy of the add list supplied to Mrs Rawle. The add list should be extended to contain the customer details needed by Mrs Rawle.

Our comments have been discussed with your finance director and the chief accountant and these matters will be considered by us again during future audits. We look forward to receiving your comments on the points made. Should you require any further information or explanations please do not hesitate to contact us.

We should like to take this opportunity to thank your staff for their co-operation and assistance during the course of our audit.

Yours faithfully.

XYZ & Co.

Answer 8.3

Tests of control over completeness of recording of sales include:

(a) Sequence tests on sales orders, despatch notes, invoices and credit notes to ensure that there are no missing numbers or two documents with the same number

(b) Comparisons of despatch notes with order and invoices, checking documents are cross-referenced to each other

(c) Checking posting of sales day book to sales ledger control account and sales ledger

(d) Checking control account reconciliations have been carried out and have been reviewed by senior staff

(e) Controls over computerised input including control totals, checking of output to source documents and procedure over resubmisson of rejected inputs.

Answer 8.4

(a) All purchases may not be recorded.
Goods and services may be purchased which are not required.
The company may fail to buy at the best prices.

(b) Goods may be accepted which have not been ordered.
Goods may be damaged or the quantity may be wrong.

(c) Invoices may be received for goods that have not been ordered.
Invoices may be incorrect.
Accounts may not be correctly updated.

Answer 8.5

(a) Controls over the file containing suppliers' details will include the following. These should prevent fraud by the creation of a fictitious supplier.

(i) All amendments/additions/deletions to the data should be authorised by a responsible official. A standard form should be used for such changes.

(ii) The amendment forms should be input in batches (with different types of change in different batches), sequentially numbered and recorded in a batch control book so that any gaps in the batch numbers can be investigated. The output produced by the computer should be checked to the input.

(iii) A listing of all such adjustments should automatically be produced by the computer and reviewed by a responsible official, who should also check authorisation.

(iv) A listing of suppliers' accounts on which there has been no movement for a specified period (6 months, 12 months) should be produced to allow decisions to be made about possible deletions, thus ensuring that the data is current. The buying department manager might also recommend account closures on a periodic basis.

(v)   Users should be controlled by use of passwords. This can also be used as a method of controlling those who can amend data.

(vi)   Periodic listings of data should be produced in order to verify details (for example addresses) with suppliers' documents (invoices/ statements).

(b)   The input of authorised purchase invoices and credit notes should be controlled in the following ways.

(i)   Authorisation should be evidenced by the signature of the responsible official (say the Chief Accountant). In addition, the invoice or credit note should show initials to demonstrate that the details have been agreed: to a signed GRN; to a purchase order; to a price list; for additions and extensions.

(ii)   There should be adequate segregation of responsibilities between the posting function, stock custody and receipt, payment of suppliers and changes to data.

(iii)   Input should be restricted by use of passwords linked to the relevant site number.

(iv)   A batch control book should be maintained, recording batches in number sequence. Invoices should be input in batches using pre-numbered batch control sheets. The manually produced invoice total on the batch control sheet should be agreed to the computer generated total. Credit notes and invoices should be input in separate batches to avoid one being posted as the other.

(v)   A program should check calculation of VAT at standard rate and total (net + VAT = gross) of invoice. Non-standard VAT rates should be highlighted.

(vi)   The input of the supplier code should bring up the supplier name for checking by the operator against the invoice.

(vii)   Invoices for suppliers which do not have an account should be prevented from being input. Any sundry suppliers account should be very tightly controlled and all entries reviewed in full each month.

(viii)   An exception report showing unusual expense allocation (by size or account) should be produced and reviewed by a responsible official. Expenses should be compared to budget and previous years.

(ix)   There should be monthly reconciliations of purchase ledger balances to suppliers' statements by someone outside the purchasing (accounting) function.

Answer 8.6

	ICQ question	Internal control objective	Audit tests	Consequences
1	Does an appropriate official authorise rates of pay?	Employees are paid amounts authorised	Test rates of pay from payroll to schedule of authorised pay rates (personnel files, board minutes etc)	Incorrect rates of pay could lead to over/under statement of profit
2	Are written notices required for employing and terminating employment?	All employees paid through payroll exist	Check a sample of employees from payroll files for authorisation of employment or termination Check details for cheque or credit transfer salary payments to personnel files	Payroll may include fictitious employees

	ICQ question	Internal control objective	Audit tests	Consequences
3	Are formal records such as time cards used for time keeping?	Employees are only paid for work done	Review time records to ensure they are properly completed and controlled Observe procedures for time recording Check time records where absences are recorded to payroll to ensure they have been accounted for Review the wages account and investigate any large or unusual amounts	Overstatement of payroll costs. Employees over/under paid
4	Does anyone verify rates of pay, overtime hours and computation of gross pay before wage payments are made?	Employees are paid the correct amount	Examine payroll for evidence of verification Recompute gross pay (including overtime) Check wage rates to authorised schedule	Misstatement of payroll costs
5	Does the accounting system ensure the proper recording of payroll costs in the financial records?	Payroll costs are properly recorded	Check posting of payroll costs to the nominal ledger	Misstatement of payroll costs

Chapter 9   Tests of control: asset cycles

Chapter topic list

1   Introduction

2   The cash system

3   The stock system

4   Fixed assets and general procedures

Learning objectives

On completion of this chapter you will be able to:

	Performance criteria	Range statement
• Describe how controls are tested in the following accounting systems:	17.1.4, 17.1.7,	17.1.1-17.1.3,
○ Cash/petty cash	17.2.1-17.2.4	17.2.1-17.2.3
○ Stock		
○ Fixed assets and investments		

BPP
PUBLISHING

1   INTRODUCTION

1.1   This chapter deals with other areas of the accounts for which significant controls are likely to exist.

1.2   Controls over **cash** and **bank balances** cannot be seen in complete isolation from controls over the sales, purchases/expenses and wages cycle. In this chapter we concentrate on controls over and testing of the safe **custody** and **recording** of cash. You should note in particular the emphasis on prompt recording of receipts and payments, and prompt banking of cash and cheques received. Bear in mind also when you work through the section on bank and cash that controlling cheque receipts and payments is significantly easier than controlling cash receipts and payments.

1.3   For **stock**, there should obviously be **proper security arrangements** and **prompt recording**. You should note however the other aspects of control of stock, particularly reviews of the condition of stock, and stockholding policies designed to ensure that the business is not holding too much or too little stock. These controls interest auditors since they may impact upon how stock is valued. We shall discuss valuation of stock further in Chapter 12.

1.4   With **fixed assets**, controls over the **recording** and **condition** of fixed assets are important, also the **custody** of portable fixed assets such as computer equipment. Given that much fixed asset expenditure is for significant amounts, auditors will also be interested in **controls** over the **acquisition** and **disposal** of fixed assets, particularly **authorisation** controls.

2   THE CASH SYSTEM

Aims of controls

2.1   The most important aims of the control system relating to cash receipts and payments are:

- All **monies received** are **recorded**
- All **monies received** are **banked**
- **Cash** and **cheques** are **safeguarded** against loss or theft
- All **payments** are **authorised, made** to the **correct recipients** and **recorded**

2.2   Segregation of duties is particularly important here. The person responsible for receiving and recording cash when it arrives in the post should not be the same as the person responsible for banking it. Ideally the cash book should be written up by a further staff member, and a fourth staff member should reconcile the various records of amounts received.

2.3   Records of cash are obviously also at the heart of a company's accounting records; therefore if these accounting records are to fulfil Companies Act requirements, cash must be recorded **promptly.**

2.4   The following detailed matters should be considered.

Control considerations

Cash at bank and in hand - receipts

2.5   Recording of receipts by post

- **Safeguards** to **prevent interception of mail** between receipt and opening

- Appointment of **responsible person** to supervise mail
- **Protection** of **cash and cheques** (restrictive crossing)
- **Amounts received listed** when post opened
- **Post stamped** with date of receipt

2.6 Recording of cash sales and collections

- **Restrictions** on **receipt of cash** (by cashiers only, or by salesmen etc)

- **Evidencing** of receipt of cash

   ° Serially numbered receipt forms
   ° Cash registers incorporating sealed till rolls

- **Clearance** of cash offices and registers

- **Agreement** of **cash collections** with **till rolls**

- **Agreement** of **cash collections** with **bankings** and cash and sales records

- **Investigation** of cash shortages and surpluses

2.7 General controls over recording

- **Prompt maintenance** of **records** (cash book, ledger accounts)

- **Limitation** of **duties** of receiving cashiers

- **Holiday arrangements**

- **Giving** and **recording** of **receipts**

   ° Retained copies
   ° Serially numbered receipts books
   ° Custody of receipt books
   ° Comparisons with cash book records and bank paying in slips

2.8 Banking

- **Daily bankings**

- **Make-up** and **comparison** of **paying-in** slips against initial receipt records and cash book

- **Banking** of receipts **intact**/control of disbursements

2.9 Safeguarding of cash and bank accounts

- **Restrictions** on **opening new bank accounts**

- **Limitations** on **cash floats** held

- **Restrictions** on **payments** out of **cash received**

- **Restrictions** on **access** to cash registers and offices

- **Independent checks** on cash floats

- **Surprise cash counts**

- **Custody** of **cash outside office hours**

- **Custody** over **supply** and issue of cheques

- **Preparation** of **cheques** restricted (person responsible should be separate from purchase ledger)

- **Safeguarding** of **IOUs**, cash in transit

- **Safeguards** over **mechanically signed cheques**/cheques carrying printed signatures

- **Restrictions** on issue of **blank** or **bearer** cheques

- **Insurance arrangements**

- **Bank reconciliations**

  ○ Issue of bank statements
  ○ Frequency of reconciliations by independent person
  ○ Reconciliation procedures
  ○ Treatment of longstanding unpresented cheques
  ○ Stop payment notice on unpresented cheques
  ○ Sequence of cheque numbers is confirmed as complete
  ○ Comparison of reconciliation with cash books

Cash at bank and in hand - payments

2.10 The arrangements for controlling payments will depend to a great extent on the nature of business transacted, the volume of payments involved and the size of the company.

2.11 The cashier should generally not be concerned with keeping or writing-up books of account other than those recording disbursements nor should he have access to, or be responsible for the custody of, securities, title deeds or negotiable instruments belonging to the company.

2.12 The person responsible for preparing cheques or traders' credit lists should not himself be a cheque signatory. Cheque signatories in turn should not be responsible for recording payments.

2.13 Cheque payments

- **Cheque requisitions**

  ○ Appropriate supporting documentation
  ○ Approval by appropriate staff
  ○ Presentation to cheque signatories
  ○ Cancellation (crossing/recording cheque number)

- **Authority** to sign cheques

  ○ Signatories should not also approve cheque requisitions
  ○ Limitations on authority to specific amounts
  ○ Number of signatories (all cheques/larger cheques require more than one signature)
  ○ Prohibitions over signing of blank cheques
  ○ Cancellation of supporting documentation

- **Prompt despatch** of signed **cheques**

- **Obtaining** of paid **cheques** from **banks**

- Payments **recorded promptly** in **cash book** and **ledger**

2.14 Cash payments

- **Authorisation** of **expenditure**
- **Cancellation** of **vouchers** to ensure cannot be paid
- **Limits** on **disbursements**
- **Rules** on **cash advances** to employees, IOUs and cheque cashing

Tests of controls

2.15 Auditors will carry out the following tests to ensure receipts are being recorded. Note that as well as testing controls over receipts, auditors are also obtaining evidence to support the assertion that sales and receipts are **completely** recorded.

2.16 Receipts received by post

- Observe procedures for post opening are being followed.

- **Observe** that **cheques** received by post are immediately **crossed** in the company's favour.

- For items entered in the rough cash book (or other record of cash, cheques etc received by post), **trace entries** to:
  - **Cash book**
  - **Paying-in book**
  - **counterfoil** or carbon copy receipts

- **Verify amounts entered** as **received** with remittance advices or other supporting evidence.

2.17 Cash sales, branch takings

- For a sample of cash sales summaries/branch summaries from different locations:
  - **Verify with till rolls** or copy cash sale notes
  - **Check to paying-in slip** date-stamped and initialled by the bank
  - **Verify that takings** are banked intact daily
  - **Vouch expenditure** out of takings

2.18 Collections

- For a sample of items from the original collection records:
  - **Trace amounts** to **cash book** via collectors' cash sheets or other collection records
  - **Check entries** on **cash sheets** or collection records with collectors' receipt books
  - **Verify** that **goods delivered** to travellers/salesmen have been regularly **reconciled** with sales and stocks in hand
  - **Check numerical sequence** of collection records

2.19 Receipts cash book

- For cash receipts for several days throughout the period:
  - **Check to entries in rough cash book**, receipts, branch returns or other records
  - **Check to paying-in slips** obtained direct from the bank, observing that there is no delay in banking monies received. Check additions of paying-in slips
  - **Check additions of cash book**
  - **Check postings to the sales ledger**
  - **Check postings to the general ledger**, including control accounts

- **Scrutinise the cash book** and **investigate items** of a **special** or **unusual nature**

2.20 Auditors will be concerned with whether **payments** have been **authorised** and are to the **correct payee**. The following tests will be performed on the payments cash book.

- For a sample of payments:
  - ° **Compare** with paid cheques to ensure payee agrees
  - ° **Check** that **cheques** are **signed** by the **persons authorised** to do so within their authority limits
  - ° **Check** to **suppliers' invoices** for goods and services. Verify that supporting documents are signed as having been **checked** and **passed for payment** and have been stamped 'paid'
  - ° **Check** supplier details and amounts to **suppliers' statements**
  - ° **Check** details to **other documentary evidence**, as appropriate (agreements, authorised expense vouchers, wages/salaries records, petty cash books etc)

2.21 When checking the **recording** of **payments**, auditors will carry out the following tests.

- **Check the sequence of cheque numbers** and enquire into missing numbers
- **Trace transfers** to other bank accounts, petty cash books or other records, as appropriate
- **Check additions**, including extensions, and balances forward at the beginning and end of the months covering the periods chosen
- **Check postings** to the **purchase ledger**
- **Check postings** to the **general ledger**, including the control accounts

2.22 When checking that bank and cash are **secured** auditors should consider the security arrangements over bank cheques and cash. Bank reconciliations are also a very important control and auditors should carry out the following tests on these.

- **Verify** that **reconciliations have been prepared and reviewed** at **regular intervals** throughout the year
- **Scrutinise reconciliations** for **unusual items**

Auditors should also perform the substantive tests on bank reconciliations detailed in Chapter 14.

2.23 The following tests should be carried out on petty cash.

- For a sample of payments:
  - ° **Check** to supporting vouchers
  - ° **Check** whether they are properly **approved**
  - ° **See** that **vouchers** have been **marked and initialled** by the cashier to prevent their re-use
- For a sample of weeks:
  - ° **Trace amounts** received to **cash books**
  - ° **Check additions** and **balances carried** forward
  - ° **Check postings** to the **nominal ledger**

3 THE STOCK SYSTEM

3.1 The stock system can be very important in an audit because of the high value of stock or the complexity of its audit. It is closely connected with the sales and purchases systems covered in Chapter 8.

Aims of controls

3.2 The most important aims of the control system relating to stock are:

Recording

- All **stock movements** are **authorised** and **recorded**
- **Stock records** only **include items** that **belong** to the client
- **Stock records include stock** that **exists** and is **held** by the client
- **Stock quantities** have been **recorded correctly**
- **Cut-off procedures** are **properly applied** to stock

Protection of stock

- **Stock** is **safeguarded** against loss, pilferage or damage

Valuation of stock

- The **costing system values stock correctly**
- **Allowance** is **made** for **slow-moving, obsolete** or **damaged stock**

Stock-holding

- **Levels** of **stock held** are **reasonable**

Control considerations

3.3 Significant controls are as follows.

Recording of stock

- **Segregation** of duties; custody and recording of stocks

- **Reception, checking** and **recording** of goods inwards

- **Stock issues supported** by **appropriate documentation**

- **Maintenance** of **stock records**

    ° Stock ledgers
    ° Bin cards
    ° Transfer records

Protection of stock

- **Precautions** against **theft, misuse** and **deterioration**

    ° Restriction of access to stores

    ° Controls on stores environment (right temperature, precautions against damp etc).

- **Security** over **stock** held by third parties, and third party stock held by entity

- **Stocktaking** (see also Chapter 12)
  - ° Regular stocktaking
  - ° Fair coverage so that all stock is counted at least once a year
  - ° Counts by independent persons
  - ° Recording
  - ° Cut-off for goods in transit and time differences
  - ° Reconciliation of stock count to book records and control accounts

Valuation of stock

- **Computation** of **stock valuation**
  - ° Accords with SSAP 9
  - ° Checking of calculations

- **Review** of **condition** of stock
  - ° Treatment of slow-moving, damaged and obsolete stock
  - ° Authorisation of write-offs

- **Accounting** for **scrap** and **waste**

Stockholding

- **Control** of **stock levels**
  - ° Maximum stock limits
  - ° Minimum stock limits
  - ° Re-order quantities and levels

- Arrangements for dealing with **returnable containers**

Tests of controls

3.4 Most of the testing relating to stock has been covered in the purchase and sales testing outlined in Chapter 8. Auditors will primarily be concerned at this stage with ensuring that the business keeps track of stock. To confirm this, checks must be made on how stock **movements** are **recorded** and how **stock** is **secured**.

- **Select** a sample of **stock movements records** and **agree** to **goods received** and **goods despatched notes, confirming** that **movements** have been **authorised** as appropriate

- **Select** a sample of **goods received** and **goods despatched** notes and agree to **stock movement records**

- **Check sequence** of stock records

3.5 Other tests that auditors are likely to perform include:

- **Test** check **stock counts** carried out from time to time (eg monthly) during the period and confirm:
  - ° **All discrepancies** between **book** and **actual** figures have been fully investigated
  - ° **All discrepancies** have been **signed off** by a senior manager
  - ° **Obsolete, damaged or slow-moving goods** have been **marked accordingly** and written down to NRV

- **Observe security arrangements** for stocks

- **Consider environment** in which stocks are held

Auditors will carry out extensive tests on the **valuation** of stock at the substantive testing stage (see Chapter 12).

Activity 9.1

Jonathan is the sole shareholder of Furry Lion Stores Ltd, a company which owns five stores in the west of England. The stores mainly stock food and groceries, and four of the stores have an off-licence as well.

Each store is run by a full-time manager and three or four part-time assistants. Jonathan spends on average ½ a day a week at each store, and spends the rest of his time at home, dealing with his other business interests.

All sales are for cash and are recorded on till rolls which the manager retains. Shop manager wages are paid monthly by cheque by Jonathan. Wages of shop assistants are paid in cash out of the takings.

Most purchases are made from local wholesalers and are paid for in cash out of the takings. Large purchases (over £250) must be made by cheques signed by the shop manager and countersigned by Jonathan.

Shop managers bank surplus cash once a week, apart from a float in the till.

All accounting records including the cash book, wages and VAT records are maintained by the manager. Jonathan reviews the weekly bank statements when he visits the shops. He also has a look at stocks to see if stock levels appear to be about right. All invoices are also kept in a drawer by a manager and marked with a cash book reference, and where appropriate a cheque number when paid.

Task

Discuss the weaknesses in the control systems of Furry Lion Stores Ltd, and how the weaknesses can be remedied.

4 FIXED ASSETS AND GENERAL PROCEDURES

4.1 These systems tend to be of lesser importance, although this depends on the nature of the business.

Aims of controls

4.2 The most important aims of the control system relating to fixed assets are to ensure:

- Fixed assets are **properly accounted** for and **recorded**
- **Security arrangements** over fixed assets are sufficient
- Fixed assets are **maintained properly**
- Fixed asset **acquisitions are authorised**
- Fixed asset **disposals are authorised** and proceeds of disposals are accounted for
- **Depreciation rates are reasonable**
- All **income is collected** from income-yielding fixed assets

Control considerations

4.3 Key controls are as follows.

- **Segregation** of **duties**; authorisation, custody and recording

Recording

- **Maintenance** of **accounting records** (including distinction between capital and revenue expenditure)

Security and maintenance

- **Maintenance** of plant and property **registers**
    - ° Agreement with general ledger
    - ° Inspection of assets recorded
- **Inspection** of fixed assets to ensure **properly maintained** and **used**

Acquisition and disposal

- **Authorisation** of capital expenditure
- **Authorisation** of **sales,** scrapping or transfer of fixed assets

Depreciation

- **Authorisation** of **depreciation rates**
- **Calculation** and **checking** of depreciation rates
    - ° Arithmetical check
    - ° Assessment of asset lives

Income from fixed assets

- **Identification** of income **producing assets**
    - ° Monitoring of income
    - ° Receipt of cash
- Adequate **insurance cover**

Tests of controls

4.4 A key concern of auditors will be proper controls over **movements** during the year, ie acquisitions and disposals.

- For a sample of fixed asset purchases during the year in the general ledger:
    - ° **Check authorisation** (and board approval if necessary)
    - ° **Vouch purchase price** to invoice and cash book
    - ° **Check** asset has been **recorded** in the **fixed asset register**
    - ° **Check correct depreciation** rates applied

- For a sample of fixed asset disposals during the year:
    - ° **Check disposal authorised** by senior official
    - ° **Check invoice** issued for any proceeds
    - ° **Agree recording** of proceeds in the cash books
    - ° Check **asset** has been **removed** from fixed asset register
    - ° **Check calculations of profit** or loss on disposal

4.5 Auditors should also carry out some testing on **security, maintenance** and **recording** of fixed assets.

- For a sample of fixed assets from the fixed asset register:
    - ° **Check physical existence** of asset
    - ° **Ensure asset** in **good condition**
    - ° Consider whether asset **value** should be **written down**
- Check whether fixed asset register has been **reconciled to general ledger.**
- For a sample of fixed assets of all varieties:
    - ° **Agree existence** to fixed asset register
    - ° **Consider whether write down required**

Activity 9.2

Describe the main controls that a business should implement in order to ensure safe custody of:

(a) Stock
(b) Tangible fixed assets

General procedures

4.6   As well as testing based on individual components of the accounting system, the auditor will also perform some general tests, including the following.

- **Test postings** from **books of prime entry** to the general ledger
- **Check** that the **general ledger** is regularly **balanced**
- **Test vouch** a sample of **journal entries** to **original documentation**

Key learning points

- Controls over cash receipts and payments should prevent fraud or theft.
- Key controls over **receipts** include:
  - ° Proper **post-opening** arrangements
  - ° **Prompt recording**
  - ° **Prompt banking**
  - ° **Reconciliation** of records of cash received and banked
- Key controls over **payments** include:
  - ° **Restriction of access** to cash and cheques
  - ° Procedures for **preparation and authorisation** of payments
- A further important control is **regular independent bank reconciliations**
- **Stock controls** are designed to ensure safe custody. These include:
  - ° Restriction of access to stock
  - ° Documentation and authorisation of movements
- Other important controls over stock include regular **independent stock-taking** and **review of stock condition**.
- Important controls over **tangible fixed assets** include **physical custody** and authorisation of **purchases** and **disposals**.
- Tangible fixed assets should be recorded in a **fixed asset register**.
- Controls over investments should include maintenance of an **investment register** and **investment control account** and **custody** of documents of title

---

Quick quiz

1   How frequently should cashiers bank money received?

2   What are the key controls over a system of cheque requisitions?

3   What are the most important controls over the signing of cheques?

4   If the client has a system of regular stocktakes, what are the most important features this system should have?

5   What controls should businesses exercise over stock levels?

6   What tests would auditors normally carry out on controls over fixed asset purchases?

BPP PUBLISHING

Answers to quick quiz

1   Cash receipts should ideally be banked every day.

2   The key controls over a system of cheque requisition are as follows.

  (a)   Requisitions should be supported by appropriate documentation.

  (b)   Requisitions should be approved by appropriate staff, who should not be the same as the staff authorised to sign cheques.

  (c)   Requisitions should be presented to the cheque signatories.

  (d)   Once a cheque has been drawn, requisitions should be cancelled and marked with the cheque number.

3   The most important controls over the signing of cheques are as follows.

  (a)   Signatories should not also approve cheque requisitions.
  (b)   All cheques/cheques for larger amounts should be signed by more than one person.
  (c)   Signatories should be restricted to signing cheques for a prescribed maximum amount.
  (d)   Documentation supporting cheques should be cancelled once the cheque has been signed.
  (e)   The signing of blank cheques should be prohibited.

4   (a)   The stocktakes should be carried out regularly.
  (b)   All stock should be counted at least once a year.
  (c)   Counts should be carried out by staff independent of the stock/stores function.
  (d)   The results of the stocktakes should be properly recorded, and take account of goods in transit.
  (e)   The results of the stocktakes should be reconciled to book stock records.

5   Clients should set maximum and minimum stock levels, also stock levels at which stock should be ordered and the normal re-order quantities.

6   Auditors should normally check that:

  (a)   Fixed asset purchases have been authorised.
  (b)   The purchase price can be confirmed to supporting documentation.
  (c)   The asset has been recorded in the cash book and fixed asset register.
  (d)   An appropriate depreciation rate has been chosen and has been applied correctly to the asset.

Answers to activities

Answer 9.1

Weaknesses in the system, and their remedies are as follows.

Stock

Weaknesses

The shops do not appear to have any stock movement records. This would appear to breach the Companies Act s 221 requirement for the company to maintain proper accounting records. Jonathan has also only a very approximate indication of stock levels. Hence it will be difficult to detect whether stock levels are too high, or too low with a risk of running out of stock. Theft of stock would also be difficult to detect.

Remedies

The company should therefore introduce stock movement records, detailing values and volumes.

In addition regular stock counts should be made either by Jonathan or by staff from another shop. Discrepancies between the stock records and the actual stock counted should be investigated.

Cash controls

Weaknesses

Too much cash appears to be held on site. In addition the fact that most payments appear to be for cash may mean inadequate documentation is kept.

Remedies

The level of cash on site can be decreased by daily rather than weekly bankings. In addition the need for cash on site can be decreased by paying wages by cheque, and by paying all but the smallest payments by cheque.

The cash book should obviously still be maintained but cheque stubs should also show details of amounts paid. The cash book should be supported by invoices and other supporting documentation, and should be cross-referenced to the general ledger (see below).

Cash reconciliations

Weaknesses

There is no indication of the till-rolls that are kept being reconciled to cash takings.

Remedies

There should be a daily reconciliation of cash takings and till rolls; this should be reviewed if not performed by the shop manager.

Bank reconciliations

Weaknesses

There is no mention of bank reconciliations taking place.

Remedies

Bank reconciliations should be carried out at least monthly by the shop manager, and reviewed by the owner.

Purchases

Weaknesses

There is no formal system for recording purchases. Invoices do not appear to be filed in any particular way. It would be difficult to see whether accounting records were complete, and hence it would be difficult to prepare a set of accounts from the accounting records available. In addition the way records are maintained means that accounts would have to be prepared on a cash basis, and not on an accruals basis, as required by the Companies Act.

Remedies

A purchase day book should be introduced. Invoices should be recorded in the purchase day book, and filed in a logical order, either by date received or by supplier.

General ledger

Weaknesses

There is no general ledger, and again this means that annual accounts cannot easily be prepared (and also management accounts).

Remedies

A general ledger should be maintained with entries made from the cash book, wages records and purchase day book. This will enable accounts to be prepared on an accruals basis.

Supervision

Weaknesses

Jonathan does not take a very active part in the business, only signing cheques over £250, and visiting the shops only half a day each week. This may mean that assets can easily go missing, and Jonathan cannot readily see whether the business is performing as he would wish.

Remedies

Jonathan should review wage/VAT/cash book reconciliations. Management accounts should also be prepared by shop managers for Jonathan.

Answer 9.2

(a) The most important controls over the safe custody of stock are as follows.

(i) **Physical**

Access to the stock-rooms should be restricted to authorised staff. Outside working hours, the stock area should be locked.

(ii) **Segregation of duties**

Stock movements should be recorded by different staff from those responsible for ensuring the safe custody of stocks.

(iii) **Stock records**

Appropriate documentation should be maintained including stores ledger accounts giving details of movements, quantities held and pricing of stock lines, bin cards giving details of movements and quantities held, and materials requisitions and return notes.

(iv) **Controls over movements**

(1) Stock being delivered should be logged in by goods received notes and goods inwards records, which should be reconciled with supplier delivery notes and purchase orders.

(2) All internal movements of stock should be authorised.

(3) Stock should only be despatched if a sales order has been received, and should only be despatched to authorised customers. Stock despatches should be recorded on despatch notes and in goods outwards records, and these should subsequently be reconciled to sales order and invoices.

(v) **Stocktakes**

Regular stocktakes should be carried out by someone who is independent of the stores department. All stock should be counted at least once a year. Stock counted should be compared with stock records, and differences investigated.

(b) The most important controls over the custody of tangible fixed assets are as follows.

(i) **Physical**

As with stock, fixed assets, particularly portable ones should be locked away when not in use or outside business hours. Companies may also mark fixed assets with identification codes.

(ii) **Segregation of duties**

There should be segregation of duties between the people responsible for authorising fixed asset purchases and disposals, those responsible for custody and those responsible for recording fixed assets.

(iii) **Fixed asset register**

Fixed assets held should be recorded in a fixed asset register, maintained separately from the company's general ledger and cash systems.

(iv) **Purchases and disposals**

All fixed asset purchases, disposals and scrappings should be authorised by staff of appropriate seniority. Major purchases and disposals should be authorised by the board.

(v) **Reconciliations**

The fixed asset register should be reconciled to the general ledger on a regular basis by someone other than the staff member who maintains the fixed asset register. There should also be comparisons made by independent staff to check if fixed assets recorded in the fixed asset register are actually held, and to check that assets held are recorded in the fixed asset register.

Chapter 10 Computer controls

Chapter topic list

1   Introduction

2   Controls in a computer environment

3   Controls in on-line and real-time systems

4   Control problems in small computer systems

Learning objectives

On completion of this chapter you will be able to:

	Performance criteria	Range Statement
• Describe the additional controls needed in computerised accounting systems, in particular security controls	17.1.4,17.1.7, 17.2.1-17.2.5	17.1.1-17.1.3, 17.2.1-17.2.3

1 INTRODUCTION

1.1 Having looked at controls in individual audit areas, we now go on to see how auditors view controls within computerised systems.

1.2 **Controls** which should operate **over computerised systems** include controls over computer **operations** and controls over the **environment** in which those operations take place. Certain systems have many controls, and we list a number of examples in Section 2. However many the controls, the ultimate objectives of most systems are few. The most important objectives are that the system should ensure the **accuracy** and **completeness** of the data **held** and **processing procedures**. A business should also have **proper security arrangements** over its systems and **disaster retrieval procedures** should catastrophes occur.

1.3 **Security** can be a major problem. Security procedures may operate over the entire system, and also over specific data held and specific operations performed within the system. We discuss in Sections 3 and 4 the security problems that can occur in systems where information is passed and processed from a number of different sites, and in small computer systems.

1.4 You may be asked in the devolved assessment about the use of controls in particular areas for example sales. Other questions may focus on general controls such as access, systems development and disaster retrieval controls.

2 CONTROLS IN A COMPUTER ENVIRONMENT

2.1 The expansion in the use of computers for accounting purposes will certainly continue. Auditors must therefore be able to cope with the special problems that arise when auditing in a computer environment and keep abreast of technical innovation. Broad guidance is provided for the auditor in the form of the old Auditing Practices Committee operational guideline *Auditing in a computer environment*.

2.2 Internal controls over computer-based accounting systems may be considered under the following two main headings, application controls (relating to specific controls over the transaction and data) and general controls (which relate to the whole environment in which computerised operations take place).

KEY TERMS

Application controls relate to the transactions and standing data appertaining to each computer-based accounting system and are therefore specific to each such application.

The objectives of application controls, which may be manual or programmed, are to ensure the completeness and accuracy of the accounting records and the validity of the entries made in these records resulting from both manual and programmed processing.

General controls are controls, other than application controls, which relate to the environment within which computer based accounting systems are developed, maintained and operated, and which are therefore applicable to all the applications. The objectives of general controls are to ensure the proper development and implementation of applications and the integrity of program and data files and of computer operations. Like application controls, general controls may be either manual or programmed.

2.3 Application controls and general controls are inter-related. Strong general controls contribute to the assurance which may be obtained by an auditor in relation to application controls. On the other hand, unsatisfactory general controls may undermine strong application controls or exacerbate unsatisfactory application controls.

2.4 The following points will particularly influence the auditors' approach.

(a) Before auditors place reliance on application controls which involve computer programs, they need to obtain reasonable assurance that the programs have **operated properly**, by evaluating and testing the effect of relevant general controls or by other tests on specific parts of the programs.

(b) Sometimes a programmed accounting procedure may not be subject to effective application controls. In such circumstances, in order to put themselves in a position to limit the extent of substantive procedures, the auditors may choose to perform tests of controls by **testing** the **relevant general controls** either manually or by using CAATs, to gain assurance of the continued and proper operation of the programmed accounting procedure.

(c) In a computer environment there is the possibility of **systematic errors**. This may take place because of program faults or hardware malfunction in computer operations. However, such errors should be prevented or detected by general controls over the development and implementation of applications, the integrity of the program and data files, and of computer operations.

(d) The extent to which the auditors can rely on general controls may be **limited** because many of these controls might not be evidenced, or because they could have been performed inconsistently.

Examples of application controls

2.5 To achieve the overall objectives of application controls identified above, the specific requirements are controls over:

- **Completeness, accuracy** and **authorisation** of **input**
- **Completeness** and **accuracy** of **processing**
- **Maintenance** of **master files** and the **standing data files**

(Standing data is data that will be used over and over again eg staff grades, rates of pay. Master files use this data and store an **accumulation** of **transactions**.)

Controls over input

2.6 Control techniques for ensuring the **completeness** of input in a timely fashion include:

- **Manual** or **programmed agreement** of control totals
- **One for one checking** of **processed output** to source documents
- **Manual** or **programmed sequence checking**
- **Programmed matching** of **input** to a **control file**, containing details of expected input
- **Procedures** over **resubmission** of **rejected inputs**

2.7 Controls over the **accuracy** of input are concerned with the data fields on input transactions. Control should be exercised not only over **value** fields, such as invoice amounts, but also important **reference** fields, such as account number or date of payment.

2.8 Techniques to ensure accuracy include:

- **Programmed check digit verification** (a check digit included in a reference number is arithmetically checked to ensure that it bears the required relationship to the rest of the number)

- **Programmed reasonableness checks,** including checking the logical relationship between two or more files

- **Programmed existence checks** against valid codes

- **Manual scrutiny of output** and **checking** to **source documents**

- **Manual** or **programmed agreements** of control totals

2.9 Controls over **authorisation** involve checking:

- All transactions are authorised
- The individual who authorised each transaction was empowered to do so

This will generally involve a clerical review of input transactions, although a programmed check to detect transactions that exceed authorisation limits may be possible.

Controls over processing

2.10 Controls are required to ensure:

- **Processing** of all input data

- Use of **correct master files** and **standing data** files

- **Accurate processing** of each transaction

- **Accurate** and **authorised updating of data**, and any new data generated during processing

- **Completeness and accuracy of output reports**

2.11 The control techniques used to ensure the completeness and accuracy of input may also be used to ensure the completeness and accuracy of processing. The techniques must be applied to the results of processing, such as a batch reconciliation produced after the update and not the one produced after the initial edit.

Controls over master files and standing data

2.12 Techniques for ensuring the completeness, accuracy and authorisation of amendments to master files and standing data files and for ensuring the completeness and accuracy of the processing of these amendments are similar to the techniques for transaction input.

2.13 The following controls may be particularly important.

- **One to one checking** because of the importance of master files and standing data
- **Cyclical review** of all **master files** and **standing data**
- **Controls** over the **deletion** of accounts which contain a current balance
- **Record counts** and **hash totals** every time master files are used.

(Record counts are counts of the total number of documents processed. Hash totals are the totals of for example the payroll numbers of all staff members on a payroll. That total can be used as a check that all records have been processed, but is otherwise of no significance)

Examples of general controls

2.14 To achieve the overall objectives of general controls above, controls may be needed in the following areas.

GENERAL CONTROLS	
Development of computer applications	Standards over **systems design, programming and documentation**
	Full **testing procedures** using test data
	Approval by **computer users** and **management**
	Segregation of duties so that those responsible for design are not responsible for testing
	Installation procedures so that data is not corrupted in transition
	Training of staff in new procedures and availability of adequate documentation
Prevention of unauthorised program changes	**Segregation of duties**
	Full records of program **changes**
	Password protection of programs so that access is limited to computer operations staff.
	Restricted access to **central computer**
	Maintenance of programs logs
	Virus checks on software
	Back-up copies of programs being taken and stored in other locations
	Control copies of programs being preserved and regularly **compared** with **actual programs**
	Stricter controls over certain programs (utility programs)
Testing and documentation of program changes	Complete **testing procedures**
	Documentation standards
	Approval of changes by computer users and management
	Training of staff using programs
Prevention of the use of wrong programs or files	**Operation controls** over programs
	Libraries of programs
	Proper job scheduling
Prevention of unauthorised changes to data files	See section below on real-time systems
Controls to ensure continuity of operation	**Storing extra copies** of programs and data files off site
	Protection of equipment against fire and other hazards
	Back-up power sources
	Emergency procedures
	Disaster recovery procedures eg availability of back-up computer facilities.
	Maintenance agreements and **insurance**

Activity 10.1

You are responsible for the audit of purchases and creditors in Tigger Limited. All data is processed through the computer, by full-time computer operators in the creditors section. You are about to start the audit, and want to find out more about the controls operated over processing in the creditors section.

Task

List the main questions you would ask to ascertain whether computer controls over purchases and creditors were effective.

Activity 10.2

Six months ago fire destroyed most of the manual accounting records of Big Ted Ltd. Rather than set up the manual accounting system again, the company has decided to computerise its accounting process. However the managing director is (perhaps not surprisingly) worried about what will happen if the company suffers another fire.

Task

Advise the managing director of the steps that can be taken to minimise the risk to the computerised system of fire.

3 CONTROLS IN ON-LINE AND REAL-TIME SYSTEMS

Nature of on-line and real-time systems

3.1 Whilst traditional batch processing is still a common method of using a computer to process accounting data there is a rapid increase in the use of an on-line system, including those in real-time.

3.2 **On-line** systems provide the facilities for data to be passed to and from the central computer via remote terminals. **Real-time** systems are a further development of on-line systems and permit immediate updating of computer held files. The data input and file update phases are therefore merged and the system accepts individual transactions rather than batches of data.

Controls in real-time systems

3.3 There are certain control problems associated with most real-time systems. The main points to remember are as follows. We are concerned primarily with larger, multi-user systems. By **terminals** we mean either dumb terminals or networked PCs.

Segregation of duties

3.4 The same person is often responsible for producing *and* processing the same information. To compensate for the reduction in internal check, supervisory controls should be strengthened.

Data file security

3.5 The ability of a person using a remote terminal to gain access to databases at will results in the need for special controls to ensure that files are neither read nor written to (nor destroyed), either accidentally or deliberately, without proper authority.

(a) The controls may be partly **physical**. For example:

(i) **Access to terminals** is **restricted** to authorised personnel.

(ii) The **terminals** and the **rooms** in which they are kept are **locked** when not in use.

(b) They may be partly controlled by the **operating system**, including the following.

(i) The use of **passwords** (or lockwords), or **special badges** or keys, sometimes linked to a user's personal identification code which must be used before the terminal operator can gain access to the computer/particular files.

In some systems one password or other identification is required before it is possible to read a file, a second before it is possible to write new data and yet a third if both operations are permitted. Obviously, the code given to a particular individual will depend on his job function and status within the organisation.

(ii) **Restriction** by the operating system of **certain users** to **certain files**. For example, the PC in the wages department may only be given access to the wages files.

(iii) **Logging** of all **attempted violations** of the above controls possibly accompanied by the automatic shut down of the PC or terminal used. Obviously all violations should be speedily and thoroughly investigated.

(c) **Application controls** may include validity checks on input and reporting of unusual transactions.

DEVOLVED ASSESSMENT ALERT

The guidance for this Unit has stressed the importance of security controls.

Back-ups

3.6 Back-up copies of data must be taken at least daily, and separately on a weekly basis. In a real time system it may be necessary to have a cut off time after which no further transactions are ever posted. Attempts to open a file when a back-up is in progress can sometimes corrupt the process. Stray transactions posted after the back-up has been done could be lost if there is some sort of accident and the back-up data has to be restored in full the next day.

3.7 On the other hand, immediate access to files allows more sophisticated checks to be performed. For example it allows more extensive use of computer matching, where the information input may be checked for accuracy against that held on file.

3.8 Moreover, in spite of the potential for abuse, there is a distinct advantage to enabling users to correct certain types of error immediately.

Database management systems (DBMS)

3.9 DBMS are normally designed for use in real-time environments. They enable elements of data to be accessed by different programs. This avoids the duplication of data which inevitably occurs in a traditional system.

3.10 As data is normally only stored once, and may be accessible to all users that require it, the principal control problems raised concern the authorisation of data amendments and restriction of access to data. Any data amendments must take into account the requirements of all the users. An **administration function** should be set up to run and control the day to day operation of the database, thereby enhancing segregation of duties (this function will be independent of the systems development personnel and programmers and data processing manager).

4 CONTROL PROBLEMS IN SMALL COMPUTER SYSTEMS

4.1 In this section we look at the control and audit problems peculiar to small computer systems concentrating on personal computers (PCs).

Summary of the control problems

4.2 The majority of the potential problems arise due to the departure from the formal structure of the traditional data processing department, where a controlled environment was provided over the acquisition, maintenance and distribution of computer information. In the world of the PC this controlled structure does not exist and the environment is more informal.

Lack of planning over the acquisition and use of PCs

4.3 When an organisation sets out to acquire a computer system, a series of steps should be undertaken before making the decision to purchase.

Authorisation

4.4 A **feasibility study** should be carried out, examining the requirements, the costs and the benefits, to ensure that the expense is justified. Suppliers should be invited to tender, and responses from the suppliers should be evaluated and compared. All interested parties within the organisation should be identified and involved throughout the whole procedure.

Suitability

4.5 There is a risk that the client will not have the expertise to evaluate the relative merits of systems. Many first time users tend to purchase **standard software packages** which creates an even greater risk as regards suitability, for such systems may not fit precisely the company's trading methods.

Support facilities

4.6 The support facilities offered by the supplier and/or software house should be ascertained and a maintenance contract entered. The client should ensure that in the event of machine breakdown, **prompt service** and, if necessary, backup facilities are available and **adequate** systems **documentation** and operator manuals have been provided.

Standards

4.7 In a formal data processing environment there will normally be standards covering controls and accounting principles to which all procedures regarding hardware and software should conform. With PCs, where the time taken from ordering, through installation to operation, may be a matter of weeks only, there is great danger that standards are not set.

4.8 Strict disciplines must be imposed to ensure that **recognised systems development controls** are **applied** and **sufficient administration procedures** are implemented.

Lack of documentary evidence

4.9 We have identified that many PCs operate in real time via VDUs, which allows users to have direct access to the computer thus enabling them to input data, update files and make one-off enquiries on data held on files.

4.10 Control can be enhanced by ensuring that **edit programs** are **in-built** at the **design stage** and by incorporating into the system a user-usage file which logs details of the user's identification, the application involved, the records accessed or updated and so on. Such a file can be reviewed periodically by a responsible official and the auditor.

Lack of security and confidentiality

Lack of segregation of duties

4.11 Poor segregation of duties all too easily occurs since frequently the **same person prepares** the **data, feeds** it into the computer, **supervises** the **processing** and **acts as end user**. This lack of division of duties leads to enhanced opportunities for fraud, the user having access to assets and the recording and disposal of assets. The auditors may well have to perform extensive substantive verification work to compensate for this serious lack of control.

Lack of control over users

4.12 Because PCs do not require a protected environment the **terminals** are **readily available** to any user. In order to safeguard the records, controls to prevent unauthorised users from using the computer are necessary (use of passwords and so on).

Lack of control over alterations to programs

4.13 We have emphasised that a lack of expertise, particularly in the case of first time users, may lead to imprudent purchase in terms of capacity and compatibility. Conversely, there are dangers arising because of the relative ease with which expertise may be acquired once a machine is installed and operational. PCs employ high level languages and a working knowledge can be grasped within a short time. In the wrong hands there is a danger that **programs** might be **altered** without **detection** or that programs are written at the time data is being processed without adequate testing.

4.14 Stringent supervisory arrangements are required to prevent unauthorised personnel from having access to the programs together with **programmed controls preventing unauthorised running**. A degree of security will be guaranteed to the extent that the programs are permanently etched onto silicon chips and are hence an integral part of the hardware ('ROMs'). Such programs can only be altered by specialist electronics engineers.

Activity 10.3

What controls can a small company implement over a PC based system?

BPP
PUBLISHING

Key learning points

- You must recognise the practical impact of computerisation in recent years and the fact that all auditors will encounter computer-based systems in their professional work.

- **Application controls** should ensure:
  - The completeness, accuracy and authorisation of input
  - The completeness and accuracy of processing
  - The proper maintenance of master files and standing data

- **General controls** are required to:
  - Ensure proper application development
  - Prevent or detect unauthorised changes to programs
  - Ensure that all program changes are adequately tested and documented
  - Prevent or detect errors during use of programs
  - Prevent unauthorised amendments to data files
  - Ensure that systems software is properly installed and maintained
  - Ensure that proper documentation is kept
  - Ensure continuity of operations

- The majority of modern systems are **real-time systems**, where users have instant and direct access to data. Important real-time controls are:
  - Segregation of duties
  - Data file security
  - Program security
  - Back-ups

- Many small computer systems use **personal computers (PCs).** The major problems with use of PCs are lack of:
  - Planning over acquisition and use
  - Documentary evidence
  - Security and confidentiality

Quick quiz

1   What application controls can help ensure the completeness of input?

2   What are the major objectives of controls over processing?

3   What are the key controls over the testing and documentation of program changes?

4   What controls can be operated to ensure the integrity of a Database Management System?

5   What support facilities should a supplier offer the user of a small computer system?

Answers to quick quiz

1   Completeness of input can be ensured by:

(a) Manual or programmed agreement of control totals
(b) One for one checking of processed output to source documents
(c) Manual or programmed sequence checking
(d) Programmed matching of input to a control file, containing details of expected inputs
(e) Procedures for re-submission of rejected inputs

2   The major objectives of controls over processing are to ensure that:

(a) All input data is processed.
(b) The correct master files and standing data files are used.
(c) The processing of each transaction is accurate.
(d) The updating of data/new data is accurate and authorised.

(e) Output reports are complete and accurate.

3 The key controls over testing and documentation of program changes are:

(a) Testing procedures
(b) Documentation controls and standards
(c) Approval of changes by users and computer management
(d) Internal audit involvement and segregation of duties
(e) Training and supervision of staff

4 The integrity of a DBMS can be preserved by:

(a) Restriction of access to the data dictionary
(b) Segregation of duties
(c) Liaison between the database administration function and systems development personnel
(d) Preparation and update of user manuals

5 The support facilities that should be obtained include:

(a) Prompt service and back-up facilities in the event of a breakdown

(b) Dealing with bugs

(c) Making minor modifications to programs promptly

(d) Provision of adequate documentation including program documentation, operator instructions and user manuals

(e) Adequate instruction given to operators

Answers to activities

Answer 10.1

The questions to be asked in order to review the computer controls in existence over purchases and creditors must cover controls over input, processing, access, files and output. The following questions could be asked of the accountant responsible for the creditors section.

(a) What systematic action is taken to ensure the completeness, accuracy and authorisation of input of purchase invoices, credit notes, journal entries, cash and so on? For example, batch totalling, sequence checking, programmed matching of input to control files containing details of expected input, and authorisation limits and reasonableness checks.

(b) By what methods is it established that all input is fully and accurately processed? Examples are batch reconciliation after records update, summary totals, programmed validity checks.

(c) What controls are in place to prevent or detect unauthorised amendments to programs and data files (for example, restrictions of access to programs and to users of the on-line terminals)?

(d) What controls exist over the work done by computer operators (for example, division of duties, job scheduling, computer logs, cross-checks to input control, authorisation of file issue)?

(e) What procedures are in operation to ensure the continuing correctness of master files and the standing data they contain? For example, record counts or hash totals for the files, produced and checked each time they are used, regular checks of all contents, run-to-run control totals.

(f) Are there procedures for the review and despatch of output by the computer operators? Examples are: comparison of output with prelist totals of input, checking all queries have been properly dealt with, distribution list for all output and close control over exception reports, audit totals and so on.

(g) Is the reasonableness of output tested? For example, is output tested against file totals after update, and compared with manually prepared totals and balances on individual debtors accounts?

(h) Is there an adequate management (audit) trail of generated data and regular listing of ledger balances and creditor analysis?

(i) Is there an accounting manual in existence, detailing all procedures and clerical processes relating to the purchases and creditors system, and is it up to date?

Answer 10.2

The following procedures should be undertaken to prevent fire from damaging the system.

(a) The computer room should be constructed of fire-proof materials.

(b) The computer room should have an adequate alarm system which not only warns of fire but also of high-risk conditions, for example the room becoming too hot, so that emergency procedures can be operated.

(c) The computer room should be fitted with fire extinguishers and sprinklers to minimise the effect of fire.

(d) Emergency procedures should be tested regularly.

If fire does damage computer equipment the following precautions can minimise the damage.

(a) Regular back-up copies should be taken of files processed, and these should be held in fire-proof accommodation away from the computer room.

(b) A second computer in a different location within the company can be used as a back-up system if the main computer is damaged by fire.

(c) The company may enter maintenance and repair agreements to ensure back-up facilities are provided externally, and damage to the main computers can be quickly repaired.

Answer 10.3

Possible controls over small company computer systems include the following.

(a) Accounting controls such as batching and reconciliations can be used over input.

(b) Programmed procedures within the computer can ensure correctness of processing. Examples include check digits, sequence checks and hash totals.

(c) The computer can produce reports on changes to master files for example sales prices.

(d) The computer should also be able to produce exception reports of transactions requiring authorisation or investigation, in accordance with parameters set down by the organisation.

(e) Output should be checked for reasonableness.

(f) Standing data should be checked on a regular basis.

(g) File menus can be used to help users run programs in the correct sequence and for example prevent processing for a new period before the previous period was closed down.

(h) Password systems can be used to aid security. These should be confidential and subject to frequent change. The more sensitive the application, the more passwords should be required, operated in hierarchical systems.

(i) Physical security arrangements may also be used, for example physical controls by senior staff over vital programs.

(j) The software house used by the company should supply adequate systems documentation, training and prompt service if the systems break down.

(k) Proper back-up procedures should be in place. These include copying of hard disk files onto floppy disks, and storing the files offsite in secure accommodation.

(l) The information on the system should be regularly checked and out of date or inaccurate information deleted.

(m) Hardware should be maintained on a regular basis.

(n) Small companies should have contingency plans if the system does break down. These include additional computers and ability to process data manually.

Part D
Substantive testing

Chapter 11 Substantive testing: general considerations

Chapter topic list

1   Introduction

2   Designing substantive tests

3   Analytical procedures

4   Estimates

Learning objectives

On completion of this chapter you will be able to:

	Performance criteria	Range statement
• Use analytical review techniques including ratio analysis and prior year comparisons	17.1.5,17.1.7, 17.2.1-17.2.4	17.1.1-17.1.3, 17.2.1-17.2.3
• Explain how accounting estimates are audited	17.1.5,17.1.7, 17.2.1-17.2.4	17.1.1-17.1.3, 17.2.1-17.2.3

1 INTRODUCTION

1.1 Having looked at tests of control in detail, we now move onto **substantive testing**. In Chapters 12-15 we shall consider substantive testing in each of the major audit areas. In this chapter we recap the general principles of substantive testing and we consider two general auditing issues that affect substantive tests generally, analytical review and the audit of estimates.

1.2 **Analytical review** impacts upon the whole audit process. We mentioned briefly in Chapter 4 that auditors are required to carry out analytical procedures when **planning** an audit; this chapter goes into more detail. We then go on to discuss how substantive analytical review can provide **audit evidence**. Lastly analytical review is required at the final stage of the audit, as a key part of the **overall review** of the final accounts. The purpose of analytical review at this stage is to answer the question 'Do the figures make sense?'

1.3 We shall then examine **accounting estimates**. We have mentioned in previous chapters that judgement has to be used in accounting for several figures in the accounts. Often these judgements depend on uncertain future events - what percentage of outstanding debtors will fail to pay their debts, or for how much will stock which has been in the warehouse eventually sell. Since there may be a range of plausible answers to questions such as these, estimates can cause problems for auditors. We shall see that there are a number of possible ways in which estimates can be tested, and auditors will often wish to use a combination of procedures to obtain the required assurance.

2 DESIGNING SUBSTANTIVE TESTS

2.1 As we discussed earlier in this Text, substantive tests are designed to confirm the **completeness, accuracy** and **validity** of the items in the accounts or the accounting records. Tests are also carried out to confirm that there are **no material omissions** in the accounts or accounting records. Substantive tests will always be required even if all risks are assessed as low.

2.2 We stated in Chapter 5 that substantive tests are designed to obtain evidence relating to the financial statement assertions.

Activity 11.1

List the financial statement assertions.

2.3 Some of the financial statement assertions relate to assets and liabilities, some to transactions. In practice also some balance sheet assertions are more important for specific balance sheet items than others.

2.4 We also discussed in Chapter 5 the different types of tests auditors can use to obtain evidence. Consideration will be needed of how different tests can by themselves or in combination with other tests give the required level of assurance.

2.5 As we will see in the next section of this chapter, analytical review can be a significant substantive test.

2.6 Auditors should also consider the need to test individual items. **Sampling**, testing of a representative selection of individual items, is one way of doing this but it is not the only way. Auditors may in certain circumstances, be able to gain the assurance they require, by testing **all items over a certain amount**, or **testing key items**, items which are particularly prone to error.

2.7 Auditors should in any event **scrutinise all** areas of the accounts and the accounting records and investigate all unusual or suspicious items. This is a key test in particular in the areas of fraud and error, compliance with laws and regulations and related party transactions. We shall discuss these areas further in later chapters.

Activity 11.2

Complete the following table showing standard audit tests for each balance sheet objective.

Audit objective	*Typical audit tests*
Completeness	
Rights and obligations	
Valuation	
Existence	
Disclosure	

---

3   ANALYTICAL PROCEDURES

3.1 We defined analytical procedures briefly in Chapter 4 and this definition is reproduced below. SAS 410 *Analytical procedures* deals with the subject.

KEY TERM

Analytical procedures are the analysis of relationships:

(a) between items of financial data, or between items of financial and non-financial data, deriving from the same period; or

(b) between comparable financial information deriving from different periods to identify consistencies and predicted patterns or significant fluctuations and unexpected relationships, and the results of investigation thereof.

Nature and purpose of analytical procedures

3.2 The SAS states that analytical procedures include:

(a) The **consideration of comparisons** of this year's financial information with:

    (i) **Similar information** for **prior periods**

    (ii) **Anticipated results** of the client

    (iii) **Predictions** prepared by the auditors

    (iv) **Industry information,** such as a comparison of the client's ratio of sales to trade debtors with industry averages, or with the ratios relating to other entities of comparable size in the same industry

(b) Those between **elements of financial information** that are **expected to conform** to a predicted pattern based on experience, such as the relationship of gross profit to sales

(c) Those between **financial information** and **relevant non-financial information,** such as the relationship of payroll costs to number of employees

3.3 A variety of methods can be used to perform the procedures discussed above, ranging from **simple comparisons** to **complex analysis** using statistics, on a company level, branch level or individual account level. The choice of procedures is a matter for the auditors' professional judgement.

Analytical procedures in planning the audit

SAS 410.2

Auditors should apply analytical procedures at the planning stage to assist in understanding the entity's business, in identifying areas of potential audit risk and in planning the nature, timing and extent of other audit procedures.

3.4 Analytical procedures at the planning stage have to be seen in conjunction with risk analysis and materiality as means of identifying key audit areas.

3.5 Possible **sources of information** about the client include:

- Interim financial information
- Budgets
- Management accounts
- Non-financial information

- Bank and cash records
- VAT returns
- Board minutes
- Discussions or correspondence with the client at the year-end.

Auditors may also use specific industry information or general knowledge of current industry conditions to assess the client's performance.

3.6 As well as helping to determine the nature, timing and extent of other audit procedures, such analytical procedures may also indicate aspects of the business of which the auditors were previously unaware. Auditors are looking to see if developments in the client's business have had the expected effects. They will be particularly interested in changes in audit areas where problems have occurred in the past.

3.7 SAS 410 *Analytical procedures* states that auditors must decide whether using available analytical procedures as substantive procedures will be effective and efficient in reducing **detection risk** for specific financial statement assertions. Auditors may efficiently use analytical data produced by the entity itself, provided they are satisfied that it has been properly prepared.

3.8 The SAS lists a number of factors which the auditors should consider when deciding whether to use analytical procedures as substantive procedures.

Factors to consider	Example
Plausibility and predictability of the relationships identified for comparison and evaluation	The strong relationship between certain selling expenses and turnover in businesses where the sales force is paid by commission
Objectives of analytical procedures and extent to which their results are reliable	
Degree to which information can be **disaggregated**	Analytical procedures may be more effective when applied to financial information on individual sections of an operation such as individual factories or shops
Availability of information	Financial: budgets or forecasts
	Non-financial: eg the number of units produced or sold
Relevance of available information	Whether budgets are established as results to be expected rather than as tough targets (which may well not be achieved)
Comparability of available information	Comparisons with average performance in an industry may be of little value if a large number of businesses differ significantly from the average.
Knowledge gained during previous audits	The effectiveness of the accounting and internal control systems
	The types of problems giving rise to accounting adjustments in prior periods

Reliance on analytical procedures

3.9 From our earlier coverage of audit evidence we can see that the information used in analytical procedures will be more reliable if it comes from sources independent from, rather than internal to, the client. Information produced independently outside the accounting function is more reliable than that originating from within it. The results of **other audit procedures** will help to determine the reliability of the information used in analytical procedures, as will the importance of the results of the procedure for the auditors' opinion.

3.10 The SAS identifies other factors which should be considered when determining the reliance that the auditors should place on the results of substantive analytical procedures.

Reliability factors	Example
Other audit procedures directed towards the same financial statements assertions	Other procedures auditors undertake in reviewing the collectability of debtors, such as the review of subsequent cash receipts, may confirm or dispel questions arising from the application of analytical procedures to a profile of customers' accounts which lists for how long monies have been owed
The **accuracy** with which the expected results of analytical procedures can be predicted	Auditors normally expect greater consistency in comparing the relationship of gross profit to sales from one period to another than in comparing expenditure which may or may not be made within a period, such as research or advertising
The **frequency** with which a relationship is observed	A pattern repeated monthly as opposed to annually

3.11 Reliance on the results of analytical procedures depends on the auditors' assessment of the **risk** that the procedures may identify relationships (between data) do exist, whereas a material misstatement exists (ie the relationships, in fact, do not exist). It depends also on the **results of investigations** that auditors have made if substantive analytical procedures have highlighted significant fluctuations or unexpected relationships (see below).

Analytical review at the final stage

3.12 SAS 410 goes on to look at analytical procedures as part of the overall review when completing the audit. The key aim of procedures is to see whether the overall accounts appear reasonable.

> ### SAS 410.3
>
> When completing the audit, auditors should apply analytical procedures in forming an overall conclusion as to whether the financial statements as a whole are consistent with their knowledge of the entity's business.

3.13 The conclusions from these analytical procedures should be consistent with the conclusions formed from other audit procedures on parts of the financial statements. However, these analytical procedures may highlight areas which require further investigation and audit.

Investigating significant fluctuations or unexpected relationships

> ### SAS 410.4
>
> When significant fluctuations or unexpected relationships are identified that are inconsistent with other relevant information or that deviate from predicted patterns, auditors should investigate and obtain adequate explanations and appropriate corroborative evidence.

3.14 Investigations will start with **enquiries** to management and then **confirmation** of management's responses.

(a) By **comparing them** with the auditors' knowledge of the entity's business and with other evidence obtained during the course of the audit

(b) By **carrying out additional audit procedures** where appropriate to confirm the explanations received

3.15 If explanations cannot be given by management, or if they are insufficient, the auditors must determine which further audit procedures to undertake to explain the fluctuation or relationship.

Practical techniques

3.16 When carrying out analytical procedures, auditors should remember that every industry is different and each company within an industry differs in certain respects.

Important accounting ratios	Gross profit margin = $\dfrac{\text{Gross profit}}{\text{Turnover}} \times 100\%$
	This should be calculated in total and by product, area and month/quarter if possible.
	Debtors turnover period = $\dfrac{\text{Debtors}}{\text{Sales}} \times 365$
	Stock turnover ratio = $\dfrac{\text{Cost of sales}}{\text{Stock}}$
	Current ratio = $\dfrac{\text{Current assets}}{\text{Current liabilities}}$
	Quick or acid test ratio = $\dfrac{\text{Current assets (excluding stock)}}{\text{Current liabilities}}$
	Gearing ratio = $\dfrac{\text{Loans}}{\text{Share capital and reserves}} \times 100\%$
	Return on capital employed = $\dfrac{\text{Profit before tax}}{\text{Total assets - current - liabilities}}$
Significant items	Creditors and purchases
	Stocks and cost of sales
	Fixed assets and depreciation, repairs and maintenance expense
	Intangible assets and amortisation
	Loans and interest expense
	Investments and investment income
	Debtors and bad debt expense
	Debtors and sales

3.17 Ratios mean very little when used in isolation. They should be **calculated for previous periods** and for **comparable companies**. The permanent file should contain a section with summarised accounts and the chosen ratios for prior years.

3.18 In addition to looking at the more usual ratios the auditors should consider examining **other ratios** that may be **relevant** to the particular **clients' business,** such as revenue per passenger mile for an airline operator client, or fees per partner for a professional office.

3.19 One further important technique is to examine **important related accounts** in conjunction with each other. It is often the case that revenue and expense accounts are related to balance sheet accounts and comparisons should be made to ensure that the relationships are reasonable.

3.20 Other areas that might be investigated as part of the analytical procedures include the following.

- **Examine changes** in **products, customers and levels** of **returns**

- **Assess** the effect of **price and mix changes** on the cost of sales

- **Consider** the effect of **inflation, industrial disputes, changes in production methods** and **changes in activity** on the charge for wages

- **Obtain explanations** for all **major variances** analysed using a standard costing system. Particular attention should be paid to those relating to the over or under absorption of overheads since these may, inter alia, affect stock valuations

- **Compare trends in production and sales** and assess the effect on any provisions for obsolete stocks

- **Ensure** that **changes in the percentage labour or overhead content** of production costs are also reflected in the stock valuation

- **Review other profit and loss expenditure,** comparing:
  - Rent with annual rent per rental agreement
  - Rates with previous year and known rates increases
  - Interest payable on loans with outstanding balance and interest rate per loan agreement
  - Hire or leasing charges with annual rate per agreements
  - Vehicle running expenses to vehicles
  - Other items related to activity level with general price increase and change in relevant level of activity (for example telephone expenditure will increase disproportionately if export or import business increases)
  - Other items not related to activity level with general price increases (or specific increases if known)

- **Review** profit and loss account for **items** which may have been **omitted** (eg scrap sales, training levy, special contributions to pension fund, provisions for dilapidation etc).

- **Ensure expected variations** arising from the following have occurred:
  - Industry or local trends
  - Known disturbances of the trading pattern (for example strikes, depot closures, failure of suppliers)

3.21 Certain of the comparisons and ratios measuring liquidity and longer-term capital structure will assist in evaluating whether the company is a **going concern**, in addition to contributing to the overall view of the accounts. We shall see in Chapter 16, however, that there are factors other than declining ratios that may indicate going concern problems.

3.22 The working papers must contain the completed results of analytical procedures. They should include:

- The **outline programme** of the work
- The **summary of significant figures** and relationships for the period
- A **summary** of **comparisons made** with budgets and with previous years
- Details of all **significant fluctuations** or **unexpected relationships** considered
- Details of the **results of investigations** into such fluctuations/relationships
- The **audit conclusions** reached
- **Information considered necessary** for assisting in the planning of subsequent audits

DEVOLVED ASSESSMENT ALERT

In the devolved assessment you may be given a set of figures (as in Activity 11.4 below), and asked to calculate changes, key ratios etc. Hence you will have to identify significant areas of the accounts, and are likely to be asked what audit work will be required on these significant areas.

When analysing figures, make sure that the points which you make are consistent with each other.

Activity 11.3

(a) What are the purposes of analytical procedures?
(b) At what stages of the audit should and can analytical procedures be carried out?

Activity 11.4

The following information has been provided to you in advance of the finalisation of the audit for the year to 30 June 20X7 of Moony plc, a large sports goods and sportswear manufacturer.

PROFIT AND LOSS ACCOUNTS	20X7	20X6
	£'000	£'000
Turnover	62,200	51,000
Cost of sales	46,000	35,800
	16,200	15,200
Distribution costs*	6,650	6,500
Administration expenses*	4,400	4,350
	11,050	10,850
Trading profit	5,150	4,350
Interest paid	1,800	850
Profit before taxation	3,350	3,500
*Note. Depreciation included as part of these figures	4,950	4,400

BALANCE SHEETS	20X7	20X6
	£'000	£'000
Fixed assets	50,350	50,100
Current assets		
Stock	10,800	8,650
Debtors	9,150	5,200
	19,950	13,850
Current liabilities		
Trade creditors	5,750	5,400
Other creditors	1,200	1,000
Bank overdraft	3,600	2,050
	10,550	8,450
Net current assets	9,400	5,400
Total assets less current liabilities	59,750	55,500
Long-term loan (repayable 20X9)	15,600	12,800
	44,150	42,700
Share capital	5,000	5,000
Reserves	39,150	37,700
	44,150	42,700

Required

(a) Identify five matters which you consider require special attention when auditing the accounts of Moony plc.

(b) For each of these state why you consider them to be of importance.

4 ESTIMATES

4.1 SAS 420 *Audit of accounting estimates* provides guidance on the audit of accounting estimates contained in financial statements.

> **KEY TERM**
>
> An **accounting estimate** is an approximation of the amount of an item in the absence of a precise means of measurement.

4.2 SAS 420 gives these examples.

- Allowances to reduce stocks and debtors to their estimated realisable value
- Depreciation provisions
- Accrued revenue
- Provision for a loss from a lawsuit
- Profits or losses on construction contracts in progress
- Provision to meet warranty claims

4.3 **Directors and management** are responsible for making accounting estimates included in the financial statements. These estimates are often made in conditions of **uncertainty** regarding the outcome of events and involve the use of judgement. The risk of a material misstatement therefore increases when accounting estimates are involved (and thus inherent risk is higher). **Audit evidence** supporting accounting estimates is generally less than conclusive and so auditors need to exercise **significant judgement**.

The nature of accounting estimates

4.4 Accounting estimates may be produced as part of the routine operations of the accounting system, or may be a non-routine procedure at the period end. Where, as is frequently the case, a **formula** based on past experience is used to calculate the estimate, it should be reviewed regularly by management (eg actual vs estimate in prior periods).

Examples: nature of accounting estimates

From a routine operation: a warranty provision calculated automatically as a percentage of sales revenue.

From a non-routine operation: a provision for legal costs and damages payable in an impending legal dispute.

Using a standard formula: the use of standard rates for depreciating each category of fixed assets.

Audit procedures

SAS 420.2

Auditors should obtain sufficient appropriate evidence as to whether an accounting estimate is reasonable in the circumstances and, when required, is appropriately disclosed.

4.5 The auditors should gain an understanding of the procedures and methods used by management to make accounting estimates. This will aid the auditors' planning of their own procedures.

SAS 420.3

Auditors should adopt one or a combination of the following approaches in the audit of an accounting estimate:

(a) review and test the process used by management or the directors to develop the estimate;

(b) use an independent estimate for comparison with that prepared by management or the directors; or

(c) review subsequent events.

Review and testing the process

4.6 The auditors will carry out these steps.

- **Evaluate the data** and **consider the assumptions** on which the estimate is based
- **Test the calculations** involved in the estimate
- **Compare estimates** made for **prior periods** with **actual results** of those periods
- **Consider management's**/directors' **review and approval procedures**

Use of an independent estimate

4.7 Such an estimate (made or obtained by the auditors) may be compared with the accounting estimate. The auditors should **evaluate** the **data, consider** the **assumptions** and **test the**

calculation procedures used to develop the independent estimate. Prior period independent assessments and actual results could also be compared.

Review of subsequent events

4.8   The auditors should review transactions or events after the period end which may reduce or even remove the need to test accounting estimates (as described above).

Evaluation of results of audit procedures

> ### SAS 420.4
>
> Auditors should make a final assessment of the reasonableness of the accounting estimate based on their knowledge of the business and whether the estimate is consistent with other audit evidence obtained during the audit.

4.9   Auditors must assess the differences between the amount of an estimate supported by evidence and the estimate calculated by management. If the auditors believe that the difference is unreasonable then an adjustment should be made. If the directors or management refuse to revise the estimate, then the difference is considered a misstatement and will be treated as such.

Key learning points

- Substantive tests may include **testing of individual items** and **analytical procedures**. **Scrutiny tests** should always be carried out.

- **Analytical procedures** cover comparisons of financial data with other financial or non-financial data of the same or previous periods, also comparisons of financial data with expected data.

- Analytical procedures aim to **identify inconsistencies** or **significant fluctuations**.

- Analytical procedures must be undertaken at the **planning** stage of audits.

- Analytical procedures can be used as substantive procedures, depending on the **available information** and the plausibility and predictability of the relationships.

- Analytical review should be undertaken at the **final stage** of an audit on the final accounts.

- **Significant fluctuations** and **unexpected variations** should be investigated by enquiries of management, comparisons with other evidence and further audit procedures as required.

- Accounts may contain **accounting estimates** in a number of areas.

- Auditors can test accounting estimates by:

   - **Reviewing** and **testing** the management process
   - **Using an independent estimate**
   - **Reviewing subsequent events**

Quick quiz

1   Give four examples of information that can be compared with this year's financial information.

2   Give four examples of sources of information for analytical procedures at the planning stage.

3   According to SAS 410, what factors determine the reliance that auditors can place on analytical procedures.

4   What are:

(a) The current ratio
(b) The acid test ratio
(c) The return on capital employed

5   (a) What is an accounting estimate?
    (b) Give three examples of an accounting estimate.

6   When auditors are testing the process that management use to arrive at estimates what procedures should they undertake?

Answers to quick quiz

1   Examples include:

(a) Comparable information for prior periods
(b) Anticipated results
(c) Predictive estimates
(d) Industry information

2   Examples include:

(a) Interim financial information
(b) Budgets
(c) Management accounts
(d) Non-financial information
(e) Bank and cash records
(f) VAT returns
(g) Board minutes
(h) Discussions or correspondence with the client at the year end

3   The reliance auditors can place on substantive analytical procedures is determined by:

(a) Other audit procedures directed towards the same assertions
(b) The accuracy with which results can be predicted
(c) The frequency with which a relationship is observed

4   (a) $\text{Current ratio} = \dfrac{\text{Current assets}}{\text{Current liabilities}}$

(b) $\text{Acid test ratio} = \dfrac{\text{Current assets (excluding stock)}}{\text{Current liabilities}}$

(c) $\text{Return on capital employed} = \dfrac{\text{Profit before tax}}{\text{Total assets less current liabilities}}$

5   (a) An accounting estimate is an approximation of the amount of an item in the absence of a precise means of measurement.

(b) Examples of accounting estimates include:

(i)   Provisions against stocks and debtors
(ii)   Depreciation provisions
(iii) Accrued revenue
(iv)   Provision for loss from a lawsuit
(v)   Profits or losses on construction contracts in progress
(vi)   Provision to meet warranty claims

6   When testing the management process, auditors should:

(a) Evaluate the data and consider the assumptions on which the estimate is based.
(b) Test the calculations involved in the estimate.
(c) Compare estimates made in prior periods with actual results for those periods.
(d) Consider review and approval procedures.

Answers to activities

Answer 11.1

Existence. An asset or liability exists at a given date.

Rights and obligations. An asset or liability pertains to the entity at a given date.

Occurrence. A transaction or event took place which pertains to the entity during the relevant period.

Completeness. There are no unrecorded assets, liabilities, transactions or events, or undisclosed items.

Valuation. An asset or liability is recorded at an appropriate carrying value.

Measurement. A transaction or event is recorded in the proper amount and revenue or expense is allocated to the proper period.

Presentation and disclosure. An item is disclosed, classified and described in accordance with the applicable reporting framework (eg relevant legislation and applicable accounting standards).

You may also have included **accuracy**, that all assets, liabilities, transactions and events are recorded accurately.

Answer 11.2

Audit objective	Typical audit tests
Completeness	(1) Review of post balance sheet items (2) Cut off (3) Analytical review (4) Confirmations (5) Reconciliations to control account (6) Sequence checks
Rights and obligations	(1) Checking invoices for proof that item belongs to the company (2) Confirmations with third parties
Valuation	(1) Checking to invoices (2) Recalculation (3) Accounting policy consistent and reasonable (4) Review of post balance sheet payments and invoices
Existence	(1) Physical verification (2) Third party confirmations (3) Cut off testing
Disclosure	(1) Check compliance with CA 1985 and SSAPs and FRSs (2) True and fair override invoked

Answer 11.3

(a) Analytical procedures are used to identify relationships between financial data or between financial and non-financial data. Their purpose is to identify consistencies and patterns, or significant fluctuations and unexpected relationships. They assist in increasing auditors' understanding of a business and can be used to aid audit efficiency by highlighting risk areas and providing an alternative means of audit assurance to extensive sampling tests.

(b) Analytical procedures can be carried out:

(i)   At the planning stage of an audit, to ascertain which areas of the accounts require particular attention

(ii)   As a substantive test, to provide evidence for the various financial statement assertions

(iii) As part of the final review of the accounts, to see if the accounts are consistent with the auditors' knowledge of the business

Answer 11.4

(a) The matters which require special attention include (any five of) the following.

(i)   The increase in turnover by 22%
(ii)   The fall in gross profit percentage from 29.8% to 26.0%
(iii) The 18% increase in trading profit
(iv)   The reason why profit before taxation has fallen despite increased turnover
(v)   Fixed asset additions/revaluation amounting to a minimum £5.2 million
(vi)   The 25% increase in stock
(vii) The increase in debtor days from 37 days to 54 days
(viii) The 76% increase in bank overdraft
(ix)   The £2.8 million increase in long-term loan

(b) Each of the matters is important for the following reasons.

(i)   Turnover might be overstated as the result of including post year end sales. The same error could have understated stocks. Analysing sales on a monthly basis might reveal inconsistencies, for example unusually high sales in June 19X7 and unusually low sales in July 19X7.

(ii)   The gross profit percentage may have fallen due to changed trading conditions such as increased supplier prices, or a change in the company's pricing policy to boost turnover. There may however have been errors which have misstated purchases or stock.

(iii) The increase in trading profits suggests that distribution costs or administrative expenses may be incorrect. Distribution costs have only increased by 3% while turnover has increased by 22%. Normally, distribution costs would be expected to increase in line with turnover.

(iv)   Profit before taxation is affected by the further figure of interest paid. Interest paid could be over- or under-stated. Understatement could result from failing to accrue for all interest payable up to the year end.

(v)   All additions should be checked to ensure that cost has been correctly recorded, and that the additions have been authorised. If revaluations of fixed assets have taken place, it is important to check that the revaluations are reasonable.

(vi)   A misstatement in the stock valuation has a direct effect on profit. The large increase in stock could indicate overvaluation of stocks held. Increased stock levels alternatively suggest that there may be significant quantities of stock which cannot be sold (for example obsolete stock).

(vii) The rise in debtor days could indicate possible bad debts for which provision should be made. However, it will be more useful if debtor days were calculated using monthly sales figures: it may be that much of the increased turnover for 19X6/7 occurred in the final months of the year, in which case the debtors' collection position may not be as bad as our figures suggest.

(viii) The bank overdraft may have increased because of cash flow problems brought about by excessive purchases of stock or failure to collect money from debtors.

(ix)   The reasons for the increase in the loan should be ascertained. It may be due to increased investment in fixed assets, but it may be of concern if it has resulted from cash flow problems mentioned in (viii).

Chapter 12 Stocks and work in progress

Chapter topic list

Learning objectives

On completion of this chapter you will be able to:

	Performance criteria	Range statement
• Explain why auditors attend stocktake and describe auditing procedures at the stocktake	17.1.5, 17.1.7, 17.2.1-17.2.4	17.1.1-17.1.3, 17.2.1-17.2.3
• Explain the importance of cut-off and describe the procedures used to test cut-off	17.1.5, 17.1.7, 17.2.1-17.2.4	17.1.1-17.1.3, 17.2.1-17.2.3
• Describe the procedures for confirming stock valuation and identify the relevant disclosures required in the accounts	17.1.5, 17.1.7, 17.2.1-17.2.4	17.1.1-17.1.3, 17.2.1-17.2.3

1   INTRODUCTION

1.1   Stock causes more problems for auditors than any other audit area. As you will know from your accounting studies, closing stock appears on both the profit and loss account and balance sheet and often has a material effect on both. However stock does *not* form part of the double entry; hence it is not possible to find errors in stock as a result of finding errors in other areas. Stock errors can arise for a number of reasons.

1.2   Verifying the **existence** and **completeness** of stock can cause problems. Stock often is very portable and hence easy to steal. Companies face problems controlling stock because stock is often held in a number of different locations or is held by third parties.

1.3   Another very difficult aspect of stock is **stock valuation** for the following reasons:

   (a)   If a company sells a large number of different products, then stock will be made up of a large number of diverse items with different unit values.

   (b)   Different stock valuation methods are allowed under by the Companies Act and by SSAP 9 *Stocks and long term contracts* although they must be applied consistently.

   (c)   Stock does get damaged; other stock may be difficult to sell because fashions change or technology has moved on. The Companies Act requires stock to be written down to its ultimate selling price if that price is below the cost of the stock. However identifying stock which has selling price below cost is a subjective process and can prove difficult.

   (d)   Valuing work in progress can also be difficult. Its valuation depends on the state of completion it has reached; this may be quite difficult to gauge.

   (e)   For both stock and work in progress, valuation will include overheads, production overheads and other overheads attributable to bringing the product or service to its present location or condition. Which overheads constitute overheads attributable is again a subjective decision.

1.4   How should auditors view stock? They must understand how stock is **accounted for** and thus we summarise firstly in this chapter the relevant provisions of the Companies Act and SSAP 9.

1.5   The central audit procedure in auditing stock is **attending the stocktake.** Most companies carry out a stocktake at the year-end and auditors should aim to attend the stocktake. The reason for this is that the stocktake can provide evidence of completeness, existence, ownership and valuation (by observing the condition of stock).

1.6   Much audit time after the stocktake will be taken up checking the **valuation** of stock. This has several aspects. Partly it involves checking costs to invoices, and it also involves review of the absorption of overheads. Auditors may also have seen at the stocktake stock which appeared to be old or in poor condition, and will follow this up by reviewing post year end sales. General analytical procedures on stock are also important.

2   ACCOUNTING FOR STOCK

2.1   The rules surrounding the audit of stocks and the related reporting requirements come from three sources:

   (a)   Companies Act 1985 (disclosure and basis of valuation)

   (b)   SSAP 9 *Stocks and long-term contracts* (disclosure and valuation)

(c) The auditing standards and guidelines relating to the audit of stock (audit approach and valuation)

Companies Act 1985

2.2 The Companies Act 1985 lays out the format of the balance sheet and under stock in current assets the following headings must be used.

1 Raw materials and consumables
2 Work in progress
3 Finished goods and goods for resale
4 Payments on account

2.3 In terms of valuation, CA 1985 states that all current assets should be stated at the lower of their **purchase price** or production cost and their **net realisable value**. 'Purchase price' can be interpreted as 'fair value'. 'Production cost' is determined according to the provision of SSAP 9.

2.4 CA 1985 allows certain methods of identifying cost, because it recognises that it is impossible to identify cost for each item individually. The methods allowed are:

- First in first out (FIFO)
- Last in first out (LIFO)
- Weighted average cost
- Other similar methods

SSAP 9 does *not* allow last in first out (LIFO) as a method of valuation except on rare occasions.

SSAP 9 *Stocks and long-term contracts*

> ### KEY TERMS
>
> **Net realisable value** is the estimated or actual selling price (net of trade discounts but before settlement discounts) less all further costs to completion and all costs to be incurred in marketing, selling and distributing the good or service.
>
> **Cost** is that expenditure which has been incurred in the normal course of business in bringing the product or service to its present location and condition. This includes the purchase price plus production costs appropriate to the location and condition of the stock.

2.5 **Production costs** (costs of conversion) include:

(a) Costs specifically attributable to units of production

(b) Production overheads

(c) Other overheads attributable to bringing the product or service to its present location and condition

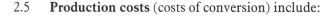

Activity 12.1

Why is the audit of stock and work-in-progress one of the most difficult areas of the audit?

BPP PUBLISHING

3   THE STOCKTAKE

RESPONSIBILITIES IN RELATION TO STOCK	
Management	Ensure stock figure in accounts: • Represents stock that **exists** • Includes all stock **owned** Ensure accounting records include **stocktaking statements**
Auditors	**Obtain sufficient audit evidence** about stock figure from: • Stock records • Stock control systems • Results of stocktaking • Test counts by auditors **Attend stocktaking if** stock is material and evidence of existence is provided by management stocktake

Methods of stocktaking

3.1   A business may take stock by one or a combination of the following methods.

(a)   **Stocktaking** at the **year-end**

From the viewpoint of the auditor, often the best method

(b)   **Stocktaking before** or **after** the **year-end**

Provides audit evidence of varying reliability depending on:

(i)   The **length of time** between the stocktake and the year-end; the greater the time period, the less the value of the stocktake as audit evidence

(ii)   The business's system of **internal controls**

(iii)   The **quality of records** of stock movements in the period between the stocktake and the year-end

(c)   **Continuous stocktaking** where management has a programme of stock-counting throughout the year

3.2   If continuous stocktaking is used, auditors will check that:

(a)   Management maintains **adequate stock records** that are kept up-to-date.

(b)   The client has **satisfactory procedures** for **stocktaking** and **test-counting**. Auditors should confirm the stocktaking instructions are as rigorous as those for a year-end stock-take. Crucially the auditors should confirm that all stock lines are counted at least once a year.

(c)   The client **investigates** and **corrects** all **material differences**.

Auditors should **attend one** of the **stock counts** (to observe and confirm that instructions are being adhered to). They should also **review** the **year's stock counts** to confirm the extent of counting, the treatment of discrepancies and the overall accuracy of records. If matters are not satisfactory, auditors will only be able to gain sufficient assurance by a full count at the year-end.

Work-in-progress

3.3 Evidence of the existence of work-in-progress should be obtained by **attending** a **stocktake,** or **reviewing management controls** over completeness and accuracy of accounting records and inspection of work-in-progress. (These procedures will be required if the nature of work-in-progress means that a stocktake is impractical.)

3.4 The auditors need to do this to gain assurance that the stock-checking system as a whole is effective in maintaining accurate stock records from which the amount of stocks in the financial statements can be derived.

The main stocktaking procedures

3.5 The following paragraphs set out the principal procedures which may be carried out by an auditors when attending a stocktake. Other procedures may also be appropriate.

PLANNING STOCKTAKE	
Gain knowledge	**Review** previous year's **arrangements**
	Discuss with **management stock-taking arrangements** and **significant changes**
Assess key factors	The **nature** and **volume** of the **stocks**
	The **identification** of **high value items**
	Method of accounting for stocks
	Location of stock and how it affects stock control and recording
	Internal control and **accounting systems** to identify potential areas of difficulty
Plan procedures	**Ensure** a **representative selection** of **locations, stocks** and **procedures** are covered
	Ensure sufficient attention is given to **high value items**
	Arrange to obtain from **third parties confirmation** of stocks they hold
	Consider the need for **expert help**

Review of stock-taking instructions

REVIEW OF STOCK-TAKING INSTRUCTIONS	
Organisation of count	**Supervision** by senior staff including senior staff not normally involved with stock
	Tidying and **marking** stock to help counting
	Restriction and **control** of the production process and stock movements during the count
	Identification of damaged, obsolete, slow-moving, third party and **returnable** stock
Counting	**Systematic counting** to ensure all stock is counted
	Teams of **two counters,** with one counting and the other checking or two **independent counts**
Recording	**Serial numbering, control** and **return** of all stock sheets
	Stock sheets being **completed** in **ink** and **signed**
	Information to be recorded on the **count records** (location and identity, count units, quantity counted, conditions of items, stage reached in production process)
	Recording of **quantity, conditions** and **stage of production** of **work-in-progress**
	Recording of last numbers of **goods inwards** and **outwards** records and of internal transfer records
	Reconciliation with **stock records** and **investigation** and correction of any **differences**

During the stocktaking

3.6 Key tasks during the stocktake are as follows.

- **Check** the **client's staff** are following instructions

- **Make test counts** to ensure procedures and internal controls are working properly

- Ensure that the **procedures** for **identifying damaged, obsolete** and **slow-moving** stock operate properly; the auditors should **obtain information** about the stocks' **condition, age, usage** and in the case of work in progress, its **stage of completion**

- Confirm that **stock held** on behalf of **third parties** is separately identified and accounted for

- Ensure that **proper account** is taken of **stock movements** during the stocktake, and noting the last numbers of stock documentation for cut-off purposes (see below)

- Conclude whether the **stocktaking** has been **properly carried out** and is sufficiently reliable as a basis for determining the existence of stocks

- Consider whether any **amendment** is necessary to subsequent **audit procedures**

3.7 When carrying out test counts the auditors should select items from the count records and from the physical stocks and check in both directions, to confirm the accuracy of the count records. The auditors should concentrate on high value stock. If the results of the test counts are not satisfactory, the auditors may request stock be recounted.

3.8 The auditors should conclude by trying to gain an **overall impression** of the levels and values of stocks held so that they may, in due course, judge whether the figure for stocks appearing in the financial statements is reasonable.

3.9 The auditors' working papers should include:

- Details of their **observations** and **tests**

- The manner in which **points** that are **relevant** and **material** to the stocks being counted or measured have been dealt with by the client

- Instances where the **client's procedures** have **not been satisfactorily carried out**

- **Items for subsequent testing**, such as photocopies of rough stocksheets

- **Details** of the **sequence** of **stocksheets**

- The **auditors' conclusions**

After the stocktaking

3.10 After the stocktaking, the matters recorded in the auditors' working papers at the time of the count or measurement should be followed up.

3.11 Key tests include the following.

- **Trace items** that were **test counted** during the stocktake to final stocksheets

- **Check all count** records have been **included** in final stocksheets

- **Check final stocksheets** are **supported by** count records

- **Ensure** that **continuous stock records** have been **adjusted** to the amounts physically counted or measured, and that differences have been investigated

- **Confirm cut-off** by using details of the last serial number of goods inwards and outwards notes; and of movements during the stocktake (see below)

- **Check replies** from **third parties** about stock held by or for them

- **Confirm** the client's final **valuation** of stock has been calculated correctly

- **Follow up queries** and **notifying problems** to management

---

Activity 12.2

How can stocktaking instructions ensure that stock is counted completely and accurately?

Activity 12.3

What planning procedures should auditors undertake when planning attendance at a stock-take?

---

4 STOCK CUT-OFF

4.1 Auditors should consider whether management has instituted adequate cut-off procedures: procedures intended to ensure that movements into, within and out of stocks are properly identified and reflected in the accounting records in the **correct accounting period**.

4.2 Cut-off is most critical to the accurate recording of transactions in a manufacturing enterprise at particular points in the accounting cycle.

- **Point of purchase** and **receipt** of **goods** and **services**
- **Requisitioning** of **raw materials** for production
- **Transfer** of **completed work-in-progress** to **finished goods stocks**
- **Sale** and **despatch** of **finished goods**

4.3 Purchase invoices should be recorded as liabilities only if the goods were received *prior* to the stock count. A schedule of 'goods received not invoiced' should be prepared, and items on the list should be accrued for in the accounts.

4.4 Sales cut-off is generally more straightforward to achieve correctly than purchases cut-off. Invoices for goods despatched after the stock count should not appear in the profit and loss accounts for the period.

4.5 Prior to the stock-take management should make arrangements for cut-off to be properly applied.

(a) **Appropriate systems of recording** of receipts and despatches of goods should be in place, and also a system for documenting materials requisitions. Goods received notes (GRNs) and goods despatched notes (GDNs) should be sequentially pre-numbered.

(b) **Final GRN and GDN** and **materials requisition numbers should be noted**. These numbers can then be used to check subsequently that purchases and sales have been recorded in the current period.

(c) **Arrangements** should be made to ensure that the **cut-off arrangement** for stock held by **third parties** are satisfactory.

4.6 There should ideally be no movement of stocks during the stock count. Preferably, receipts and despatches should be suspended for the full period of the count. It may not be practicable to suspend all deliveries, in which case any deliveries which are received during the count should be segregated from other stocks and carefully documented.

Audit procedures on cut-off

4.7 At the stocktake the auditors should carry out the following procedures.

- **Record all movement notes** relating to the period, including:
  - All interdepartmental requisition numbers
  - The last goods received notes(s) and despatch note(s) prior to the count
  - The first goods received notes(s) and despatch note(s) after the count

- **Observe** whether correct cut-off procedures are being followed in the despatch and receiving areas

- **Discuss procedures** with company staff performing the count to ensure they are understood

- **Ensure** that **no goods finished** on the day of the count are **transferred** to the warehouse

4.8 During the final audit, the auditors will use the cut-off information from the stocktake to perform the following tests.

- **Match up** the last **goods received notes** with **purchase invoices** and ensure the **liability** has been **recorded** in the **correct period** (Only goods received before the year end should be recorded as purchases)

- **Match up** the last **goods despatched notes** to **sales invoices** and ensure the **income** has been **recorded** in the **correct period** (Only stocks despatched before the year-end should be recorded as sales)

- **Match up** the **requisition notes** to the **work in progress** details for the receiving department to ensure correctly recorded

5   VALUATION OF STOCK

Assessment of cost and net realisable value

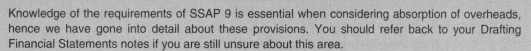

DEVOLVED ASSESSMENT ALERT

You must know the audit work needed to confirm valuation of stock is correct and consistent when overheads have been absorbed, and to confirm stocks that are excess, slow-moving, obsolete or defective are reduced to net realisable value.

Knowledge of the requirements of SSAP 9 is essential when considering absorption of overheads, hence we have gone into detail about these provisions. You should refer back to your Drafting Financial Statements notes if you are still unsure about this area.

5.1   Auditors must understand how the company determines the cost of an item for stock valuation purposes. Cost, for this purpose, should include an appropriate proportion of overheads, in accordance with SSAP 9.

5.2   There are several ways of determining cost. Auditors must ensure that the company is **applying** the method **consistently** and that each year the method used **gives** a **fair approximation** to cost. They may need to support this by additional procedures.

- **Reviewing price changes** near the year-end
- **Ageing the stock** held
- **Checking gross profit margins** to reliable management accounts

Valuation of raw materials and brought in components

5.3   The auditors should check that the correct prices have been used to value raw materials and brought in components valued at actual costs, by **referring** to **suppliers' invoices**. Reference to suppliers' invoices will also provide the auditors with assurance as regards ownership.

5.4   If standard costs are used, auditors should **check** the **basis** of the **standards, compare standard costs** with **actual costs** and **confirm** that **variances** are being **accounted for appropriately.**

Valuation of work in progress and finished goods
(other than long-term contract work in progress)

5.5   As we saw above, SSAP 9 defines 'cost' as comprising the cost of purchase plus the costS of conversion (production costs). The costs of conversion comprise:

- Costs **specifically attributable** to units of production

- **Production overheads**

- Other **overheads attributable** to bringing the product or service to its present **location and condition**

Audit procedures

5.6   The audit procedures will depend on the methods used by the client to value work in progress and finished goods, and on the adequacy of the system of internal control.

Reasonableness tests

5.7   The auditors should consider what tests they can carry out to check the reasonableness of the valuation of finished goods and work in progress. **Analytical procedures** may assist comparisons being made with stock items and stock categories from the previous year's stock summaries. A **reasonableness check** will also provide the auditors with **assurance** regarding **completeness**.

Costs attributable to production

5.8   The auditors should carry out the following tests.

- For materials:
    ○ **Check costs being used** to **invoices** and **price lists**
    ○ **Confirm appropriate basis** of **valuation** (eg FIFO) is being used
    ○ **Confirm correct quantities** are being used when calculating raw material value in work in progress and finished goods

- For labour costs:
    ○ **Check labour costs** to **wage records**
    ○ **Check labour hours** to **time summaries** and production reports
    ○ **Review standard labour costs** in the light of actual costs and production

Overhead allocation

5.9   The auditors should ensure that the client includes a proportion of overheads **appropriate** to **bringing** the **stock** to its **present location** and **condition**. The basis of overhead allocation should be **consistent** with **prior years** and **calculated** on the **normal level** of **production activity**.

5.10   Thus, overheads arising from **reduced levels** of **activity, idle time** or **inefficient production should be written off** to the profit and loss account, rather than being included in stock.

5.11   In an appendix to SSAP 9 there is general guidance on the allocation of overheads which the auditors should follow. SSAP 9 comments that auditors should note that overheads are **classified by function** when being allocated (eg whether they are a function of production, marketing, selling or administration).

(a)   All **abnormal conversion** costs (such as idle capacity) must be **excluded**.

(b)   Where **firm sales contracts** have been entered into for the provision of goods or services to customer's specification, **design, marketing and selling costs** incurred before manufacture may be **included**.

(c)   The costs of **general management**, as distinct from functional management, are not directly related to current production and are, therefore, **excluded**.

(d) The allocation of costs of **central service departments** should depend on the function or functions that the department is serving. **Only** those costs that can reasonably be allocated to the **production function** should be **included**.

(e) In determining what constitutes 'normal' activity, a number of factors need to be considered:

    (i) The **volume of production** which the **production facilities** are **designed** to achieve

    (ii) The **budgeted level of activity** for the **year** under review and for the **ensuing year**

    (iii) The **level of activity achieved** both in the **year** under review and in **previous years**

    Although temporary changes in the load of activity may be ignored, persistent variation should lead to revision of the previous norm.

5.12 Difficulty may be experienced if the client operates a system of total overhead absorption. It will be necessary for those overheads that are of a general, non-productive nature to be identified and excluded from the stock valuation.

Cost vs Net Realisable Value

5.13 Auditors should **compare cost and net realisable value** for each item of stock of all types - raw materials, work in progress and finished goods. Where this is impracticable, the comparison may be done by stock group or category.

5.14 Net realisable value is likely to be less than cost when there has been:

- An **increase in costs** or a fall in selling price
- **Physical deterioration** of stocks
- **Obsolescence** of products due for example to changes in technology
- A **decision** as part of a company's **marketing strategy** to sell products at a loss
- **Errors in production** or **purchasing**

5.15 The following audit tests are important.

- **Review and test the client's system** for **identifying slow-moving, obsolete** or **damaged stock**

- **Follow up** any such **items** that were **identified** at the **stocktaking,** ensuring that the client has made adequate provision to write down the items to net realisable value

- **Examine stock records** to identify slow-moving items; it may be possible to incorporate into a computer audit program certain tests and checks such as listing items whose value or quantity has not moved over the previous year

- **Examine the prices** at which finished goods have been sold after the year-end and ascertain whether any finished goods items need to be reduced below cost

- **Review quantities of goods sold after the year end** to determine that year end stock has, or will be, realised

- If significant quantities of finished goods stock remain unsold for an unusual time after the year-end, **consider** the **need** to make **appropriate provision**

5.16 For work in progress, the **ultimate selling price** should be **compared** with the **carrying value** at the year end plus **costs to be incurred** after the year end to bring work in progress to a finished state.

Activity 12.4

(a) What types of stock might be valued at less than cost?

(b) What audit work would you carry out to find stock that should be carried at net realisable value, and to confirm the value at which that stock should be carried?

Activity 12.5

What general analytical procedures can be applied to test whether the valuation of stock is reasonable?

Activity 12.6

What are the major tasks auditors should carry out:

(a) During a stocktake
(b) After a stocktake

Key learning points

- The audit of stocks and work in progress is difficult and time consuming, because of problems of control over stock (affecting **existence and cut-off**) and **problems over valuation**.

- The **valuation** and **disclosure** rules for stock are laid down in SSAP 9 and CA 1985.

- An old APC guideline on the auditors' attendance at the stocktake still demonstrates best practice.

- Stocktake procedures are vital as they provide evidence which cannot be obtained elsewhere or at any other time about the quantities and conditions of stocks and work in progress.

  ° Before the stocktake auditors should ensure audit **coverage** of **stock-taking** is **appropriate**, and that the client's **stock-taking instructions** have been reviewed.

  ° During the stocktake the auditors should **check the stock count** is being carried out according to instructions, carry out **test counts**, and watch for **third party, slow moving stock, cut-off problems.**

  ° After the stocktake the auditors should check that **final stock sheets** have been **properly compiled** from stock count records and that **book stock records** have been **appropriately adjusted**.

- Auditors should check **cut-off** by noting the **serial numbers** of items received and despatched just before and after the year-end, and subsequently checking that they have been included in the correct period.

- Auditing the valuation of stock includes:

  ° Checking the **allocation of overheads** is appropriate
  ° Confirming stock is carried at the lower of **cost** and **net realisable value**

Quick quiz

1   Under what headings does the Companies Act 1985 require stock to be classified?

2   What methods of identifying cost of stock does the Companies Act allow to be used? Which method is not allowed by SSAP 9?

3   How does SSAP 9 define net realisable value?

4   What factors determine the reliability of an annual stocktake which takes place other than at the year-end?

5   What should auditors include in their working papers concerning the work that they have carried out at a stock-take?

6   At what points of the accounting cycle is cut-off of most importance?

7   What tests should auditors carry out to check the valuation of raw materials and brought in components which are valued at actual cost?

8   How should auditors test whether work-in-progress is being carried at the lower of cost and net realisable value?

Answers to quick quiz

1   Companies Act 1985 prescribes the following headings.

(a)   Raw materials and consumables
(b)   Work in progress
(c)   Finished goods and goods for resale
(d)   Payments on account

2   Companies Act 1985 allows the following methods of stock valuation to be used.

(a)   First in first out (FIFO)
(b)   Last in first out (LIFO) (not allowed by SSAP 9)
(c)   Weighted average cost
(d)   Other similar methods

3   SSAP 9 defines net realisable value as the estimated or actual selling price, net of trade discounts but before settlement discounts less all further costs to completion and all costs to be incurred in marketing, selling or distributing the good or service.

4   The factors which determine the reliability of a stocktake other than at the year-end are

(a)   The length of time between the stock-take and the year-end
(b)   The internal control system
(c)   The quality of stock movement records

5   Auditors' working papers should include:

(a)   Details of their observations and tests
(b)   How the client has dealt with material points
(c)   Instances where client procedures have not been carried out satisfactorily
(d)   Items for subsequent testing
(e)   Details of the sequence of stocksheets
(f)   The auditors' conclusions

6   Stock cut-off is particularly important at the following points of the cycle.

(a)   The point of purchase and receipt of goods and services
(b)   The requisitioning of raw materials for production
(c)   The transfer of completed work-in-progress to finished goods stocks
(d)   The sale and despatch of finished goods

7   Auditors should check that raw materials and brought in components are valued at actual cost by referring to suppliers' invoices.

8   For work-in-progress, auditors should compare the ultimate selling price with the carrying value at the year-end plus costs to be incurred after the year-end to bring work-in-progress to a finished state.

Answers to activities

Answer 12.1

Stock can pose auditors particular problems for the following reasons.

(a) Closing stock does not normally form part of the double entry bookkeeping system; thus a misstatement cannot be detected by finding corresponding errors in other audit areas.

(b) Stock existence must generally be verified by attendance at stocktake and follow-up procedures.

(c) Control over stocktaking can be difficult to achieve if it is taking place in a number of locations.

(d) Cut-off may be difficult to test because it may be necessary to move stock during the stock-take.

(e) Valuation of stock can be difficult for a number of reasons.

   (i) Stock is often made up of a large number of different items.

   (ii) The Companies Act and SSAP 9 allow a variety of methods to be used to value stock.

   (iii) The allocation of overheads which is required by Companies Act and SSAP 9 is a subjective process.

   (iv) Assessment of the valuation of work-in-progress depends on assessment of its state of completion, which is generally subjective.

   (v) Assessment of the valuation of slow-moving, obsolete and damaged stock is also subjective.

Answer 12.2

If instructions are to ensure stock is counted completely and accurately, they must be clear, and include the following features.

(a) Someone, preferably someone not normally responsible for stock, should supervise the count and deal with queries.

(b) Stock should be tidied and laid out in an orderly manner.

(c) All stock should be clearly identified.

(d) Goods received on the day of the stocktake should be physically segregated until the count has been completed.

(e) Goods due to be despatched to customers or issued internally on the day should be separately identified so that they are not included in stock.

(f) Records should be kept of goods received or issued during the day.

(g) Prenumbered stock sheets should be issued to counters.

(h) Counters should be given responsibility for a specific area.

(i) All stock should be marked after being counted so that it is evident it has been counted.

(j) Each area should be subject to a recount.

(k) One of the counts should be by someone who is not normally responsible for stock.

(l) All stock sheets should be accounted for at the end of the audit.

Answer 12.3

In planning attendance at a stocktake the auditors should carry out the following tests

(a) Review previous year's audit working papers and discuss any developments in the year with management.

(b) Obtain and review a copy of the company's stocktaking instructions.

(c) Arrange attendance at stockcount planning meetings, with the consent of management.

(d) Gain an understanding of the nature of the stock and of any special stocktaking problems this is likely to present, for example liquid in tanks, scrap in piles.

(e) Consider whether expert involvement is likely to be required as a result of any circumstances noted in (d) above.

(f) Obtain a full list of all locations at which stock is held, including an estimate of the amount and value of stock held at different locations.

(g) Using the results of the above steps, plan for audit attendance by appropriately experienced audit staff at all locations where material stocks are held, subject to other factors (for example rotational auditing, reliance on internal controls).

(h) Consider the impact of internal controls upon the nature and timing of the stocktaking attendance.

(i) Ascertain whether stocks are held by third parties and if so make arrangements to obtain written confirmation of them or, if necessary, to attend the stocktake of them.

Answer 12.4

(a) Stock which may be worth less than cost will include:

   (i)   Slow moving stock
   (ii) Obsolete or superseded stock
   (iii) Seconds stock and items that have been damaged
   (iv) Stock which is being, or is soon likely to be, sold at reduced prices
   (v)   Discontinued stock lines

(b) (i) To identify stock which may be worth less than cost the following work will be carried out.

   (1) Examine the computerised stock control system and list items showing an unacceptably low turnover rate. An unacceptable rate of turnover may be different for different items, but stock representing more than six months' sales is likely to qualify.

   (2) Check the stock printout for items already described as seconds or recorded as damaged.

   (3) Discuss with management the current position regarding slow moving stock and their plans and expectations in respect of products that may be discontinued. The standard system must be carefully considered and estimates obtained of the likely selling price of existing stock. The most likely outcome regarding the use and value of discontinued components must be decided.

   (4) At the stocktake, look for stock which is dusty, inaccessible and in general not moving and mark on the stock sheets.

   (5) Find out whether any lines are unreliable and therefore frequently returned for repairs as these may be unpopular.

   (6) Check with the trade press or other sources to see whether any of the equipment is out of date.

   (ii) To determine the net realisable value of the stock the following tests should be carried out.

   (1) Find the actual selling prices from the latest sales invoice. For items still selling, invoices will be very recent, but for slow moving and obsolete items the invoiced prices will be out of date and allowance will have to be made for this (probably a reduction in estimating the most likely sale price of the stock concerned).

   (2) Estimate the value of marketing, selling and distribution expenses using past figures for the types of finished goods concerned as a base. I would update and check for reasonableness against the most recent accounting records.

   (3) Discuss with management what selling prices are likely to be where there is little past evidence. Costs to completion will be questioned where these are difficult to estimate and where there are any unusual assembly, selling or distribution problems.

   (4) Discuss any large differences between auditor estimation of net realisable value and management estimation, and consider the basis for the company's estimates.

   (5) Value any damaged stock at zero since it is unlikely to fetch any money.

   (6) Conclude line by line what stock ought to be carried at cost, and what at net realisable value.

Answer 12.5

The figures calculated should be broken down as far as possible, by product or by location. Comparisons that can be made include the following.

(a) Comparisons of stock ratios with previous years; these include gross profit margins and stock turnover

(b) Comparisons of values of stock held with previous years

(c) Comparisons of quantities of stock held with previous years

(d) Comparisons of stock provisions, both in absolute terms and as a percentage of stock held; auditors should consider whether provisions made in previous years were excessive or insufficient

(e) Comparisons of costings with previous years, auditors should consider unit stock prices, also percentage of material, labour and overhead in production costs

(f) If standard costing is used, auditors should ascertain the reasons for changes in standards and also significant variances

(g) Comparisons of selling prices to those charged elsewhere

Auditors should consider levels and costs of stock held in the light of what they know about what is happening in the industry. In particular auditors might have to consider the effect of new technology and new fashions, and hence the possible risk of stock obsolescence.

Answer 12.6

(a) During a stocktake the auditors should carry out the following procedures.

(i) Check that the client's staff are following instructions. If auditors see a breach of instructions for example client staff counting stock together when one should be counting and one checking, they should draw this to the attention of whoever is supervising the stock count.

(ii) Make test counts. Auditors should compare count records with actual stock and vice versa, concentrating on high value stock. If the results of these are not satisfactory, auditors may have to request the stock to be recounted.

(iii) Ensure that the procedures for identifying damaged, obsolete and slow-moving stock are operating. Auditors should record details of stock likely to be valued at lower than cost including condition, age and usage.

(iv) Ensure that stock held on behalf of third parties is separately identified and accounted for.

(v) Ensure that proper account is taken of stock movements during the stock-take, and noting the last numbers of stock documentation for cut-off purposes.

(vi) Conclude whether the stock-take provides sufficient evidence of the existence of stocks.

(vii) Consider whether any amendment is necessary to subsequent audit procedures.

(viii) Gain an overall impression of the valuation of stock.

(b) After the stocktake, auditors should carry out the following tests.

(i) Trace items that were test counted during the stock count to the final stock sheets.

(ii) Check all count records have been included in the final stock sheets.

(iii) Check final stock sheets are supported by count records.

(iv) Ensure that book stock records have been adjusted to reflect actual stock counted, and differences have been investigated.

(v) Confirm cut-off by checking correct treatment of last goods inwards and outwards before the stock-take, and first goods inwards and outwards after the stock-take. Auditors should also check that stock movements during the stock-take have been treated correctly.

(vi) Check confirmations by third parties of stock held by them.

(vii) Discuss queries and problems with management.

(viii) Conclude whether the final valuation of stock has been calculated correctly.

Chapter 13 Fixed assets

Chapter topic list

Learning objectives

On completion of this chapter you will be able to:

	Performance criteria	Range statement
• Describe the procedures used to audit tangible fixed assets, intangible fixed assets and investments	17.1.5, 17.1.7, 17.2.1-17.2.4	17.1.1-17.1.3, 17.2.1-17.2.3

1 INTRODUCTION

1.1 In this chapter we discuss the audit of fixed assets, which may include intangible and tangible fixed assets and also investments.

1.2 We shall concentrate first on **tangible fixed assets** such as land and buildings, plant and machinery and motor vehicles. These will be the major items that many companies own, and hence the figure for tangible fixed assets is likely to be very material in the accounts. That said, the major tangible fixed assets tend to be few in number, so that not many items have to be tested in order to gain assurance about a large proportion of the amount shown.

1.3 Assertions of particular significance for tangible fixed assets are **rights and obligations** (ie ownership), **existence and valuation**. Different tests will be needed on ownership and existence. Although ownership may be verified by inspecting appropriate documentation (for example land deeds or vehicle registration documents) those documents do not guarantee that the asset still exists. Physical inspection of the asset may be required to prove existence.

1.4 Valuation is the other important assertion generally. The auditors will concentrate on **testing** any **valuations** made **during the year**, and also whether asset values appear reasonable given asset usage and condition. A very important aspect of testing valuation is **reviewing depreciation rates**. Auditors should check that the rates used appear reasonable and are consistently applied from year to year.

1.5 Fewer companies have **intangible fixed assets**. These include patents, trademarks, goodwill and research and development. Many are capitalised because of **expectations** management has about the **future income** they will yield, so auditors will need to consider whether those **expectations** appear to be **reasonable**. There are specific accounting standards on research and development and goodwill, so auditors will need to confirm that the requirements of these standards have been followed.

1.6 We shall lastly consider **investments**. Gaining sufficient assurance concerning the client's **ownership** of investments can be a particular problem in this area.

1.7 Two topics which we covered in earlier chapters may well be important in the audit of fixed assets, using the work of an expert and the usefulness of third party confirmations. You should refer back to your notes in these subjects.

1.8 You may be asked in the devolved assessment about the audit work required on fixed assets, or whether a proposed accounting treatment is acceptable.

2 TANGIBLE FIXED ASSETS

Internal control considerations

2.1 As we have seen, a key element of a good internal control system is a **fixed asset register**, which should help identify assets. In any event auditors should record movements in fixed assets in their working papers.

2.2 Auditors should also ensure that the company has good controls over substantial asset expenditure and disposals.

Activity 13.1

What do you think the auditors can do if a company does not maintain a fixed asset register?

Summary of audit procedures

> **DEVOLVED ASSESSMENT ALERT**
>
> You should know how to audit certain aspects of tangible fixed assets (such as valuation). In the assessment you may be given a specific example and asked what audit work you would carry out (for example, X Limited has revalued its properties by £40,000 this year using a valuation by a director).

2.3 Completeness

- **Obtain** or **prepare** a **summary** of tangible fixed assets showing:

  ° **Gross book value**
  ° **Accumulated depreciation**
  ° Net **book value**

  and **reconcile** with the **opening position**

- **Compare fixed assets** in the general ledger with the **fixed assets register** and **obtain explanations** for **differences**

- **Check** whether **assets** which **physically exist** are **recorded** in the **fixed asset register**

- If a fixed asset register is not kept, **obtain** a **schedule** showing the original costs and present depreciated value of major fixed assets

- **Reconcile** the **schedule** of fixed assets with the **general ledger**

Existence

- **Confirm** that the **company physically inspects** all items in the fixed asset register each year

- **Inspect assets,** concentrating on high value items and additions in year. Confirm items inspected:

  ° Exist
  ° Are in use
  ° Are in good condition

- **Review records** of **income yielding assets** to see whether **all income** has been received

- **Reconcile** opening and closing **vehicles** by numbers as well as amounts

Valuation

- **Verify valuation** to valuation certificate

- **Consider reasonableness** of **valuation**, reviewing:

  ° Experience of valuer
  ° Scope of work
  ° Methods and assumption used

- **Check revaluation surplus** has been **correctly calculated**

- **Consider** whether **permanent diminution** in value of assets has occurred

Ownership

- **Verify title** to land and buildings by inspection of:
  - ○ Title deeds
  - ○ Land registry certificates
  - ○ Leases

- Obtain a certificate from solicitors/bankers:
  - ○ **Stating purpose** for which the deeds are being held (custody only)
  - ○ **Stating deeds** are **free** from **mortgage** or **lien**

- **Inspect registration documents** for vehicles held

- **Confirm** all vehicles used for the **client's business**

- **Examine documents** of **title** for other assets (including purchase invoices, architects' certificates, contracts, hire purchase or lease agreements)

Additions (to confirm rights and obligations, valuation and completeness)

- **Verify purchase price of additions** by inspection of architects' certificates, solicitors' completion statements, suppliers' invoices etc.

- **Check capitalisation** of **expenditure** is correct by considering for fixed assets additions and items in relevant expense categories (repairs, motor expenses, sundry expenses) whether:
  - ○ Capital/revenue distinction correctly drawn
  - ○ Capitalisation in line with consistently applied company policy

- Check **purchases** have been **properly allocated** to correct fixed asset accounts

- **Check purchases** have been **authorised** by directors/senior management

- **Ensure** that appropriate **claims** have been made for **grants**, and grants received and receivable have been received

- **Check additions** have been **recorded** in fixed asset register and general ledger

Self-constructed assets

- **Verify material** and **labour** costs and **overheads** to invoices, wage records etc.

- **Ensure expenditure** has been **analysed correctly** and **properly charged** to capital

- **Check no profit element** has been included in costs

Disposals (to confirm rights and obligations, valuation and completeness)

- **Verify disposals** with supporting documentation, checking transfer of title, sales price and dates of completion and payment

- **Check calculation** of profit or loss

- **Check** that **disposals** have been **authorised**

- **Consider** whether **proceeds** are **reasonable**

- If the property was **used as security**, ensure **release from security** has been correctly made

- For **significant disposals**, consider impact upon other areas of business and whether disposal should be disclosed under FRS 3

Depreciation

- **Review depreciation rates** applied in relation to:
  - ° Asset lives
  - ° Replacement policy
  - ° Past experience of gains and losses on disposal
  - ° Consistency with prior years and accounting policy
  - ° Possible obsolescence

- Check **depreciation** has been **charged on all** assets with a limited useful life

- For **revalued assets,** ensure that the charge for **depreciation** is **based** on the **revalued amount**

- **Check calculation** of depreciation rates

- **Compare ratios** of depreciation to fixed assets (by category) with:
  - ° Previous years
  - ° Depreciation policy rates

- **Ensure no further depreciation** provided on **fully depreciated assets**

- **Check** that **depreciation policies and rates are disclosed** in the accounts

Charges and commitments

- **Review for evidence** of charges in statutory books and by company search

- **Review leases** of leasehold properties to ensure that company has fulfilled covenants set out in the leases

- **Examine invoices received after year-end, orders and minutes** for evidence of capital commitments

Insurance

- **Review insurance policies** in force for all categories of tangible fixed assets and consider the adequacy of their insured values and check expiry dates

DEVOLVED ASSESSMENT ALERT

You may need to consider whether the rates used in specific circumstances are reasonable.

Activity 13.2

The following material items have been included in the fixed asset note of the year-end accounts of Growler Ltd. Explain the audit tests you would carry out on them.

(a) Plant and machinery additions of £80,000.
(b) A depreciation charge of £15,000 for motor vehicles.

Activity 13.3

You are the audit manager in charge of the audit of Freddo Ltd. The audit senior has contacted you with a number of problems he has encountered when considering the audit of fixed assets.

(a) The client has stated that the motor vehicles the senior wished to inspect cannot be inspected, as they are all being driven by salesmen who are not due to return to office until after the accounts are signed.

(b) The client has capitalised furniture in its new office block, although furniture has not previously been capitalised. The furniture has an expected life of three years.

(c) A large crane, previously written off by the client has been brought back into use at a valuation of £10,000 because of problems with its replacements. The £10,000 has been included as a re-valuation in this year's accounts.

Task

Outline the audit work that should be carried out in the light of the problems found.

---

3 INTANGIBLE FIXED ASSETS

3.1 The types of asset we are likely to encounter under this heading include patents, licences, trade marks, development costs and goodwill. All intangibles have a finite economic life and should hence be amortised.

Tests on intangible assets

3.2 General

- **Prepare analysis** of movements on cost and amortisation accounts

Ownership

- **Obtain confirmation** of all **patents** and **trademarks** held by a patent agent
- **Verify payment** of **annual renewal fees**

Valuation

- **Review specialist valuations** of intangible assets, considering:
  - ° Qualifications of valuer
  - ° Scope of work
  - ° Assumptions and methods used

- **Confirm carried down balances** represent **continuing value**, which are proper charges to future operations.

Additions

- **Inspect purchase agreements, assignments** and **supporting documentation** for purchase prices of intangible assets acquired in period
- **Confirm purchases** have been **authorised**
- **Verify amounts capitalised** of patents developed by the company with supporting costing records

Amortisation

- **Review amortisation**
  - ° Check computation
  - ° Confirm that rates used are reasonable

Income from intangibles

- **Review sales returns** and **statistics** to verify the reasonableness of income derived from patents, trademarks, licences etc.

- **Examine audited accounts** of third party sales covered by a patent, licence or trademark owned by the company

226

Goodwill

3.3 Key tests are as follows.

- **Agree consideration** to a **sales agreement**

- **Confirm valuation** of assets acquired is reasonable

- **Check purchased goodwill** is **calculated correctly** (it should reflect the difference between the fair value of the consideration given and the aggregate of the fair values of the separable net assets acquired)

- **Check goodwill** does **not include non-purchased goodwill**

- **Review amortisation**
  - Test calculation
  - Assess whether amortisation rates are reasonable

- **Ensure valuation** of **goodwill** is **reasonable** by reviewing prior year's accounts and discussion with the directors

Development costs

3.4 The key audit tests largely reflect the criteria laid down in SSAP 13.

- **Check accounting records** to confirm:
  - **Project** is **clearly defined** (separate cost centre or nominal ledger codes)
  - **Related expenditure** can be **separately identified**, and certified to invoices, timesheets

- **Confirm feasibility** and **viability**
  - Examine market research reports, feasibility studies, budgets and forecasts
  - Consult client's technical experts

- **Review budgeted revenues** and **costs** by examining results to date, production forecasts, advance orders and discussion with directors

- **Review calculations** of **future cash flows** to ensure resources exist to complete the project

- **Review previously deferred expenditure** to ensure SSAP 13 criteria are still justified

- **Check amortisation:**
  - Commences with production
  - Charged on a systematic basis

3.5 The good news for the auditors in this audit area is that many companies adopt a prudent approach and write off research and development expenditure in the year it is incurred. The auditors' concern in these circumstances is whether the profit and loss account charge for research and development is complete, accurate and valid.

4 INVESTMENTS

4.1 This section applies to companies where dealing in investments is secondary to the main objectives of the company. Under the general heading of 'investments' four distinct items are considered.

- Investment properties (not covered here)
- Investments in companies, whether listed or unlisted, fixed interest or equity
- Income arising from the investments
- Investment in subsidiary and associated companies

(*Note*. The following comments apply equally to investments treated as fixed or current.)

Internal control considerations

4.2 Controls over investments were discussed in detail in Chapter 9. The key controls are:

(a) **Authorisation** over investment dealing. Authorisation from high level management should be required.

(b) **Segregation of duties:**

(i) The recording and custody roles should be kept separate.

(ii) As investments may be misappropriated by being pledged as collateral, those responsible for custody should not have access to cash.

Existence and rights and obligations

4.3 Stockbrokers should not normally be entrusted with the safe custody of share certificates on a continuing basis since they have ready access to the Stock Exchange. Auditors should not therefore rely on a certificate from a broker stating that he holds the company's securities. If securities are being transferred over the year-end the auditors should nevertheless obtain a broker's certificate but the transaction should be further verified by examining contract notes, and in the case of purchases, examination of the title documents after the year-end.

4.4 Substantive tests

- **Examine certificates** of **title** to investments listed in investment records and confirm that they are:

    ° Bona fide complete title documents
    ° In the client's name
    ° Free from any charge or lien

- **Examine confirmation** from **third party investment custodians** (such as banks) and check:

    ° Investments are in client's name
    ° Investments are free from charge or lien

- **Inspect certificates** of **title** which are held by third parties who are not bona fide custodians

- **Inspect blank transfers** and **letters of trust** to confirm client owns shares in name of nominee

- **Review minutes** and **other statutory books** for evidence of charging and pledging

Additions and disposals

4.5 Substantive tests should include the following.

Additions

- **Verify purchase prices** to agreements, contract notes and correspondence

- **Confirm purchases** were **authorised**

- **Check** with Stubbs, Extel or appropriate financial statements that all **reported capital changes** (bonus or rights issues) have been correctly **accounted for** during the period

Disposals of investments

- **Verify disposals** with contract notes, sales agreements correspondence etc.

- **Check** whether investment **disposals** have been **authorised**

- **Confirm** that **profit** or **loss** on sale of investments has been **correctly calculated** taking account of:

  ○ Bonus issue of shares
  ○ Consistent basis of identifying cost of investment sold
  ○ Rights issues
  ○ Accrued interest
  ○ Taxation

Valuation

4.6 The auditors should establish that the company's policy on valuing investments has been correctly applied and is consistent with previous years, for example cost or market value.

4.7 Substantive tests

- **Confirm** the **value** of **listed investments** by reference to the Stock Exchange Daily Lists or the quotations published in the Financial Times or Times; the middle market value should be used

- Review accounts of unlisted investments and:

  ○ Check the **basis on** which the **shares** are **valued** (expert help may be required)
  ○ **Ensure** that the **valuation** of the investment is **reasonable**

- **Check** that **no substantial fall** in the value of the investments has taken place since the balance sheet date

- **Consider** whether there are any **restrictions** on **remittance** of **income** and ensure these are properly disclosed

- **Check** whether **current asset investments** are included at the **lower of cost** or **net realisable value**

Investment income

4.8 The basis of recognising investment income may vary from company to company particularly for dividends, for example:

- Credit taken only when received (cash basis)
- Credit taken when declared
- Credit taken after ratification of the dividend by the shareholders in general meeting

A consistent basis must be applied from year to year.

4.9 Substantive tests

- **Check** that all **income** due has been **received**, by reference to Stubbs or Extel cards for listed investments, and financial statements for unlisted investments

- **Review investment income** account for **irregular** or unusual **entries,** or those not apparently pertaining to investments held (particular attention should be paid to investments bought and sold during the year)

- **Ensure** that the **basis** of **recognising** income is **consistent** with previous years

- **Compare investment income** with **prior years** and **explain** any **significant fluctuations**

- **Consider whether** there are likely to be any **restrictions** on **realisation** of the investment or remittance of any income due (especially for investments abroad) and ensure these are properly disclosed in the financial statements

4.10 If the client is a charity or pension scheme, auditors should check that tax deducted at source has been reclaimed from the Inland Revenue.

General tests

4.11 Other tests that are likely to be carried out include the following.

- **Obtain** or prepare a **statement** to be placed on the current file **reconciling the book value** of listed and unlisted investments at the last balance sheet date and the current balance sheet date (tests completeness)

- **Ensure** that the **investments** are **properly disclosed and categorised** in the financial statements into listed and unlisted

---

Activity 13.4

You are auditing the accounts of the Crossroads Motel trust. The trust owns significant investments, the income from which is used to support retired stars of television soap operas. The investments include large investments in the shares of listed companies.

Tasks

(a) Explain how you would confirm the trust's ownership of the listed company shares.
(b) Explain how you would check that all income due during the year has been received.
(c) Explain what work you would carry out on the disposals of investments.

Key learning points

- The disclosure and valuation requirements for all fixed assets under CA 1985 are relevant here.

- Key areas when testing **tangible fixed assets** are:

  - **Confirmation** of ownership
  - **Inspection** of fixed assets to confirm **existence**
  - **Valuation** by third parties
  - **Adequacy** of **depreciation** rates

- **Intangible assets** may cause audit problems in the areas of:

  - Capitalisation (whether the assets should be capitalised)
  - Amortisation

- **Investments** (if quoted) should be **valued** at **mid-market price** at the balance sheet date.

- Auditors may need to **inspect share certificates** to confirm ownership.

Quick quiz

1   What documentation should auditors inspect when reviewing deeds to registered land?

2   How should auditors check whether a company has capitalised expenditure correctly?

3   What are the major audit tests that should be carried out on the disposal of fixed assets?

4   What audit work should be carried out in order to check whether a company has capital commitments and charges on fixed assets?

5   How should auditors test income from intangible assets?

6   In what circumstances can development expenditure be deferred under SSAP 13?

7   How would an auditor test whether the valuation of listed investments is reasonable?

Answers to quick quiz

1   When inspecting title to registered land, auditors should inspect the land registry certificate which is conclusive evidence of title. Other documents should only normally be inspected in cases of doubt.

2   When checking capitalisation of expenditure, auditors should check fixed asset additions and expense categories which may contain capital items such as repairs or motor expenses. They should check whether the capital/revenue distinction has been correctly drawn, and whether the capitalisation is consistent with company policy.

3   Auditors should carry out the following work on disposals.

   (a)   Verify disposals with supporting documentation.
   (b)   Check the calculation of profit or loss on disposal.
   (c)   Check disposals have been authorised.
   (d)   Consider whether proceeds received appear reasonable.

4   Auditors should review statutory books and carry out company searches for evidence of charges. They should review invoices raised after the year-end, orders and board minutes for evidence of capital commitments.

5   Auditors should test income from intangible fixed assets by reviewing sales returns and statistics to verify the reasonableness of income. They should also examine audited accounts of third party sales, when the third parties are operating under a patent, licence or trademark owned by the company.

6   Development expenditure can be deferred and carried as an intangible fixed asset when:

   (a)   There is a clearly defined project.

   (b)   The expenditure on the project is separately identifiable.

   (c)   The outcome of the project has been assessed with reasonable certainty. Consider:

      (i)   Its technical feasibility
      (ii)   Its ultimate commercial viability
      (iii)   Its costs being more than covered by future revenues

   (d)   Adequate resources will be available to complete the project.

7   The valuation of listed investments should be confirmed by referring to the Stock Exchange Daily Lists, or the quotations published in the *Financial Times* or *Times*.

Answers to activities

Answer 13.1

If a company does not maintain a fixed asset register, the auditors should ask the client for a schedule listing the major items of fixed assets. This schedule should show the original cost and estimated depreciated value; it should also indicate additions and disposals during the year. (Alternatively auditors may have a schedule from previous years on file, and would need information about movements in fixed assets to update it.)

The schedule should be reconciled to the draft accounts.

Auditors should verify additions to supporting documentation and should inspect assets acquired.

Auditors may have problems obtaining evidence on the completeness of disposals. If they have a schedule from previous years, they can inspect the assets recorded on it to see if they still exist and can confirm ownership to appropriate supporting documentation. If however the auditors do not have information about what was held at the start of the year they will have to scrutinise the cash book for any large unexplained receipts, and also inspect board minutes for reference to disposals.

Auditors should also use their knowledge of the business to consider whether fixed asset additions should have resulted in corresponding disposals (for example new motor vehicles replacing old). Alternatively changes in the business such as discontinuation of certain products may be expected to result in disposals.

Ultimately auditors may be forced to conclude that they have insufficient evidence on fixed assets.

Answer 13.2

(a) We should carry out the following work on plant and machinery additions.

(i) Check that the purchase has been authorised by examining board minutes or other evidence of authorisation.

(ii) Confirm the purchase price paid to suppliers' invoice and cash book.

(iii) Inspect the new plant and machinery to confirm its existence.

(iv) Check whether any security has been granted over the plant and machinery; if it has, we should ensure that it has been properly recorded and disclosed in the accounts.

(b) We should carry out the following work on the depreciation charge.

(i) Check whether the depreciation charge is consistent with charges for previous years, and consistent with the company's accounting policies relating to depreciation.

(ii) Check the calculation of the depreciation charge for individual vehicles/in total.

(iii) Review the profits or losses on disposals of motor vehicles during the year to ensure that the charge is not excessive.

(iv) Check that depreciation rates appear reasonable in the light of vehicle usage and replacement policy.

(v) Check that all vehicles are being depreciated.

(vi) Check that no further depreciation is being charged on fully depreciated vehicles.

(vii) Check that the client's depreciation policy and depreciation charge are disclosed in the accounts.

Answer 13.3

(a) Alternative means of obtaining evidence of the existence of vehicles include the following.

(i) Insurance policies

(ii) Evidence of repair and maintenance expenditure

(iii) MOT certificate

(iv) Correspondence with the salesmen, including acknowledgement by the salesmen that they have the cars

(b) We should consider whether:

(i) The change in accounting policy is reasonable; the new office block may have meant the company has purchased furniture that is significantly more expensive than previously.

(ii) The furniture purchased is expensive enough to warrant capitalisation.

(iii) The expected life of the furniture is reasonable (has the board decided that all furniture will be replaced after three years?).

Audit work on the furniture should include:

(i) Confirm costs to purchase invoices.

(ii) Inspect the furniture to confirm its existence and condition, and to check if the expected life appears reasonable.

(c)   Audit work should include:

(i)   Inspect the crane to confirm its condition and the fact that it is still being used.

(ii)   Check the invoices which detail the expenditure on the crane.

(iii) If the client has used internal labour in bringing the crane back into use, check labour costs to wage records.

(iv)   Check the insurance policy on the crane for evidence of valuation.

Answer 13.4

(a)   Ownership could be verified by the following tests.

(i)   Select a sample of fixed interest investments held at the year end and inspect the relevant certificates. These should be in the trust's name.

(ii)   For listed companies, again select a sample of investments held at the year end and agree to the share certificate in the trust's name.

(iii) Compare the list of investments held with the list of income received and investigate any discrepancies between the two.

(iv)   Check dividend and interest vouchers for trust's name and number of shares held.

(b)   Income is received from two sources - fixed interest stocks and shares in listed companies.

(i)   For fixed interest stocks, verify the overall income in the accounts by analytical review. In overall terms as the income is fixed the expected income can be calculated. It will be necessary to take into account tax reclaimed from the Inland Revenue and opening and closing debtors for tax.

(ii)   For fixed interest stocks, test individual receipts to the cash books to ensure that the expected interest was received, and check the calculations.

(iii) For shares in listed companies select a sample of investments and obtain from Extel or a similar reference details of dividend payments made during the year.

(iv)   Trace receipt of these dividends to the cash book via dividend vouchers.

(v)   For shares in listed companies, reconcile total income in accounts to total income in cash book.

(vi)   Carry out comparison of dividends received as compared with previous year and check changes to Extel.

(vii) For shares disposed of in year, check to Extel or broker's note that all dividends to which the trust was entitled have been received in the year.

(viii) For shares bought in year, check to Extel or broker's note that dividends to which the trust was entitled have been received.

(ix)   Review the reclaims of tax made by the trust to the Inland Revenue to ensure that all reclaims had been made.

(c)   The following tests should be carried out on investments disposed of during the year.

(i)   Verify disposals to contract notes, sales agreements or other relevant information.

(ii)   Check whether the disposal of shares had been authorised.

(iii) Confirm that the profit or loss on the sale of investments has been correctly calculated, taking account of:

(1)   Basis of identifying costs of investment
(2)   Bonus issues of shares
(3)   Rights issues
(4)   Accrued interest
(5)   Taxation

Chapter 14 Debtors and cash

Chapter topic list

1   Introduction

2   Debtors and sales

3   Bank and cash

Learning objectives

On completion of this chapter you will be able to:

	Performance criteria	Range Statement
Describe the procedures used to audit:	17.1.5,17.1.7,	17.1.1-17.1.3,
° Debtors and sales	17.2.1-17.2.4	17.2.1-17.2.3
° Bank and cash		

1 INTRODUCTION

1.1 Having dealt with stock in Chapter 12, in this chapter we deal with the other major current assets, debtors and bank and cash and debtors, also considering sales when testing debtors.

1.2 With debtors, auditors are primarily concerned to prove that:

(a) Debtors represent **amounts** due to the company (the assertions of existence and rights and obligations).

(b) **Adequate provision** has been made for bad debts, discounts and returns (valuation).

(c) **Cut-off of goods** despatched and invoiced is satisfactory (measurement, rights and obligations).

1.3 The primary procedure for obtaining evidence of the correctness of rights and obligations of debtor balances is the **debtors' circularisation**, asking debtors for confirmation of balances owed. Satisfactory responses to the circularisation are strong audit evidence, as they are **written evidence** from **third parties**. You need to know the specific procedures auditors follow when carrying out a circularisation. Inevitably auditors will not always obtain exact confirmation from all of the debtors circularised, and you should be aware of what auditors do in those circumstances.

1.4 Although debtors may agree that they owe the amount stated in the client's books, that does not mean that they will pay that amount. Therefore auditors will also need to carry out tests to confirm the **valuation** of debtors and the **adequacy** of **bad debt provisions**. Provision for bad debts may be made against specific debts. Alternatively there may be a general provision, say X% of trade debtors, or X% of all overdue debts.

1.5 Finally **cut-off** will need to be tested. Most often this will be done along with testing of stock and purchases cut-off.

1.6 The main concern of auditors when testing sales will be that sales have been **completely** recorded.

1.7 The other major current asset is **cash at bank** and in hand. Cash at bank will be confirmed by obtaining confirmation in the form of a **bank letter** from the clients' bank(s) of balances held at the year-end. Auditors will then check that the balances shown in the bank letter can be reconciled to the balances shown in the client's records by carrying out a bank reconciliation or checking the reconciliation that the client has prepared.

1.8 **Cash in hand** can be confirmed by a **cash count**. Cash counts are not carried out on many audits since cash balances held as floats are small. However you need to know the procedures involved, because cash counts may be necessary when the amount of cash passing through a business is large (retail operations, for example), or a cash count is performed to test controls over cash as well as to substantiate the balances held.

2 DEBTORS AND SALES

Debtors' listing and aged analysis

2.1 Much of the auditors' detailed work will be based on a selection of debtors' balances chosen from a listing of sales ledger balances, prepared by the client or auditors. Ideally the list should be aged, showing the period or periods of time money has been owed. The following substantive procedures are necessary to check the **completeness** and **accuracy** of a client-prepared list.

- **Check** the **balances** from the **individual sales ledger accounts** to the **list of balances** and vice versa

- **Check** the **total** of the **list** to the **sales ledger control account**

- **Cast** (ie add up) the **list of balances** and the **sales ledger control account**

- **Confirm** whether **list of balances reconciles** with the **sales ledger control account**

The debtors' circularisation

When circularisation is used

2.2 The verification of trade debtors by contacting them directly to confirm balances (direct circularisation) is the normal means of checking whether debtors owe *bona fide* amounts due to the company.

2.3 Circularisation should produce a written statement from each debtor contacted that the amount owed at the date of the circularisation is correct. This is, *prima facie*, reliable audit evidence, being from an independent source and in 'documentary' form.

Timing

2.4 Ideally the circularisation should take place immediately after the year-end and hence cover the year-end balances to be included in the balance sheet. However, time constraints may make it impossible to achieve this ideal. In these circumstances it may be acceptable to carry out the circularisation **prior to the year-end** provided that circularisation occurs no more than three months before the year-end and internal controls are strong.

Client's mandate

2.5 Circularisation is essentially an act of the **client**, who alone can authorise third parties to divulge information to the auditors. Should the client refuse to co-operate in the circularisation the auditors will have to consider whether they should **qualify** their **audit report,** as they may not be able to satisfy themselves, by means of other audit procedures, as to the validity and accuracy of the debtor balances.

Positive v negative circularisation

2.6 When circularisation is undertaken the method of requesting information from the debtor may be either 'positive' or 'negative'.

(a) Under the **positive** method the debtor is requested to confirm the accuracy of the balance shown or state in what respect he is in disagreement.

(b) Under the **negative** method the debtor is requested to reply *only* if the amount stated is disputed.

2.7 The positive method is generally preferable as it is designed to encourage definite replies from those circularised. The negative method may be used if the client has good internal control, with a large number of small accounts. In some circumstances, say where there is a small number of large accounts and a large number of small accounts, a combination of both methods may be appropriate.

2.8 The following is a specimen 'positive' confirmation letter.

MANUFACTURING CO LIMITED
15 South Street
London

Date

Messrs   (debtor)

In accordance with the request of our auditors, Messrs Arthur Daley & Co, we ask that you kindly confirm to them directly your indebtedness to us at (insert date) which, according to our records, amounted to £.......... as shown by the enclosed statement.

If the above amount is in agreement with your records, please sign in the space provided below and return this letter direct to our auditors in the enclosed stamped addressed envelope.

If the amount is not in agreement with your records, please notify our auditors directly of the amount shown by your records, and if possible detail on the reverse of this letter full particulars of the difference.

Yours faithfully,

For Manufacturing Co Limited

Reference No: ....

....

(Tear off slip)

The amount shown above is/is not * in agreement with our records as at

Account No   ....   Signature   ....

Date   ....   Title or position   ....

* The position according to our records is shown overleaf.

Note:

- The letter is on the client's paper, signed by the client.
- A copy of the statement is attached.
- The reply is sent directly to the auditor in a pre-paid envelope.

2.9   The statements will normally be prepared by the client's staff, from which point the auditors, as a safeguard against the possibility of fraudulent manipulation, must maintain **strict control** over the **checking** and **despatch** of the statements. Precautions must also be taken to ensure that undelivered items are returned, not to the client, but to the auditors' own office for follow-up by them.

Sample selection

2.10   Auditors will normally only circularise a sample of debtors. If this sample is to yield a meaningful result it must be based upon a complete list of all debtor accounts. In addition, when constructing the sample, the following classes of account should receive special attention:

- **Old unpaid accounts**
- **Accounts written off** during the period under review
- **Accounts** with **credit balances**
- **Accounts** settled by **round sum payments**

Similarly, the following should not be overlooked:

- **Accounts** with **nil balances**
- **Accounts** which have been **paid** by the date of the examination

2.11 Auditors may apply stratification techniques to ensure that a sufficient proportion of debtors are confirmed.

Follow-up procedures

2.12 Auditors will have to carry out further work in relation to those debtors who:

- **Disagree** with the **balance stated** (positive and negative circularisation)
- **Do not respond** (positive circularisation only)

2.13 In the case of disagreements, the debtor response should have identified specific amounts which are disputed.

2.14 Disagreements can arise for the following reasons.

(a) There is a **dispute** between the client and the customer. The reasons for the dispute would have to be identified, and provision made if appropriate against the debt.

(b) **Cut-off problems** exist, because the client records the following year's sales in the current year or because goods returned by the customer in the current year are not recorded in the current year. Cut-off testing may have to be extended (see below).

(c) The customer may have sent the **monies before** the year-end, but the monies were **not recorded** by the client as receipts until **after** the year-end. Detailed cut-off work may be required on receipts.

(d) Monies received may have been posted to the **wrong account** or a cash-in-transit account. Auditors should check if there is evidence of other mis-posting. If the monies have been posted to a cash-in-transit account, auditors should ensure this account has been cleared promptly.

(e) Customers who are also suppliers may **net off balances** owed and owing. Auditors should check that this is allowed.

(f) **Teeming and lading, stealing** monies and **incorrectly posting** other receipts so that no particular debtor is seriously in debt is a fraud that can arise in this area. If auditors suspect teeming and lading has occurred, detailed testing will be required on cash receipts, particularly on prompt posting of cash receipts.

2.15 When the positive request method is used the auditors must follow up by all practicable means those debtors who **fail to respond**. Second requests should be sent out in the event of no reply being received within two or three weeks and if necessary this may be followed by telephoning the customer, with the client's permission.

2.16 After two, or even three, attempts to obtain confirmation, a list of the outstanding items will normally be passed to a responsible company official, preferably independent of the sales accounting department, who will arrange for them to be investigated.

2.17 If it proves impossible to get confirmations from individual debtors, alternative procedures include the following.

- **Check receipt of cash** after date
- **Verify valid purchase** orders if any

- **Examine the account** to see if the balance outstanding represents specific invoices and **confirm** their **validity**

- **Obtain explanations** for **invoices remaining unpaid** after subsequent ones have been paid

- **Check** if the **balance** on the account is **growing,** and if so, why

- **Test company's control** over the issue of **credit notes** and the **write-off of bad debts**

Additional procedures where circularisation is carried out before year-end

2.18 The auditors will need to carry out the following procedures where their circularisation is carried out before the year-end.

- **Review** and **reconcile entries** on the **sales ledger control account** for the intervening period

- **Verify sales entries** from the control account by checking sales day book entries, copy sales invoices and despatch notes

- **Check** that **appropriate credit entries** have been made for goods returned notes and other evidence of returns/allowances to the sales ledger control account

- **Select a sample** from the **cash received records** and **ensure** that **receipts** have been **credited** to the control account

- **Review** the **list of balances** at the **circularisation** date and year end and **investigate** any **unexpected movements** or lack of them (it may be prudent to send further confirmation requests at the year end to material debtors where review results are unsatisfactory)

- **Carry out analytical review** procedures, comparing debtors' ratios at the confirmation date and year-end

- **Carry out** year end **cut-off tests,** in addition to any performed at the date of the confirmation (see below)

Evaluation and conclusions

2.19 All circularisations, regardless of timing, must be properly recorded and evaluated. All **balance disagreements** and **non-replies** must be **followed up** and their effect on total debtors evaluated. **Differences** arising that merely represent **invoices** or **cash in transit** (normal timing differences) generally do not require adjustment, but disputed amounts, and errors by the client, might require adjustments.

Activity 14.1

(a) How reliable a source of audit evidence is a debtors' circularisation?

(b) Describe the audit procedures that should be followed when planning and performing a circularisation to be carried out at the client's year end. (You are not required to consider follow-up procedures.)

(c) Describe the audit work you would carry out on the following replies to a debtors' circularisation.

    (i) Balance agreed by debtor

    (ii) Balance not agreed by debtor

    (iii) Debtor is unable to confirm the balance because of the form of records kept by the debtor

    (iv) Debtor does not reply to the circularisation

Bad debts

2.20 The extent of testing is likely to depend on the strength of controls over credit terms and slow payers, the client's previous record of bad debts, and the proportion of debts that are overdue.

2.21 The following procedures will be important.

- **Confirm necessity/adequacy** of provision against **write-off** of debts by review of correspondence, solicitors' debt collection, agencies' letters, liquidation statements

- Examine customer files on overdue debts, and **assess** whether **provision** is required in the circumstances

- **Consider** whether **amounts owed** may be **not recovered** where there have been:
  - ° Round sum payments on account
  - ° Invoices unpaid after subsequent invoices paid

- **Review customer files/correspondence** from solicitors for evidence of potential bad debts

- **Confirm general provisions** for bad debts
  - ° Calculation correct
  - ° Formula used reasonable and consistent with previous years

- **Examine credit notes** issued after the year-end for **provisions** that should be made against current period balances.

- **Check accuracy** of **aged debtor analysis** by comparing analysis with dates on invoices

- **Investigate unusual features** on aged debtors analysis, such as:
  - ° Unapplied credits
  - ° Unallocated cash

- **Investigate unusual items** in the sales ledger, such as:
  - ° Journal entries transferring balances from one account to another
  - ° Journal entries that clear post year-end debtor balances
  - ° Balances not made up of specific invoices
  - ° Sales ledger accounts with significant adjustments or credit notes

2.22 Auditors should also consider the collectability of material debtor balances other than those contained in the sales ledger. Auditors should request certificates of loan balances from employees and others, and inspect the authority if necessary.

Sales

2.23 Debtors will often be tested in conjunction with sales. Auditors are seeking to obtain evidence that sales are **completely** and **accurately recorded**. This will involve carrying out certain procedures to test for **completeness** of sales and also testing **cut-off**.

Completeness and occurrence of sales

2.24 **Analytical review** is likely to be important when testing completeness. Auditors should consider the following.

- The **level of sales** over the year, compared on a month-by-month basis with the previous year

- The effect on sales value of **changes in quantities** sold

- The effect on sales value of changes in **products** or **prices**

- The level of **goods returned, sales allowances** and **discounts**

- The **efficiency of labour** as expressed in sales or pre-tax profit per employee

2.25 In addition auditors must record reasons for changes in the **gross profit margin** ($\frac{\text{Gross profit}}{\text{Turnover}} \times 100\%$). Analysis of the gross profit margin should be as detailed as possible, ideally broken down by **product area** and **month or quarter**.

2.26 As well as analytical review, auditors may feel that they need to test completeness of recording of individual sales in the accounting records. To do this, auditors should start with the documents that first record sales (**goods despatched notes** or **till rolls** for example). They should trace details of sales recorded in these through intermediate documents such as the sales **day book invoices** and **summaries through** to the **sales ledger**.

2.27 Auditors must **ensure** that the **population of documents** from which the sample is originally taken is itself complete, by checking for example the completeness of the sequence of goods despatched notes. Auditors should also **review reconciliations** of the sales ledger control account and other relevant reconciliations, and **investigate unusual items**.

DEVOLVED ASSESSMENT ALERT

You must remember the direction of this test. Since we are checking the completeness of recording of sales in the sales ledger, we cannot take a sample from the ledger since the sample cannot include what has not been recorded.

2.28 If on the other hand, the auditors suspect that sales may have been **invalidly** recorded (may **not** have **occurred**), then the sample will be taken from the sales ledger and confirmed to supporting documentation (orders, despatch notes etc).

Measurement of sales

2.29 Other tests that may be carried out on sales include:

- Check the **pricing calculations** and **additions** on invoices
- Check whether **discounts** have been **properly calculated**
- **Check** whether **VAT** has been **added appropriately**
- **Check casting** of the **sales ledger accounts** and **sales ledger control account**

2.30 Auditors should also check the **measurement** and **validity** of **credit notes** by tracing debits in the sales account to credit notes, and **checking credit notes** to **supporting documentation** for **authorisation**, and evidence that the sales did take place.

Sales cut-off

2.31 During the stocktake the auditors will have obtained details of the last serial numbers of goods outward notes issued before the commencement of the stocktaking.

2.32 The following substantive procedures are designed to test that goods taken into stock are not also treated as sales in the year under review and, conversely, goods despatched are treated as sales in the year under review and not also treated as stock.

- **Check goods despatched** and **returns inwards** notes around year-end to ensure:

  ○ **Invoices** and **credit notes** are **dated** in the **correct period**

  ○ **Invoices** and **credit notes** are **posted** to the **sales ledger** and **general ledger** in the correct period

- **Reconcile entries** in the **sales ledger control account** around the **year-end** to daily batch invoice totals ensuring batches are posted in correct year

- **Review sales ledger control account** around year-end for **unusual items**

- **Review material after-date invoices, credit notes** and **adjustments** and ensure that they are properly treated as following year sales

Other tests on debtors and sales

Goods on sale or return

2.33 Care should be exercised to ensure that goods on sale or return are properly treated in the accounts. Except where the client has been notified of the sale of the goods they should be reflected in the accounts as **stock** at cost and not as debtors, otherwise profits may be incorrectly anticipated.

Inter-company indebtedness

2.34 Where significant trading occurs between group companies the auditors should have ascertained as a result of their tests of controls whether trading has been at arm's length. As regards the balances at the year end, the following substantive procedures are suggested

- **Confirm balances** owing from group and associated companies (current and loan accounts) with the other companies' records (directly, or by contacting other group members' auditors)

- **Ensure** that **cut-off procedures** have operated properly regarding inter company transfers

- **Assess reliability** of amounts owing

- **Ascertain** the **nature** of the entries comprised in the balances at the year end.

- **Ensure** that any **management charges** contained therein have been **calculated** on a **reasonable** and **consistent basis** and have been acknowledged by the debtor companies

Prepayments

2.35 The extent of audit testing will depend on the materiality of the amounts.

- **Verify prepayments** by reference to the cash book, expense invoices, correspondence and so on

- **Check calculations** of prepayments

- **Review** the **detailed profit and loss account** to ensure that all likely prepayments have been provided for

- **Review** the **prepayments** for **reasonableness** by comparing with prior years and using analytical procedures where applicable

---

Activity 14.2

Itchy and Scratchy Ltd do not normally provide against specific bad debts, but normally make a general bad debt provision. This year the general provision is 5% of debtors.

Tasks

State the audit work you would perform on the company's bad debt provision.

---

3   BANK AND CASH

Bank balances

3.1   The audit of bank balances will need to cover **completeness, existence, rights and obligations** and **valuation**. All of these elements can be audited directly through the device of obtaining third party confirmations from the client's banks and reconciling these with the accounting records, having regard to cut-off.

3.2   As preparation, the auditors should update details of bank accounts held, ensuring the client holds accounts with bona fide banks.

Bank reports

3.3   The Auditing Practices Board issued Practice Note 16 *Bank reports for audit purposes* in August 1998. The note sets out a revised process for auditors when requesting information from the banks. It draws a distinction between standard and supplementary information. The standard request consists of information about account and balance details, facilities, securities, and additional banking relationships. The request for supplementary information is concerned with requests for trade finance information, and derivatives and commodity trading information.

3.4   The procedure is simple but important.

(a)   The banks will require **explicit written authority** from their client to disclose the information requested.

(b)   The **auditors' request** must **refer** to the **client's letter** of authority and the date thereof. Alternatively it may be countersigned by the client or it may be accompanied by a specific letter of authority.

(c)   In the case of joint accounts, **letters of authority** signed by all **parties** will be necessary.

(d)   Such **letters** of **authority** may either **give permission** to the bank to disclose information for a specific request or grant permission for an indeterminate length of time.

(e)   The request should **reach** the **branch manager** at least **two weeks in advance** of the client's **year-end** and should state both that year-end date and the previous year-end date.

(f)   The **auditors** should themselves **check** that the bank response covers all the information in the standard and other responses.

3.5   **Bank confirmation request letter - illustration**

[XXXXXX Bank plc
25 XXX Street
Warrington
Cheshire
WA1 1XQ]

Dear Sirs,

In accordance with the agreed practice for provision of information to auditors, please forward information on our mutual client(s) as detailed below on behalf of the bank, its branches and subsidiaries. This request and your response will not create any contractual or other duty with us.

COMPANIES OR OTHER BUSINESS ENTITIES
(attach a separate listing if necessary)

[Parent Company Ltd
Subsidiary 1 Ltd
Subsidiary 2 Ltd]

AUDIT CONFIRMATION DATE (30 APRIL 2000)

Information required	Tick
Standard	
Trade finance	
Derivative and commodity trading	
Custodian arrangements	
Other information (see attached)	

The authority to disclose information signed by your customer is attached / already held by you (delete as appropriate). Please advise us if this authority is insufficient for you to provide full disclosure of the information requested.

The contract name is [John Caller]   Telephone [01 234 5678]

Yours faithfully,
[XXX Accountants]

Standard request for information

3.6   The following information should always be disclosed by banks upon receipt of a request for information for audit purposes. Responses should be given in the order below and if no information is available then this must be stated as 'None' in the response.

1 **Account and balance details**

Give full titles of all bank accounts including loans, (whether in sterling or another currency) together with their account numbers and balances. For accounts closed during the 12 months up to the audit confirmation date give the account details and date of closure.

Note. Also give details where your customer's name is joined with that of other parties and where the account is in a trade name.

State if any account or balances are subject to any restriction(s) whatsoever. Indicate the nature and extent of the restriction, eg garnishee order.

2 **Facilities**

Give the following details of all loans, overdrafts and associated guarantees and indemnities:

- Term
- Repayment frequency and/or review date
- Details of period of availability of agreed finance, ie finance remaining undrawn
- Detail the facility limit

3 **Securities**

With reference to the facilities detailed in (2) above give the following details:

- Any security formally charged (date, ownership and type of charge). State whether the security supports facilities granted by the bank to the customer or to another party.

  Note. Give details if a security is limited in amount or to a specific borrowing or if to your knowledge there is a prior, equal or subordinate charge.

- Where there are any arrangements for set-off of balances or compensating balances eg back to back loans, give particulars (ie date, type of document and accounts covered) of any acknowledgement of set-off, whether given by specific letter of set-off or incorporated in some other document.

4 **Additional banking relationships**

State if you are aware of the customer(s) having any additional relationships with branches or subsidiaries of the Bank not covered by the response. Supply a list of branches etc.

Request for supplementary information

3.7 The Practice Note also gives example letters if information about **trade finance**, **derivatives** and **custodian arrangements** is required.

Cut-off

3.8 Care must be taken to ensure that there is no **window dressing,** by checking cut-off carefully. Window dressing in this context is usually manifested as an attempt to overstate the liquidity of the company by:

(a) Keeping the cash book open to take credit in the year for **remittances actually received after** the year end, thus enhancing the balance at bank and reducing debtors

(b) **Recording cheques** as **paid** in the period under review which are not actually despatched until after the year end, thus decreasing the balance at bank and reducing creditors

A combination of (a) and (b) can contrive to present an artificially healthy looking current ratio.

3.9 With the possibility of (a) above in mind, where lodgements have not been cleared by the bank until the new period the auditors should **examine** the **paying-in slip** to ensure that the amounts were actually paid into the bank on or before the balance sheet date.

3.10 As regards (b) above, where there appears to be a particularly **large number** of **outstanding cheques** at the year-end, the auditors should check whether these were **cleared within** a **reasonable time** in the new period. If not, this may indicate that despatch occurred after the year-end.

Summary of bank balance procedures

3.11 The following suggested substantive balance sheet tests summarise the principal audit procedures discussed above relevant to bank balances. The procedures apply to all bank accounts.

- **Obtain standard bank confirmations** from each bank with which the client conducted business during the audit period

- **Check arithmetic** of bank reconciliation

- **Trace cheques shown as outstanding** from the bank reconciliation to the cash book prior to the year-end and to the **after date bank statements** and **obtain explanations** for any large or unusual **items not cleared** at the time of the audit

- **Verify** by checking pay-in slips that **uncleared bankings** are **paid in** prior to the year end, and check uncleared bankings are cleared quickly after the year-end

- **Verify** balances per cash book according to the reconciliation with **cash book** and **general ledger**

- **Verify** the **bank balances** with reply to **standard bank letter** and with the bank statements

- **Scrutinise** the cash book and bank statements before and after the balance sheet date for **exceptional entries** or **transfers** which have a material effect on the balance shown to be in hand

- **Identify** whether any **accounts** are **secured** on the **assets** of the company

- **Consider** whether there is a **legal right** of **set-off** of overdrafts against positive bank balances

- **Determine** whether the **bank accounts** are **subject** to any **restrictions**

- **Obtain explanations** for **all items** in the **cash book** for which there are **no corresponding entries** in the **bank statement** and vice versa

Cash balances

3.12 Cash balances/floats are often individually immaterial. They may require some audit emphasis because of the opportunities for fraud that could exist where internal control is weak due for example to lack of segregation of duties, failure to bank receipts promptly or inadequate custody arrangements. However, in enterprises such as hotels, the amount of cash in hand at the balance sheet date could be considerable; the same goes for retail organisations.

3.13 Where the auditors determine that cash balances are potentially material they may conduct a cash count, ideally at the balance sheet date. Rather like attendance at stocktaking, the conduct of the count falls into three phases: planning, the count itself and follow up procedures.

Planning

3.14 Planning is an essential element, for it is an important principle that all cash balances are counted at the same time as far as possible. Cash in this context may include unbanked cheques received, IOUs and credit card slips, in addition to notes and coins.

3.15 As part of their planning procedures the auditors will hence need to determine the **locations** where cash is held and which of these locations warrant a count.

3.16 Planning decisions will need to be recorded on the current audit file including:

- **Precise** time of the count(s) and location(s)
- **Names** of the **audit staff** conducting the counts
- **Names** of the **client staff** intending to be present at each location

Where a location is not visited it may be expedient to obtain a letter from the client confirming the balance.

Cash count

3.17 The following matters apply to the count itself.

(a) All cash/petty **cash books** should be **written up** to date in ink (or other permanent form) at the time of the count.

(b) All **balances** must be **counted** at the **same time**.

(c) All **negotiable securities** must be **available** and **counted** at the time the cash balances are counted.

(d) At **no time** should the **auditors** be left **alone** with the cash and negotiable securities.

(e) **All cash** and securities **counted** must be **recorded** on working papers subsequently filed on the current audit file, reconciliations should be prepared where applicable (for example imprest petty cash float).

Follow-up procedures

3.18 Follow up procedures should ensure that:

(a) **Certificates** of **cash-in-hand** are **obtained** as appropriate.

(b) **Unbanked cheques/cash receipts** have subsequently been **paid in** and agree to the bank reconciliation.

(c) **IOUs** and cheques cashed for employees have been **reimbursed.**

(d) **IOUs or cashed cheques outstanding** for **unreasonable periods** of time have been provided for.

(e) The **balances** as **counted** are **reflected** in the **accounts** (subject to any agreed amendments because of shortages and so on).

Activity 14.3

(a) List the contents of a standard bank letter for audit purposes.

(b) What tests should auditors normally carry out on the bank reconciliation?

DEVOLVED ASSESSMENT ALERT

Remember that the bank letter contains the balance held by the client at the bank **per the bank's records**. This must be reconciled to the balance held with the bank **per the client's records**.

Key learning points

- **Circularisation** of debtors is a major procedure. Generally circularisation will be **positive** (debtors confirm client's figures are correct).

- Auditors must follow up:
  ° Debtor disagreements
  ° Failure by debtors to respond

- Testing of the **bad debt provision** and sales **cut-off** is also important.

- Bank balances are usually confirmed directly with the **bank** by a bank letter. Balances confirmed by the bank must be reconciled to the balances shown in the client cash book.

- **Cash balances** should be **checked** if irregularities are suspected.

Quick quiz

1 In what circumstances might it be acceptable to carry out a debtors' circularisation prior to the year end?

2 (a) What is the difference between a positive and negative debtors' circularisation?
  (b) In what circumstances might a negative circularisation be undertaken?

3 What types of account require special attention when selecting a sample for a debtors' circularisation?

4 What audit work should be carried out on prepayments?

5 What must auditors get in order to obtain a response to a bank letter from a client's bank?

6 How far in advance of the year-end should a bank letter normally be sent?

7 Give two examples of 'window-dressing' of year-end bank balances?

8 What are the main procedures that auditors should perform when carrying out a cash count?

Answers to quick quiz

1 A debtors' circularisation can be carried out prior to the year-end provided:

(a) The circularisation takes place not more than two or three months before the year-end.

(b) The internal control system is strong enough to ensure that the circularisation plus work on the intervening period gives auditors sufficient assurance.

2   (a)   A positive circularisation is when the debtor is requested to reply whether or not he disagrees with the balance stated. A negative circularisation is where the debtor is requested to reply only when he disagrees with the balance stated.

    (b)   A negative circularisation can be used when the client has a good internal control system and debtors consist of a large number of small balances. It can also be used to confirm smaller balances in a ledger with positive circularisation being used for larger balances.

3   The following accounts require special attention in a debtors' circularisation.

    (a)   Old unpaid accounts
    (b)   Accounts written off during the period under review
    (c)   Accounts with credit balances
    (d)   Accounts settled by round-sum payments

4   Prepayments should be tested by using the following tests.

    (a)   Verify amounts provided to supporting evidence such as cash book, expense invoices and correspondence.

    (b)   Check calculations.

    (c)   Review the profit and loss account to see whether all likely prepayments have been provided.

    (d)   Review for reasonableness by comparing with previous years and using appropriate analytical procedures.

5   Clients must give explicit written authority for the bank to disclose balances held.

6   Bank letters should normally be sent so as to reach the bank at least two weeks in advance of the year end.

7   Two examples of window dressing are:

    (a)   Including cash received after the year-end as cash receipts during the year

    (b)   Recording cheques as paid during the year, but not sending the cheques out until after the year-end

8   When counting cash, auditors should:

    (a)   Ensure all records are written up to date in ink.

    (b)   Count all balances of cash and negotiable securities at the same time.

    (c)   Count cash in the presence of the individuals responsible (auditors should not be left alone with the cash).

    (d)   Record all amounts counted and confirm balances to accounting records.

Answers to activities

Answer 14.1

(a)   The debtors circularisation can often provide strong evidence of the existence and valuation of a balance shown as outstanding from a customer. This is because the circularisation provides confirmation from an independent third party and in documentary form, and is therefore the most reliable type of audit evidence available.

Because of the quality of evidence it produces, a debtors circularisation is normally considered a standard procedure and only omitted under special circumstances. It can be strengthened by asking customers who disagree with the balance to state the make-up of their purchase ledger balance.

However on occasions the assurance provided by the circularisation will be limited for the following reasons.

(i)   The circularisation is generally carried out on a sample, and hence there is sampling risk that the circularisation will show an incorrect result.

(ii)   Some debtors confirm balances automatically without checking the circularisation letter to their own records.

(iii) Some debtors report that they cannot confirm the balance from their accounting records. However this sort of reply does at least provide evidence that the balance exists.

(iv) Some debtors will disagree with the balance, and the client's balance is correct. Usually this is due to cash or purchases in transit, or customer failure to update its purchase ledger.

(v) A debtors' circularisation may confirm debtors agree that the money is owed, but it does not confirm that they will pay the money. Hence further tests will be required on recoverability.

The above observations apply to a positive circularisation. On occasions a negative circularisation (asking the debtor to reply only if he disagrees with the balance) will be used. However this procedure is weaker than a positive circularisation because of the risk that debtors will not reply even though their records show different balances to the client's.

(b) The debtors' circularisation should normally take place immediately after the year-end covering balances outstanding at the year-end. When planning the debtors' circularisation, auditors should obtain a list of debtor balances, reconciled to the total in the sales ledger control account. The auditors should review the list for any obvious omissions or misstatements (customers where large balances were expected).

The auditors should then select a sample from the list, concentrating on the following accounts:

(i) Overdue accounts
(ii) Accounts written off in the period under review
(iii) Accounts with credit balances
(iv) Accounts settled by round-sum payments

The sample should also include:

(i) Accounts with nil balances
(ii) Accounts that had been paid since the year-end

The auditors should ensure a letter is prepared for each debtor sampled. The letter should be on the client's headed notepaper and should be signed by the client. It should authorise the debtor to contact the auditors about the amount owed. A pre-paid envelope addressed to the auditors should be provided for this purpose. The letter would normally state that if the debtor agrees with the amount, they should sign the letter to indicate agreement. If they do not agree with the amount, they should notify the auditors directly of the amount they believe is owed, and if possible give full details of the difference.

The letter should be accompanied by a debtors' statement which should be prepared by the client at the year-end.

Auditors should check the letters and statements to the debtors' listing prior to despatch, and should supervise despatch themselves.

(c) The audit work required on the various replies to a debtors' circularisation would be as follows.

(i) *Balances agreed by debtor*

Where the balance has been agreed by the debtor all that is required would be to ensure that the debt does appear to be collectable. This would be achieved by reviewing cash received after date or considering the adequacy of any provision made for a long outstanding debt.

(ii) *Balances not agreed by debtor*

All balance disagreements must be followed up and their effect on total debtors evaluated. Differences arising that merely represent invoices or cash in transit (which are normal timing differences) generally do not require adjustment, but disputed amounts, and errors by the client, may indicate that further substantive work is necessary to determine whether material adjustments are required.

(iii) *Debtor is unable to confirm the balance because of the form of records he or she maintains*

Certain companies, often computerised, operate systems which make it impossible for them to confirm the balance on their account. Typically in these circumstances their purchase ledger is merely a list of unpaid invoices. However, given sufficient information the debtor will be able to confirm that any given invoice is outstanding. Hence the auditors can circularise such enterprises successfully, but they will need to break down the total on the account into its constituent outstanding invoices.

(iv) *Debtor does not reply to circularisation*

When the positive request method is used the auditors must follow up by all practicable means those debtors who fail to respond. Second requests should be sent out in the event of no reply being received within two or three weeks and if necessary this may be followed by telephoning the customer with the client's permission.

If no reply has been received a list of the outstanding items will normally be passed to a responsible company official, preferably independent of the sales department, who will arrange for them to be investigated.

Other auditing tests that can establish that there existed a valid debt from a genuine customer at the date of the verification are as follows.

(1) Check receipt of cash after date.
(2) Verify valid purchase orders, if any.
(3) Examine the account to see if the balance represents specific outstanding invoices.
(4) Obtain explanations for invoices remaining unpaid after subsequent ones have been paid.
(5) See if the balance on the account is growing, and if so, why.
(6) Test the company's control over the issue of credit notes and the write-off of bad debts.

Answer 14.2

I would carry out the following tests on Itchy and Scratchy Ltd's bad debt provision.

(a) Check that the basis used is consistent with previous years.

(b) Consider whether the basis was reasonable, reviewing recent years to see the provision made had been adequate but not excessive.

(c) Review the sales ledger for this year, checking the ageing of debtors, and considering whether the pattern of debtors had changed in terms of amounts owed and collection period.

(d) Review the sales ledger for all large debts against which specific provision might be required.

(e) Check the calculation of the provision.

(f) Confirm that the debtors' balances used agreed with the adjusted control account provision.

(g) Confirm that the provision had been posted to the accounting records.

Answer 14.3

(a) The main elements of a standard bank letter are as follows.

   (i) Titles, numbers and balances on all bank accounts including loans

   (ii) Details of accounts where the customer's name is joined with that of other parties or where the account is in a trade name

   (iii) Account details and date of closure for accounts closed during the twelve months up to the audit confirmation date

   (iv) Details of loans, overdrafts and associated guarantees and indemnities
   (1) Term
   (2) Repayment frequency and/or review date
   (3) Detail of period of availability of agreed finance ie finance remaining undrawn
   (4) The facility limit

   (v) In relation to the facilities:

   (1) Details of any supporting security formally charged
   (2) Details if a security is limited in amount or to a specific borrowing, or if there is another charge

   (vi) Set-off arrangements

   (vii) Additional relationships with other branches or subsidiaries of the bank

(b) The following tests should be carried out on the bank reconciliation.

   (i) Check the arithmetic of the bank reconciliation.

   (ii) Trace cheques shown as unpresented on the bank reconciliation to the cash book before the year-end and the bank statement after the year-end.

   (iii) Check uncleared bankings per the bank reconciliation to paying-in-slips to confirm that they have been paid in prior to the year-end, and check they appear on bank statements soon after the year-end.

   (iv) Investigate other reconciling items.

   (v) Verify balance per cash book on reconciliation with cash book and general ledger.

   (vi) Verify balance per bank on reconciliation with bank statements and bank letter.

   (vii) Scrutinise cash book and bank statements before and after the year-end for unusual items which may materially affect the bank balance.

Chapter 15 Liabilities, share capital, reserves and statutory books

---

Chapter topic list

1   Introduction

2   Current liabilities, purchases and expenses

3   Long-term liabilities

4   Share capital, reserves and statutory books

Learning objectives

On completion of this chapter you will be able to:

	Performance criteria	Range Statement
Describe the procedures used to audit:	17.1.5,17.1.7, 17.2.1-17.2.4	17.1.1-17.1.3, 17.2.1-17.2.3

- Describe the procedures used to audit:

  ○ Current liabilities
  ○ Long term liabilities
  ○ Share capital, share issues and redemptions
  ○ Types of reserve and their treatment and disclosure
  ○ Statutory books

1 INTRODUCTION

1.1 In this chapter we deal with the testing of creditors, purchases and expenses share capital and reserves. **Creditors** is often one of the most sensitive areas of a company's accounts. It significantly affects the company's liquidity, and may be closely related to limits on bank borrowing or loan agreements. There may thus be significant incentives for a company to carry creditors at less than their true value.

1.2 Testing of creditors therefore is designed primarily to obtain evidence that the balances owed to creditors are **completely** and **accurately recorded**. Testing for completeness of creditors can be particularly difficult. We shall see how auditors can gain some assurance on completeness from a variety of sources, and also have to use their knowledge of the business.

1.3 **Testing of purchases and expenses** is primarily concerned with testing that the amounts shown are for **valid expenditure**.

1.4 We shall consider in a separate section of this chapter **long-term liabilities** such as loans and debentures. These may be major long-term sources of finance for a company. Auditors will thus be concerned with how **onerous the terms** are that the company has to fulfil, and whether the company has kept up with the **repayments** it is required to make.

1.5 We then go to consider **share capital** and **reserves**, and also **statutory books** and **transactions with directors**. The Companies Act has detailed provisions governing all of these, and auditors must obtain evidence that the statutory requirements have been met.

2 CURRENT LIABILITIES, PURCHASES AND EXPENSES

2.1 The purchases cycle tests of controls will have provided the auditors with some assurance as to the completeness of liabilities.

2.2 Auditors should however be particularly aware, when conducting their balance sheet work, of the possibility of understatement of liabilities.

2.3 As regards **trade creditors**, auditors should particularly consider the following.

(a) Is there a **satisfactory cut-off** between goods received and invoices received, so that purchases and trade creditors are recognised in the correct year?

(b) Do trade creditors represent **all the bona fide amounts due** by the company?

2.4 Before we ascertain how the auditors design and conduct their tests with these objectives in mind, we need to establish the importance, as with trade debtors, of the list of balances.

Trade creditors listing and accruals listing

2.5 The list of balances will be one of the principal sources from which the auditors will select their samples for testing. The listing should be extracted from the purchase ledger by the client. The auditors will carry out the following substantive tests to verify that the extraction has been properly performed and is **complete**.

- **Check** from the **purchase ledger accounts** to the **list of balances** and *vice versa*
- **Reconcile** the **total** of the list with the **purchase ledger control account**
- **Cast** the **list** of balances and the purchase ledger control account

The client should also prepare a detailed schedule of trade and sundry accrued expenses.

Completeness and accuracy of trade creditors

2.6   The most important test when considering **trade creditors** is comparison of suppliers' statements with purchase ledger balances. This provides evidence of **existence, rights and obligations** and **completeness.**

2.7   When selecting a sample of creditors to test, auditors must be careful not just to select creditors with large year-end balances. Remember, it is errors of **understatement** that auditors are primarily interested in when reviewing creditors, and errors of understatement could occur equally in creditors with low or nil balances as with high balances. Hence when comparing supplier statements with year-end purchase ledger balances, auditors should include within their sample creditors with nil or negative purchase ledger balances. Auditors should be particularly wary of low balances with major suppliers.

2.8   You may be wondering as we normally carry out a debtors' circularisation whether we would also circularise creditors. The answer is generally no. The principal reason for this lies in the nature of the purchases cycle: third party evidence in the form of suppliers' invoices and even more significantly, suppliers' statements, is available as part of the standard documentation of the cycle.

2.9   In the following circumstances the auditors may, however, determine that a circularisation is necessary.

   (a)   Where **suppliers' statements** are, for whatever reason, **unavailable** or **incomplete**

   (b)   Where **weaknesses in internal control** or the nature of the client's business make possible a material misstatement of liabilities that would not otherwise be picked up

   (c)   Where it is thought that the **client** is **deliberately** trying to **understate creditors**

   (d)   Where the **accounts** appear to be **irregular** or if the nature or size of balances or transactions is abnormal

In these cases confirmation requests should be sent out and processed in a similar way to debtors' confirmation requests. 'Positive' requests will be required.

Purchases

2.10   When testing purchases, auditors are testing whether they have **occurred**, are **measured correctly** and have been made for **valid reasons,** (that goods and services purchased have provided benefits to the company). They are also checking for **accuracy of recording** of purchases so again cut-off procedures will be important.

Validity of purchases

2.11   As with sales, **analytical procedures** will be important. Auditors should consider:

   •   The **level of purchases** over the year, compared on a month-by-month basis with the previous year

   •   The effect on value of purchases of **changes in quantities purchased**

   •   The effect on value of purchases of changes in **products** purchased (for example a change in ingredients), or **prices of products**

   •   How the **ratio of trade creditors to purchases** compares with previous years

   •   How the **ratio of trade creditors to stock** compares with previous years

   •   How **major expenses** other than purchases compare with previous years

255

2.12 In addition auditors may carry out the following additional substantive tests on individual purchases or expenses.

- **Check purchases and expenses recorded** in the **general or purchase ledger** or **cash book** to supporting documentation (books of prime entry, invoices, delivery notes, purchase orders) considering:

  - ° Whether **purchases** and **expenses** are **valid** (invoices addressed to the client, for goods and services ordered by the client, for the purposes of the business)

  - ° Whether **purchases** and **expenses** have been allocated to the correct **purchase** or **general ledger** account

  - ° Whether amounts have been **calculated correctly**

- Consider **reasonableness of deductions** from purchases or expenses by reference to subsequent events

- Consider whether **valid debts** are **recorded** in **purchase ledger** by **checking credit notes**

2.13 If auditors are concerned about the completeness of recording of purchases, the following tests may be necessary.

- **Check** a **sample** of **purchase orders/goods received notes** to **purchase invoices**

- **Review the file** of **unprocessed invoices** and **obtaining explanations**

- **Check** the **total** of the **purchase day book** to the **general ledger**

- Analytically **review** the **gross profit percentage** and obtaining explanations for fluctuations

Purchases cut-off

2.14 The procedures applied by the auditors will be designed to ascertain whether:

- **Goods received** for which **no invoice** has been **received** are **accrued.**
- **Goods received** which have been **invoiced** but **not yet posted** are **accrued.**
- **Goods returned prior** to the **year-end** are **excluded** from **stock** and **trade creditors.**

2.15 At the year-end stocktaking the auditors will have made a note of the last serial numbers of goods received notes. Suggested substantive procedures are as follows.

- **Check from goods received notes** with serial numbers before the year-end to ensure that invoices are either:

  - ° Posted to purchase ledger prior to the year-end, or
  - ° Included on the schedule of accruals

- **Review the schedule of accruals** to ensure that goods received after the year-end are not accrued

- **Check from goods returned notes prior to year-end** to ensure that **credit notes** have been **posted** to the purchase ledger prior to the year-end or accrued

- **Review large invoices** and **credit notes** included after the year-end to ensure that they refer to the following year

- **Reconcile daily batch invoice totals** around the year-end to purchase ledger control ensuring batches are posted in the correct year

- **Review** the **control account** around the year-end for **any unusual items**

256

Purchase of goods subject to reservation of title clauses

2.16 We have already mentioned briefly the existence of transactions where the seller may retain legal ownership of goods passed to a 'purchaser' in the context of the audit of debtors. The main burden is, however, on the auditors of the **purchaser not the seller**. We now look at the audit implications of such 'reservation of title clauses' in more detail.

2.17 The cases of *Borden (UK) Limited v Scottish Timber Products*, *Re Bond Worth* and *Romalpa* suggest that a reservation of title clause will only be upheld if it states that the seller has a charge over the goods and any products made from them, and any sale proceeds are kept separately and are readily identifiable.

2.18 The existence of this type of transaction will place an additional burden on the auditor of the purchaser.

2.19 Generally, the auditors' approach should be as follows.

- **Ascertain** how the **client identifies suppliers selling** on terms which **reserve title** by enquiry of those responsible for purchasing and the board

- **Review** and test the **procedures** for **quantifying** or **estimating** the **liabilities**

- **Consider** whether **disclosure** is **sufficient** by itself if the directors have decided quantification is impractical

- **Consider** the adequacy of the **disclosures** in the accounts

- **Review the terms of sale** of **major suppliers** to confirm that liabilities not provided for do not exist or are immaterial

Verification of accruals

2.20 Checking the **completeness** and **valuation** of accruals is an area that lends itself to analytical procedures and reconciliation techniques. Care must be taken with statutory liabilities such as PAYE and VAT where there is, arguably, an expectation that the auditors verify these liabilities regardless of materiality.

2.21 You should note in particular with accruals the variety of sources which may indicate possible accruals. These include **last year's accruals, expense items** where an accrual would be expected, and **invoices received** and **cash paid** after the year-end. Auditors should also use their **knowledge** of the **business** to consider whether there are accruals which they would expect to be there, but which may not be invoiced or paid until long after the year-end.

2.22 The following substantive procedures are suggested.

- Check that **accruals** are **fairly calculated** and **verify** by reference to **subsequent payments** and **supporting documentation**

Note. For PAYE and VAT the following approach should be adopted.

- **PAYE.** Normally this should represent one month's deductions. **Check amount paid to Inland Revenue** by inspecting receipted annual declaration of tax paid over, or returned cheque

- **VAT. Check reasonableness** to **next VAT return** (either the year-end will coincide with a VAT period-end, in which case the accounts should agree with the VAT return, or the liability should be an appropriate part of the liability for the first period ending after the year-end). **Verify last amount paid** in year per cash book to VAT return

- **Review the profit and loss account** and **prior years'** figures and consider liabilities inherent in the trade to **ensure** that all **likely accruals have been provided**

- **Scrutinise payments** and **invoices** received made **after year-end** to ascertain whether they should be accrued

- **Consider basis** for **round sum accruals** and ensure it is consistent with prior years

- **Ascertain** why any **payments on account** are being **made** and **ensure** that the **full liability is provided**

- For provisions (other than provisions for depreciation, tax and bad debts):

  ° **Prepare a schedule** of any **provisions** indicating their purpose and basis, showing details of movement during the period

  ° **Decide** whether any of the **provisions** are **sufficiently material** to be separately disclosed in the accounts; in particular consider whether any provisions need to be disclosed in accordance with FRS 3

Wages and salaries

2.23 Although auditors may test other expenses solely by analytical review, they may carry out more detailed testing on wages and salaries, partly because of the consequences of failure to deduct PAYE and NIC correctly.

2.24 Analytical procedures will nonetheless be used to give some assurance on wages and salaries. Auditors should consider:

- **Wages and salaries levels** month-by-month with **previous years**
- **Effect on wages and salaries of salary changes** during the year
- **Average wage** per month **over the year**
- **Sales/profits per employee**

2.25 In addition auditors may carry out the following substantive tests.

Occurrence

- **Check individual remuneration** per payroll to **personnel records, records of hours** worked, **salary agreements** etc.

- **Confirm existence of employees** on payroll by meeting them, attending wages payout etc.

- **Check benefits** (pensions) on payroll to **supporting documentation.**

Measurement

- **Check accuracy of calculation** of **benefits**

- **Check whether calculation of statutory deductions** (PAYE, NIC) is **correct**

- **Check validity of other deductions** (pension contributions, share save etc) by agreement to supporting documentation (personnel files, conditions of pension scheme) and **check accuracy of calculation** of other deductions

Completeness

- **Check** a sample of employees from **personnel records** and ensure **included** in **payroll records**

- **Check details** of **joiners** and ensure **recorded** in **correct month**

- **Check casts of payroll records**

- **Confirm payment of net pay** per payroll records to **cheque or bank transfer** summary

- **Agree net pay** per cash book to **payroll**

- **Scrutinise payroll** and **investigate** unusual items

DEVOLVED ASSESSMENT ALERT

Wages and salaries is an important profit and loss account topic.

Inter-company indebtedness

2.26 The same procedures apply as discussed in the section on inter-company indebtedness in the last chapter.

Activity 15.1

You are carrying out the audit of creditors and accruals of Rodney Rabbit Limited, which manufactures baskets and hutches to be sold in pet shops.

The company operates a central warehouse to which all raw materials are delivered. Stores reception checks all deliveries for quantity and quality to the delivery note, and the stores receptionist completes a goods received note, keeping one copy and sending one copy to the bought ledger department.

The bought ledger department receives invoices, and when details have been checked as correct, invoices are posted to the bought ledger. Accounts with suppliers are settled monthly.

Tasks

Describe the audit work you will carry out:

(a) To confirm purchase cut-off is correct

(b) To confirm balances on the purchase ledger

(c) To confirm accruals (you can assume the only accruals are VAT, PAYE and time-apportioned expenses)

3 LONG-TERM LIABILITIES

3.1 We are concerned here with long-term liabilities comprising debentures, loan stock and other loans repayable at a date more than one year after the year-end.

3.2 Auditors will primarily try and determine:

(a) **Completeness:** whether all long-term liabilities have been disclosed

(b) **Measurement:** whether interest payable has been calculated correctly and included in the correct accounting period

(c) **Disclosure:** whether long-term loans and interest have been correctly disclosed in the financial statements

Substantive procedures applicable to all audits

3.3 The following suggested substantive procedures are relevant.

- **Obtain/prepare schedule of loans** outstanding at the balance sheet date showing, for each loan: name of lender, date of loan, maturity date, interest date, interest rate, balance at the end of the period and security

- **Compare opening balances** to previous year's working papers

- **Test the clerical accuracy** of the analysis

- **Compare balances** to the **general ledger**

- **Check name** of **lender** etc, to **register** of **debenture holders** or equivalent (if kept)

- **Trace new borrowings** and **repayments** to **entries** in the **cash book**

- **Confirm repayments** are in accordance with **loan agreement**

- **Examine cancelled cheques** and **memoranda of satisfaction** for **loans repaid**

- **Verify** that **borrowing limits** imposed either by articles or by other agreements are **not exceeded**

- **Examine signed Board minutes** relating to **new borrowings/repayments**

- **Obtain direct confirmation** from **lenders** of the amounts outstanding, accrued interest and what security they hold

- **Verify interest charged** for the period and the adequacy of accrued interest

- **Confirm assets charged** have been **entered** in the **register of charges** and **notified** to the **Registrar**

- **Review restrictive covenants** and provisions relating to default:
  - ○ **Review** any **correspondence** relating to the loan
  - ○ **Review confirmation** replies for non-compliance
  - ○ If a **default appears** to exist, **determine** its **effect**, and **schedule findings**

- **Review minutes, cash book** to **check** if all **loans have been recorded**

4 SHARE CAPITAL, RESERVES AND STATUTORY BOOKS

4.1 This section discusses three areas which, although only tenuously related, are often bracketed together for audit purposes. The audit objectives are to ascertain that:

(a) **Share capital** has been **properly classified** and **disclosed** in the financial statements and **changes** properly **authorised**.

(b) **Movements** on reserves have been properly **authorised** and, in the case of statutory reserves, **only used** for **permitted purposes.**

(c) **Statutory records** have been **properly maintained** and returns properly and expeditiously dealt with.

Share capital, reserves and distributions

4.2 The issued share capital as stated in the accounts must be **agreed** in total with the **share register**. An examination of transfers on a test basis should be made in those cases where a company handles its own registration work. Where the registration work is dealt with by independent registrars, auditors will normally examine the reports submitted by them to the company, and obtain from the registrars at the year-end a certificate of the share capital in issue.

4.3   Company law prescribes that:

(a)   The directors must have the **general powers of management** to be able to allot shares.

(b)   The directors must not exercise that power without **authority** from the **members**. That authority may either be given by the company's **articles** or by **resolution** passed in **general meeting** (s 80 of the Companies Act).

(c)   The directors must respect the **pre-emption rights** of **existing members**. Under s 89 of the Companies Act directors must first offer shares to holders of similar shares in proportion to their holdings. A private company can permanently exclude these rules in its memorandum and articles. Any company can decide by special resolution that the rules should not apply on a specific occasion.

4.4   Auditors should take particular care if there are any movements in reserves that cannot be distributed, and should **confirm** that these movements are **valid**.

4.5   The following suggested substantive procedures are relevant.

Share capital

- **Agree** the **authorised share capital** with the **memorandum** and **articles of association**

- **Agree changes** to **authorised share capital** with **properly authorised resolutions**

Issue of shares

- **Verify any issue** of share capital or other changes during the year with general and board **minutes**

- **Ensure issue or change** is within the **terms** of the **memorandum** and **articles** of association, and directors possess appropriate authority to issue shares

- Confirm that **cash** or **other consideration** has been **received** or **debtor(s) is included** as called up share capital not paid

- **Confirm** that any **premium** on issue of shares has been **credited** to the **share premium** account

- Where a public company has issued shares for **non-cash consideration,** check fair **value** has been **received for** the shares, and that valuation reports have been obtained

- For **redeemable shares** issued, check their **terms provide** for payment on **redemption**

Transfers of shares

- **Verify transfers of shares** shown in the register of members by reference to:

    ◦   Correspondence
    ◦   Completed and stamped transfer forms
    ◦   Cancelled share certificates
    ◦   Minutes of directors' meeting if director approval is required for transfers

- **Check the balances** on **shareholders' accounts** in the register of members and the total list with the amount of issued share capital in the general ledger

Dividends

- **Agree dividends** paid and proposed to **authority** in minute books and **check calculation** with **total share capital** issued to ascertain whether there are any outstanding or unclaimed dividends

- **Check dividend payments** with **documentary evidence** (say, the returned dividend warrants)

- **Check** that **dividends do not contravene** the distribution provisions of the **Companies Act 1985**

Reserves

- **Check movements on reserves** to **supporting authority**

- **Ensure that movements on reserves do not contravene** the **Companies Act 1985** and the memorandum and articles of association

- **Confirm** that the **company** can **distinguish** those reserves at the balance sheet date that are **distributable** from those that are **non-distributable**

- **Ensure appropriate disclosures** are made in the company's accounts. (These include the requirement to show movements on reserves during the year, and the FRS 3 requirement to include a statement of total gains and losses, and a statement of shareholders' funds)

Statutory books

4.6   Suggested substantive procedures are as follows.

Register of directors and secretaries

- **Update permanent file** giving details of directors and secretary

- **Verify** any **changes** with the **minutes** and ensure that the necessary details have been filed at Companies House

- **Verify** that the **number of directors complies** with the **articles**

Register of directors' interests in shares and debentures

- **Ensure** that **directors' interests** are **noted** on the permanent file for cross-referencing to directors' reports

- **Ensure** that **directors' shareholdings comply** with the **articles**

Minute books of directors' and general meetings

- **Obtain photocopies** or **prepare extracts** from the **minute books** of meetings concerning financial matters, cross-referencing them to appropriate working papers

- **Ensure** that **extracts** of **agreements** referred to in the minutes are **prepared** for the permanent file

- **Check agreements** with the company's seal book where one is kept

- **Note the date** of the last **minute reviewed**

- **Check** that **meetings** have been **properly convened** and that quorums attended them

Register of interests in shares (if applicable)

- **Scrutinise register** and verify that it appears to be in order
- **Ensure** that **significant interests** are **noted on** the permanent file

Register of charges

- **Update permanent file schedule** from the register

- **Ensure** that **any assets** which are **charged** as security for loans from third parties are disclosed in the accounts

- **Obtain confirmation** that there are **no charges** to be recorded if no entries are recorded in the register

- **Consider carrying out company search** at Companies House to verify the accuracy of the register

Accounting records

- Consider whether the accounting records are adequate to:

    ○ **Show** and **explain** the **company's transactions**

    ○ **Disclose** with **reasonable accuracy**, at any time, the **financial position** of the **company**

    ○ **Comply** with the **Companies Act** by recording money received and expended, assets and liabilities, year-end stock and stock-taking, sales and purchases

    ○ **Enable** the **directors** to **ensure** that the **accounts** give a **true and fair view**

General ledger and journals

- **Check opening balances** in general ledger to **previous year's audited accounts**

- **Check additions** of **general ledger accounts**

- **Review general ledger accounts** and ensure significant transfers and unusual items are *bona fide*

- **Review the journal** and ensure that **significant entries** are **authorised** and properly **recorded**

- **Check extraction** and **addition** of **trial balance** (if prepared by the clients)

Returns

- **Check** that the **following returns** have been **filed properly**:

    ○ Annual return and previous year's accounts
    ○ Notices of change in directors or secretary
    ○ Memoranda of charges or mortgages created during the period
    ○ VAT returns
    ○ Other tax returns

Directors' service contracts

- **Inspect copies** of directors' service contracts or memoranda

- **Ensure** that they are **kept** at either:

    ○ The registered office
    ○ The principal place of business
    ○ The place where the register of members is kept, if not the registered office

- Verify that long-term service contracts (lasting more than five years) have been approved in general meeting

BPP
PUBLISHING

Activity 15.2

What audit work should normally be carried out on:

(a) Issues of shares, and

(b) Transfers of shares

in a private company?

Directors' emoluments

4.7 The auditors have a duty to include in their report the required disclosure particulars of directors' emoluments and transactions with directors, if these requirements have not been complied with in the accounts (s 237).

Audit approach

4.8 The auditors will have carried out an evaluation of salaries payroll procedures, including the system in operation for directors' salaries, earlier in the audit. At the year end, they can probably concentrate on limited substantive work designed to ensure that **the final figures in** the **accounting records** are **complete** and the **disclosure requirements** in respect of directors have been **complied with.**

4.9 Auditors may have particular problems here in relation to **non-recurring payments** and **benefits in kind,** as, if the auditors have no previous knowledge of the existence of such items, they are often difficult to detect. Consideration should always be given as to whether some of the more common types of benefit exist (for example a company car or cheap loans).

4.10 The auditors should carry out the following general procedures.

- **Ascertain** whether **monies payable or benefits** in kind provided have been **properly approved** in accordance with the company's memorandum and articles of association and that they are not prohibited by the Act

- **Confirm** that all **monies payable** and **benefits receivable** in relation to the current accounting period have been **properly accounted for,** unless the right to any of these has been waived by inspecting:

    ° Salary records
    ° Service contracts
    ° Board minutes
    ° Other relevant records

- **Review directors' service contracts**

- **Review** the **company's procedures** to ensure that **all directors advise** the board of all disclosable **emoluments**

- **Review** the **procedures** for ensuring that any **payments made to former directors** of the company are **identified** and **properly disclosed**

- **Consider** the **need** for any **amounts** included in directors' remuneration to be **further disclosed** in accordance with the Companies Act 1985 (for example property rented by directors from a company at below market rental)

Valuation of benefits in kind

4.11   In accordance with the Companies Act 1985 the amount to be disclosed for a benefit in kind is its **estimated money value**.

4.12   Where the value used is based upon estimates the auditors must ensure that such estimates are made at an appropriate level (for example by the board of directors). On occasions it may be almost impossible to place a meaningful value on the benefit. In such cases it might be advisable for the directors to provide an explanatory note at the foot of the directors' emoluments note.

Golden hellos

4.13   Under the Companies Act 1985 rules emoluments in respect of a person's accepting office as director shall be treated as emoluments in respect of his services as director.

Related parties

4.14   The auditing standard SAS 460 *Related parties* is closely aligned to FRS 8 *Related party disclosures*, adopting the same definitions and general approach.

> **KEY TERMS**
>
> **Related parties** are two or more parties are related parties when at any time during the financial period:
>
> (a)   one party has direct or indirect control of the other party; or
>
> (b)   the parties are subject to common control from the same source; or
>
> (c)   one party has influence over the financial and operating policies of the other party to an extent that that other party might be inhibited from pursuing at all times its own separate interests; or
>
> (d)   the parties, in entering a transaction, are subject to influence from the same source to such an extent that one of the parties to the transaction has subordinated its own separate interests.

4.15   FRS 8 requires disclosure of:

(a)   Information on related party transactions

(b)   The name of the party controlling the reporting entity and, if different, that of the ultimate controlling party whether or not any transactions between the reporting entity and those parties have taken place

SAS 460 *Related parties*

> **SAS 460.1**
>
> The auditors should plan and perform the audit with the objective of obtaining sufficient audit evidence regarding the adequacy of the disclosure of related party transactions and control of the entity in the financial statements.

Inherent difficulties of detection

4.16 An audit cannot be expected to detect all material related party transactions. The risk that undisclosed related party transactions will not be detected by the auditors is especially high when:

(a) Related party transactions have taken place **without charge.**

(b) Related party transactions are **not self-evident** to the auditors or management.

(c) Transactions are with a party that the auditors could **not reasonably be expected to know is a** related party.

(d) **Active steps** have been taken by directors or management to **conceal** either the full terms of a transaction, or that a transaction is, in substance, with a related party.

Responsibilities of the directors

4.17 The directors are responsible for the identification of related party transactions. Such transactions should be properly approved as they are frequently not at arm's length. The directors are also responsible for the **disclosure** of related party transactions.

Identification of related parties and transactions

4.18 Control systems should be instituted by the directors to identify related party transactions. In general, the higher the auditors' assessment of control risk, with respect to related parties, the more emphasis is placed on substantive procedures when developing the audit programme.

SAS 460.3

The auditors should review for completeness information provided by the directors identifying material transactions with those parties that have been related parties for any part of the financial period.

4.19 The following examples are given of audit procedures.

- **Review minutes** of meetings of shareholders and directors and other relevant statutory records such as the register of directors' interests

- **Review accounting records** for large or unusual transactions or balances, in particular transactions recognised at or near the end of the financial period

- **Review confirmations of loans receivable** and payable and confirmations from banks, such a review may indicate the relationship, if any, of guarantors to the entity

- **Review investment transactions,** for example purchase or sale of an interest in a joint venture or other entity

4.20 The following substantive procedures are suggested, the extent of which should be determined as a result of tests of controls and the procedures listed above.

- **Enquire of management** and the directors as to whether transactions have taken place with related parties that are required to be disclosed by the disclosure requirements, such as FRS 8, that are applicable to the entity

- **Review prior year working papers** for names of known related parties

- **Enquire** as to the **names** of all pension and other trusts established for the benefit of employees and the names of their management and trustees

- **Enquire** as to the **affiliation** of directors and officers with other entities

- **Review the register of interests in shares** to determine the names of principal shareholders

- **Enquire of other auditors** currently involved in the audit, or predecessor auditors, as to their knowledge of additional related parties

- **Review the entity's tax returns**, listing documents supplied to Stock Exchanges, returns made under companies legislation and other information supplied to regulatory agencies for evidence of the existence of related parties

- **Review invoices and correspondence** from lawyers for indications of the existence of related parties or related party transactions

SAS 460.4

The auditors should be alert for evidence of material related party transactions that are not included in the information provided by the directors.

4.21 The following evidence is suggested of the type mentioned in SAS 460.4.

- Transactions which have **abnormal terms of trade**, such as unusual prices, interest rates, guarantees and repayment terms

- Transactions which appear to **lack a logical business reason** for their occurrence

- Transactions in which **substance differs from form**

- Transactions **processed or approved in a non-routine manner** or by personnel who do not ordinarily deal with such transactions

- **Unusual transactions** which are entered into shortly before or after the end of the financial period

Examining identified related party transactions and disclosures

SAS 460.5

The auditors should obtain sufficient appropriate audit evidence that material identified related party transactions are properly recorded and disclosed in the financial statements.

4.22 The following procedures are suggested when the audit evidence about a related party transaction is limited.

- **Discuss** the **purpose** of **the transaction** with management or the directors

- **Confirm** the **terms** and **amount** of the **transaction** with the related party

- **Corroborate** with the **related party** the **explanation** of the purpose of the transaction and, if necessary, confirm that the transaction is *bona-fide*

Disclosure relating to control of the entity

> **SAS 460.6**
>
> The auditors should obtain sufficient appropriate audit evidence that disclosures in the financial statements relating to control of the entity are properly stated.

Directors' representations

> **SAS 460.7**
>
> The auditors should obtain written representations from the directors concerning the completeness of information provided regarding the related party and control disclosures in the financial statements.

Audit conclusions and reporting

> **SAS 460.8**
>
> The auditors should consider the implications for their report if:
>
> (a) they are unable to obtain sufficient appropriate audit evidence concerning related parties and transactions with such parties; or
>
> (b) the disclosure of related party transactions or the controlling party of the entity in the financial statements is not adequate.

Key learning points

- The largest figure in **current liabilities** will normally be **trade creditors** generally checked by comparison of **suppliers' statements** with **purchase ledger accounts.**

- A **creditors' circularisation** might be appropriate, although they are relatively rare in practice compared to the frequency of debtors' circularisations.

- **Accruals** can be significant in total. Expense accruals will tend to repeat from one year to the next. Auditors should review **after-date invoices and payments**, and consider whether anything else that would have been expected has not been accrued.

- **Long-term liabilities** are usually **authorised** by the board and should be well documented.

- Share capital, reserves and statutory books will usually be examined together in an audit.

- The main concern with **share capital and reserves** (including distributions) will be that all **transactions comply** with the Companies Act.

- When auditing **statutory books** auditors should consider whether:

  ° The company has complied with the Companies Act
  ° The records contain information that affects other areas of the audit

- Auditors should ensure that directors' emoluments have been **completely** recorded in the accounts.

- **Related parties** are often very difficult to detect and the auditors must use great care when considering whether such parties exist.

Quick quiz

1 How would you check whether a list of purchase ledger balances had been correctly extracted?

2 In what circumstances may a creditors' circularisation be necessary?

3 What tests should auditors normally carry out on:

(a) PAYE liability?
(b) VAT liability?

4 What information should be contained on a schedule of long-term loans?

5 What statutory books is a company required to maintain by the Companies Act 1985?

6 What criteria must a company's accounting records fulfil?

7 What sources of information can auditors examine to obtain assurance about the completeness of recording of directors' emoluments?

Answers to quick quiz

1 The following tests should be carried out to check the proper extraction of a list of purchase ledger balances:

(a) Check from the purchase ledger accounts to the list of balances and vice-versa.
(b) Reconcile the total of the list of balances with the purchase ledger control account.
(c) Cast the list of balances and the purchase ledger control account.

2 A creditors' circularisation may be necessary where:

(a) Suppliers' statements are unavailable or incomplete
(b) There are serious weaknesses in internal control
(c) There is a high risk that the client is trying to understate creditors
(d) The accounts appear to be irregular or the nature or size of balances is unusual

3 (a) Auditors should check whether PAYE represents one month's deduction. They should check the amount paid to the Inland Revenue by inspecting the annual declaration of tax paid over or the returned cheque.

(b) Auditors should check whether the amount of VAT paid appears reasonable to the next VAT return, and the last amount paid in the year per the cash book should be verified to the VAT return.

4 The following information should be included on a schedule of long-term loans.

(a) Name of lender
(b) Date of loan
(c) Maturity date
(d) Interest date
(e) Interest rate
(f) Balance at period-end
(g) Security

5 A company must maintain the following statutory books.

(a) Register of directors and secretaries
(b) Register of directors' interests in shares and debentures
(c) Minutes of general meetings and directors' meetings
(d) Register of interests in shares (public companies only)
(e) Register of charges
(f) Directors' service contracts
(g) Register of members

6 Per s 221 of the Companies Act, a company's accounting records must:

(a) Show and explain the company's transactions

(b) Disclose with reasonable accuracy at any time the financial position of the company

(c) Record money received and expended, assets and liabilities, year-end stock and stock-taking, sales and purchases

(d) Enable the directors to ensure the accounts give a true and fair view

7   Possible sources of information apart from the accounting records are:

(a)   Salary records
(b)   Service contracts
(c)   Board minutes

Answers to activities

Answer 15.1

(a)   The audit work I would carry out to verify that purchases cut off has been correctly carried out at the year end is as follows.

(i)   From my notes taken at the stocktake I will have the number of the last GRN that was issued before the year end.

(ii)   I will then select a sample of GRNs issued in the period immediately before and immediately after the year end. The period to be covered would be at least two weeks either side of the year end.

(iii) I will concentrate my sample on high value items, and more on those GRNs from before the year end as these represent the greatest risk of cut-off error.

(iv)   I will check that the GRNs have a correct number, according to the last GRN issued in the year and whether the goods were received before or after the year end.

(v)   For GRNs issued before the year end I will ensure that the stock has been included in the year end stock total. In addition, I will ensure that the creditor is either included in trade creditors or purchase accruals.

(vi)   For GRNs issued after the year end, I will need to ensure that the stock is only included in the stock records after the year end balance has been extracted. In addition, I will need to check to the purchase ledger to ensure that the relevant invoice has been posted to the supplier account after the year end.

(b)   The audit work I will carry out to check balances on the purchase ledger is as follows.

I will select a sample of creditors and compare suppliers' statements with purchase ledger balances. The extent of the sample will depend on the results of my tests of controls and my assessment of the effectiveness of controls within the purchases system (ie if the system of control is strong I will check fewer items).

I will select the sample on a random basis. Selection of only large balances or those with many transactions will not yield an appropriate sample as I am looking for understatement of liabilities. Nil and negative balances will also need to be included in the sample.

If no statement was available for the supplier, I would ask for confirmation of the balance from the creditor.

If the balance agrees exactly, no further work needs to be carried out.

Where differences arise these need to be categorised as either in-transit items or other (including disputed) items.

In-transit items will be either goods or cash.

If the difference relates to goods in transit, I would ascertain whether the goods were received before the year end by reference to the GRN and that they are included in year end stock and purchase accruals. If the goods were received after the year end, the difference with the suppliers' accounts is correct. If not, a cut-off error has occurred and should be investigated.

Similarly, cash in transit would arise where the payment to the supplier was made by cheque before the year end but was not received by him until after the year end. The date the cheque was raised and its subsequent clearing through the bank account after the year end should be verified by checking the cash book and the post year end bank statements.

However, if the cheque clears some while after the year end date, it may indicate that the cheque, though raised before the year end was not sent to the supplier until after the year end, and the relevant amount should be added back to year end creditors and to the end of year bank balance.

Differences which do not arise from in-transit items need to be investigated and appropriate adjustments made where necessary. These differences may have arisen due to disputed invoices, where for example the client is demanding credit against an invoice which the supplier is not willing to agree to. The client may decide not to post the invoice to the supplier account as he does not consider it to be a liability of the company. However, differences may also arise because invoices have been held back in order to reduce the level of year-end creditors.

If significant unexplained differences are discovered it may be necessary to extend my testing. There may also be a problem if sufficient suppliers' statements are not available. Alternative procedures, eg a circularisation may then need to be required.

(c) The audit work I will carry out to ensure that accruals are correctly stated is as follows.

(i) I will assess the system of control instituted by management to identify and quantify accruals and creditors. Where controls are strong, I will perform fewer substantive procedures, taking the materiality of the amounts into consideration.

(ii) From the client's sundry creditors and accruals listing I will check that accruals are calculated correctly and verify them by reference to subsequent payments. I will check that all time apportionments have been made correctly (eg for electricity).

(iii) *PAYE and VAT balance*

(1) I will check the amount paid to the Inland Revenue for PAYE and NI. The balance at the year end would normally represent one month's deductions and can be verified to the payroll records. The payment should be traced from the cash book to the PAYE payment book (if used) and subsequent bank statements.

(2) For the VAT balance I will review for reasonableness to the next VAT return. I would also ensure that the payment for the previous return was for the correct amount and had cleared through the bank.

(iv) I will review the profit and loss account and prior year figures (for any accruals which have not appeared this year or which did not appear last year) and consider liabilities inherent in the trade (eg weekly wages) to ensure that all likely accruals have been provided.

(v) I will scrutinise payments made after the year end to ascertain whether any payments made should be accrued. This will include consideration of any payments relating to the current year which are made a long time after the year-end.

(vi) I will consider and document the basis for round sum accruals and ensure it is consistent with prior years.

(vii) I will ascertain why any payments on account are being made and ensure that the full liability is provided.

(viii) Accrued interest and basic charges on loans or overdrafts can be agreed to the bank letter received for audit purposes.

Answer 15.2

(a) The following procedures should be carried out on the issue of shares.

(i) Check to the company's articles to confirm that the company has sufficient authorised share capital (issued share capital should not exceed authorised share capital).

(ii) Check that the issue otherwise complies with the company's memorandum and articles.

(iii) Check that the directors possess the appropriate authority under s 80 of the Companies Act to issue shares.

(iv) Verify the terms of the issue with board minutes and minutes of general meetings.

(v) Confirm that cash or other consideration has been received for the shares or the debtor is included in called up share capital not paid.

(vi) Confirm that any premium on the issue of shares has been credited to the share premium account.

(b) Transfers of shares shown in the register of members should be verified to:

(i) Correspondence with the members
(ii) Completed and stamped transfer forms
(iii) Cancelled share certificates
(iv) Minutes of directors' meetings if directors are required to approve the transfer.

Part E
Reporting framework

Chapter 16 Audit completion procedures

Chapter topic list

1   Introduction

2   Overall review of financial statements

3   Analytical procedures

4   Opening balances and comparatives

5   Unaudited published information

6   Subsequent events

7   Contingencies

8   Going concern

9   Management representations

10   Reporting to management

11   Completion of the audit

Learning objectives

On completion of this chapter you will be able to:

	Performance criteria	Range Statement
• Explain the purpose of an overall review of the financial statements and unaudited published financial information	17.1.5,17.1.7, 17.2.1-17.2.4	17.1.1-17.1.3, 17.2.1-17.2.3
• Describe the audit procedures used to review opening balances and comparatives	17.1.5,17.1.7, 17.2.1-17.2.4	17.1.1-17.1.3, 17.2.1-17.2.3
• Describe the audit procedures used to review subsequent events	17.1.5,17.1.7, 17.2.1-17.2.4	17.1.1-17.1.3, 17.2.1-17.2.3
• Describe the audit procedures used to review contingencies	17.1.5,17.1.7, 17.2.1-17.2.4	17.1.1-17.1.3, 17.2.1-17.2.3
• Describe the audit procedures used to assess going concern	17.1.5,17.1.7, 17.2.1-17.2.4	17.1.1-17.1.3, 17.2.1-17.2.3
• Explain why auditors obtain a letter of representation and describe its main contents	17.3.1	17.3.1
• Describe the completion procedures at the end of an audit	17.3.1-17.3.4	17.3.1

BPP PUBLISHING

1 INTRODUCTION

1.1 This chapter deals with **review** and **completion procedures** on an audit. Review procedures have two aspects. Firstly auditors need to **review** the **final accounts**, considering whether the accounts **comply** with **Companies Act requirements**, the **figures make sense** (final analytical review) and the **accounts** give a **true and fair view**. Auditors have a specific responsibility to consider **opening balances** and **comparatives**, and **information published along with** the **accounts**.

1.2 The second part of the review deals with **events** that have taken place **since the balance sheet date**, and future events that may take place after the accounts are signed but which may have some bearing on the accounts (**contingencies**).

1.3 Auditors also need to consider whether the accounts should be prepared on a **going concern** basis. This is a very important task since going concern is one of the fundamental accounting concepts, and auditor misjudgements in this area can lead to considerable bad publicity. It can be very difficult to explain why a company whose accounts did not contain any mention of going concern problems, and who received an unqualified audit report, shortly afterwards went into liquidation.

1.4 Completion procedures auditors undertake include obtaining **representations** from management in areas where those representations are significant audit evidence. Auditors may also send a final **management letter** (discussed in Chapter 7), and there are various other procedures involved in signing the accounts and tidying the audit file which are best dealt with by means of a completion checklist.

2 OVERALL REVIEW OF FINANCIAL STATEMENTS

2.1 Once the bulk of the substantive procedures have been carried out, the auditors will have a draft set of financial statements which should be supported by appropriate and sufficient audit evidence. SAS 470 *Overall review of financial statements* covers the beginning of the end of the audit process.

> **SAS 470.1**
>
> Auditors should carry out such a review of the financial statements as is sufficient, in conjunction with the conclusions drawn from the other audit evidence obtained, to give them a reasonable basis for their opinion on the financial statements.

2.2 This review requires appropriate skill and experience on the part of the auditors.

Compliance with accounting regulations

> **SAS 470.2**
>
> Auditors should consider whether the information presented in the financial statements is in accordance with statutory requirements and that the accounting policies employed are in accordance with accounting standards, properly disclosed, consistently applied and appropriate to the entity.

2.3 The SAS suggests that, when compliance with statutory requirements and accounting standards is considered, the auditors may find it useful to use a **checklist**. In fact, it is quite common, particularly in large firms which audit plcs and other complex businesses, to have a variety of pre-printed checklists for different types of client.

Review for consistency and reasonableness

> **SAS 470.3**
>
> Auditors should consider whether the financial statements as a whole and the assertions contained therein are consistent with their knowledge of the entity's business and with the results of other audit procedures, and the manner of disclosure is fair.

3   ANALYTICAL PROCEDURES

3.1   In Chapter 11 we discussed how analytical review procedures are used as part of the overall review procedures at the end of an audit.

3.2   Remember the areas that the analytical review at the final stage must cover.

- Important accounting ratios
- Related items
- Changes in products; customers
- Price and mix changes
- Wages changes
- Variances
- Trends in production and sales
- Changes in material and labour content of production
- Other profit and loss account expenditure
- Variations caused by industry or economy factors

3.3   As at other stages, significant fluctuations and unexpected relationships must be investigated and documented.

4   OPENING BALANCES AND COMPARATIVES

> **KEY TERMS**
>
> **Opening balances** are those account balances that exist at the beginning of the period. Opening balances are based upon the closing balances of the preceding period and reflect the effect of transactions of preceding periods and accounting policies applied in the preceding period.
>
> **Comparatives** are the corresponding amounts and other related disclosures from the preceding period which are part of the current period's financial statements as required by relevant legislation and applicable accounting standards. Such comparatives are intended to be read in relation to the amounts and other disclosures related to the current period.

4.1   SAS 450 *Opening balances and comparatives* covers this area. Such matters should be considered at the planning stage as well as the final stages of the audit as the relevant audit procedures could have an impact on the current year audit.

4.2   Note that the preceding period accounts, when new auditors are appointed, may have been reported on by the predecessor auditors or they may have been *unaudited*.

Opening balances

> **SAS 450.2**
>
> Auditors should obtain sufficient appropriate audit evidence that:
>
> (a)   opening balances have been appropriately brought forward;
>
> (b)   opening balances do not contain errors or misstatements which materially affect the current period's financial statements; and
>
> (c)   appropriate accounting policies are consistently applied or changes in accounting policies have been properly accounted for and adequately disclosed.

4.3   If the auditors are unable to obtain sufficient appropriate audit evidence, then they should consider the implications for their audit report. The reporting implications of this are discussed in Chapter 17.

4.4   The SAS goes on to look at opening balances from the point of view of both **continuing auditors** and **incoming auditors**.

> **KEY TERMS**
>
> **Continuing auditors** are the auditors who audited and reported on the preceding period's financial statements and continue as the auditors for the current period.
>
> **Predecessor auditors** are the auditors who previously audited and reported on the financial statements of an entity, and who have been replaced by the incoming auditors.
>
> **Incoming auditors** are the auditors who are auditing and reporting on the current period's financial statements, not having audited and reported on those for the preceding period.

Continuing auditors

4.5   Audit procedures need not extend beyond ensuring that opening balances have been **appropriately brought forward** and the current accounting policies have been **consistently applied**, *if*:

(a)   The continuing auditors issued an **unqualified report** on the preceding period's financial statements.

(b)   The audit of the current period does not reveal any matters which cast **doubt** on those financial statements.

4.6   If a **qualified audit report** was issued on the preceding period's financial statements then the auditors should consider whether the matter which gave rise to the qualification has been **adequately resolved** and properly dealt with in the **current period's financial statements**. This is in addition to the procedures in Paragraph 4.5.

Incoming auditors

4.7   This situation is obviously more difficult. Appropriate and sufficient audit evidence is required on the opening balances and this depends on matters such as the following.

(a)   The **accounting policies** followed by the entity

(b)   Whether the **preceding period's financial statements were audited** and, if so, whether the auditors' report was **qualified**

(c)   The **nature of the opening balances,** including the risk of their misstatement

(d)   The **materiality of the opening balances** relative to the current period's financial statements

4.8   The **procedures given** in Paragraph 4.5 for continuing auditors should be carried out. Other procedures suggested by the SAS are as follows.

(a)   **Consultations with management** and review of records, working papers and accounting and control procedures for the preceding period

(b)   **Substantive testing of any opening balances** in respect of which the results of other procedures are considered unsatisfactory

4.9   Consultations with predecessor auditors will not normally be necessary as the above procedures will be sufficient. Predecessor auditors have no legal or ethical duty to provide information and would not normally be expected to release relevant working papers. However:

> 'they are expected to cooperate with incoming auditors to provide clarification of, or information on, specific accounting matters where this is necessary to resolve any particular difficulties.'

Comparatives

4.10   Opening balances will, in the current year's financial statements, become comparative figures which must be disclosed. The profit and loss account will also contain comparatives for income and expenses for the preceding period.

SAS 450.3

Auditors should obtain sufficient appropriate audit evidence that:

(a)   the accounting policies used for the comparatives are consistent with those of the current period and appropriate adjustments and disclosures have been made where this is not the case;

(b)   the comparatives agree with the amounts and other disclosures presented in the preceding period and are free from errors in the context of the financial statements of the current period; and

(c)   where comparatives have been adjusted as required by relevant legislation and accounting standards, appropriate disclosures have been made.

4.11   The SAS then goes on to discuss the status of comparatives from an audit perspective.

> 'The comparatives form part of the financial statements on which the auditors express an opinion, although they are not required to express an opinion on the comparatives as such. Their responsibility is to establish whether the comparatives are the amounts which appeared in the preceding period's financial statements or, where appropriate, have been restated.'

4.12 Where the auditors are unable to obtain sufficient appropriate audit evidence to support the comparatives they must consider the implications for their report. The SAS then discusses these implications in various situations.

Continuing auditors

4.13 The extent of audit procedures for comparatives will be significantly less then those for current year balances; normally they will be limited to a **check that balances have been brought forward correctly**. Materiality of any misstatements should be considered in relationship to *current* period figures.

4.14 The auditors' report on the previous period financial statements may have been qualified. Where the qualification matter is still **unresolved**, two situations may apply.

(a) If the matter is material in the context of the current period's opening balances as well as comparatives, the report on the current period's financial statements should be **qualified regarding opening balances and comparatives**.

(b) If the matter does not affect opening balances but is material in the context of the current period's financial statements, the report on the current period's financial statements should **refer to the comparatives**.

   (i) If comparatives are **required by law or regulation**, the reference will be in the form of a **qualification on the grounds of non-compliance** with that requirement.

   (ii) If comparatives are presented solely as **good practice**, the reference should be in the form of an **explanatory paragraph**.

Incoming auditors: audited comparatives

4.15 In this situation, the preceding period's financial statements have been audited by other auditors. The incoming auditors only bear audit responsibility for the comparatives in the context of the financial statements as a whole. The incoming auditors will use the knowledge gained in the current audit to decide whether the previous period's financial statements have been properly reflected as comparatives in the current period's financial statements.

4.16 The procedures below should be considered should such a situation arise.

Incoming auditors: unaudited comparatives

4.17 In this situation (eg where the company took advantage of the small company audit exemption in the previous period) the auditors should check that there is clear **disclosure** in the current financial statements that the comparatives are unaudited. They must still undertake the duties mentioned above as far as is appropriate. If there is not sufficient appropriate evidence, or if disclosure is inadequate, the auditors should consider the implications for their reports.

Activity 16.1

Fluff Limited has recently expanded with the result that it cannot claim exemption from audit for its accounts for the year ended 28 February 19X8. Auditors have therefore been appointed to audit this year's accounts.

Tasks

Discuss the work that should be carried out on the opening balances and comparatives of Fluff Limited for the year ended 28 February 19X8.

5 UNAUDITED PUBLISHED INFORMATION

5.1 The APB's SAS 160 *Other information in documents containing audited financial statements* provides guidance for auditors in this area. However, the SAS states clearly that:

> 'Nothing in this SAS refers to other information which is released in conjunction with financial statements without the auditors' knowledge and consent.'

5.2 The SAS uses the term 'other information' by which it means financial and non-financial information *other than* the audited financial statements and the auditors' report, which an entity may include in its annual report, either by custom or statute.

- A directors' report (required by statute)
- A chairman's statement
- An operating and financial review
- Financial summaries
- Employment data
- Planned capital expenditures
- Financial ratios
- Selected quarterly data

5.3 Auditors have no responsibility to report that other information is properly stated because an audit is only an expression of opinion on the truth and fairness of the financial statements. However, they may be engaged separately, or required by statute, to report on elements of other information.

> **SAS 160.1**
>
> Auditors should read the other information. If as a result they become aware of any apparent misstatements therein, or identify any material inconsistencies with the audited financial statements, they should seek to resolve them.

Auditors' consideration of other information

> **SAS 160.2**
>
> If auditors identify an inconsistency between the financial statements and the other information, or a misstatement within the other information, they should consider whether an amendment is required to the financial statements or to the other information and should seek to resolve the matter through discussion with the directors.

5.4 A **misstatement** within other information exists when it is stated incorrectly or presented in a misleading manner.

5.5 An **inconsistency** exists when the other information contradicts, or appears to contradict information contained in the financial statements. This could lead to doubts about audit evidence or even the auditors' opinion.

Unresolved misstatements and inconsistencies

> ### SAS 160.3
>
> If, after discussion with the directors, the auditors conclude
>
> (a) that the financial statements require amendment and no such amendment is made, they should consider the implications for their report,
>
> (b) that the other information requires amendment and no such amendment is made, they should consider appropriate actions, including the implications for their report.

5.6 The auditors have a statutory duty to consider a company's directors' report. S 235 Companies Act 1985 states that:

> 'the auditors shall consider whether the information given in the directors' report for the financial year for which the accounts are prepared is consistent with those accounts; and if they are of opinion that it is not they shall state that fact in their report.'

5.7 Matters which may require resolution or reference in an explanatory paragraph within the auditors' report include:

(a) An **inconsistency between amounts or narrative** appearing in the financial statements and the directors' report

(b) An **inconsistency between the bases of preparation** of related items appearing in the financial statements and the directors' report, where the figures themselves are not directly comparable and the different bases are not disclosed

(c) An **inconsistency between figures** contained in the financial statements **and a narrative interpretation** of the effect of those figures in the directors' report

5.8 Other information may contain misstatements or inconsistencies with the financial statements and the auditors may be unable to resolve them by discussion with the directors. They may need to include within the audit report an explanatory paragraph describing the apparent misstatement or material inconsistency.

Timing considerations

5.9 SAS 600 *Auditors' reports on financial statements* (see Chapter 17) requires all other information to be approved by the entity, and the auditors to consider all necessary evidence, before the audit opinion is expressed.

6 SUBSEQUENT EVENTS

6.1 Before describing the steps taken by the auditors to obtain reasonable assurance in respect of subsequent events (also called post balance sheet events - the terms are interchangeable) we need to revise the accounting requirements of the relevant accounting standard SSAP 17 *Accounting for post balance sheet events* which you have studied in *Drafting Financial Statements*.

SSAP 17 Accounting for post balance sheet events

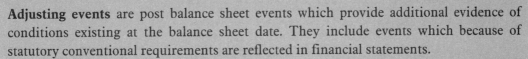

> **KEY TERMS**
>
> **Post balance sheet events** are those events, both favourable and unfavourable, which occur between the balance sheet date and the date on which the financial statements are approved by the board of directors.
>
> **Adjusting events** are post balance sheet events which provide additional evidence of conditions existing at the balance sheet date. They include events which because of statutory conventional requirements are reflected in financial statements.
>
> **Non-adjusting events** are post balance sheet events which concern conditions which did not exist at the balance sheet date.

Activity 16.2

Give two examples of an adjusting post balance sheet event and five examples of a non-adjusting post balance sheet event.

6.2 Standard practice in respect of the disclosure of post balance sheet events is as follows.

'Financial statements should be prepared on the basis of conditions existing at the balance sheet date.

A material post balance sheet event requires changes in the amounts to be included in financial statements where:

(a) it is an adjusting event; or

(b) it indicates that application of the going concern concept to the whole or a material part of the company is not appropriate.

A material post balance sheet event should be disclosed where:

(a) it is a non-adjusting event of such materiality that its non-disclosure would affect the ability of the users of financial statements to reach a proper understanding of the financial position; or

(b) it is the reversal or maturity after the year end of a transaction entered into before the year end, the substance of which was primarily to alter the appearance of the company's balance sheet.'

6.3 In respect of each disclosable post balance sheet event, the notes to the financial statements should state:

(a) The **nature** of the event

(b) An **estimate** of the financial effect, or a statement that it is not practicable to make such an estimate

> **DEVOLVED ASSESSMENT ALERT**
>
> Knowledge of the relevant accounting requirements is particularly important when dealing with post balance sheet events.

SAS 150 *Subsequent events*

KEY TERMS

Subsequent events are those relevant events (favourable or unfavourable) which occur and those facts which are discovered between the period end and the laying of the financial statements before the members or equivalent.

Relevant events are those which:

- provide additional evidence relating to conditions existing at the balance sheet date; or

- concern conditions which did not exist at the balance sheet date, but which may be of such materiality that their disclosure is required to ensure the financial statements are not misleading.

SAS 150.1

Auditors should consider the effect of subsequent events on the financial statements and on their report.

SAS 150.2

Auditors should perform procedures designed to obtain sufficient appropriate audit evidence that all material subsequent events up to the date of their report which require adjustment of, or disclosure in, the financial statements have been identified and properly reflected therein.

Audit procedures

6.4   These procedures should be applied to any matters examined during the audit which may be susceptible to change after the year end. They are in addition to tests on specific transactions after the period end, eg cut-off tests.

PROCEDURES TESTING SUBSEQUENT EVENTS	
Enquiries of management	Status of items involving **subjective judgement**/ accounted for using preliminary data
	New **commitments**, borrowings or guarantees
	Sales or destruction of **assets**
	Issues of **shares/debentures** or changes in business structure
	Developments involving **risk areas, provisions** and **contingencies**
	Unusual accounting adjustments
	Major events (eg going concern problems) affecting appropriateness of accounting policies for estimates
Other procedures	**Consider procedures** of management for identifying subsequent events
	Read minutes of general board/committee meetings
	Review latest accounting records and financial information

6.5 These procedures should be performed as near as possible to the date of the auditors' report. Reviews and updates of these procedures may be required, depending on the length of the time between the procedures and the signing of the auditors' report and the susceptibility of the items to change over time.

Subsequent events discovered after the date of the auditors' report but before the financial statements are issued

6.6 The financial statements are the directors' responsibility. The directors should therefore inform the auditors of any material subsequent events between the date of the auditors' report and the date the financial statements are issued. The auditors do *not* have any obligation to perform procedures, or make enquires regarding the financial statements *after* the date of their report.

> **SAS 150.3**
>
> When, after the date of their report but before the financial statements are issued, auditors become aware of subsequent events which may materially affect the financial statements, they should establish whether the financial statements need amendment, should discuss the matter with the directors and should consider the implications for their report, taking additional action as appropriate.

6.7 When the financial statements are amended, the auditors should extend the subsequent events procedures to the date of their new report, carry out any other appropriate procedures and issue a new audit report dated the day it is signed.

6.8 The situation where the statements are not amended but the auditors feel that they should be is discussed below.

Subsequent events discovered after the financial statements have been issued but before their laying before the members, or equivalent

> **SAS 150.4**
>
> When, after the financial statements have been issued, but before they have been laid before the members or equivalent, auditors become aware of subsequent events which, had they occurred and been known of at the date of their report, might have caused them to issue a different report, they should consider whether the financial statements need amendment, should discuss the matter with the directors, and should consider the implications for their report, taking additional action as appropriate.

6.9 The SAS gives the appropriate procedures which the auditors should undertake when the directors revise the financial statements.

- **Carry out the audit procedures** necessary in the circumstances
- **Consider**, where appropriate, whether Stock Exchange or financial services regulations require the **revision to be publicised** or a regulator to be informed
- **Review the steps taken by the directors** to ensure that anyone in receipt of the previously issued financial statements together with the auditors' report thereon is informed of the situation
- **Issue a new report** on the revised financial statements

6.10   When the auditors issue a **new report** they:

- **Refer in their report to the note to the financial statements** which more extensively discusses the reason for the revision of the previous accounts

- **Refer to the earlier report** issued by them on the financial statements

- **Date** their new report **not earlier** than the date the revised financial statements are approved

- **Have regard** to the **guidance** relating to reports on revised annual financial statements and directors' reports as set out in APB's Practice Note 8 *Reports by auditors under company legislation in the United Kingdom*

6.11   Where the directors do *not* revise the financial statements but the auditors feel they should be revised, and where the statements have been issued but not yet laid before the members; or if the directors do not intend to make an appropriate statement at the AGM, then the auditors should consider steps to take, on a timely basis, to prevent reliance on their report eg a statement at the AGM. The auditors have no right to communicate to the members directly in writing.

7   CONTINGENCIES

7.1   Again, we will revise the accounting requirements here first.

FRS 12 *Provisions, contingent liabilities and contingent assets*

7.2   The objective of FRS 12 is to ensure that contingent liabilities and assets and provisions are properly accounted for and disclosed.

KEY TERMS

A **provision** is a liability that is of uncertain timing or amount, to be settled by the transfer of economic benefits.

A **contingent liability** is either (a) a possible obligation arising from past events whose existence will be confirmed only by the occurrence of one or more uncertain future events not wholly within the entity's control; or (b) a present obligation that arises from past events but is not recognised because it is not probable that a transfer of economic benefits will be required to settle the obligation or because the amount of the obligation cannot be measured with sufficient reliability.

A **contingent asset** is a possible asset arising from past events whose existence will be confirmed only by the occurrence of one or more uncertain future events not wholly within the entity's control.

The key distinction therefore is between provisions which are accrued in the accounts, and contingent assets and liabilities, which are not accrued but which may be disclosed.

Recognition

7.3   A provision should be recognised when an entity has a **present obligation** as a result of a past event, it is **probable** that a **transfer** of **economic benefits** will be **required** to settle the obligation, and a **reasonable estimate** can be made of the amount of the obligation. Unless these conditions are met, no provision should be recognised.

Measurement

7.4   The amount recognised as a provision should be the **best estimate** of the expenditure required to settle the present obligation at the balance sheet date.

Reimbursements

7.5   Where some or all of the expenditure required to settle a provision is expected to be reimbursed by another party, the reimbursement should be recognised only when it is **virtually certain** that the reimbursement will be received if the entity settles the obligation. The reimbursement should be treated as a separate asset.

Changes in provisions

7.6   Provisions should be reviewed at each balance sheet date and adjusted to reflect the current best estimate.

CONTINGENT LIABILITIES		
Where, as a result of past events, there may be a transfer of future economic benefits in settlement of (a) a present obligation or (b) a possible obligation whose existence will be confirmed by the occurrence of one or more uncertain future events not wholly within the entity's control, and		
there is a present obligation that probably requires a transfer of economic benefits in settlement,	there is a possible obligation or a present obligation that may, but probably will not, require a transfer of economic benefits in settlement,	there is a possible obligation or a present obligation where the likelihood of a transfer of economic benefits in settlement is remote,
a provision is recognised and disclosures are required for the provision.	no provision is recognised but disclosures are required for the contingent liability.	no provision is recognised and no disclosure is required.

7.7   A contingent liability also arises in the extremely rare case **where there is a liability** that cannot be recognised because it cannot be **measured reliably**. Disclosures are required for the contingent liability.

CONTINGENT ASSETS		
Where, as a result of past events, there is a possible asset whose existence will be confirmed by the occurrence of one or more uncertain future events not wholly within the entity's control, and		
the inflow of economic benefits is virtually certain,	the inflow of economic benefits is probable but not virtually certain,	the inflow is not probable,
the asset is not contingent.	no asset is recognised but disclosures are required.	no asset is recognised and no disclosure is required.

7.8   The audit tests that should be carried out on provisions and contingent assets and liabilities are as follows.

•   **Obtain details** of all **provisions** which have been included in the **accounts** and all **contingencies** that have been disclosed

- **Obtain** a **detailed analysis** of all **provisions** showing opening balances, movements and closing balances

- **Determine** for each material provision **whether** the **company** has a **present obligation** as a result of past events by:

  ° **Review** of **correspondence** relating to the item

  ° **Discussion** with the **directors**. Have they created a valid expectation in other parties that they will discharge the obligation?

- **Determine** for each material provision **whether** it is **probable** that a **transfer of economic benefits** will be required to settle the obligation by the following tests:

  ° **Check** whether any **payments** have been **made** in the post balance sheet period in respect of the item

  ° **Review of correspondence** with solicitors, banks, customers, insurance company and suppliers both pre and post year end

  ° **Send** a **letter** to the **solicitor** to obtain their views (where relevant)

  ° **Discuss** the **position** of similar **past provisions** with the directors, were these provisions eventually settled?

  ° **Consider** the **likelihood** of **reimbursement**

- **Recalculate** all **provisions** made

- **Compare** the **amount provided** with any post year end payments and with any amount paid in the past for similar items

- In the event that it is not possible to estimate the amount of the **provision**, **check** that this **contingent liability** is **disclosed** in the accounts

- **Consider** the **nature** of the **client's business**; would you expect to see any other provisions eg warranties?

DEVOLVED ASSESSMENT ALERT

You should appreciate that the problems of accounting for provisions and contingencies makes their audit difficult.

Activity 16.3

(a) What general procedures should auditors carry out when reviewing post balance sheet events?

(b) What information relating to after the balance sheet date, might be relevant, and why, in the following audit areas.

   (i)   Stock
   (ii) Trade creditors and accruals

(c) How should auditors obtain evidence about legal claims in which clients are involved?

8   GOING CONCERN

8.1   SAS 130 *Going concern basis in financial statements* is a very important SAS because of the potential liability of the auditors should they miss the going concern problems of a client and the difficulties surrounding the determination of going concern status in any given situation.

Going concern as an accounting concept

> ### KEY TERMS
>
> The **going concern** concept: the enterprise will continue in operational existence for the foreseeable future. This means in particular that the profit and loss account and balance sheet assume no intention or necessity to liquidate or curtail significantly the scale of operation. (SSAP 2)

8.2 The SSAP definition is supported by legal requirements. Under these requirements, the financial statements of an entity are assumed to be prepared on a going concern basis.

8.3 Where the going concern basis is *not* appropriate:

- The entity may not be able to recover the amounts recorded in respect of assets.
- There may be changes in the amounts and dates of maturities of liabilities.

Therefore, if material, the amounts and classification of assets and liabilities would need to be adjusted.

8.4 Consequently, the *directors* must satisfy themselves that the going concern basis is appropriate. Even where it is, further disclosure may be required to give a true and fair view.

Activity 16.4

What factors may indicate that a business is suffering from going concern problems?

The applicability and scope of this SAS

8.5 The SAS gives guidance to auditors in the context of the going concern basis in financial statements which are required to be properly prepared under the Companies Act and to show a true and fair view.

Foreseeable future

8.6 SSAP 2 uses the term 'foreseeable future' but does not define it. The SAS recognises that any consideration of foreseeable future involves 'making a judgement, at a particular point in time, about future events which are inherently uncertain'. The SAS suggests that the following factors are relevant.

8.7 The 'foreseeable future' depends on the specific circumstances at a point in time, the degree of **uncertainty increases significantly** the **further into the future** the consideration is taken. As a consequence there can never be any certainty in relation to going concern. The auditors' judgement is only valid at that time and can be 'overturned by subsequent events'.

Consideration of going concern by the directors

8.8 The directors must assess going concern by looking at a period into the future and considering all available and relevant information. The SAS states that a minimum length for this period cannot be specified; it would be 'artificial and arbitrary' as there is no 'cut off point' after which the directors would change their approach.

Audit procedures

> ### SAS 130.1
>
> When forming an opinion as to whether financial statements give a true a fair view, the auditors should consider the entity's ability to continue as a going concern, and any relevant disclosures in the financial statements.

8.9 The audit procedures will be based on the directors' deliberations and the information they used. The auditors must assess whether the audit evidence is sufficient and whether they agree with the directors' judgement.

Audit evidence

> ### SAS 130.2
>
> The auditors should assess the adequacy of the means by which the directors have satisfied themselves that:
>
> (a) it is appropriate for them to adopt the going concern basis in preparing the financial statements; and
>
> (b) the financial statements include such disclosures, if any, relating to going concern as are necessary for them to give a true and fair view.
>
> For this purpose:
>
> (a) the auditors should make enquiries of the directors and examine appropriate available financial information; and
>
> (b) having regard to the future period to which the directors have paid particular attention in assessing going concern, the auditors should plan and perform procedures specifically designed to identify any material matters which could indicate concern about the entity's ability to continue as a going concern.

Preliminary assessment

8.10 The auditors' approach includes a preliminary assessment, when the overall audit plan is being developed, of the risk that the entity may be unable to continue as a going concern. The auditors should consider:

(a) **Whether the period** to which the directors have paid particular attention in assessing going concern is **reasonable** in the client's circumstances

(b) The **systems,** or other means (formal or informal), **for timely identification of warnings of future risks** and uncertainties the entity might face

(c) **Budget and/or forecast information** (cash flow information in particular) produced by the client, and the quality of the systems (or other means, formal or informal) in place for producing this information and keeping it up to date

(d) Whether the **key assumptions** underlying the budgets and/or forecasts appear appropriate in the circumstances, including consideration of:

• Projected profit

- Forecast levels of working capital
- The completeness of forecast expenditure
- Whether the client will have sufficient cash at periods of maximum need
- The financing of capital expenditure and long-term plans

(e) The **sensitivity of budgets and/or forecasts** to variable factors both within the control of the directors and outside their control

(f) Any **obligations, undertakings or guarantees** arranged with other entities (in particular, lenders, suppliers and group companies)

(g) The **existence, adequacy and terms of borrowing facilities**, and supplier credit

(h) The **directors' plans** for resolving any matters giving rise to the concern (if any) about the appropriateness of the going concern basis. In particular, the auditors may need to consider whether:

- The plans are realistic.
- The plans are likely to resolve any problems foreseen.
- The directors are likely to put the plans into practice effectively.

8.11 The auditors' and directors' procedures can be very simple in some cases, particularly in the case of smaller companies, where budgets and forecasts are not normally prepared and no specific systems are in place to monitor going concern matters.

The auditors' examination of borrowing facilities

8.12 The auditors will usually:

- **Obtain confirmations** of the existence and terms of bank facilities
- **Make** their own **assessment** of the intentions of the bankers relating thereto

8.13 These procedures will become more important if for example, the client is **dependent** on **borrowing facilities** shortly due for renewal, correspondence between the bankers and the entity reveals that the **last renewal** of facilities was **agreed with difficulty**, or a **significant deterioration in cash flow** is predicted.

8.14 If the auditors cannot satisfy themselves then, in accordance with the audit reporting standard (SAS 600), they should consider whether the relevant matters need to be:

(a) **Disclosed in the financial statements** in order that they give a true and fair view, and/or

(b) **Referred to in the auditors' report** (by an explanatory paragraph or a qualified opinion)

Determining and documenting the auditors' concerns

8.15 The following are given as examples of indicators of an entity's inability to continue as a going concern.

GOING CONCERN	
Financial	An excess of liabilities over assets
	Net current liabilities
	Necessary borrowing facilities have not been agreed
	Default on terms of loan agreements, and potential breaches of covenant
	Significant liquidity or cash flow problems
	Major losses or cash flow problems which have arisen since the balance sheet date and which threaten the entity's continued existence
	Substantial sales of fixed assets not intended to be replaced
	Major restructuring of debts
	Denial of (or reduction in) normal terms of trade credit by suppliers
	Major debt repayment falling due where refinancing is necessary to the entity's continued existence
	Inability to pay debts as they fall due
Operational	Fundamental changes to the market or technology to which the entity is unable to adapt adequately
	Externally forced reductions in operations (for example, as a result of legislation or regulatory action)
	Loss of key management or staff, labour difficulties or excessive dependence on a few product lines where the market is depressed
	Loss of key suppliers or customers or technical developments which render a key product obsolete
Other	Major litigation in which an adverse judgement would imperil the entity's continued existence
	Issues which involve a range of possible outcomes so wide that an unfavourable result could affect the appropriateness of the going concern basis

DEVOLVED ASSESSMENT ALERT

You may be asked to list signs that a particular client may not be a going concern.

8.16 Auditors may still obtain sufficient appropriate audit evidence in such situations to conclude that the going concern basis is still appropriate. Further procedures such as discussions with the directors and further work on forecasts may be required.

8.17 Where auditors consider that there is a significant level of concern about the going concern basis, they might write to the directors suggesting the need to take suitable advice.

Written confirmations of representations from the directors

SAS 130.4

The auditors should consider the need to obtain written confirmations of representations from the directors regarding:

(a) the directors' assessment that the company is a going concern; and
(b) any relevant disclosures in the financial statements.

8.18 Representations may be critical in terms of audit evidence. If they do *not* receive such representations the auditors should consider whether:

(a) There is a **limitation of scope** in their work and a qualified opinion is required in 'except for' or 'disclaimer' terms.

(b) The failure of the directors to provide written confirmation could indicate **concern.**

Assessing disclosures in the financial statements

SAS 130.5

The auditors should consider whether the financial statements are required to include disclosures relating to going concern in order to give a true and fair view.

8.19 The main concern here is **sufficiency** of disclosure:

- Where there are going concern worries
- Where the future period the directors have considered is less than one year

8.20 The auditors must assess whether the statements show a true and fair view and hence whether their opinion should be qualified, as well as whether all matters have been satisfactorily disclosed.

Reporting on the financial statements

8.21 The SAS summarises, in flowchart form, how auditors formulate their opinion as to whether the financial statements give a true and fair view and this is shown on the next page.

SAS 130.6

Where the auditors consider that there is a significant level of concern about the entity's ability to continue as a going concern, but do not disagree with the preparation of the financial statements on the going concern basis, they should include an explanatory paragraph when setting out the basis of their opinion. They should not quality their opinion on these grounds alone, provided the disclosures in the financial statements of the matters giving rise to the concern are adequate for the financial statements to give a true and fair view.

8.22 The following matters must be included in the financial statements for disclosure to be regarded as adequate.

- A statement that the financial statements have been prepared on the **going concern basis**

- A statement of the **pertinent facts**

- The **nature** of the concern

- A statement of the **assumptions** adopted by the directors, which should be clearly distinguishable from the pertinent facts

- (Where appropriate and practicable) a statement regarding the directors' **plans for resolving the matters** giving rise to the concern

- Details of any **relevant actions** by the directors

SAS 130.7

If the period to which the directors have paid particular attention in assessing going concern is less than one year from the date of approval of the financial statements, and the directors have not disclosed that fact, the auditors should do so within the section of their report setting out the basis of their opinion, unless the fact is clear from any other references in their report. They should not qualify their opinion on the financial statements on these grounds alone.

8.23 The auditors will also qualify their opinion if they consider that the directors have not taken adequate steps to satisfy themselves that it is appropriate for them to adopt the going concern basis. This will be a limitation in the scope of the auditors' work.

8.24 The audit report will contain the following paragraph if disclosure is considered adequate.

> **Basis of opinion: excerpt**
>
> *Going concern*
>
> In forming our opinion, we have considered the adequacy of the disclosures made in note 1 of the financial statements concerning the uncertainty as to the continuation and renewal of the company's bank overdraft facility. In view of the significance of this uncertainty we consider that it should be drawn to your attention but our opinion is not qualified in this respect.

Going concern presumption is inappropriate

8.25 Where the going concern presumption is **inappropriate**:

    (a) Even disclosure in the financial statements of the matters giving rise to this conclusion is *not* sufficient for them to give a true and fair view.

    (b) The effect on financial statements prepared on that basis is so material or pervasive that the financial statements are seriously misleading.

Accordingly, an **adverse opinion** (that the accounts do not give a true and fair view) is appropriate in such cases.

Financial statements not prepared on the going concern basis

SAS 130.9

In rare circumstances, in order to give a true and fair view, the directors may have prepared financial statements on a basis other than that of a going concern. If the auditors consider this other basis to be appropriate in the specific circumstances, and if the financial statements contain the necessary disclosures, the auditors should not qualify their opinion in this respect.

8.26 You should refer back to this section after you have studied the next chapter on the audit report. The reporting requirements relating to going concern will then be much clearer.

8.27 **Section summary**

    • Director and auditor assessment of the going concern basis should take place over the **foreseeable future.**

    • Auditors should make a **preliminary assessment** of going concern and be alert during the audit for **signs** of **going concern problems.**

- Specific audit procedures include **assessment** of **client forecasts,** examination of **borrowing facilities** and obtaining **representations** from the directors.

- Auditors may **qualify** the audit report because they disagree with the use of the **going concern basis** or **extent of disclosure.**

- Alternatively auditors may consider it appropriate to give an unqualified opinion with a **fundamental uncertainty** paragraph.

Activity 16.5

(a) What is meant by the statement 'These accounts have been prepared on a going concern basis'?

(b) What procedures should auditors carry out in order to obtain assurance that a company is a going concern? (You may assume auditors have no initial reasons to doubt the company's ability to continue as a going concern.)

---

9 MANAGEMENT REPRESENTATIONS.

9.1 The auditors receive many representations during the audit and some may be critical to obtaining sufficient appropriate audit evidence. Representations may also be required for general matters, eg full availability of accounting records.

9.2 Written confirmation of oral representations avoids confusion and disagreement. The written confirmation may take the form of:

(a) A **representation letter** from **management** (see example below)

(b) A **letter from the auditors** outlining their understanding of management's representations, duly acknowledged and confirmed in writing by management

(c) **Minutes of meetings of the board** or directors, or similar body, at which such representations are approved

Acknowledgement by directors of their responsibility for the financial statements

> **SAS 440.2**
>
> The auditors should obtain evidence that the directors acknowledge their collective responsibility for the preparation of the financial statements and have approved the financial statements.

9.3 Auditors normally do this when they receive a signed copy of the financial statements which incorporate a relevant statement of the directors' responsibilities.

Representations by management as audit evidence

9.4 In addition to representations relating to responsibility for the financial statements, the auditors may wish to rely on management representations as audit evidence.

> **SAS 440.3**
>
> Auditors should obtain written confirmation of representations from management on matters material to the financial statements when those representations are critical to obtaining sufficient appropriate audit evidence.

*Going concern and reporting
on the financial statements*

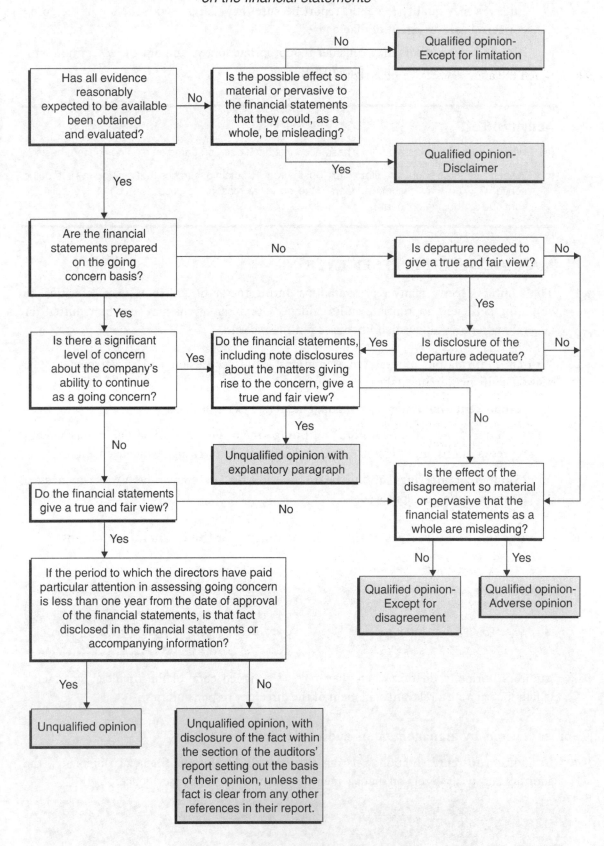

9.5   Such matters should be discussed with those responsible for giving the written confirmation, to ensure that they understand what they are confirming. Written confirmations are normally required of appropriately senior management. Only matters which are material to the financial statements should be included in a letter of representation.

9.6   When the auditors receive such representations they should:

(a)   **Seek corroborative audit evidence**

(b)   **Evaluate** whether the **representations** made by management appear **reasonable** and are **consistent** with other audit evidence obtained, including other representations

(c)   Consider whether the individuals making the representations can be **expected** to be **well-informed** on the particular matters

9.7   The SAS then makes a very important point.

> 'Representations by management cannot be a substitute for other (expected) audit evidence. If auditors are unable to obtain sufficient appropriate audit evidence regarding a matter which may have a material effect on the financial statements and such audit evidence is expected to be available, this constitutes a limitation in the scope of the audit, even if a representation from management has been received on the matter.'

9.8   There are two instances given in the SAS where management representations *may* be the only audit evidence available.

(a)   **Knowledge of the facts is confined to management**, eg the facts are a matter of management intention.

(b)   **The matter is principally one of judgement or opinion**, eg the trading position of a particular customer.

9.9   There may be occasions when the representations received do not agree with other audit evidence obtained.

SAS 440.4

If a representation appears to be contradicted by other audit evidence, the auditors should investigate the circumstances to resolve the matter and consider whether it casts doubt on the reliability of other representations.

9.10   Investigations of such situations will normally begin with further enquiries of management; the representations may have been misunderstood or, alternatively, the other evidence misinterpreted. If explanations are insufficient or unforthcoming, then further audit procedures may be required.

Basic elements of a management representation letter

9.11   A management representation letter should:

- Be **addressed** to the **auditors**
- Contain the **specified information**
- Be **appropriately dated**
- Be **approved** by those with **specific knowledge** of the relevant matters

9.12   The auditors will normally request that the letter is:

(a) Discussed and agreed by the board of directors (or equivalent)

(b) Signed on its behalf by the chairman and secretary before the auditors approve the financial statements

9.13 The letter will usually be **dated on** the day the financial statements are **approved**, but if there is any significant delay between the representation letter and the date of the auditors' report, then the auditors should consider the need to obtain further representations.

Action if management refuses to provide written confirmation of representations

> ### SAS 440.5
>
> If management refuses to provide written confirmation of a representation that the auditors consider necessary, the auditors should consider the implications of this scope limitation for their report.

9.14 In these circumstances, the auditors should consider whether it is appropriate to rely on other representations made by management during the audit.

Example of a management representation letter

9.15 An *example* of a management representation letter is provided in an appendix to the SAS. It is *not* a standard letter, and representations do not have to be confirmed in letter form.

(Company letterhead)

(To the auditors)   (Date)

We confirm to the best of our knowledge and belief, and having made appropriate enquiries of other directors and officials of the company, the following representations given to you in connection with your audit of the financial statements for the period ended 31 December 19...

(1) We acknowledge as directors our responsibilities under the Companies Act 1985 for preparing financial statements which give a true and fair view and for making accurate representations to you. All the accounting records have been made available to you for the purpose of your audit and all the transactions undertaken by the company have been properly reflected and recorded in the accounting records. All other records and related information, including minutes of all management and shareholders' meetings, have been made available to you.

(2) The legal claim by ABC Limited has been settled out of court by a payment of £258,000. No further amounts are expected to be paid, and no similar claims have been received.

(3) In connection with deferred tax not provided, the following assumptions reflect the intentions and expectations of the company:

    (a) capital investment of £450,000 is planned over the next three years;

    (b) there are no plans to sell revalued properties; and

    (c) we are not aware of any indications that the situation is likely to change so as to necessitate the inclusion of a provision for tax payable in the financial statements.

(4) The company has not had, or entered into, at any time during the period any arrangement, transaction or agreement to provide credit facilities (including loans, quasi-loans or credit transactions) for directors or to guarantee or provide security for such matters.

(5) There have been no events since the balance sheet date which necessitate revision of the figures included in the financial statements or inclusion of a note thereto.

As minuted by the board of directors at its meeting on .... (date)

....

Chairman   Secretary

9.16 Examples of other issues which may be the subject of representations from [...] include:

(a) The extent of the purchase of goods on terms which include reservation of t[...] suppliers

(b) The absence of knowledge of circumstances which could result in losses on long-term contracts

(c) The reasons for concluding that an overdue debt from a related party is fully recoverable

(d) Confirmation of the extent of guarantees, warranties or other financial commitments relating to subsidiary undertakings or related parties

DEVOLVED ASSESSMENT ALERT

The most important points to remember about a letter of representation are:

(a) The circumstances in which it can be used
(b) The auditors' response if the client fails to agree to it

You should also be able to draft appropriate representations if asked.

Activity 16.6

(a) What are the main purposes of a letter of representation and how far can auditors rely on the audit evidence it provides?

(b) Draft appropriate representations to cover the following circumstances.

  (i) A long-term material balance of £200,000 owed by an associated company, Y Limited, has been outstanding for nine months at the year-end. The reason for the delay in repayment has been cash flow problems, but the associate's cash flow has improved since the year-end and the directors are confident the debt can be recovered.

  (ii) A major customer has sued the company for £50,000. The directors have disclosed this claim in the accounts, but believe it will be settled in the company's favour. The directors also believe that the reasons why the claim arose are one-off, and do not apply to other customers, or other transactions with this customer.

10   REPORTING TO MANAGEMENT

10.1 As we discussed in Chapter 7, a management letter is likely to be sent at the final stage of the audit.

10.2 The final letter will cover not only weaknesses in control, but matters which caused delays or problems in the audit and may have resulted in increased costs.

10.3 Auditors may also highlight some of the results of their analytical review if they believe these will be of use to management.

BPP PUBLISHING

...he financial statements give a true a fair view, auditors should assess the ...ate of uncorrected misstatements.

...e aggregate of uncorrected misstatements comprises:

(a) **Specific misstatements** identified by the auditors, including uncorrected misstatements identified during the audit of the previous period if they affect the current period's financial statements

(b) Their **best estimate** of **other misstatements** which cannot be quantified specifically

11.2 If the auditors consider that the aggregate of misstatements may be material, they must consider reducing audit risk by extending audit procedures or requesting the directors to adjust the financial statements (which the directors may wish to do anyway).

11.3 The auditors should consider the implications for their audit report if:

(a) The directors refuse to adjust.

(b) The extended audit procedures do not enable the auditors to conclude that the aggregate of uncorrected misstatements is not material.

11.4 The summary of errors will not only list errors from the current year, but also those in the previous year(s). This will allow errors to be highlighted which are reversals of errors in the previous year, such as in the valuation of closing/opening stock. Cumulative errors may also be shown, which have increased from year to year.

SCHEDULE OF UNADJUSTED ERRORS

		20X2				20X1			
		P & L account		Balance sheet		P & L account		Balance sheet	
		Dr	Cr	Dr	Cr	Dr	Cr	Dr	Cr
		£	£	£	£	£	£	£	£
(a)	ABC Ltd debt unprovided	10,470			10,470	4,523			4,523
(b)	Opening/ closing stock under-valued*	21,540			21,540		21,540	21,540	
(c)	Closing stock undervalued		34,105	34,105					
(d)	Opening unaccrued expense:								
	Telephone*		453	453		453			453
	Electricity*		905	905		905			905
(e)	Closing unaccrued expenses								
	Telephone	427			427				
	Electricity	1,128			1,128				
(f)	Obsolete stock write off	2,528			2,528	3,211			3,211
Total		36,093	35,463	35,463	36,093	9,092	21,540	21,540	9,092
	*Cancelling items	21,540			21,540				
			453	453					
			905	905					
		14,553	34,105	34,105	14,553				

11.5 The schedule will be used by the audit manager and partner to decide whether the client should be requested to make adjustments to the financial statements.

Completion checklists

11.6 Audit firms frequently use checklists which must be signed off to ensure that all final procedures have been carried out, all material amounts are supported by sufficient appropriate evidence, etc. An example is shown overleaf.

Key learning points

- The auditors must perform and document an **overall review** of the financial statements before they can reach an opinion, covering:

  - Compliance with statute and accounting standards
  - Consistency with audit evidence
  - Overall reasonableness

- **Analytical procedures** should be used at the final stage of audit. The review should cover:

  - Key business ratios
  - Related items in accounts
  - The effect of known changes on the accounts

- Specific procedures must be applied to **opening balances** at a new audit client.

- The auditors' responsibilities for **comparatives** relate mainly to **consistency**, although comparatives and opening balances can have an impact on current results.

- **Unaudited published information** includes the **directors' report,** and other statements such as the **chairman's statement** and an **operating and financial review.** Auditors have a statutory responsibility to report inconsistencies between the directors' report and accounts.

- Auditors should consider the effect of **subsequent events** (after the balance sheet date) on the accounts.

- Auditors have a responsibility to **review subsequent events** before they sign their audit report, and may have to take action if they become aware of subsequent events between the date they sign their audit report and the date the financial statements are laid before members.

- The audit of **contingencies** involves reviewing the company's dealing with solicitors, and is generally connected to the subsequent events review.

- Evaluation of going concern is most important. Auditors should consider the **future plans** of directors and any signs of **going concern problems** which may be noted throughout the audit. **Bank facilities** may have to be confirmed.

- When reporting on the accounts, auditors should consider whether the going concern basis is **appropriate,** and whether **disclosure** of going concern problems is **sufficient**.

- **Representations from management** should generally be restricted to matters that cannot be verified by other audit procedures.

- Any representations should be **compared** with other evidence and their **sufficiency** assessed.

- As part of their completion procedures, auditors should consider whether the **aggregate of uncorrected misstatements** is material.

Quick quiz

1 What matters should auditors consider when examining accounting policies?

2 What are the principal considerations in a review of the financial statements for consistency and reasonableness?

3 What checks should continuing auditors carry out on opening balances if their report on the previous year's accounts was unqualified?

4 What does SAS 450 say about communications with predecessor auditors?

Audit completion checklist

Client:
Period ended:

Instructions:
1 All questions must be answered by ticking one of the columns as appropriate.
2 Any 'No' answer must be referenced to the 'points for partner' schedule.

Section I - To be completed by the manager

	Yes	No	N/A	Reference to points for partner schedule
Permanent audit file				
1 Have the following been updated in the course of the audit:				
(a) Flowcharts and related documentation for:				
(i) computer systems?				
(ii) non-computer systems?				
(b) Internal /key control evaluation questionnaire conclusions?				
(c) Details of the client organisation?				
(d) Financial history?				
2 Is a current letter of engagement in force?				
Transaction (interim) audit file				
3 Were walk-through tests performed to confirm our record of the accounting systems?				
4 Was the audit programme tailored?				
5 Was adequate audit attention given to internal control weaknesses?				
6 Were levels of audit testing (compliance and substantive) appropriate?				
7 Have audit programmes been signed off as complete?				
8 Are there adequate explanations of work done and are conclusions drawn?				
9 Is there evidence of the review of work?				
10 Have weaknesses arising on the interim audit been reported to management in a formal letter				
11 Has the client replied to the weaknesses already notified in respect of matters arising from the previous year's audit?				
12 Have major internal control weaknesses previously notified been rectified?				
Final (balance sheet) audit file				
13 Have lead schedules been prepared for each audit area and cross-referenced and agreed with the financial statements?				
14 Have all the working papers been initialled and dated by the members of staff who prepared them?				

	Yes	No	N/A	Reference to points for partner schedule
15 Have all the working papers been cross-referenced?				
16 Do the working papers show comparative figures where appropriate?				
17 Have audit conclusions been drawn for each balance sheet audit area as appropriate?				
18 Has the balance sheet audit programme been completed, initialled and cross-referenced to the working papers?				
19 Have the necessary profit and loss account schedules been prepared and do they agree with the detailed accounts?				
20 Current assets:				
(a) Were debtors circularised and were the results satisfactory?				
(b) Was the client's stocktaking attended and were the results satisfactory?				
(c) Is the basis of stock and work in progress valuation satisfactory and correctly disclosed in the accounts?				
21 Liabilities:				
(a) Were creditors circularised and were the results satisfactory?				
(b) Have all liabilities, contingent liabilities, and capital commitments been fully accounted for or noted in the accounts?				
Audit completion				
22 Have formal representations been obtained or has a draft letter been set up (including representations in respect of each director regarding transactions involving himself and his connected persons required to be disclosed by the Companies Act 1985)?				
23 Have all audit queries been satisfactorily answered?				
24 Post balance sheet event review:				
(a) Has a comprehensive review been performed and evidenced?				
(b) Has the review been carried out at the most recent date possible with regard to the anticipated date of the audit report?				
25 Have all audit queries been satisfactorily answered?				
26 Have all closing adjustments been agreed with the client?				
27 Are you satisfied that all material instances where we have not received the information and explanations we require have been referred to in the points for partner schedule?				

	Yes	No	N/A	Reference to points for partner schedule
37 Has the directors' report been reviewed for consistency with the financial statements?				
38 Has other financial information to be issued with the audited financial statements (eg contained in the Chairman's Statement or Employee Accounts) been reviewed for consistency with the financial statements?				

.... Audit Manager   .... Date

Section II - To be completed by the reporting partner

	Yes	No	Comments
1 Has Section I of the checklist been satisfactorily completed?			
2 Have all the points on the 'points for partner' schedule been satisfactorily resolved or are there any material matters outstanding which should be referred to the audit panel?			
3 Has your review of the current and permanent file indicated that the working paper evidence is sufficient to enable you to form an opinion on the financial statements, having regard to the firm's audit manual procedures?			
4 Are the conclusions you have drawn from your overall review of the financial statements based on your knowledge of the client, consideration of the analytical review memorandum, review of post balance sheet events and where appropriate, client risk evaluation questionnaire, consistent with those contained in the detailed working papers?			
5 Have all improvements which you consider could be made in the conduct of future audits been noted on 'points forward' (for consideration at the audit debriefing)?			
6 (a) Are there any specialist areas in which the client could benefit from our expertise, for example tax planning?			
(b) Has the provision of such services been drawn to his attention?			

I confirm that the report of the auditors will be unqualified*/unqualified with an explanatory paragraph*/ qualified* as set out in the attached draft financial statements.

.... Reporting Partner   .... Date

*Delete as appropriate

	Yes	No	N/A	Reference to points for partner schedule
28 Review of working papers?				
(a) Have you reviewed all the working papers? (If not, briefly describe review procedure adopted)				
(b) Have arrangements been made for the financial statements to be reviews by:				
(i) a second partner (a brief review or special review)? and/or				
(ii) the audit review panel?				
(c) Has the planning memorandum and, where applicable, client risk evaluation questionnaire been completed?				
Subsidiary and associated companies				
29 Where secondary auditors have been involved in the audit of subsidiary and associated companies, have we:				
(a) Sent our group accounts audit questionnaire?				
(b) Received satisfactory answers? or				
(c) Reviewed and approved the working papers of secondary auditors?				
30 Have all accounts of subsidiary and associated companies been approved by the directors and audited?				
31 If any of the audit reports have been qualified has the fact and nature of the qualification been referred to in the points for partner schedule?				
Financial statements and directors' report				
32 Is the financial statements layout in accordance with the firm's standard accounts pack?				
33 Has the analytical review memorandum been properly completed and are the review conclusions consistent with the conclusions drawn in respect of our other audit work?				
34 Is the reliance placed on analytical review reasonable in the circumstances?				
35 Is any proposed dividend covered by the distributable profits as disclosed in the financial statements?				
36 Has the firm's accounting disclosure checklist been completed to ensure that the financial statements and directors' report comply with:				
(a) the Companies Act 1985?				
(b) Statements of Standard Accounting Practice and Financial Reporting Standards?				
(c) Stock Exchange requirements?				
(d) Other reporting requirements?				

5   What are the inconsistencies between the accounts and the directors' report to which auditors may have to refer in their audit report?

6   What is the difference between an adjusting and non-adjusting post balance sheet event?

7   What procedures should auditors undertake as a result of revisions to the accounts by the directors after the accounts have been issued?

8   What are the consequences regarding the realisation of assets and liabilities if the going concern basis is not appropriate?

9   What circumstances may lead to auditors examining a client's borrowing requirements?

10   What criteria should auditors use to judge whether disclosure about going concern problems is sufficient?

11   What forms may written confirmations of representation take?

12   What types of misstatement might be included in the aggregate of uncorrected misstatements?

Answers to quick quiz

1   When examining accounting policies, auditors should consider:

(a)   Policies commonly adopted in particular industries

(b)   Policies for which there is substantial authoritative support

(c)   Whether any departures from applicable accounting standards are necessary for the financial statements to give a true and fair view

(d)   Whether the financial statements reflect the substance of the underlying transactions and not merely their form

2   When reviewing accounts for consistency and reasonableness auditors should consider:

(a)   Whether the accounts reflect the information and explanations and the conclusions reached during the audit

(b)   Whether the review reveals any new factors which may affect the presentation and disclosure of the accounts

(c)   The results of analytical procedures at the end of the audit

(d)   Whether the presentation of the accounts may have been unduly influenced by the directors

(e)   The effect of the aggregate of uncorrected misstatements

3   Continuing auditors should check opening balances have been appropriately brought forward and the current accounting policies consistently applied.

4   The SAS suggests that communications with predecessor auditors on opening balances will not normally be necessary, but predecessor auditors should provide clarification of, or information on, specific accounting matters where it is necessary to resolve any particular difficulty.

5   Inconsistencies between the accounts and directors' report include:

(a)   Inconsistencies between amounts or narrative

(b)   Inconsistencies between the bases of preparation (where the different bases are not disclosed)

(c)   Inconsistencies between figures in the accounts and narrative interpretation of the figures in the directors' report

6   An adjusting post balance sheet event provides additional evidence of conditions existing at the balance sheet date. A non-adjusting event concerns conditions which did not exist at the balance sheet date.

7   Auditors should undertake the following procedures if accounts are changed:

(a)   Whatever audit procedures are required to verify the changes

(b)   Consideration of whether the revision should be publicised in accordance with Stock Exchange regulations

(c)   Consideration of whether the change ought to be reported to the appropriate regulator

(d)   Review of how the directors have informed anyone who received a copy of the previously issued accounts

(e)   Issue of a new report on the accounts

8   If the going concern basis is not appropriate, the entity may not be able to recover the amounts recorded in respect of assets, and there may be changes in the amounts and dates of maturity of liabilities.

9   Auditors may examine a client's borrowing requirements when:

(a)   There is a low margin of available financial resources.
(b)   The client is dependent on borrowing facilities shortly due for renewal.
(c)   The last renewal was agreed with difficulty, or banks have imposed further conditions.
(d)   A significant deterioration in cash flow is predicted.
(e)   The value of assets granted as security for the borrowings is declining.
(f)   The entity has breached the terms of the borrowing covenants.

10   Auditors should consider whether disclosures about going concern problems include the following:

(a)   A statement that the accounts have been prepared on a going concern basis
(b)   A statement of the pertinent facts
(c)   The nature of the concern
(d)   The directors' assumptions
(e)   The directors' plans
(f)   Relevant actions by the directors

11   Representations may take the form of board minutes or a written representation from directors.

12   Misstatements that may be included in the statement are specific misstatements identified by the auditors, and the auditors' best estimate of other misstatements.

Answers to activities

Answer 16.1

Under SAS 450 auditors have a responsibility to obtain sufficient appropriate audit evidence that amounts derived from preceding period's accounts have been properly brought forward and included in this year's accounts.

Opening balances

For opening balances, this means obtaining appropriate audit evidence that:

(a)   Opening balances have been appropriately brought forward.

(b)   Opening balances do not contain material misstatements which affect the current year's accounts.

(c)   Accounting policies are consistently applied or changes in accounting policies are appropriate and fully disclosed.

Auditors' procedures should include consultations with management. They should check that balances in last year's trial balance have been brought forward to this year's accounting records, and should consider whether the accounting policies which affect the opening balances are appropriate.

They should review the accounting records, accounting procedures and internal controls that were in operation during the last accounting period.

Often these procedures will suffice since auditors can gain assurance on the correctness of opening balances by obtaining assurance on this year's closing balances and transactions during the year. However audit verification work may be required on opening balances if the review procedures mentioned above do not provide sufficient evidence. SAS 450 suggests that verification procedures are more likely when, as here, the previous year's accounts were not audited.

If additional verification procedures are required, auditors should concentrate on those areas which are material to this year's accounts, particularly areas where there have been significant changes as compared with last year.

Comparatives

SAS 450 requires auditors to obtain sufficient appropriate audit evidence that:

(a) Accounting policies used for comparatives are consistent with those used for the current period, or appropriate adjustments and disclosures have been made.

(b) The comparatives agree with the accounts and other disclosures presented in the previous periods and are free from errors.

(c) Where comparatives have been adjusted, appropriate disclosures have been made.

Unlike with opening balances, it should not be necessary to carry out verification work on comparatives. Auditors should ensure comparatives have been correctly brought forward and appropriately classified for Fluff Ltd, and they should check that the comparatives are clearly disclosed in the accounts as being unaudited.

If the auditors become aware that the comparatives have been materially misstated, they should encourage the directors either to restate the comparatives or reissue last year's accounts. If the comparatives are re-stated in this year's accounts, auditors should ensure the re-statement is adequately disclosed. If the comparatives are not re-stated, the audit opinion is likely to have to be qualified.

Answer 16.2

(a) The following are normally examples of adjusting post balance sheet events.

(i) Subsequent determination of the price of assets bought or sold before the year-end

(ii) A property valuation which indicates a permanent diminution in property value which occurred before the year-end

(iii) Receipt of accounts from a long-term investment which indicates a permanent diminution in the value of that investment

(iv) Indications of the net realisable value of stocks such as the sales prices

(v) Renegotiation of amounts owed by debtors or the insolvency of a debtor

(vi) Declaration of dividends by investments relating to periods before the balance sheet date

(vii) Receipt of information regarding rates of tax

(viii) Amounts received in respect of insurance claims being negotiated prior to the year-end

(ix) Discoveries of errors or frauds

(b) The following are usually examples of non-adjusting events.

(i) Mergers and acquisitions
(ii) Reconstructions and proposed reconstructions
(iii) Issues of shares and debentures
(iv) Purchases and sales of fixed assets and investments
(v) Losses of fixed assets due to fire or flood
(vi) Opening new trading activities or extending trading activities
(vii) Closing significant trading activities (other than closures fulfilling FRS 3 requirements)
(viii) Post year-end decline in the value of property and investments
(ix) Changes in the rate of foreign exchange
(x) Government action
(xi) Labour disputes
(xii) Changes in pension benefits

Answer 16.3

(a) Auditors should carry out the following procedures as part of their post balance sheet events review.

(i) Consider the procedures management has established in order to ensure post balance sheet events are correctly treated. Auditors will be concerned with how post balance sheet events have been identified, considered and properly evaluated as to their effect on the financial statements.

(ii) Review post year-end accounting records which contain further evidence of conditions existing at the balance sheet date. This review will include review of debtors for evidence of receipt from cash from debtors, and review of bank and cash for evidence of clearance of cheques which were uncleared at the year-end.

(iii) Review budgets, profit forecasts, cash flow projections and management accounts. These may indicate significant income or expenditure which needs to be disclosed, and will also give general indications about the company's trading position.

(iv) Search for evidence about known risk areas and contingencies. This includes a review of documentation relating to legal matters (see (d)).

(v) Read the minutes of directors' meetings which took place after the year-end. These may provide evidence of significant decisions which may need to be disclosed. Auditors should find out details of what has happened at meetings for which minutes are not yet available.

(vi) Review relevant sources of evidence that are external to the client, such as knowledge of competitors, suppliers and customers and industry trends.

(vii) Discuss with management whether any events have occurred that may affect the accounts. Examples include new commitments, changes in assets or events which bring into question the accounting policies or estimates used in the accounts.

(b) (i) The main use of after-date evidence in stock is to determine the client's ability to sell its stock and hence to determine what net realisable value should be. The following information may be relevant:

    (1) After-date sales made or orders received
    (2) Details of planned reductions in sales prices
    (3) Industry trends and details, particularly prices and performance of competitors
    (4) Details of increases in average age of stock
    (5) Details of stock scrapped

(ii) The main uses of information on trade creditors and accruals are:

    (1) Trade creditors and accruals have been completely recorded
    (2) Stock cut-off has been correctly applied

Relevant information includes:

    (1) Information received after the year-end for goods or services received prior to the year-end
    (2) Credit notes received after the year-end for goods returned before the year-end
    (3) Suppliers' statements received after the year-end relating to periods prior to the year-end
    (4) Payments made after the year-end relating to goods or services received before the year-end

(c) Auditors should carry out the following procedures to obtain evidence about legal actions.

(i) Discuss with management the arrangements for instructing solicitors or barristers.

(ii) Examine board minutes for indications of legal actions.

(iii) Examine correspondence with, and bills rendered by, solicitors and obtain confirmation that no bills are outstanding.

(iv) Obtain a list of matters referred to solicitors.

(v) Obtain written assurances that directors or other officials are not aware of any outstanding matters other than those disclosed.

(vi) If appropriate (due to problems with other evidence), obtain confirmation from solicitors about the directors' assessment of likely outcomes of legal actions, and of whether the information provided by the directors is complete.

Answer 16.4

Factors indicating going concern problems include the following.

(a) Financial factors such as cash flow problems, net current liabilities or inability to pay debts
(b) Operational factors such as changes in market, loss of key staff, suppliers or customers
(c) Other factors such as major litigation

A more detailed list is given in paragraph 8.15 of this chapter.

Answer 16.5

(a) Going concern is one of the fundamental accounting principles which underpin the preparation of accounts. The statement that accounts have been prepared on a going concern basis means that the business will continue to be in operational existence for the foreseeable future. That means assets will be realised in the normal course of business without the necessity for forced sales at knockdown prices, and that no liability will arise other than those incurred in the normal course of business.

(b) In order to gain sufficient audit evidence to be able to form an opinion on the going concern status of a company, the auditors should review the following.

(i) Whether the period to which the directors have paid particular attention in assessing going concern is reasonable in the entity's circumstances and in the light of the need for the directors to consider the ability of the entity to continue in operational existence for the foreseeable future

(ii) The systems, or other means (formal or informal), for timely identification of warnings of future risks and uncertainties the entity might face

(iii) Budget and/or forecast information (cash flow information in particular) produced by the entity, and the quality of the systems (or other means, formal or informal) in place for producing this information and keeping it up to date

(iv) Whether the key assumptions underlying the budgets and/or forecasts appear appropriate in the circumstances

(v) The sensitivity of budgets and/or forecasts to variable factors both within the control of the directors and outside their control

(vi) Any obligations, undertakings or guarantees arranged with other entities (in particular, lenders, suppliers and group companies) for the giving or receiving of support

(vii) The existence, adequacy and terms of borrowing facilities, and supplier credit

(viii) The directors' plans for resolving any matters giving rise to the concern (if any) about the appropriateness of the going concern basis. In particular, the auditors may need to consider whether:

(1) The plans are realistic.

(2) There is a reasonable expectation that the plans are likely to resolve any problems foreseen.

(3) The directors are likely to put the plans into practice effectively.

Answer 16.6

(a) The purpose of a letter of representation is to obtain evidence about matters which are critical to the audit where that evidence is not available by other means.

SAS 440 suggests that matters where representations are obtained will mainly be where knowledge of the facts is confined to management, or where the directors have used judgement or opinion in the preparation of the accounts.

The fundamental weakness of representations is that they are not a substitute for stronger, independent evidence. Therefore representations will be insufficient if other stronger evidence is expected to be available.

If other evidence would not be expected to be available, auditors will consider the following:

(i) The fact that making misleading representations to auditors is an offence under the Companies Act

(ii) Whether other evidence that the auditors have sought to corroborate the representations, does do so

(iii) Whether the representations are consistent with other evidence obtained during the course of audit

(iv) Whether those making the representations are able to do so knowledgeably

(b) (i) Since the year-end, the cash flows of Y Limited, an associated company, have improved significantly. As a result we believe that amounts of £200,000 which have been owed since WW will be fully recoverable.

(ii) We are confident that the legal claim made by X Limited for £50,000 will be successfully defended and the disclosures made in the accounts concerning the claim are sufficient. No similar claims from X Limited or other customers have been received or are expected to be received.

Chapter 17 The external audit opinion

Chapter topic list

Learning objectives

On completion of this chapter you will be able to:

	Performance criteria	Range Statement
• Describe the importance and content of the audit report	17.3.1-17.3.4	17.3.1
• Draft an unqualified audit report	17.3.1-17.3.4	17.3.1
• Decide which type of audit report is relevant in different circumstances and draft appropriate qualifications and explanatory paragraphs	17.3.1-17.3.4	17.3.1

1 INTRODUCTION

1.1 We deal in detail in this chapter with the audit report, the public product of the auditors' work.

1.2 We start by stating the matters on which the auditor reports explicitly (truth and fairness, and preparation in accordance with the Companies Act), and those on which the auditor reports by exception.

1.3 We shall then revise the form of the **audit report**. Remember the current version of the audit report is designed to close the **expectations gap** by stating the responsibilities of auditors and directors, and setting out the work which auditors perform to obtain a basis for their opinion.

1.4 We shall then examine **qualified audit reports**. These are given when the auditors are not satisfied that the accounts give a true and fair view, and hence have to give a qualification (or qualifications) to the audit opinion. **Qualifications** arise for two reasons. Firstly if the auditors are not **convinced** that they have **obtained all the evidence** that ought to be available to them, they qualify their audit opinion on grounds of limitation of scope. Secondly if the auditors **do not agree** with amounts, accounting policies or disclosures in the financial statements, they issue a qualification on the grounds of disagreement.

1.5 A further problem for auditors concerns areas where they do have all the evidence that they can expect to obtain, but there nevertheless remain considerable **uncertainties** surrounding those areas. If significant uncertainties of this sort exist, auditors must make reference to them in the audit report, but will *not* qualify their audit report if they are happy with the way the uncertainties have been treated in the accounts.

1.6 The last section of the chapter deals with auditor reporting on small and medium-sized company accounts.

2 STATUTORY REQUIREMENTS

Unqualified report

2.1 An *unqualified* audit report communicates an assurance to the user, that an independent examination of the accounts has discovered no material problems and that the accounts show a **true and fair view**. We will discuss truth and fairness in the next section of this chapter.

2.2 An unqualified report also conveys certain implications. These are unstated because the auditors only report **by exception**. In other words, these assumptions will only be mentioned (by a **qualified** audit report) if they do not hold true. An unqualified report implies that (under s 237 Companies Act 1985):

(a) **Proper accounting records** have been kept and proper returns adequate for the audit received from branches not visited.

(b) The **accounts** agree with the **accounting records** and **returns.**

(c) **All information and explanations** have been **received** as the auditors think necessary and they have had access at all times to the company's books, accounts and vouchers.

(d) **Details** of **directors' emoluments** and **other benefits** have been correctly **disclosed** in the financial statements.

(e) Particulars of **loans** and **other transactions** in favour of **directors** and others have been correctly disclosed in the financial statements.

(f) The **information** given in the **directors' report** is **consistent** with the **accounts.**

3 TRUE AND FAIR

3.1 The accounts of a limited company are required by s 226(2) of the Companies Act 1985 to show a **true and fair view** of the company's financial position as at the balance sheet date and of its profit or loss for the year ending on that date. The auditors are required to state in their report whether, in their opinion, the accounts satisfy that requirement.

3.2 Most commentators give definitions of truth and fairness along the following lines.

> **KEY TERMS**
>
> **True:** Information is factual and conforms with reality, not false. In addition the information conforms with required standards and law. The accounts have been correctly extracted from the books and records.
>
> **Fair:** Information is free from discrimination and bias and in compliance with expected standards and rules. The accounts should reflect the commercial substance of the company's underlying transactions.

3.3 The Accounting Standards Committee (ASC), the predecessor to the Accounting Standards Board, obtained the following opinion.

> 'A SSAP is a declaration by the ASC, on behalf of its constituent professional bodies, that save in exceptional circumstances accounts which do not comply with the standard will not give a true and fair view.'

3.4 This opinion also made these points:

(a) 'Accounts will not be true and fair unless the information they contain is **sufficient** in **quantity** and **quality** to satisfy the reasonable expectations of readers to whom they are addressed.'

(b) The expectations of readers will have been influenced by the **normal practices of accountants**.

(c) **SSAPs** serve the following purposes.

   (i) They **crystallise professional opinion** about what may be expected in accounts that are true and fair.

   (ii) Because accounts are obliged to comply with SSAPs, **readers** will thus **expect accounts to conform** with SSAPs.

(d) SSAPs therefore have an indirect but important effect on truth and fairness.

3.5 The main thrust of recent developments in company law and standard setting has been to strengthen considerably the previous opinion that compliance with accounting standards indicates that a true and fair view is being shown. The implication is that companies which do *not* follow accounting standards are presumed 'guilty', ie their accounts do *not* show a true and fair view.

4 SAS 600 AUDITORS' REPORT ON FINANCIAL STATEMENTS

> **SAS 600.1**
>
> Auditors' reports on financial statements should contain a clear expression of opinion, based on review and assessment of the conclusions drawn from evidence obtained in the course of the audit.

4.1   The auditors' report should be placed before the financial statements. The directors' responsibilities statement (explained later) should be placed before the auditors' report.

Basic elements of the auditors' report

SAS 600.2

Auditors' reports on financial statements should include the following matters:

(a)   a title identifying the person or persons to whom the report is addressed;
(b)   an introductory paragraph identifying the financial statements audited;
(c)   separate sections, appropriately headed, dealing with:
    (i)   respective responsibilities of directors (or equivalent persons) and auditors;
    (ii)   the basis of the auditors' opinion;
    (iii)   the auditors' opinion on the financial statements;
(d)   the manuscript or printed signature of the auditors; and
(e)   the date of the auditors' report.

4.2   The following is given as an example of an unqualified audit report in an appendix to the SAS.

Example 1. Unqualified opinion: company incorporated in Great Britain

AUDITORS' REPORT TO THE SHAREHOLDERS OF XYZ PLC

We have audited the financial statements on pages ... to ... which have been prepared under the historical cost convention (as modified by the revaluation of certain fixed assets) and the accounting policies set out on page ....

Respective responsibilities of directors and auditors
As described on page ... the company's directors are responsible for the preparation of financial statements. It is our responsibility to form an independent opinion, based on our audit, on those statements and to report our opinion to you.

Basis of opinion
We conducted our audit in accordance with Auditing Standards issued by the Auditing Practices Board. An audit includes examination, on a test basis, of evidence relevant to the amounts and disclosures in the financial statements. It also includes an assessment of the significant estimates and judgements made by the directors in the preparation of the financial statements, and of whether the accounting policies are appropriate to the company's circumstances, consistently applied and adequately disclosed.

We planned and performed our audit so as to obtain all the information and explanations which we considered necessary in order to provide us with sufficient evidence to give reasonable assurance that the financial statements are free from material misstatement, whether caused by fraud or other irregularity or error. In forming our opinion we also evaluated the overall adequacy of the presentation of information in the financial statements.

Opinion
In our opinion the financial statements give a true and fair view of the state of the company's affairs as at 31 December 20.. and of its profit (loss) for the year then ended and have been properly prepared in accordance with the Companies Act 1985.

Registered auditors   *Address*

Date

---

* A reference to the convention draws attention to the fact that the values reflected in the financial statements are not current but historical and, where appropriate, to the fact that there is a mixture of past and recent values.

4.3 The report recommends the use of standard format as an aid to the reader, including headings for each section, for example 'Qualified opinion'. The title and addressee and the introductory paragraph are fairly self explanatory. You may have noticed that the audit report does not refer to the company's cash flow statement in the opinion paragraph. This is discussed in the next section.

Statements of responsibility and basic opinion

SAS 600.3

(a) Auditors should distinguish between their responsibilities and those of the directors by including in their report:

   (i) a statement that the financial statements are the responsibility of the reporting entity's directors;

   (ii) a reference to a description of those responsibilities when set out elsewhere in the financial statements or accompanying information; and

   (iii) a statement that the auditors' responsibility is to express an opinion on the financial statements.

(b) Where the financial statements or accompanying information (for example the directors' report) do not include an adequate description of directors' relevant responsibilities the auditors' report should include a description of those responsibilities.

Example wording of a description of the directors' responsibilities for inclusion in a company's financial statements

4.4 A description of the directors' responsibilities is given in an example in an appendix. It can be produced by the directors or included by the auditors in their report.

> Company law requires the directors to prepare financial statements for each financial year which give a true and fair view of the state of affairs of the company and of the profit or loss of the company for that period. In preparing those financial statements, the directors are required to:
>
> (a) select suitable accounting policies and then apply them consistently;
>
> (b) make judgements and estimates that are reasonable and prudent;
>
> (c) state whether applicable accounting standards have been followed, subject to any material departures disclosed and explained in the financial statements (large companies only);
>
> (d) prepare the financial statements on the going concern basis unless it is inappropriate to presume that the company will continue in business (if not separate statement on going concern is made by the directors).
>
> The directors are responsible for keeping proper accounting records which disclose with reasonable accuracy at any time the financial position of the company and to enable them to ensure that the financial statements comply with the Companies Act 1985. They are also responsible for safeguarding the assets of the company and hence for taking reasonable steps for the prevention and detection of fraud and other irregularities.

This wording can be adapted to suit the specific situation.

Explanation of auditors' opinion

> ### SAS 600.4
>
> Auditors should explain the basis of their opinion by including in their report:
>
> (a) a statement as to their compliance or otherwise with Auditing Standards, together with the reasons for any departure therefrom;
>
> (b) a statement that the audit process includes:
>
>   (i) examining, on a test basis, evidence relevant to the amounts and disclosures in the financial statements;
>
>   (ii) assessing the significant estimates and judgements made by the reporting entity's directors in preparing the financial statements;
>
>   (iii) considering whether the accounting policies are appropriate to the reporting entity's circumstances, consistently applied and adequately disclosed;
>
> (c) a statement that they planned and performed the audit so as to obtain reasonable assurance that the financial statements are free from material misstatement, whether caused by fraud or other irregularity or error, and that they have evaluated the overall presentation of the financial statements. (SAS 600.4)

4.5 Other than in exceptional circumstances, a departure from an auditing standard is a limitation on the scope of work undertaken by the auditors.

Expression of opinion

> ### SAS 600.5
>
> An auditors' report should contain a clear expression of opinion on the financial statements and on any further matters required by statute or other requirements applicable to the particular engagement.

4.6 An unqualified opinion on financial statements is expressed when in the auditors' judgement they give a true and fair view (where relevant) and have been prepared in accordance with relevant accounting or other requirements. This judgement entails concluding whether *inter alia*:

(a) The financial statements have been prepared using **appropriate, consistently applied accounting policies**.

(b) The financial statements have been **prepared** in accordance with **relevant legislation, regulations** or **applicable accounting standards** (and that any departures are justified and adequately explained in the financial statements).

(c) There is **adequate disclosure** of all information relevant to the proper understanding of the financial statements.

Date and signature of the auditors' report

> **SAS 600.9**
>
> (a) Auditors should not express an opinion on financial statement until those statements and all other financial information contained in a report of which the audited financial statements form a part have been approved by the directors, and the auditors have considered all necessary available evidence.
>
> (b) The date of an auditors' report on a reporting entity's financial statements is the date on which the auditors sign their report expressing an opinion on those statements.

4.7 If the date on which the auditors sign the report is later than that on which the directors approve the financial statements, then the auditors must check that the post balance sheet event review has been carried out up to the date they sign their report and that the directors would also have approved the financial statements on that date.

Forming an opinion on financial statements

4.8 Appendix 1 of the SAS considers the process of forming an audit opinion using the flowchart shown on the next page. The flowchart is drawn up on the basis that the directors make no further amendments to the financial statements following the audit.

4.9 The principal matters which auditors consider in forming an opinion may be expressed in three questions.

(a) Have they **completed all procedures necessary** to meet auditing standards and to obtain all the information and explanations necessary for their audit?

(b) Have the financial statements been **prepared in accordance** with the **applicable accounting requirements**?

(c) Do the financial statements, as prepared by the directors, give **a true and fair view**?

Note. Requirements are referred to in terms of generally accepted accounting principles.

Activity 17.1

The following is a series of extracts from an unqualified audit report which has been signed by the auditors of Little Panda Limited.

AUDITORS' REPORT TO THE SHAREHOLDERS OF LITTLE PANDA LIMITED

We have audited *the financial statements on pages .... to ....* which have been prepared under the historical cost convention.

We have conducted our audit *in accordance with Auditing Standards* issued by the Auditing Practices Board. An audit includes examination on a test basis of evidence relevant to the amounts and disclosures in the financial statements.

In our opinion the financial statements give a true and fair view of the state of the company's affairs as at 31 December 20X7 and of its profit for the year then ended and have been properly prepared in accordance with the Companies Act 1985.

Tasks

Explain the purpose and meaning of the following phrases taken from the above extracts of an unqualified audit report.

(a) '... the financial statements on pages .... to ....'
(b) '... in accordance with Auditing Standards.'
(c) 'In our opinion ...'

FORMING AN OPINION ON FINANCIAL STATEMENTS

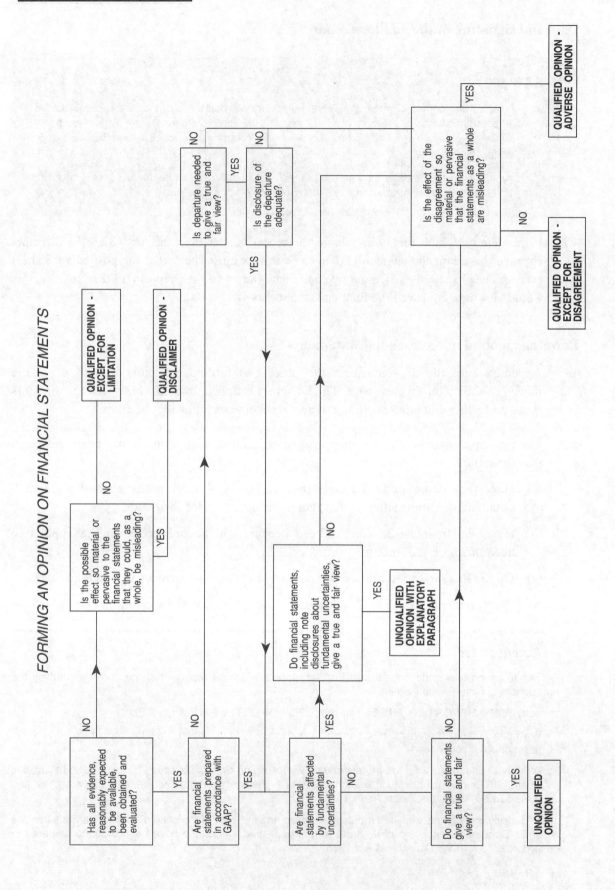

5 QUALIFICATIONS IN AUDIT REPORTS

5.1 Qualified audit reports arise when auditors do not believe they can state without reservation that the accounts give a true and fair view.

The qualification 'matrix'

5.2 SAS 600 gives the circumstances in which each type of qualification would be appropriate. Where the auditors are unable to report affirmatively on the matters contained in the paragraphs about which they have reservations, they should give:

- A full explanation of the **reasons** for the qualification
- Whenever possible, a **quantification** of its effect on the financial statements

Where appropriate, reference should be made to non-compliance with relevant legislation and other requirements.

5.3 The standard stresses the fact that **a qualified audit report should leave the reader in no doubt as to its meaning and its implications for an understanding of the financial statements**.

5.4 The Auditing Practices Board takes the view that the nature of the circumstances giving rise to a qualification of the auditor's opinion will generally fall into one of two categories:

(a) Where there is a **limitation in the scope of work** which prevents the auditors from forming an opinion on a matter (uncertainty - see SAS 600.7)

(b) Where the auditors are able to form an opinion on a matter but this **conflicts** with the view given by the financial statements (disagreement - see SAS 600.8)

5.5 Either case, uncertainty or disagreement, may give rise to alternative forms of qualification. This is because the uncertainty or disagreement can be:

- Material but not fundamental
- Of fundamental importance to the overall true and fair view

The standard requires that the following forms of qualification should be used in the different circumstances outlined below.

QUALIFICATION MATRIX

Nature of circumstances	Material but not fundamental	Fundamental
Limitation in scope	Except for .. might	Disclaimer of opinion
Disagreement	Except for ...	Adverse opinion

Except for . . . might	Auditors disclaim an opinion on a particular aspect of the accounts which is not considered fundamental.
Disclaimer of opinion	Auditors state they are unable to form an opinion on truth and fairness.
Except for	Auditors express an adverse opinion on a particular aspect of the accounts which is not considered fundamental.
Adverse opinion	Auditors state the accounts do not give a true and fair view.

Limitations in the scope of the audit

5.6 Scope limitations will arise where auditors are unable for any reason to obtain all the information and explanations which they consider necessary for the purpose of their audit, arising from:

(a) **Absence** of proper **accounting records**

(b) An **inability** to carry out **audit procedures** considered necessary as, for example, where the auditors are unable to obtain satisfactory evidence of the existence or ownership of material assets

---

SAS 600.7

When there has been a limitation on the scope of the auditors' work that prevents them from obtaining sufficient evidence to express an unqualified opinion:

(a) the auditors' report should include a description of the factors leading to the limitation in the opinion section of their report;

(b) the auditors should issue a disclaimer of opinion when the possible effect of a limitation on scope is so material or pervasive that they are unable to express an opinion on the financial statements;

(c) a qualified opinion should be issued when the effect of the limitation is not as material or pervasive as to require a disclaimer, and the wording of the opinion should indicate that it is qualified as to the possible adjustments to the financial statements that might have been determined to be necessary had the limitation not existed.

5.7 When giving this type of qualified opinion, auditors should assess:

(a) The **quantity and type of evidence** which may reasonably be expected to be available to support the figure or disclosure in the financial statements

(b) The **possible effect** on the financial statements of the matter for which insufficient evidence is available

5.8 SAS 600 gives the following examples.

Example 8. Qualified opinion: limitation on the auditors' work

(Basis of opinion: excerpt)

.... or error. However, the evidence available to us was limited because £... of the company's recorded turnover comprises cash sales, over which there was no system of control on which we could rely for the purposes of our audit. There were no other satisfactory audit procedures that we could adopt to confirm that cash sales were properly recorded.

In forming our opinion we also evaluated the overall adequacy of the presentation of information in the financial statements.

Qualified opinion arising from limitation in audit scope

Except for any adjustments that might have been found to be necessary had we been able to obtain sufficient evidence concerning cash sales, in our opinion the financial statements give a true and fair view of the state of the company's affairs as at 31 December 20.. and of its profit (loss) for the year then ended and have been properly prepared in accordance with the Companies Act 1985.

In respect alone of the limitation on our work relating to cash sales:

(a) we have not obtained all the information and explanations that we considered necessary for the purpose of our audit; and

(b) we were unable to determine whether proper accounting records had been maintained.

Example 9. Disclaimer of opinion

(Basis of opinion: excerpt)

.... or error. However, the evidence available to us was limited because we were appointed auditors on (date) and in consequence we were unable to carry out auditing procedures necessary to obtain adequate assurance regarding the quantities and condition of stock and work in progress, appearing in the balance sheet at £... . Any adjustment to this figure would have a consequential significant effect on the profit for the year.

In forming our opinion we also evaluated the overall adequacy of the presentation of information in the financial statements.

Opinion: disclaimer on view given by financial statements

Because of the possible effect of the limitation in evidence available to us, we are unable to form an opinion as to whether the financial statements give a true and fair view of the state of the company's affairs as at 31 December 20.. or of its profit (loss) for the year then ended. In all other respects, in our opinion the financial statements have been properly prepared in accordance with the Companies Act 1985.

In respect of the limitation on our work relating to stock and work-in-progress:

(a)   we have not obtained all the information and explanations that we considered necessary for the purpose of our audit; and

(b)   we were unable to determine whether proper accounting records had been maintained.

Note. Because of the length of the audit report, we have only shown those parts of each qualified report which differ from the unqualified report shown in Section 3.

5.9   SAS 601 *Imposed limitation of audit scope* provides guidance for auditors when then directors of those who appoint the auditors place limitations upon the scope of the audit.

> **SAS 601.1**
>
> If the auditors are aware, before accepting an audit engagement, that the directors of the entity, or those who appoint its auditors, will impose a limitation on the scope of the audit work which they consider likely to result in the need to issue a disclaimer or opinion on the financial statements, they should not accept that engagement, unless required to do so by statute.

5.10   The SAS points out that agreeing to such a limitation would threaten the independence of auditors and make it possible for them to meet the requirements of auditing standards. The APB also believe that in accepting such a limited engagement, the auditors are complicit in the client evading the spirit of the legal requirement to be audited.

> **SAS 601.2**
>
> If the auditors become aware, after accepting an audit engagement, that the directors of the entity, or those who appointed them as auditors, have imposed a limitation on the scope of their work which they consider likely to result in the need to issue a disclaimer on the financial statements, they should request the removal of the limitation. If the limitation is not removed, they should consider resigning from the audit engagement.

5.11   If the auditors do not consider it necessary to resign but do issue a disclaimer, the audit report should give full details of why the disclaimer was given.

Circumstances giving rise to disagreements

5.12   The explanatory notes to SAS 600 suggest that circumstances giving rise to disagreement include the following.

(a) **Inappropriate accounting policies**

(b) **Disagreement** as to the **facts or amounts** included in the financial statements

(c) **Disagreement** as to the **manner or extent of disclosure** of facts or amounts in the financial statements

(d) **Failure to comply** with **relevant legislation** or **other requirements**

SAS 600.8

Where the auditors disagree with the accounting treatment or disclosure of a matter in the financial statements, and in the auditors' opinion the effect of that disagreement is material to the financial statements:

(a) the auditors should include in the opinion section of their report:

  (i) a description of all substantive factors giving rise to the disagreement;
  (ii) their implications for the financial statements;
  (iii) whenever practicable, a quantification of the effect on the financial statements;

(b) when the auditors conclude that the effect of the matter giving rise to disagreement is so material or pervasive that the financial statements are seriously misleading, they should issue an adverse opinion;

(c) in the case of other material disagreements, the auditors should issue a qualified opinion indicating that it is expressed except for the effects of the matter giving rise to the disagreement.

Example 7. Qualified opinion: disagreement

Qualified opinion arising from disagreement about accounting treatment

Included in the debtors shown on the balance sheet is an amount of £Y due from a company which has ceased trading. XYZ plc has no security for this debt. In our opinion the company is unlikely to receive any payment and full provision of £Y should have been made, reducing profit before tax and net assets by that amount.

Except for the absence of this provision, in our opinion the financial statements give a true and fair view of the state of the company's affairs as at 31 December 20.. and of its profit (loss) for the year then ended and have been properly prepared in accordance with the Companies Act 1985.

Example 10. Adverse opinion

Adverse opinion

As more fully explained in note ... no provision has been made for losses expected to arise on certain long-term contracts currently in progress, as the directors consider that such losses should be off-set against amounts recoverable on other long-term contracts. In our opinion, provision should be made for foreseeable losses on individual contracts as required by Statement of Standard Accounting Practice 9. If losses had been so recognised the effect would have been to reduce the profit before and after tax for the year and the contract work in progress at 31 December 20.. by £.. .

In view of the effect of the failure to provide for the losses referred to above, in our opinion the financial statements do not give a true and fair view of the state of the company's affairs as at 31 December 19.. and of its profit (loss) for the year then ended. In all other respects, in our opinion the financial statements have been properly prepared in accordance with the Companies Act 1985.

6   REPORTING INHERENT UNCERTAINTY

Inherent and fundamental uncertainty

> **KEY TERMS**
>
> An **inherent uncertainty** is an uncertainty whose resolution is dependent upon uncertain future events outside the control of the reporting entity's directors at the date the financial statements are approved.
>
> A **fundamental uncertainty** is an inherent uncertainty where the magnitude of its potential impact is so great that, without clear disclosure of the nature and implications of the uncertainty, the view given by the financial statements would be seriously misleading.

6.1   Inherent uncertainties about the outcome of future events frequently affect a wide range of components of the financial statements. These uncertainties are uncertainties which remain even though auditors have obtained all the evidence they can expect to obtain about the components.

6.2   SAS 600 gives details of how auditors should approach inherent uncertainties.

> **SAS 600.6**
>
> (a)   In forming their opinion on financial statements, auditors should consider whether the view given by the financial statements could be affected by inherent uncertainties which, in their opinion, are fundamental.
>
> (b)   When an inherent uncertainty exists which:
>
>   (i)   in the auditors' opinion is fundamental; and
>   (ii)   is adequately accounted for and disclosed in the financial statements;
>
>   the auditors should include an explanatory paragraph referring to the fundamental uncertainty in the section of their report setting out the basis of their opinion.
>
> (c)   When adding an explanatory paragraph, auditors should use words which clearly indicate that their opinion on the financial statements is not qualified in respect of its concepts.

6.3   In forming an opinion, auditors take into account:

(a)   The **appropriateness of the accounting policies**

(b)   The **adequacy of the accounting treatment**

(c)   **Estimates and disclosures of inherent uncertainties** in the light of evidence available at the date they express their opinion

6.4   Inherent uncertainties are regarded as **fundamental** when they involve a **significant level** of concern about the validity of the **going concern basis** or other matters whose potential effect on the fundamental statements is unusually great. A common example of a fundamental uncertainty is the outcome of major litigation.

6.5   The auditor will need to consider:

(a)   The possibility that the estimate included in the accounts may be **subject to change**

(b)   The **possible range of values** it may take

(c) The **consequences** of that range of potential values on the view shown in the financial statements

---

Example 4. Unqualified opinion with explanatory paragraph describing a fundamental uncertainty.

Fundamental uncertainty (insert just before opinion paragraph)

In forming our opinion, we have considered the adequacy of the disclosures made in the financial statements concerning the possible outcome to litigation against B Limited, a subsidiary undertaking of the company, for an alleged breach of environmental regulations. The future settlement of this litigation could result in additional liabilities and the closure of B Limited's business, whose net assets included in the consolidated balance sheet total £... and whose profit before tax for the year is £... . Details of the circumstances relating to this fundamental uncertainty are described in note .... . Our opinion is not qualified in this respect.

Activity 17.2

What do the following forms of qualified audit opinion represent?

(a) Disagreement
(b) Adverse opinion
(c) Disclaimer

Activity 17.3

You are an audit partner and are reviewing the audit files of four clients, on each of which there is a significant matter arising.

(a) The audit team were not informed about the year-end stocktake until after it had taken place. Stock is material in the financial statements.

(b) No provision has been made against a material amount owed by a debtor who is now in liquidation.

(c) A substantial claim has been lodged against the company by a major customer. The matter is fully explained in the notes to the accounts, but no provision has been made for legal costs or has compensation payable as it is not possible to determine with reasonable accuracy the amounts, if any, which may become payable.

The directors have received legal advice which appears to be reliable that the claim can be successfully defended.

Task

What impact would each of these matters have on the audit report of these clients?

---

7 SMALL AND MEDIUM-SIZED COMPANIES

7.1 Certain companies defined as 'small' or 'medium-sized' can file an abbreviated set of accounts with the Registrar of Companies in substitution for the 'full accounts' etc. Abbreviated accounts should not be confused with summary financial statements issued to shareholders or with non-statutory ('abridged') accounts.

Criteria for determining size

Category	Criteria	
Small	Turnover not more than	£2.8m
	Balance sheet total (total assets) not more than	£1.4m
	Average number of employees not more than	50
Medium-sized	Turnover not more than	£11.2m
	Balance sheet total (total assets) not more than	£5.6m
	Average number of employees not more than	250

7.2 All non-dormant companies must continue to prepare **full** accounts for **presentation** to their **shareholders** and the exemptions only affect what has to be filed with the Registrar of Companies. (Regulations passed during recent years have decreased the amount of information small companies' full accounts must contain.)

7.3 When using the above criteria the following definitions are used.

Turnover

7.4 If the accounting period of a company is not a period of twelve calendar months, then the maximum figure of turnover set out in the table will have to be proportionately adjusted.

Balance sheet total

7.5 This should be taken as the sum of all the assets, *without* any deduction for liabilities.

Average number of employees

7.6 The figure must be determined on a monthly basis. The number of full-time plus part-time employees (who are each treated as one for this purpose) in each month of the year must be totalled. The sum of the monthly totals is then divided by the number of months in the accounting period (usually 12) to arrive at the average.

Excluded companies

7.7 Certain companies are excluded from being able to file abbreviated accounts. These are:

- Public companies

- Banking or insurance companies

- An authorised person under the Financial Services Act 1986

- Companies which are members of an ineligible group (basically an ineligible group is one which contains any company falling within category (a) or (c) above)

7.8 A company may be regarded as small or medium-sized in the financial year to which the accounts relate if it meets the required conditions in respect of both the current year and the previous year. If a company fails to meet the required conditions in a future year its status will not be lost in that year. However, if the failure were to run into a second consecutive year, then the status would be lost.

7.9 If a company is not small or medium sized, or loses its small or medium-sized status, it will have to meet the **required conditions** for **two consecutive years** before the status can be obtained or regained.

7.10 However a newly incorporated company may be regarded as being small or medium-sized in its first year of trading if it meets the required condition for that year.

Small companies

7.11 A small company need only file abbreviated accounts with the Registrar of Companies comprising:

- An abbreviated version of its normal balance sheet
- Certain specified notes

7.12 A small company need *not* file:

- A **profit and loss account**
- A **directors' report**
- Any **information** relating to the **emoluments** of directors
- A cash flow statement

Abbreviated balance sheet

7.13 The abbreviated balance sheet need only show the total amount for each category of asset and liability, as designated by a letter or Roman numeral in the two permissible balance sheet formats in Schedule 4 of the 1985 Act.

Notes to the accounts

7.14 Under the exemptions for small companies, only the following requirements of Schedule 4 apply in respect of the notes to the financial statements.

- Accounting policies
- Share capital
- Particulars of allotments
- Particulars of creditors payable in over five years and particulars of security given
- The basis used in translating foreign currency amounts into sterling
- Details of debtors and creditors receivable and payable in more than one year
- Movements in total asset categories

Note. A set of 1992 regulations has allowed small companies to produce less information for their *full* accounts as well.

Medium-sized companies

7.15 A medium-sized company may file accounts which will comprise a **full balance sheet, notes and directors' report**, but only an **abbreviated** version of its **profit and loss account**. In respect of the profit and loss account, this means that the following items can be combined and shown as one item under the heading of 'gross profit or loss'.

(a) **In the formats where expense are classified by function**: turnover, cost of sales, gross profit or loss and other operating income

(b) **In the formats where expenses are classified by type**: turnover, charge in stocks of finished goods and in work-in-progress, own work capitalised, other operating income, raw materials and consumables, and other external charges

7.16 In addition to the above, the notes to the financial statements may omit the analysis of turnover and profit or loss before taxation called for in Schedule 4 paragraph 55 of the 1985 Act.

Auditors' responsibilities

7.17 Where abbreviated accounts are filed for individual companies, the balance sheet must include, above the directors' signatures, a statement by the *directors* that they are entitled to file abbreviated accounts. An example of such a statement would be as follows.

> 'We have relied on the exemptions for individual accounts, in accordance with ss 246 to 247 Companies Act 1985, on the grounds that XYZ Limited is entitled to the benefit of those exemptions as a (small/medium-sized) company.'

7.18 Assuming the company has not claimed exemption from audit before abbreviated accounts are filed, the company's auditors should consider whether the conditions required for exemption have been satisfied. If not satisfied, the auditors must report this fact to the directors. In this situation, the company could not properly proceed with the production of abbreviated accounts. If they are satisfied, the auditors must prepare a 'special report' to this effect.

Terms of auditors' report

7.19 The terms of the special report are as follows.

    (a) The report is addressed to the company.

    (b) The scope of the report is *only* the abbreviated accounts.

    (c) The report should state that the auditing standards were not followed as the auditors' work was limited to checking the s 247 and s 249 entitlements and examining the accounts to ensure proper preparation.

    (d) It expresses the auditors' opinion that:

        (i) The company is entitled to deliver abbreviated accounts prepared in accordance with the relevant provisions to the registrar.

        (ii) The accounts have been 'properly prepared' (ie accurately produced from the full financial statements) in accordance with Schedule 8 of the Act.

    (e) It should be dated as soon as possible on or after the date the full report is signed.

    (f) It should be delivered to the Registrar with the abbreviated accounts.

7.20 An audit as such is *not* required: the abbreviated accounts are not intended to give a true and fair view. APB Bulletin 1997/1 *The Special Auditors' Report on Abbreviated Accounts in Great Britain* gives advice on how auditors should approach reporting on abbreviated accounts and gives the following example auditors' report.

Auditors report to XYZ Limited under section 247B of the Companies Act 1985

We have examined the abbreviated accounts set out on pages ... to ..., together with the financial statements of the company for the year ended ... prepared under section 226 of the Companies Act 1985.

Respective responsibilities of directors and auditors
The directors are responsible for preparing the abbreviated accounts in accordance with section 246 of the Companies Act 1985. It is our responsibility to form an independent opinion as to whether the company is entitled to deliver abbreviated accounts prepared in accordance with sections 246(5) and (6) of the Act to the registrar of companies and whether the accounts to be delivered are properly prepared in accordance with those provisions and to report our opinion to you.

Basis of opinion
We have carried out the procedures we consider necessary to confirm, by reference to the financial statements, that the company is entitled to deliver abbreviated accounts and that the abbreviated accounts to be delivered are properly prepared. The scope of our work for the purpose of this report did not include examining or dealing with events after the date of our report on the financial statements.

Opinion
In our opinion the company is entitled to deliver abbreviated accounts prepared in accordance with sections 246(5) and (6) of the Companies Act 1985, and the abbreviated accounts on pages ... to ... are properly prepared in accordance with those provisions.

Other information
    ...

Registered auditors   *Address*
Date

Inclusion of the full audit report

7.21   The report on the abbreviated accounts need not include the audit report on the full accounts if the report on the full accounts was **unqualified**.

7.22   If however the report on the full accounts was qualified, the report on the abbreviated accounts must give the report on the full accounts in full, together with any further material necessary to understand the qualification.

7.23   If the audit report on the full accounts contains any of the following statements, the report on the abbreviated accounts must set out the statement in full.

- The accounting records or returns are inadequate.
- The accounts do not agree with the accounting records.
- The auditors have failed to obtain the necessary information and explanations.

7.24   The APB Bulletin also recommends that a fundamental uncertainty paragraph in an unqualified audit report on the full accounts should be included in the report on the abbreviated accounts.

Effects of qualification

7.25   Where the audit report on the main financial statements has been qualified in the current or previous period on a matter which could have an effect on one of the criteria for exemption, the auditor must, in order to report, be satisfied that the maximum effect of the matter which was subject to qualification does not take the turnover and/or total assets over the exemption limits.

Dormant companies

7.26 A company can claim exemption under s 250 of the Companies Act from audit as a dormant company if no significant accounting transactions occur during the year and the company passes a special resolution. Significant accounting transactions are transactions which must be recorded in the accounting records. Banking and insurance companies and Financial Service Act companies cannot claim this exemption.

Key learning points

- The Companies Act requires **specific reference** in the audit report to:
  - ○ The truth and fairness of the state of the company's affairs at the period-end
  - ○ The truth and fairness of the profit or loss
  - ○ Whether the accounts have been properly prepared in accordance with the Companies Act

- The Companies Act requires certain matters to be reported on by **exception**:
  - ○ Proper accounting records kept and proper returns received
  - ○ Accounts in agreement with the accounting records and returns
  - ○ All information and explanations received
  - ○ Details of directors' emoluments correctly disclosed
  - ○ Details of loans and other transactions in favour of directors and related parties correctly disclosed
  - ○ Information given in the directors' report consistent with the accounts

- SAS 600 *Auditors' report on financial statements* radically altered the form of both unqualified and qualified audit reports.

- The main elements of an **unqualified audit report are**:
  - ○ A **title** identifying the addressee
  - ○ An **introductory paragraph** identifying the **financial statements audited**
  - ○ Sections dealing with:
    - \- **Responsibilities** of **directors** and **auditors**
    - \- **Basis** of the **auditors' opinion**
    - \- A **clear statement of opinion**

- Auditors may qualify their audit opinion on the grounds of **uncertainty or limitation of scope**; these may be **material** or **fundamental.**

- Auditors are principally concerned with the correct **treatment** and **disclosure** of **inherent** and **fundamental uncertainties**, which relate to uncertain future events.

- Auditors should include an **explanatory paragraph** in their audit report if **fundamental uncertainties** exist.

Quick quiz

1 What should auditors do if the accounts do not contain the details required by the Companies Act concerning directors' emoluments?

2 How according to SAS 600.3 should auditors distinguish between their responsibilities and those of the directors?

3   According to the example given in SAS 600, what must the directors do when preparing financial statements?

4   On what must the auditors conclude in order to be able to give an unqualified opinion?

5   What should auditors do if the date on which they sign their audit report is after than the date on which the financial statements are approved?

6   Give two examples of scope limitations on the audit.

7   According to SAS 600, why might auditors issue a qualified opinion on the grounds of disagreement?

8   When forming an opinion on the treatment in the accounts of inherent uncertainties, what should auditors consider?

9   How should auditors qualify their report if the information in the directors' report is inconsistent with the financial statements, and the auditors believe that the financial statements are correct?

Answers to quick quiz

1   If the accounts do not contain the disclosures of directors' emoluments required by statute, auditors should qualify their audit report and give the required disclosures in their report.

2   According to SAS 600.3, auditors should state that the financial statements are the responsibility of the directors, make reference to the description of directors' responsibilities if set out elsewhere in the accounts, and state the auditors' responsibility is to express an opinion on the financial statements.

3   When preparing financial statements, directors should:

(a)   Select suitable accounting policies and apply them consistently.

(b)   Make judgements and estimates that are reasonable and prudent.

(c)   State whether applicable accounting standards have been followed, with material departures disclosed and explained (large companies only).

(d)   Prepare the financial statements on the going concern basis unless inappropriate.

4   Auditors must conclude that:

(a)   The financial statements have been prepared using appropriate, consistently applied accounting policies.

(b)   The financial statements have been prepared in accordance with relevant legislation, regulations or applicable accounting standards.

(c)   There is adequate disclosure of all relevant information.

5   If auditors sign later than the directors, they must extend their post balance sheet event review up to the date on which they sign their report.

6   Scope limitations can arise because of:

(a)   Absence of proper accounting records
(b)   An inability to carry out audit procedures considered necessary

7   Auditors might qualify on the grounds of disagreement because of:

(a)   Inappropriate accounting policies
(b)   Disagreements on the facts and amounts included in the accounts
(c)   Disagreement on the manner and extent of disclosure of facts or amounts
(d)   Failure to comply with relevant legislation or other requirements

8   When considering inherent uncertainties, auditors should take into account:

(a)   The appropriateness of the accounting policies
(b)   The adequacy of the accounting treatment
(c)   The estimates and disclosures of inherent uncertainties in the light of available evidence

9   If there is an inconsistency with the directors' report and the financial statements are right, auditors should draw attention to the disagreement in a separate paragraph below the main opinion paragraph. The opinion paragraph should not be qualified.

Answers to activities

Answer 17.1

(a)   '...the financial statements on pages ... to ...'

Purpose
The purpose of this phrase is to make it clear to the reader of an audit report the part of a company's annual report upon which the auditors are reporting their opinion.

Meaning
An annual report may include documents such as a chairman's report, employee report, five year summary and other voluntary information. However, under the Companies Act, only the profit and loss account, balance sheet and associated notes are required to be audited in true and fair terms. Thus the page references (for instance, 8 to 20) cover only the profit and loss account, balance sheet, notes to the accounts, cash flow statement and statement of total recognised gains and losses. The directors' report, although examined and reported on by exception if it contains inconsistencies, is not included in these page references.

(b)   '...in accordance with Auditing Standards...'

Purpose
This phrase is included in order to confirm to the reader that best practice, as laid down in Auditing Standards, has been adopted by the auditors in both carrying out their audit and in drafting their audit opinion. This means that the reader can be assured that the audit has been properly conducted, and that should he or she wish to discover what such standards are, or what certain key phrases mean, he or she can have recourse to Auditing Standards to explain such matters.

Meaning
Auditing Standards are those auditing standards prepared by the Auditing Practices Board.

These prescribe the principles and practices to be followed by auditors in the planning, designing and carrying out various aspects of their audit work, the content of audit reports, both qualified and unqualified and so on. Members are expected to follow all of these standards.

(c)   'In our opinion ...'

Purpose
Under the Companies Act, auditors are required to report on every balance sheet, profit and loss account or group accounts laid before members. In reporting, they are required to state their *opinion* on those accounts. Thus, the purpose of this phrase is to comply with the statutory requirement to report an opinion.

Meaning
An audit report is an expression of opinion by suitably qualified auditors as to whether the financial statements give a true and fair view, and have been properly prepared in accordance with the Companies Act. *It is not a certificate*; rather it is a statement of whether or not, in the professional judgement of the auditors, the financial statements give a true and fair view.

Answer 17.2

(a)   A qualification on the grounds of disagreement may arise for the following reasons.

  (i)   Inappropriate accounting policies

  (ii)   Disagreements on the facts or amounts included in the accounts

  (iii) Disagreement about the disclosure of the facts or amounts in the accounts

  (iv)   Failure to comply with relevant legislation (Companies Act) or other requirements (accounting standards or for listed companies Stock Exchange requirements)

If the agreement is material but does not result in the accounts being misleading, an except for qualification would be used. The opinion paragraph would state that the accounts give a true and fair view apart from this one item.

Details of the reasons for the disagreement would generally be included in a separate paragraph immediately above the opinion paragraph. The opinion section would be headed "qualified opinion arising from [specific matter]".

(b)   An adverse opinion is given whether the disagreement is not just material but fundamental. The auditors believe that the disputed matters render the accounts misleading. The reasons why this type of matter might arise are listed in section (a).

BPP
PUBLISHING

In the opinion paragraph the auditor will state that the accounts do not give a true and fair view. The opinion paragraph may, if appropriate, also say that the accounts have not been properly prepared in accordance with the Companies Act.

As with a disagreement, an explanation for the reasons for the qualification will be given immediately above the opinion paragraph. The section should be headed "adverse opinion".

(c) A disclaimer is a qualification due to a fundamental uncertainty. There will have been a limitation on the scope of the audit and the limitation is such that the auditors feel that they cannot give an opinion on the truth and fairness of the accounts.

The opinion paragraph should state that the auditors are unable to form an opinion on the accounts. Generally the auditors should be able to state that the accounts have been properly prepared in accordance with the Companies Act.

Immediately below the opinion paragraph, the auditors would generally state that in respect of the matter about which there was uncertainty, they had not obtained all the information and explanations that they considered necessary for the purposes of the audit. They may also have to state that they are unable to determine whether proper accounting records had been kept.

The opinion section should be headed up as a disclaimer.

A detailed description of the limitation of scope would normally appear in the basis of opinion section of the audit report. The auditors would normally state that they planned their audit so as to obtain the necessary information and explanations, but that the evidence available was limited in respect of the specific matter.

Answer 17.3

(a) The auditing guideline on stocktaking states that auditors should attend the stock-taking where stocks are material in the company's financial statements, and the auditor is placing reliance upon management's stocktake in order to provide evidence of existence.

There appears to have been therefore a material limitation of scope on the audit.

The basis of opinion section of the audit report should state that the evidence available to us, as auditors, was limited because we could not attend the stock-take and (presumably) were unable to carry out alternative procedures necessary to give sufficient assurance. The paragraph should state the amount of stock involved.

The opinion section of the audit report should be headed up as an opinion qualified due to limitation of scope. The section should state that the accounts give a true and fair view except for any adjustments that may have been necessary had we been able to obtain sufficient assurance concerning stock.

The opinion section also should state in a separate paragraph that in respect of the limitation on the work relating to stock, we did not obtain all the information and explanations that we considered necessary for the purpose of our audit, and we were unable to determine whether proper accounting records had been kept.

(b) It appears that there is no prospect that the monies owed will be recovered.

The audit opinion should therefore be qualified on the grounds of disagreement. The opinion section should be headed up as qualified opinion arising from disagreement about provision for debtor.

Details of the disagreement should be given in a paragraph above the opinion paragraph. We should state that the debtor has ceased trading and is unlikely to make any payment. We should also specific the amount of the provision that we believe should be made.

The opinion paragraph should state that the accounts give a true and fair view except for the failure to provide against the debtor.

(c) We need to decide whether the legal claim is a material matter and whether it is fundamental to the view given by the financial statements. Because of the importance of the customer, it may be that an adverse judgement will have serious consequences for the whole of the company's business, and thus the matter is fundamental.

If we agree that the disclosure is adequate, and on balance, we believe no provision is required, the impact on the audit report will depend on whether the inherent uncertainty involved is material or fundamental. If it is material, we do not need to mention it in the audit report. If it is fundamental, the audit report should include a separate paragraph, headed fundamental uncertainty. This should give details of the circumstances and amounts involved, and make reference to the note in which further details are given. The paragraph should also state that the audit report is not qualified in respect of this matter.

No reference to the claim should be made in the opinion section of the audit report.

Chapter 18 Auditor's liability and audit responsibility

Chapter topic list

1 Introduction

2 Liability under contract law

3 Liability to third parties in tort

4 Fraud and error

5 Law and regulations

Learning objectives

On completion of this chapter you will be able to:

	Performance criteria	Range Statement
• Describe the legal responsibilities of auditors (contract, negligence and liability to third parties)	all	all
• Describe the auditors' responsibilities in relation to fraud	all	all
• Describe the audit procedures used to assess compliance with laws and regulations	all	all

BPP PUBLISHING

1   INTRODUCTION

1.1   The main part of this chapter deals with **auditor liability** for professional negligence. This is a subject of great concern to auditors. Press reports of actions against auditors for large financial damages have become more common over the last few years. Audit firms can take out professional indemnity insurance to protect their assets, but this has its drawbacks, since arguably it provides a ready source of compensation which therefore makes auditors easy targets.

1.2   Auditors face potential liability to clients under the **law of contract**. A client who brings an action under contract law does so to enforce upon auditors responsibility for loss which has occurred through the failure of auditors to carry out their duties imposed by the contract with the client. In this chapter we shall discuss what these duties are, what a client has to prove in order to bring a successful action under the law of contract and whether auditors have any defences.

1.3   Auditors may also be liable under the **law of tort**. We cannot discuss the law of tort in detail but its effect may be to impose upon auditors a duty of care over and above what is imposed by statute or contract. In theory clients may sue in tort, but in practice the law of contract will most likely offer them better remedies. The law of tort is more likely to be a remedy for third parties. In this chapter we shall see how far auditor liability stretches, emphasising in particular the importance of the **Caparo case** which restricted the scope of auditor liability in this area.

1.4   One reason why auditors may face court actions is because of misunderstandings over the role of auditors - the expectation gap which we discussed in Chapter 1. In the remainder of this chapter we deal with auditor responsibilities in two important areas- **fraud and error**, and **law and regulations**. With fraud and error, audit procedures are designed to give the auditors reasonable assurance that they have detected material fraud and error. The laws and regulations that auditors are mainly concerned with are those that affect the content of the financial statements and those that are central to the client's ability to carry on business.

2   LIABILITY UNDER CONTRACT LAW

2.1   When auditors accept appointment, they enter into a contract which imposes certain obligations upon them. These obligations arise from the terms of the contract.

2.2   Both **express** and **implied** terms of contracts impact upon auditors. Express terms are those stated explicitly in the contract.

Express terms

2.3   The express terms of the audit contract cannot over-ride the Companies Act by restricting company auditors' statutory duties or imposing restrictions upon auditors' statutory rights which are designed to assist them in discharging those duties.

2.4   Express terms will however be significant if auditors and client agree that auditor responsibilities should be extended beyond those envisaged by the Companies Act. Additionally if auditors are involved a non-statutory audit, the express terms will only be those contained in any specific contract that may exist with the client.

2.5   In these circumstances auditors are always likely to be judged on the content of any report which they have issued, and so they should always ensure that their report clearly states the effect of any limitations that there have been upon the extent and scope of their work. The auditors must take special care to ensure that their report does not in any way imply that they have in fact done more work than that required by the terms of his contract.

Implied terms

2.6 'Implied terms' are those which the parties to a contract may have left unstated because they consider them too obvious to express, but which, nevertheless, the law will impart into a contract.

2.7 The 'implied terms' which the law will impart into a contract of the type with which we are currently concerned are as follows:

- The auditors have a duty to exercise **reasonable care**.
- The auditors have a duty to carry out the work required with **reasonable expediency**.
- The auditors have a right to **reasonable remuneration**.

The auditors' duty of care

2.8 The auditors' duty of care arose under the Supply of Goods Act 1982; a higher degree of care arises in work of a specialised nature or where negligence is likely to cause substantial loss.

2.9 Auditors should use generally accepted auditing techniques. In addition, if auditors' suspicions are aroused (they are put upon enquiry) they must conduct further investigations until the suspicions are confirmed or put to rest.

2.10 When the auditors are exercising judgement they must act both honestly and carefully. Obviously, if auditors are to be 'careful' in forming an opinion, they must give due consideration to all relevant matters. Provided they do this and can be seen to have done so, then their opinion should be above criticism.

2.11 However if the opinion reached by the auditors is one that no reasonably competent auditor would have been likely to reach then they would still possibly be held negligent. This is because however carefully the auditors may appear to have approached their work, it clearly could not have been careful enough, if it enabled them to reach a conclusion which would be generally regarded as unacceptable.

Actions for negligence against auditors

KEY TERM

Negligence is some act or omission which occurs because the person concerned has failed to exercise the degree of professional care and skill, appropriate to the case, which is expected of accountants or auditors.

2.12 If a client is to bring a successful action against an auditors then the client, as the plaintiff, must satisfy the court in relation to three matters, all of which must be established.

(a) *Duty of care*

There existed a duty of care enforceable at law.

    (b) *Negligence*

        In a situation where a duty of care existed, the auditors were negligent in the performance of that duty, judged by the accepted professional standards of the day.

    (c) *Damages*

        The client has suffered some monetary loss as a direct consequence of the negligence on the part of the auditors.

2.13   A good early example of a client action for negligence is that of *Wilde & Others v Cape & Dalgleish 1897*. In this case the auditors were held to have been negligent in failing to detect defalcations, the primary reason for this being that they did not examine the bank pass books contrary to generally accepted best practice.

Excluding or restricting liability to a client

2.14   An agreement with a client designed to exclude or restrict an accountant's liability may not always be effective in law. S 310 Companies Act 1985 makes void (same in exceptional circumstances), any provision in a company's articles or any contractual arrangement purporting to **exempt the auditors from** or to **indemnify** them against, any **liability** for negligence, default, breach of duty or breach of trust. In addition the Unfair Contract Terms Act 1977 (UCTA 1977) introduced extensive restrictions upon the enforceability of exclusions of liability for negligence and breaches of contract.

3   LIABILITY TO THIRD PARTIES IN TORT

3.1   An accountant may be liable for negligence not only in contract, but also in tort if a person to whom he owed a **duty of care** has suffered **loss** as a result of the accountant's negligence. The key question in the law of tort is to whom does an auditor owe a duty of care.

3.2   An accountant will almost always owe a duty of care to his own client. However that duty is likely to be co-existent with his contractual duty. In practice, the possibility of liability in tort will be important mainly in the context of claims by third parties.

3.3   Certain relatively recent decisions of the courts appeared to expand the classes of case in which a person professing some special skill (as an accountant does) may be liable for negligence to someone other than his own client: *Hedley Byrne & Co Ltd v Heller & Partners 1963 AC 465* and *Anns v Merton London Borough Council 1978 AC 728*.

3.4   However, since 1963 there have been other cases which are important in considering the consequences of *Hedley Byrne* and these are discussed below.

Jeb Fasteners Ltd v Marks Bloom & Co 1980
The facts: Jeb Fasteners acquired the entire share capital of another company, and then suffered substantial loss because of inflated stock figures. Jeb Fasteners sued Marks Bloom who had audited the company's accounts on which they had relied.

Decision: A duty of care was owed by the auditors to the plaintiff, even though they did not know of his existence, or that any takeover bid was being planned. Mr Justice Woolf held the appropriate test was whether the auditors knew or *reasonably should have foreseen* at the time at which the accounts were audited, that a person might rely on them for the purpose of deciding whether or not to take over the company and could therefore suffer loss if the accounts were inaccurate.

In this pre-*Caparo* case the judge decided there was a duty of care but Marks Bloom were excused liability because their client would have been acquired anyway; it was purchased for its management rather than its (negligently) audited balance sheet.

Littlejohn v Lloyd Cheyham 1985

The facts: The plaintiff alleged that the auditors of a trailer rental business had been negligent; it was claimed that they had failed to consider that the tyre replacement policy used was cash based rather than accruals based.

The audit client had gone into receivership a few months after the plaintiff bought a controlling interest.

The auditors' defence was that they had fully considered and documented the tyre policy, including raising it in the management letter. They had also issued a going concern qualification and generally carried out a thorough audit.

Decision: A thorough audit (in accordance with the Auditing Standards) was a good defence against claims of negligence.

Al Saudi Banque & Others v Clark Pixley 1989

The facts: Ten banks lent money to Gallic Credit Ltd, an import-export company. Of the ten banks, seven were creditors at the year end, and three went on to lend money subsequently. The company's assets largely comprised of bills of exchange accepted by customers and drawn in Gallic's favour. The banks alleged that a large part of the company's business was fraudulent; the bills of exchange were not supported by underlying transactions and effectively new borrowing was being used to repay earlier loans. The company was compulsorily wound up with a deficiency for unsecured creditors estimates at £8.6m.

Decision: No duty was owed to the three banks because there was *insufficient proximity*; and no duty of care was owed to the seven banks either because the auditors did not report to them; the banks did not appoint the auditors.

3.5 In 1990 the law was authoritatively stated in the *Caparo* case.

Caparo Industries plc v Dickman & Others 1990

The facts: In 1984 Caparo Industries purchased 100,000 Fidelity shares in the open market. On June 12 1984, the date on which the accounts (audited by Touche Ross) were published, they purchased a further 50,000 shares. Relying on information in the accounts, further shares were acquired. On September 4, Caparo made a bid for the remainder and by October had acquired control of Fidelity. Caparo alleged that the accounts on which they had relied were misleading in that an apparent pre-tax profit of some £1.3 million should in fact have been shown as a loss of over £400,000. The plaintiffs argued that Touche owed a duty of care to investors and potential investors.

Decision: (by the House of Lords)

(a) The auditors of a public company's accounts owed **no duty of care** to members of the public at large who relied upon the accounts in deciding to buy shares in the company.

(b) As a purchaser of further shares, while relying upon the auditors' report, a **shareholder stood** in the **same position** as any other investing member of the public to whom the auditors owed no duty.

(c) The purpose of the audit was simply that of fulfilling the statutory requirements of the Companies Act 1985.

(d) There was nothing in the statutory duties of company auditors to suggest that they were intended to protect the interests of investors in the market. In particular, there was no reason why any special relationship should be held to arise simply from the fact that the affairs of the company rendered it susceptible to a takeover bid.

> **DEVOLVED ASSESSMENT ALERT**
>
> This case is vital to an understanding of auditor liability.

3.6 In its report *The Financial Aspects of Corporate Governance*, the Cadbury Committee gave an opinion on the current situation as reflected in the *Caparo* ruling. It felt that *Caparo* **did not lessen** auditors' duty to use skill and care because auditors are still fully liable in negligence to the companies they audit and their shareholders collectively.

3.7 Thus the decision in *Caparo v Dickman* has considerably narrowed the auditors' **potential liability** to third parties. The judgement would appear to imply that users such as creditors, potential investors or others, will not be able to sue the auditors for negligence by virtue of their placing reliance on audited annual accounts.

ADT v BBH

3.8 In December 1995, a High Court judge awarded electronic security group ADT £65m plus interest and costs (£40m) in damages for negligence against the former BDO Binder Hamlyn (BBH) partnership.

3.9 The firm had jointly audited the 1988/89 accounts of Britannia Security Group (BSG), which ADT acquired in 1990 for £105m, but later found to be worth only £40m. Although, under *Caparo*, auditors do not owe a duty of care in general to third parties, the judge found that BBH audit partner Martyn Bishop, who confirmed that the firm stood by BSG's accounts at a meeting with ADT in the run-up to the acquisition, had thereby taken on a contractual relationship with ADT.

3.10 The case has subsequently been settled out of court.

Other recent cases

3.11 In *Yorkshire Enterprise Ltd (YEL) and another v Robson Rhodes 1998* the court held that two investors in a company which went into receivership could claim damages against the company's auditors on the basis of negligent misstatements in the company's accounts and in letters that the auditors sent to the investors. The court held that a special relationship had been established between the auditors and the investors because they knew who the investors were, the use to which the information would be put, and had consented to involvement in the transaction.

3.12 The High Court stated in *Sasea Finance Ltd (in liquidation) v KPMG (a firm)* that auditors who failed to identify that a company was insolvent could be liable to the company for a dividend that was mistakenly paid out. (In fact in this case the auditors escaped liability because the liquidators failed to find evidence that the dividend was ever paid out.)

4 FRAUD AND ERROR

4.1 The incidence of financial fraud, particularly in a computer environment, is increasing and has been a central feature in a number of financial scandals in recent years. This fact, together with the increasing sophistication of fraudsters, creates difficult problems for management and auditors. A few years ago the then Minister for Corporate and Consumer Affairs called on the profession to be 'the front line of the public's defences against fraud'.

4.2　There are some who would argue that the detection of fraud should be the auditors' principal function. This attitude clearly gives rise to a public expectation which is neither shared nor fulfilled by the profession.

4.3　SAS 110 *Fraud and error,* which is quite long and complicated, is covered briefly here.

Introduction

Auditors should plan and perform their audit procedures and evaluate and report the results thereof, recognising that fraud or error may materially affect the financial statements. (SAS 110.1)

The approach to be adopted by the auditors

When planning the audit the auditors should assess the risk that fraud or error may cause the financial statements to contain material misstatements. (SAS 110.2)

Based on their risk assessment, the auditors should design audit procedures so as to have a reasonable expectation of detecting misstatements arising from fraud or error which are material to the financial statements. (SAS 110.3)

Procedures when there is an indication that fraud or error may exist

When auditors become aware of information which indicates that fraud or error may exist, they should obtain an understanding of the nature of the event and the circumstances in which it has occurred, and sufficient other information to evaluate the possible effect on the financial statements. If the auditors believe that the indicated fraud or error could have a material effect on the financial statements, they should perform appropriate modified or additional procedures. (SAS 110.4)

When the auditors become aware of, or suspect that there may be, instances of error or fraudulent conduct, they should document their findings and, subject to any requirement to report them direct to a third party, discuss them with the appropriate level of management. (SAS 110.5)

The auditors should consider the implications of suspected or actual error or fraudulent conduct in relation to other aspects of the audit, particularly the reliability of management representations. (SAS 110.6)

Reporting to management

The auditors should as soon as practicable communicate their findings to the appropriate level of management, the board of directors or the audit committee if:

(a) they suspect or discover fraud, even if the potential effect on the financial statements is immaterial (save where SAS 110.12 applies); or

(b) material error is actually found to exist. (SAS 110.7)

Reporting to addressees of the auditors' report on the financial statements

Where the auditors conclude that the view given by the financial statements could be affected by a level of uncertainty concerning the consequences of a suspected or actual error or fraud which, in their opinion, is fundamental, they should include an explanatory paragraph referring to the matter in their report. (SAS 110.8)

Where the auditors conclude that a suspected or actual instance of fraud or error has a material effect on the financial statements and they disagree with the accounting treatment or with the extent, or the lack, of disclosure in the financial statements of the instance or of its consequences they should issue an adverse or qualified opinion. If the auditors are unable to determine whether fraud or error has occurred because of limitation in the scope of their work, they should issue a disclaimer or a qualified opinion. (SAS 110.9)

Reporting to third parties

Where the auditors become aware of a suspected or actual instance of fraud they should:

(a) consider whether the matter may be one that ought to be reported to a proper authority in the public interest; and where this is the case

(b) except in the circumstances covered in SAS 110.12, discuss the matter with the board of directors, including any audit committee. (SAS 110.10)

Where having considered any views expressed on behalf of the entity and in the light of any legal advice obtained, the auditors conclude that the matter ought to be reported to an appropriate authority in the public interest, they should notify the directors in writing of their view and, if the entity does not voluntarily do so itself or is unable to provide evidence that the matter has been reported, they should report it themselves. (SAS 110.11)

When a suspected or actual instance of fraud casts doubt on the integrity of the directors auditors should make a report direct to a proper authority in the public interest without delay and without informing the directors in advance. SAS 110.12)

Overseas activities

Where any of the activities of a company or group are carried on outside the United Kingdom or the Republic of Ireland, the auditors should take steps to ensure that the audit work in relation to the detection and reporting of any fraud and error is planned and carried out in accordance with the requirements of this SAS. (SAS 110.13)

4.4 **Fraud** comprises both the use of deception to obtain an unjust or illegal financial advantage, and intentional misrepresentation by management, employees or third parties. **Error** is an unintentional mistake.

4.5 The SAS emphasises that it is the **responsibility** of the **directors** to take reasonable steps to prevent and detect fraud. It is also their responsibility to prepare financial statements which give a true and fair view of the entity's affairs.

4.6 Auditors have a responsibility to consider, when carrying out their risk assessment, the risk that fraud or error may have a significant effect on the accounts. Following from their risk assessment, auditors should then design procedures which they would reasonably expect to detect fraud or error which had a material effect on the financial statements.

4.7 Throughout the audit auditors should be alert for signs that suggest a significant risk that fraud or error has occurred. The SAS lists the following signs.

FRAUD AND ERROR	
Previous experience or incidents which call into question the **integrity or competence** of management	Management dominated by one person (or a small group) and no effective oversight board or committee
	Complex corporate structure where complexity does not seem to be warranted
	High turnover rate of key accounting and financial personnel
	Personnel (key or otherwise) not taking holidays
	Significant and prolonged under-staffing of the accounting department
	Frequent changes of legal advisers or auditors
Financial reporting pressures within a client	Industry volatility
	Inadequate working capital due to declining profits or too rapid expansion
	Deteriorating quality of earnings, for example increased risk taking with respect to credit sales, changes in business practice or selection of accounting policy alternatives that improve income
	The client needs a rising profit trend to support the market price of its shares due to a contemplated public offering, a takeover or other reason
	Significant investment in an industry or product line noted for rapid change

	Pressure on accounting personnel to complete financial statements in an unreasonably short period of time
	Dominant owner-management
	Performance-based remuneration
Weaknesses in the **design** and **operation** of the **accounting** and **internal controls system**	A weak control environment within the client
	Systems that, in their design, are inadequate to give reasonable assurance of preventing or detecting error or fraud
	Inadequate segregation of responsibilities in relation to functions involving the handling, recording or controlling of the entity's assets
	Indications that internal financial information is unreliable
	Evidence that internal controls have been overridden by management
	Ineffective monitoring of the operation of system which allows control overrides, breakdown or weakness to continue without proper corrective action
	Continuing failure to correct major weakness in internal control where such corrections are practicable and cost effective
Unusual transactions	Unusual transactions, especially near the year end, that have a significant effect on earnings
	Complex transactions or accounting treatments
	Unusual transactions with related parties
	Payments for services (for example to lawyers, consultants or agents) that appear excessive in relation to the services provided
Problems in **obtaining** sufficient appropriate audit **evidence**	Inadequate records, for example incomplete files, excessive adjustments to accounting records, transactions not recorded in accordance with normal procedures and out-of-balance control accounts
	Inadequate documentation of transactions, such as lack of proper authorisation, supporting documents not available and alteration to documents (any of these documentation problems assume greater significance when they relate to large or unusual transactions)
	An excessive number of differences between accounting records and third party confirmations, conflicting audit evidence and unexplainable changes in operating ratios
	Evasive, delayed or unreasonable responses by management to audit inquires
	Inappropriate attitude of management to the conduct of the audit, eg time pressure, scope limitation and other constraints
Some factors unique to an **information systems environment** which relate to the conditions and events described above	Inability to extract information from computer files due to lack of, or non-current, documentation of record contents or programs
	Large numbers of program changes that are not documented, approved and tested
	Inadequate overall balancing of computer transactions and data bases to the financial accounts

4.8　Fraud or error found in one area may impact upon other audit areas, or indeed the whole audit. If the problems found cast doubt upon management's integrity or competence, this will have a significant impact on the auditors' overall risk assessment.

4.9　As far as reporting is concerned, you should note that normally fraud or error should be discussed with management firstly, unless there are doubts about the integrity of management. Auditors should consider whether the fraud or error has a significant impact on the accounts, and may need to qualify their audit report or include an explanatory paragraph. Fraud may also need to be reported to an appropriate authority.

5　LAW AND REGULATIONS

5.1　The SASs in SAS 120 *Consideration of law and regulations* are as follows.

Introduction

Auditors should plan and perform their audit procedures, and evaluate and report on the results thereof, recognising that non-compliance by the entity with law or regulations may materially affect the financial statements. (SAS 120.1)

When carrying out their procedures for the purpose of forming an opinion on the financial statements, the auditors should in addition be alert for instances of possible or actual non-compliance with law or regulations which might affect the financial statements. (SAS 120.4)

The auditors' consideration of compliance with law and regulations

The auditors should obtain sufficient appropriate audit evidence about compliance with those laws and regulations which relate directly to the preparation of, or the inclusion or disclosure of specific items in, the financial statements. (SAS 120.2)

The auditors should perform procedures to help identify possible or actual instances of non-compliance with those laws and regulations which provide a legal framework within which the entity conducts its business and which are central to the entity's ability to conduct its business and hence to its financial statements, by:

(a)　obtaining a general understanding of the legal and regulatory framework applicable to the entity and the industry, and of the procedures followed to ensure compliance with that framework;

(b)　inspecting correspondence with relevant licensing or regulatory authorities;

(c)　enquiring of the directors as to whether they are on notice of any such possible instances of non-compliance with law or regulations; and

(d)　obtaining written confirmation from the directors that they have disclosed to the auditors all those events of which they are aware which involve possible non-compliance, together with the actual or contingent consequences which may arise therefrom. (SAS 120.3)

When carrying out their procedures for the purpose of forming an opinion on the financial statements, the auditors should in addition be alert for instances of possible or actual non-compliance with law or regulations which might affect the financial statements. (SAS 120.4)

Procedures when possible non-compliance with law or regulations is discovered

When the auditors become aware of information which indicates that non-compliance with law or regulations may exist, they should obtain an understanding of the nature of the act and the circumstances in which it has occurred and sufficient other information to evaluate the possible effect on the financial statements. (SAS 120.5)

When the auditors become aware of or suspect that there may be non-compliance with law or regulations, they should document their findings and, subject to any requirement to report them direct to a third party, discuss them with the appropriate level of management. (SAS 120.6)

The auditors should consider the implications of suspected or actual non-compliance with law or regulations in relation to other aspects of the audit, particularly the reliability or management representations. (SAS 120.7)

Reporting to management

The auditors should, as soon as practicable (save where SAS 120.15 applies) either:

(a)   communicate with management, the board of directors or the audit committee, or

(b)   obtain evidence that they are appropriately informed,

regarding any suspected or actual non-compliance with law or regulations that comes to the auditors' attention. (SAS 120.8)

If, in the auditors' judgement, the suspected or actual non-compliance with law or regulations is material or is believed to be intentional, the auditors should communicate the finding without delay. (SAS 120.9)

Reporting to addressees of the auditors' report on the financial statements

Where the auditors conclude that the view given by the financial statements could be affected by a level of uncertainty concerning the consequences of a suspected or actual non-compliance which, in their opinion, is fundamental, they should include an explanatory paragraph referring to the matter in their report. (SAS 120.10)

Where the auditors conclude that a suspected or actual instance of non-compliance with law or regulation has a material effect on the financial statements and they disagree with the accounting treatment or with the extent, or the lack, of any disclosure in the financial statements of the instance of its consequences they should issue an adverse or qualified opinion. If the auditors are unable to determine whether non-compliance with law or regulations has occurred because of limitation in the scope of their work, they should issue a disclaimer or a qualified opinion. (SAS 120.11)

Reporting to third parties

When the auditors become aware of a suspected or actual non-compliance with law and regulations which gives rise to a statutory duty to report, they should make a report to the appropriate authority without undue delay. (SAS 120.12)

Where the auditors become aware of a suspected or actual instance of non-compliance with law or regulations which does not give rise to a statutory duty to report to an appropriate authority they should:

(a)   consider whether the matter may be one that ought to be reported to a proper authority in the public interest; and where this is the case;

(b)   except in the circumstances covered in SAS 120.15, discuss the matter with the board of directors including any audit committee. (SAS 120.13)

Where, having considered any views expressed on behalf of the entity and in the light of any legal advice obtained, the auditors conclude that the matter ought to be reported to an appropriate authority in the public interest, they should notify the directors in writing of their view and, if the entity does not voluntarily do so itself or is unable to provide evidence that the matter has been reported, they should report it themselves. (SAS 120.14)

Auditors should report a matter direct to a proper authority in the public interest and without discussing the matter with the entity if they conclude that the suspected or actual instance of non-compliance has caused them no longer to have confidence in the integrity of the directors. (SAS 120.15)

Overseas activities

Where any of the activities of a company or group are carried on outside the United Kingdom or the Republic of Ireland, the auditors should take steps to ensure that the audit work in relation to the detection and reporting of any non-compliance with local law and regulations is planned and carried out in accordance with the requirements of this SAS. (SAS 120.16)

5.2 The SAS makes clear the distinction between the responsibilities of the directors and the responsibilities of the auditors.

5.3 The **directors** should take the appropriate steps and establish arrangements to **ensure compliance** with law and regulations and to prevent and detect any non-compliance. In addition, they are responsible for the financial statements showing a true and fair view.

5.4 Auditor responsibilities for detection of non-compliance with laws and regulations are similar to those for detection of fraud or error. Auditors should design procedures which will give them a reasonable expectation of detecting non-compliance which significantly affects the accounts. However auditors cannot be expected to identify all instances of non-compliance with laws and regulations.

5.5 Many clients are subject to laws and regulations of many different kinds, and the question therefore arises of how much work auditors are expected to do in this area. SAS 120 draws an important distinction between three types of laws and regulations

(a) Laws and regulations that directly **affect the contents** of the **financial statements**. Auditors must check that these have been obeyed.

(b) Laws and regulations that are **central** to the **client's ability** to carry on its business. Auditors should understand what these are, and carry out certain procedures to check the client's systems of compliance. These procedures include inspecting correspondence with regulatory authorities, and discussing compliance with the client.

(c) Other laws and regulations. Auditors have no responsibility to carry out specific procedures to check compliance with this type. If however auditors become aware that there is non-compliance with laws and regulations, and that non-compliance may seriously impact upon the accounts, they should try and assess the effect.

5.6 In practice the distinction between (b) and (c) may not always be easy to apply. SAS 120 gives examples of the following types of laws and regulations as being central to the client's business.

(a) Where compliance is a pre-requisite of obtaining a licence to operate in the business concerned (for example authorisation under the Financial Services Act

(b) Where non-compliance may cause the client to cease to trade (either because non-compliance accounts for a significant proportion of profits or because non-compliance is likely to be punished by heavy fines or other penalties)

5.7 SAS 120 provides a similar list to SAS 110 of signs that may indicate that the client is not complying with laws and regulations.

- Investigation by government departments or payment of fines or penalties

- Payments for unspecified services or loans to consultants, related parties, employees or government employees

- Sales commissions or agents' fees that appear excessive in relation to those normally paid by the entity or in its industry or to the services actually received

- Purchasing at pricing significantly above or below market price

- Unusual payments in cash, purchases in the form of cashiers' cheques payable to bearer or transfers to numbered bank accounts

- Unusual transactions with companies registered in tax havens

- Payments for goods or services made other than to the country from which the goods or services originated

- Existence of an accounting system that fails, whether by design or by accident, to provide adequate audit trail or sufficient evidence

- Unauthorised transactions or improperly recorded transactions

- Media comment

5.8 When considering how non-compliance should be reported, auditors should discuss matters with management unless there are specific legal reasons not to do so, or auditors doubt the integrity of management.

5.9 Auditors should consider the effect of **non-compliance** on the **accounts**. Laws and regulations which directly affect the content of the accounts will obviously be important here. Auditors should also consider whether provisions need to made for **legal expenses**, and the possibility of **uncertainties** due to going concern problems or lack of explanations by management.

5.10 As regards reporting to third parties, auditors are under a statutory duty to report certain instances of non-compliance, for example breaches of the Financial Services Act. On other occasions it may be in the public interest to report, and legal advice may be required.

Activity 18.1

You are the auditor of Falmouth Ltd and are currently planning this year's audit. You have just had a planning meeting with the company's Managing Director, during which he has told you about two anonymous tip-offs he has received concerning frauds at the two largest of the company's five branches.

(a) He has been told at one branch that the manager has been submitting false claims for travel expenses and false invoices for non-existent purchases in order to fund his own tastes for expensive cars and his girlfriend's tastes for jewellery and foreign holidays.

(b) At another branch, the stores staff have been acting in collusion to steal significant quantities of stock. They have done this by claiming that certain stock is damaged or scrap, and has therefore been disposed of for nil value.

What actions will you take as auditor to investigate these allegations?

Key learning points

- Auditors can be **criminally liable** under a number of statutes.

- Auditors can also suffer **civil liability** under statute in insolvency cases.

- Auditors are most likely to be subject to civil liability to clients under the **law of contract**. Clients must show:

    ° A duty of care
    ° Auditor negligence
    ° Damage has been suffered

- Auditors are unlikely to be able to **restrict liability** to clients under contract law.

- Auditors may be liable to third parties (and rarely to clients) in **tort.**

- However to be liable in **tort proximity** must be established and the **Caparo** case has made this difficult.

- **Proximity** *may* be established by direct assurances from the auditors on the accounts (**BBH v ADT** case).

- **Directors** (not auditors) are responsible for preventing fraud. Auditors should design procedures so as to have a **reasonable expectation** of **detecting material misstatements**, whether intentional or unintentional, in the accounts.

- Auditors' main responsibilities under SAS 120 on **law and regulations** relate to the law and regulations which:

    ° Relate to the **accounts**
    ° Provide the **legal framework** and are **central** to the client's ability to conduct its business

Quick quiz

1   Give three examples of legislation under which auditors may be criminally liable.

2   What are the implied terms which the courts will normally impute into a contract entered into by auditors?

3   What has the APB said about how courts will treat APB pronouncements?

4   What must a client prove to bring a successful action against auditors in contract?

5   How does s 310 Companies Act affect the liability of auditors?

6   What did the judgement in *Caparo* say about auditors' duties to investors?

7   How much assurance of detecting fraud or error should auditors seek to obtain from audit procedures?

8   According to SAS 110 what are possible indicators of fraud in an information systems environment?

9   What audit work should auditors carry out to test client compliance with laws and regulations which are central to the client's ability to conduct its business?

10 Under what circumstances should auditors report non-compliance with law and regulations to the proper authority?

Answers to quick quiz

1   Legislation under which auditors may be criminally liable includes:

    (a) Theft Act 1986
    (b) Insolvency Act 1986
    (c) Financial Services Act 1986

2   The implied terms which will normally be imputed are that the auditors have:

(a)   A duty to exercise reasonable care
(b)   A duty to carry out the work required with reasonable expediency
(c)   A right to reasonable remuneration

3   The APB have stated courts will take into account all APB pronouncements and in particular Auditing Standards when assessing the adequacy of auditors' work.

4   To bring a successful action in contract, a client must prove:

(a)   A duty of care enforceable at law existed.

(b)   The auditors were negligent in performance of that duty, judged by accepted contemporary professional standards.

(c)   The client has suffered pecuniary loss as a result of auditor negligence.

5   S 310 of Companies Act makes void any provision exempting auditors from liability.

6   The *Caparo* judgement stated that auditors owed no duty of care to anyone (members or non-members) who used the accounts in making investment decisions.

7   Auditors should seek to have a reasonable expectation of detecting material misstatements arising from fraud or error.

8   Possible indicators of fraud in an information systems environment include:

(a)   Inability to extract information from computer files due to lack of, or non-current, documentation of record contents or programs

(b)   Large numbers of program changes that are not documented, approved or tested

(c)   Inadequate overall balancing of computer transactions and databases

9   Auditors should carry out the following procedures on compliance with laws and regulations:

(a)   Obtain a general understanding of the legal and regulatory framework and the procedures followed to ensure compliance with the framework.

(b)   Inspect correspondence with relevant licensing or regulatory authorities.

(c)   Make enquiries of directors.

(d)   Obtain written confirmation of full disclosure from directors.

10   Auditors should report on non-compliance directly to the proper authority when:

(a)   There is a statutory duty to report.

(b)   They believe it is in the public interest to report, and either the client has not reported non-compliance, or the auditors no longer have confidence in the integrity of the directors.

Answers to activities

Answer 18.1

As auditor, I have a responsibility under SAS 110 to plan procedures that give reasonable assurance of detecting fraud that has a material effect on the company's financial statements. The indications are that the amounts involved are material, and I have also been warned by the managing director that there may be potential problems. I would therefore investigate the allegations as part of the audit.

(a)   I would discreetly try and check if the branch manager had a lifestyle that appeared to be unduly lavish. There may be legitimate reasons for expensive purchases, for example a legacy or lottery win.

I would also consider the general behaviour of the manager during the audit. Signs of particular concern would include a lack of co-operation, evidence that the branch's staff were cowed, and general evidence of limited central control of the branch, as well as lack of the specific controls outlined below.

Travel expenses

I would carry out analytical review on travel expenses to see how they compared with previous years and also with the levels of expenses at other branches. I would investigate significant variations, although there may be legitimate reasons for these, for example special sales promotions.

BPP PUBLISHING

I would also consider the controls operated by head office over the expenses. Strong controls would include head office booking of tickets or hotel accommodation, and approval of other travel expenses.

I would also examine the documentation for individual expenses, considering whether the amounts claimed appeared reasonable, and checking with other evidence that the travel had been undertaken, for example evidence of sales arising

Purchases

I would also consider analytical evidence here. As well as comparing levels of purchases with previous years and other branches, I would also consider profit margins, and attempt to reconcile amounts purchased with amounts sold and in stock.

I would consider internal controls over purchases. I would assess the strength of the system, for example whether suppliers were chosen from an approved list, and whether payments to suppliers could be made without being supported by a valid purchase invoice or purchase order. I would also ascertain the degree of involvement of the branch manager in the purchasing process, whether he chose suppliers, or whether there were any suppliers that he handled directly outside the normal purchase system.

I would also scrutinise the records of suppliers to see if any appeared to have unusual addresses such as box numbers or an address which was the same as the home address of the branch manager. I would examine individual invoices to see if they had unusual features such as missing addresses or phone numbers, incomplete or inadequate product descriptions or were photocopies. I would also be alert for different suppliers with the same address or with similar business stationery.

(b)   *Stock*

I would scrutinise the records of stock written off and ascertain the reasons for write-off. If the company had a policy for scrapping stock, I would ascertain whether the write-offs fulfilled that policy. If stock had to be written off for reasons such as deterioration due to damp, I would check whether the problem had been remedied. I would also consider whether stock write-offs had to be authorised; I would gain comfort if write-offs had to be authorised by someone who was independent of stores.

I would also carry out an analytical review of stock write-offs, considering the amounts written off and the proportion of stock held that was written off. I would compare these figures with write-offs for previous years and write-offs for other branches. I would also consider whether stock orders appeared to be in excess of requirements, as some stock might be ordered just to be stolen.

I would review the records of internal stock-takes carried out during the year. I would check whether they were carried out by staff who were independent of the stock section, and whether they identified particular problems at the branch with obsolete or slow-moving stock.

Lastly I would also attend the end of year stocktake. I would pay particular attention to the instructions for dealing with obsolete or slow-moving stock, and check at the stocktake that these instructions were being put into practice. I would also consider the condition of stock identified as damaged or obsolete to see if the assessment appeared reasonable.

Chapter 19 Internal and group audits

Chapter topic list

1   Introduction

2   Internal audit

3   Group audits

Learning objectives

On completion of this chapter you will be able to:

		Performance criteria	Range statement
•	Describe the purpose of:		
	° Internal audit	17.1.4, 17.1.7	17.1.1-17.1.3
	° External audit reliance on the internal audit function	17.2.1-17.2.4	17.2.1-17.2.3
	° Group audits	17.2.1-17.2.4	17.2.1-17.2.3

BPP
PUBLISHING

1 INTRODUCTION

1.1 The first part of this chapter deals with the reliance auditors place on other auditors. In chapter 1 we contrasted the role of **internal audit** and external audit. The objectives of the two differ; external auditors seek to obtain enough evidence to be able to form an opinion on the accounts, whereas internal audit's objectives are set by management. In addition internal auditors are employees of the client with obvious implications for their independence.

1.2 Nevertheless internal audit can be a very effective internal control by for example checking the operation of other internal controls. Since internal audit is an internal control, external auditors may wish to place reliance on it. We shall therefore discuss in this chapter what external auditors need to consider when deciding how much reliance to place on internal audit.

1.3 We then go on to consider **group audits**. Often the auditors who express an opinion on the accounts of the group and parent company will not be the same as the auditors of some of the subsidiaries. This situation can present the auditors of the group accounts with problems. On the one hand they do not want to re-perform the audits of the subsidiaries in order to gain sufficient assurance that the subsidiaries' figures are materially correct in the group accounts, as they would be duplicating the work of the subsidiaries' auditors. However they need to gain enough assurance about the subsidiaries somehow. We shall therefore examine the chapter the different methods the group auditors can use to gain the assurance they need.

2 INTERNAL AUDIT

> **KEY TERM**
>
> **Internal audit** is an appraisal or monitoring activity established by management and directors, for the review of the accounting and internal control systems as a service to the entity. It functions by, amongst other things, examining, evaluating and reporting to management and the directors on the adequacy and effectiveness of components of the accounting and internal control systems.

2.1 Remember what we said earlier about internal audit: large organisations may appoint full time staff whose function is to monitor and report on the running of the company's operations. The corporate governance reports of the 1990s (Cadbury and Hampel) emphasised the importance of internal audit; they saw internal audit as playing a key role in the **monitoring** of internal controls and procedures. The internal audit function may also undertake **investigations** on behalf of the **board** and its **audit committee**.

2.2 SAS 500 *Considering the work of internal audit* examines the relationship between external and internal audit.

> **SAS 500.1**
>
> External auditors should consider the activities of internal audit and their effect, if any, on external audit procedures.

2.3   The SAS goes on to make a most important point.

> 'The external auditors have *sole* responsibility for the audit opinion expressed and for determining the nature, timing and extent of external audit procedures. All judgements relating to the audit of the financial statements are those of the external auditors. That responsibility is not reduced by any use made of internal audit work. However, internal audit work may serve to provide external auditors with audit evidence.'

Scope and objectives of internal audit

2.4   The scope and objectives of internal audit vary widely. Normally however, internal audit operates in one or more of the following broad areas.

- Review of the **accounting** and **internal control systems**
- Examination of **financial** and **operating information**
- Review of **economy, efficiency and effectiveness**
- Review of **compliance** with **laws and regulations**
- **Special investigations**

Relationship between internal and external auditors

2.5   The objectives of internal audit will differ from those of the external auditors. However, some of the means of achieving their respective objectives are often similar, and so some of the internal auditors' work may be used by the external auditors.

Understanding and assessment of the role and scope of internal audit

> **SAS 500.2**
>
> The external auditors should obtain sufficient understanding of internal audit activities to assist in planning the audit and developing an effective audit approach

2.6   An effective internal audit function may reduce, modify or alter the timing of external audit procedures, but it can *never* eliminate them entirely. Where the internal audit function is deemed ineffective, it may still be useful to be aware of the internal audit conclusions.

> **SAS 500.3**
>
> During the course of their planning the external auditors should perform an assessment of the internal audit function if they consider that it may be possible and desirable to rely on certain internal audit work in specific audit areas for the purpose of the external audit of the financial statements.

2.7   The following important criteria will be considered by the external auditors.

ASSESSMENT OF INTERNAL AUDIT	
Organisational status	Consider **to whom** internal audit **reports** (should be board), whether internal audit has any **operating responsibilities** and constraints or restrictions on the function
Scope of function	Consider **extent** and **nature** of **assignments** performed and the action taken by management as a result of internal audit reports
Technical competence	Consider whether internal auditors have adequate **technical training** and proficiency
Due professional care	Consider whether internal audit is **properly planned**, **supervised**, **reviewed** and **documented**

Timing of liaison and co-ordination

2.8   All timing of internal audit work should be agreed as early as possible, and in particular how it co-ordinates with the external auditors' work. Liaison with the internal auditors should take place at regular intervals throughout the audit. Information on tests and conclusions should be passed both to and from internal audit.

Evaluating specific internal audit work

SAS 500.4

When the external auditors use specific internal audit work to reduce the extent of their audit procedures, they should evaluate that work to confirm its adequacy for their purposes.

2.9   The evaluation here will consider the scope of work and related audit programmes *and* whether the assessment of the internal audit function remains appropriate. This may include consideration of whether:

(a)   The work is performed by persons having **adequate technical training** and **proficiency** as internal auditors.

(b)   The work of assistants is **properly supervised, reviewed and documented**.

(c)   **Sufficient appropriate audit evidence** is obtained to afford a reasonable basis for the conclusions reached.

(d)   The **conclusions** reached are **appropriate** in the circumstances.

(e)   Any **reports** prepared by internal audit are **consistent** with the results of the work performed.

(f)   Any **exceptions** or unusual matters disclosed by internal audit are **properly resolved**.

(g)   **Amendments** to the external audit programme are **required** as a result of matters identified by internal audit work.

(h)   There is a need to **test the work of internal audit** to confirm its adequacy.

2.10   If the external auditors decide that the internal audit work is not adequate, they should extend their procedures in order to obtain appropriate evidence.

Activity 19.1

(a) What are the major differences between internal and external audit?

(b) What should external auditors consider when deciding whether to rely on the work of internal auditors?

3 GROUP AUDITS

KEY TERMS

Principal auditors are the auditors with responsibility for reporting on the financial statements of an entity when those financial statements include financial information of one or more components audited by other auditors.

Other auditors are auditors, other than the principal auditors, with responsibility for reporting on the financial information of a component which is included in the financial statements audited by the principal auditors. Other auditors include affiliated firms, whether using the same name or not, and correspondent firms, as well as unrelated auditors.

Component is a division, branch, subsidiary, joint venture, associated undertaking or other entity whose financial information is included in financial statements audited by the principal auditors.

Responsibility of principal auditors

3.1 The duty of the principal auditors is to report on the group accounts, including therefore all entities included in the group accounts.

3.2 The principal auditors have **sole responsibility** for this opinion even where the group financial statements include amounts derived from accounts which have not been audited by them. As a result, they cannot discharge their responsibility to report on the group financial statements by an unquestioning acceptance of component companies' financial statements, whether audited or not.

Rights of principal auditors

3.3 The principal auditors have the following rights:

(a) The **right to require from the other auditors** of a UK-incorporated company such **information and explanations** as they may reasonably require (s 389A(3) CA 1985)

(b) The right to **require the parent company** to take all reasonable steps to **obtain reasonable information** and explanations from the subsidiary and this will include foreign subsidiaries (s 389A(4) CA 1985)

3.4 Even where their responsibilities in this regard are not set down by statute (for example where the component company is an associated company not a subsidiary), the other auditors should appreciate that the component company's financial statements will ultimately form a part of the group financial statements. In principle, the other auditors should therefore be prepared to co-operate with the principal auditors and make available such information as the principal auditors may require in order to discharge their duties as auditors of the group financial statements.

Principal auditors and other auditors

3.5 The principal auditors must decide how to take account of the work carried out by the other auditors.

3.6 The extent of the procedures adopted by the principal auditors will be determined by the **materiality** of the amounts derived from the financial statements of components of the group, and the **level of risk** that the auditors are willing to accept that such statements contain material errors.

3.7 The APB has produced an auditing standard on this subject. SAS 510 *The relationship between principal auditors and other auditors.*

Acceptance as principal auditors

> **SAS 510.2**
>
> Auditors should consider whether their own participation is sufficient to enable them to act as principal auditors

3.8 The principal auditors should not be so far removed from large parts of the group audit that they are unable to form an opinion. The SAS suggests that, in this context, the principal auditors should consider the following.

- The **materiality** of the portion of the financial statements which they do not audit

- The **degree of their knowledge** regarding the business of the components

- The **nature of their relationship** with the firms acting as other auditors

- Their **ability** where necessary to **perform additional procedures** to enable them to act as principal auditors

- The **risk of material misstatements** in the financial statements of the components audited by other auditors

> **DEVOLVED ASSESSMENT ALERT**
>
> In addition to these points, the prospective auditor should also consider the general points relating to acceptance of appointment discussed in Chapter 3.

Principal auditors' procedures

> ### SAS 510.3
>
> When planning to use the work of other auditors, principal auditors should consider the professional qualifications, experience and resources of the other auditors in the context of the specific assignment.

3.9 The initial enquires of this nature will be concerned with:

(a) The other auditors' **membership of a professional body**

(b) The **reputation** of any firm to which the other auditors are affiliated

> ### SAS 510.4
>
> Principal auditors should obtain sufficient appropriate audit evidence that the work of the other auditors is adequate for the principal auditors' purposes.

3.10 In order to obtain such evidence at the planning stage, the principal auditors should advise the other auditors of the use they intend to make of their work and make arrangement for the co-ordination of their audit efforts. The principal auditors will inform the other auditors about the following matters.

- **Areas** requiring **special consideration** (key risks, control environment)
- Procedures for the **identification** of **discloseable inter-group transactions**
- Procedures for notifying principal auditors of **unusual circumstances**
- The **timetable** for completion of the audit
- The **independence requirements**
- The **relevant accounting, auditing** and **reporting requirements**

The other auditors should give representations on independence and accounting, auditing and reporting requirements.

3.11 The nature, timing and extent of the principal auditors' procedures will depend on the individual circumstances of the engagement (risk, materiality etc) and their assessment of the other auditors.

3.12 Procedures that the principal auditors may use include the following.

- **Discussions** with the other auditors about their audit procedures

- **Review** of a **written summary** of those procedures (perhaps using a questionnaire or checklist

- **Review** of the other auditors' **working papers**

3.13 These procedures may be unnecessary if evidence has already been obtained of adequate quality control over the other auditors' work, for example, through inter-firm reviews within affiliated firms.

3.14 Having received the agreed work, documentation etc from the other auditors:

> ## SAS 510.5
>
> The principal auditors should consider the significant findings of the other auditors.

3.15 This consideration may involve the following.

- **Discussions** with the other auditors and with the directors or management of the component

- **Review** of copies of **reports to directors** or **management** issued by the other auditors

- **Supplementary tests**, performed by the principal auditors or by the other auditors, on the financial statements of the component

Co-operation between auditors

> ## SAS 510.6
>
> Other auditors, knowing the context in which the principal auditors intend to use their work, should co-operate with and assist the principal auditors.

Information supplied by other auditors

3.16 The other auditors should draw to the attention of the principal auditors any matters they discover in their audit which they feel is likely to be relevant to the principal auditors' work. They may do so:

(a) By **direct communication** (with permission from the component or where there is a statutory obligation)

(b) By **reference** in their **audit report**

3.17 If the other auditors are unable to perform any aspect of their work as requested, they should inform the principal auditors.

Information supplied by principal auditors

3.18 The other auditors have **sole responsibility** for their audit opinion on the financial statements of the component they audit. They should **not** rely on the principal auditors informing them of matters which might have an impact on the financial statements of the component. If they wish to do so, they should seek representations directly from the directors or management of the entity audited by the principal auditors.

3.19 The principal auditors have no obligation, statutory or otherwise, to provide information to other auditors. Where during the course of their audit, they discover matters which they consider may be relevant to the other auditors' work, they should discuss and agree an appropriate course of action with the directors of the entity which they audit. This may involve the principal auditors communicating directly with the other auditors, or the directors informing the component or the other auditors.

3.20 If the circumstances are such that the information cannot be passed to the other auditors, for example due to sensitive commercial considerations, the principal auditors should take

no further action. To divulge such information in these situations would be a breach of client confidentiality.

Reporting considerations

3.21 The SAS makes the following important points about the principal auditors' report.

> 'When the principal auditors are satisfied that the work of the other auditors is adequate for the purposes of their audit, *no reference* to the other auditors is made in the principal auditors' report.
>
> The principal auditors have sole responsibility for their audit opinion and a reference to the other auditors in the principal auditors' report may be misunderstood and interpreted as a qualification of their opinion or a division of responsibility, neither of which is appropriate.'

3.22 The principal auditors must consider the implications for their report when they *cannot* obtain sufficient evidence about the work of the other auditors, and it has not been possible to perform additional procedures in respect of the component's financial statements.

3.23 The reports of other auditors on the component's financial statements may contain a qualified opinion or an explanatory paragraph referring to an uncertainty. In such cases the principal auditors should consider whether the subject of the qualification or fundamental uncertainty is of **such nature and significance,** in relation to the financial statements of the entity on which they are reporting, that it should be reflected in their audit report.

DEVOLVED ASSESSMENT ALERT

Relations with other auditors and assessment of their work is a crucial part of group audits; you must be aware of the procedures involved.

Key learning points

- **Internal audit** can be a very important internal control. It can operate in the following areas.

  - Review of accounting and internal control systems
  - Examination of financial and operating information
  - Review of economy, efficiency and effectiveness
  - Review of compliance
  - Special investigations (fraud)

- **External auditors** may rely on the work of internal audit provided it has been assessed as a reliable internal control. General criteria include:

  - Organisational status
  - Scope of function
  - Technical competence
  - Due professional care

- External auditors should also evaluate **specific internal work** if they wish to use it to reduce the extent of external audit procedures.

- **Principal auditors** (group auditors) have sole responsibility for the opinion on the group accounts. They should consider whether their participation is sufficient to allow them to act as principal auditors.

- When dealing with **other auditors**, principal auditors should:

  - Identify during planning key audit issues and requirements

  - Gain sufficient assurance about other auditors' work (by discussions, checklists, review of working papers)

  - Consider the significant findings of other auditors

- **Other auditors** should co-operate with the **principal auditors**.

Quick quiz

1. What does SAS 500 say about the responsibility of external auditors for the audit of financial statements?

2. To whom should internal audit ideally report?

3. What factors should principal auditors consider when deciding whether their own participation in the audit is sufficient?

4. Give four examples of the information that should be communicated by principal auditors to other auditors at the planning stage of an audit.

5. What are likely to be the important factors that auditors will consider when assessing a group's control environment?

Answers to quick quiz

1. SAS 500 states that the external auditors have sole responsibility for the audit opinion, for determining the nature, timing and extent of external audit procedures and making the necessary judgements. The responsibility is not reduced if internal audit work is used.

2. Ideally internal audit should report to senior management, and also be able to communicate directly with the main board or audit committee.

3. When assessing whether their own participation is sufficient, principal auditors should consider:

   (a) The materiality of the portion of the financial statements which they do not audit

   (b) The degree of their knowledge regarding the business of the components

   (c) The nature of their relationship with the firms acting as other auditors

(d)   Their ability to perform additional procedures

(e)   The risk of material misstatements in the financial statements of the components audited by other auditors

4   Examples of areas that should be communicated include:

(a)   Areas requiring special consideration (key risks, control environment)
(b)   Procedures for the identification of discloseable inter-group transactions
(c)   Procedures for identifying principal auditors of unusual circumstances
(d)   Timetable for the completion of the audit
(e)   Independence requirements
(f)   Relevant accounting, auditing and reporting requirements

5   Important features of a group's control environment include:

(a)   Organisational structure of the group
(b)   Level of involvement of parent company
(c)   Degree of autonomy of management of components
(d)   Supervision of components' management by parent company
(e)   Information systems
(f)   Role of internal audit in review of components

Answers to activities

Answer 19.1

(a)   The major differences between internal and external auditors are as follows.

Scope

Statute prescribes that external auditors should report on the financial statements. In order to do so they have certain rights such as the rights to receive all the information and explanations they consider necessary for the purposes of their audit.

The scope of internal audit's work is determined by management. It varies from company to company but may include:

(i)   Review of the accounting and internal control systems
(ii)   Examination of financial and operating information
(iii) Review of economy, efficiency and effectiveness
(iv)   Review of compliance with laws and regulations
(v)   Special investigations, for example into fraud

Objectives

The main objective of the work of external auditors is to report on the truth and fairness of the accounts. The objectives of internal audit will be determined by management. A major objective is likely to be to give assurance that the system of internal controls is working properly. Although external auditors will report weaknesses in control that they find, the external audit cannot be relied on to identify every weakness that may exist in internal control.

Reporting

The audit report of external auditors is to the shareholders.

Internal auditors report to management, ideally to top-level management. They should be able to contact the board or audit committee directly.

(b)   The internal audit function is itself part of the system of internal control: it is an internal control over internal controls. As such, the external auditors should be able to test it and, if it is found to be reliable, they can rely on it.

To check the reliability of the work of the internal auditors, external auditors would consider the following matters.

(i)   *The degree of independence of the internal auditors*

External auditors should assess the organisational status and reporting responsibilities of the internal auditors and consider any restrictions placed upon them. Although internal auditors are employees of the enterprise and cannot therefore be independent of it, they should be able to plan and carry out their work as they wish and have access to senior management and the audit committee. They should be free of any responsibility which may create a conflict of interest, and of a situation where those staff on whom they are reporting are responsible for their or their staff's appointment, promotion or pay.

(ii)   *The scope and objectives of the internal audit function*

External auditors should examine the internal auditors' formal terms of reference and ascertain the scope and objectives of internal audit assignments.

(iii)   *Quality of work*

External auditors should consider whether the work of internal audit is properly planned, controlled, recorded and reviewed. Examples of good practice include the existence of an adequate audit manual, plans and procedures for supervision of individual assignments, and satisfactory arrangements for ensuring adequate quality control, reporting and follow-up.

(iv)   *Technical competence*

Internal audit should be performed by persons having adequate training and competence as auditors. Indications of technical competence may be membership of an appropriate professional body or attendance at regular training courses.

(v)   *Reports*

External auditors should consider the quality of reports issued by internal audit and find out whether management considers and acts upon such reports.

If external auditors find that where the internal auditors' work is reliable, external auditors will be able to place reliance on that work when appropriate. This may mean that they will need to carry out less audit work.

However, it should be emphasised that external auditors cannot rely totally on the internal auditors' work in relation to any particular audit objective. Internal audit work provides only one form of evidence, and the internal auditors are not independent of company management. External auditors may be able to reduce the number of items which they test, but they will not be able to leave a particular type of test (for example, a debtors' circularisation) entirely to internal audit. External auditors remain responsible for the opinion which they form on the accounts.

List of
Key Terms
and Index

BPP PUBLISHING

BPP PUBLISHING

ORDER FORM

Any books from our AAT range can be ordered by telephoning 020-8740-2211. Alternatively, send this page to our address below, fax it to us on 020-8740-1184, or email us at **publishing@bpp.com**. Or look us up on our website: www.bpp.com

We aim to deliver to all UK addresses inside 5 working days; a signature will be required. Order to all EU addresses should be delivered within 6 working days. All other orders to overseas addresses should be delivered within 8 working days.

To: BPP Publishing Ltd, Aldine House, Aldine Place, London W12 8AW

Tel: 020-8740 2211   **Fax: 020-8740 1184**   **Email: publishing@bpp.com**

Mr / Ms (full name): _____

Daytime delivery address: _____

_____

Postcode: _____   Daytime Tel: _____

Please send me the following quantities of books.

	5/00 Interactive Text	8/00 DA Kit	8/00 CA Kit
FOUNDATION			
Unit 1 Recording Income and Receipts	☐	☐	
Unit 2 Making and Recording Payments	☐	☐	
Unit 3 Ledger Balances and Initial Trial Balance	☐		☐
Unit 4 Supplying Information for Management Control	☐	☐	
Unit 20 Working with Information Technology (8/00 Text)	☐		
Unit 22/23 Achieving Personal Effectiveness	☐		
INTERMEDIATE			
Unit 5 Financial Records and Accounts	☐		☐
Unit 6 Cost Information	☐		☐
Unit 7 Reports and Returns	☐	☐	
Unit 21 Using Information Technology	☐		
Unit 22: see below			
TECHNICIAN			
Unit 8/9 Core Managing Costs and Allocating Resources	☐		☐
Unit 10 Core Managing Accounting Systems	☐	☐	
Unit 11 Option Financial Statements (Accounting Practice)	☐		☐
Unit 12 Option Financial Statements (Central Government)	☐		
Unit 15 Option Cash Management and Credit Control	☐	☐	
Unit 16 Option Evaluating Activities	☐	☐	
Unit 17 Option Implementing Auditing Procedures	☐	☐	
Unit 18 Option Business Tax FA00(8/00 Text)	☐		
Unit 19 Option Personal Tax FA00(8/00 Text)	☐		
TECHNICIAN 1999			
Unit 17 Option Business Tax Computations FA99 (8/99 Text & Kit)	☐	☐	
Unit 18 Option Personal Tax Computations FA99 (8/99 Text & Kit)	☐	☐	
TOTAL BOOKS	☐ +	☐ +	☐ = ☐

@ £9.95 each = £ ☐

Postage and packaging:

UK: £2.00 for each book to maximum of £10

Europe (inc ROI and Channel Islands): £4.00 for first book, £2.00 for each extra   P & P   £ ☐

Rest of the World: £20.00 for first book, £10 for each extra

▶ Unit 22 Maintaining a Healthy Workplace Interactive Text (postage free)   ☐ @ £3.95   £ ☐

GRAND TOTAL £ ☐

I enclose a cheque for £ _____ (cheques to BPP Publishing Ltd) or charge to **Mastercard/Visa/Switch**

Card number ☐☐☐☐ ☐☐☐☐ ☐☐☐☐ ☐☐☐☐ ☐☐☐☐

Start date _____   Expiry date _____   Issue no. (Switch only)___

Signature _____

REVIEW FORM & FREE PRIZE DRAW

All original review forms from the entire BPP range, completed with genuine comments, will be entered into one of two draws on 31 January 2001 and 31 July 2001. The names on the first four forms picked out on each occasion will be sent a cheque for £50.

Name: _____   **Address**: _____

_____

_____

How have you used this Interactive Text? *(Tick one box only)*	**During the past six months do you recall seeing/receiving any of the following?** *(Tick as many boxes as are relevant)*
☐ Home study (book only)	☐ Our advertisement in *Accounting Technician* magazine
☐ On a course: college _____	☐ Our advertisement in *Pass*
☐ With 'correspondence' package	☐ Our brochure with a letter through the post
☐ Other _____	

Why did you decide to purchase this Interactive Text? *(Tick one box only)*	**Which (if any) aspects of our advertising do you find useful?** *(Tick as many boxes as are relevant)*
☐ Have used BPP Texts in the past	☐ Prices and publication dates of new editions
☐ Recommendation by friend/colleague	☐ Information on Interactive Text content
☐ Recommendation by a lecturer at college	☐ Facility to order books off-the-page
☐ Saw advertising	☐ None of the above
☐ Other _____	

Have you used the companion Assessment Kit for this subject?   ☐ Yes   ☐ No

Your ratings, comments and suggestions would be appreciated on the following areas

	Very useful	Useful	Not useful
Introductory section (How to use this Interactive Text etc)	☐	☐	☐
Chapter topic lists	☐	☐	☐
Chapter learning objectives	☐	☐	☐
Key terms	☐	☐	☐
Assessment alerts	☐	☐	☐
Examples	☐	☐	☐
Activities and answers	☐	☐	☐
Key learning points	☐	☐	☐
Quick quizzes and answers	☐	☐	☐
List of key terms and index	☐	☐	☐
Icons	☐	☐	☐

	Excellent	Good	Adequate	Poor
Overall opinion of this Text	☐	☐	☐	☐

Do you intend to continue using BPP Interactive Texts/Assessment Kits? ☐ Yes   ☐ No

Please note any further comments and suggestions/errors on the reverse of this page.

Please return to: Nick Weller, BPP Publishing Ltd, FREEPOST, London, W12 8BR

REVIEW FORM & FREE PRIZE DRAW (continued)

Please note any further comments and suggestions/errors below

FREE PRIZE DRAW RULES

1   Closing date for 31 January 2001 draw is 31 December 2000. Closing date for 31 July 2001 draw is 30 June 2001.

2   Restricted to entries with UK and Eire addresses only. BPP employees, their families and business associates are excluded.

3   No purchase necessary. Entry forms are available upon request from BPP Publishing. No more than one entry per title, per person. Draw restricted to persons aged 16 and over.

4   Winners will be notified by post and receive their cheques not later than 6 weeks after the relevant draw date.

5   The decision of the promoter in all matters is final and binding. No correspondence will be entered into.